Ambivalent Affinities

Justice, Power, and Politics

Heather Ann Thompson and Rhonda Y. Williams, *editors*

EDITORIAL ADVISORY BOARD

Dan Berger
Peniel E. Joseph
Daryl Maeda
Barbara Ransby
Vicki L. Ruiz
Marc Stein

The Justice, Power, and Politics series publishes new works in history that explore the myriad struggles for justice, battles for power, and shifts in politics that have shaped the United States over time. Through the lenses of justice, power, and politics, the series seeks to broaden scholarly debates about America's past as well as to inform public discussions about its future.

A complete list of books published in Justice, Power, and Politics is available at https://uncpress.org/series/justice-power-politics.

Ambivalent Affinities

A Political History of Blackness and
Homosexuality after World War II

. . . .

JENNIFER DOMINIQUE JONES

The University of North Carolina Press Chapel Hill

This book was published with the assistance of the Anniversary Fund of the University of North Carolina Press.

Set in Charis by Westchester Publishing Services
Manufactured in the United States of America

Library of Congress Cataloging-in-Publication Data
Names: Jones, Jennifer Dominique, author.
Title: Ambivalent affinities : a political history of Blackness and
    homosexuality after World War II / Jennifer Dominique Jones.
Other titles: Political history of Blackness and homosexuality after
    World War II | Justice, power, and politics.
Description: Chapel Hill : The University of North Carolina Press, [2023] |
    Series: Justice, power, and politics | Includes bibliographical references
    and index.
Identifiers: LCCN 2023010382 | ISBN 9781469673561 (cloth ; alk. paper) |
    ISBN 9781469674254 (pbk. ; alk. paper) | ISBN 9781469673578 (ebook)
Subjects: LCSH: African Americans—Civil rights—United States—
    History—20th century. | African Americans—Political activity—United
    States—History—20th century. | Gay liberation movement—United
    States—History—20th century. | White supremacy movements—
    United States—History—20th century. | African Americans—Race
    identity—Political aspects. | Gays—Identity—Political aspects. |
    Lesbians—Identity—Political aspects. | United States—Race
    relations—History—20th century.
Classification: LCC E185.61 .J826 2023 | DDC 305.896/073—dc23/eng/
    20230313
LC record available at https://lccn.loc.gov/2023010382

Cover photo: *Americas (Triptych)* [*Miss America*] (1987–88) © Lyle Ashton Harris.

Contents

Figures

Abbreviations

AALGA	African American Lesbian and Gay Alliance
ABA	Atlanta Baptist Association
AGC	Atlanta Gay Center
ALCPP	Alabama Legislative Commission to Preserve the Peace
ALFA	Atlanta Lesbian Feminist Alliance
ANP	American Nazi Party
CAP	Central Atlanta Progress
CCA	Citizens' Councils of America
CCMA	Christian Council of Metropolitan Atlanta
CDA	Citizens for a Decent Atlanta
CDC	Centers for Disease Control
DAR II	Dykes of the Second American Revolution
FEPC	Fair Employment Practices Commission
GAMA	Gay Atlanta Minority Association
GPA	Gay Pride Alliance
KKK	Ku Klux Klan
LEGAL	Legislate Equality for Gays and Lesbians
MCC	Metropolitan Community Church
NAACP	National Association for the Advancement of Colored People
NAMIETP	National AIDS Minority Information Education and Training Program
NBA	National Basketball Association
NCBLG	National Coalition of Black Lesbians and Gays
NCPA	National Citizens Protective Association
NGTF	National Gay (and Lesbian) Task Force
NUL	National Urban League

RACE	Reducing AIDS through Community Education Program
SCLC	Southern Christian Leadership Conference
SCLC/ WOMEN	SCLC/Women's Organizational Movement for Equality Now
UKA	United Klans of America
VA	Veterans Administration
WAC	Women's Army Corps
WNBA	Women's National Basketball Association

A Note on Language

In the decades following World War II, the terminology for sexual, racial, and gender categories has profoundly changed. In writing about such a dynamic period, I intentionally use a shifting set of descriptors and terms. Throughout the text, I endeavor to foreground how historical subjects understood themselves, their desires, their forms of kinship, and their varied kinds of embodiment.[1] First, I use the phrases "same-sex," "gender nonconformity," sexual/gender variants, and sexual and gender dissidents to describe individuals who—at the time—would have been placed under the broad rubric of homosexuality. "Same-sex" often amends other words including intimacies, sex, and desiring/desire. Although I deploy such language, I acknowledge the limitations of these phrases (especially same-sex, which reifies a sex binary).

Second, the terms "homosexuality" and "heterosexuality" appear repeatedly throughout the text. Many of the figures in this book—who articulated binaristic formulations of sex and gender—understood heterosexuality and homosexuality as oppositional with clear boundaries. Heterosexuality encapsulates desires, sexual acts, and intimacies between two people understood contemporarily to be of different sexes. Within this schema, male identification/masculinity and female identification/femininity are understood to align with the sex assigned at birth. Homosexuality references desires, sexual acts, and intimacies between two people understood contemporarily to be members of the same sex. Also, homosexuality was often used to reference diverse forms of gender nonconformity and expansiveness—with little consideration for how historical subjects themselves understood and articulated their gender expressions and/or identities. Crucially, the hegemony of these categories was (and continues to be) incomplete and contested. Keeping these two dominant epistemological categories in view may be jarring for early twenty-first-century readers, but it is crucial to understanding the political, social, and cultural terrain upon which various subjects, collectivities, and institutions enacted and experienced privilege or marginalization. At varying moments, I use or quote other descriptors, including queer, gay, lesbian, transsexual, and transgender. I follow Susan Stryker's understanding of transgender as referring "to people who move away from the gender they were assigned at birth, people who cross over (trans-) the boundaries constructed by their culture to define and contain that gender."[2] I use the terms "gay" and / or "lesbian," to amend "rights" and "movement" in ways that index gay liberation, gay liberalism and, less often, lesbian feminist political formations that emerged in the 1960s and persisted through the 1990s. I also use the term homophile to refer to early gay and lesbian civil rights organizations founded in the 1950s. When writing about the 1990s and beyond, I utilize LGBT and LGBTQ+, usually to reference the solidarities between and shared political goals of various nonnormative gender and sexual subjects.

Third, "queer" appears frequently within this work. As the introduction will more fully explicate, "queer" functions as a multivalent term: it is an analytic that centers how power is distributed through understandings of sexual and gender norms, while also seeing those "norms" as mutually constituted with race, class, nationality, and ability. For decades, queer was often used as a slur. AIDS activists began to reclaim the term during the 1980s as they sought to challenge the profound marginalizing force of medical care, governmental policy, and public rhetoric. I also use "queer" to refer to a broad cross-section of gender and sexually non-normative subjects. Following Cathy Cohen's incisive articulation about "the radical potential of queer politics," and what Gayle Rubin has influentially called "the charmed circle," queer here refers to a broad set of subjects that lie outside of (what in any particular moment) constitutes heteronormative ways of being (which center whiteness, cis-ness, middle-class/elite status, able-bodiedness, and narrow conceptions of legitimate kinship formations).[3] Critically, I understand Black sexualities, genders, and intimacies to be always already queer by nature of the transhistorical forces that construct Blackness as gender and sexual otherness.

This book uses varying terms to describe racial categories as well. "Black," "African American," and "people of African descent" are used interchangeably (although each term has different valences regarding the ethnicities and nationalities of their constituents). I choose to capitalize Black throughout the text as a way of denoting a shared set of cultural assumptions and historical experiences that worked to marginalize those who fall within its boundaries, as well a sense of solidarity amongst those who identified with these descriptors. In doing so, I do not seek to homogenize the experiences, ethnicities, and particular interests of those who are Black. I have chosen not to capitalize white. Crucially, this work does not understand any of these terms to be siloed from each other but rather as mutually imbricated and constructed.

Ambivalent Affinities

Introduction

· ·

As he approached the podium on a sunny day in spring, Phill Wilson appeared to have history on his mind. The Black HIV/AIDS and gay rights activist was poised to address hundreds of thousands assembled for the March on Washington for Lesbian, Gay, and Bi-Equal Rights and Liberation on April 25, 1993. This march—the third such gathering in fifteen years—reflected more than ever the profound vitality and diversity of what, at the time, was increasingly called the Lesbian, Gay, Bisexual, and Transgender (LGBT) rights movement: diversity of thought, in which some articulated a liberal, assimilationist vision of gay politics while others embraced a transgressive queer politics that challenged sexual and gender norms. And diversity of racial background, in which two of the cochairs (Nadine Smith and Derek Livingston) were African American, and people of color represented 50 percent of all those officially involved in march planning.[1] Wilson's remarks centered Black queer communities while linking two political struggles imagined, by some, to be similar: the post-war Black freedom struggle and various political mobilizations by Lesbian, Gay, Bisexual, Transgender, and Queer (LGBTQ+) subjects.[2] Notably, these comparisons coexisted with a tendency to silo these two broadly imagined groups; a siloing in which Black subjects were imagined as heterosexual and LGBTQ+ subjects were assumed to be white.

Wilson began his remarks by turning to the inspiration for the 1993 mobilization—the 1963 March on Washington for Jobs and Freedom. "Thirty years ago, another people marched on Washington," Wilson declared, "urging America to be America again." The young activist reminded his audience that it was not only the iconic Dr. Martin Luther King Jr.'s vision of a just America (as articulated in his "I Have a Dream" speech) that should be remembered. Rather, he asserted that the 1963 mobilization was also the dream of Bayard Rustin, "a Black gay man." A skilled progressive organizer, Rustin assumed the role of deputy director of the march despite his homophobic ouster from Dr. King's inner circle years earlier and the objections of other march organizers. In spite of white supremacist efforts to use Rustin's criminal conviction and homosexuality to delegitimize the mobilization, the events of that day became an iconic articulation of nonviolent protest. But Wilson's genealogical vision did not end with Rustin. It included another Black queer forebearer—Langston Hughes, the famed bard, playwright, and novelist. The phrase "urging America to be American again" referenced a poem titled "Let America Be America Again," a vision of cross-racial, working-class solidarity.[3] In invoking Hughes, Wilson foregrounded a central practice of the Black gay cultural renaissance—the search for a usable Black queer past to cultivate self-esteem and affirmation.[4] For Wilson, then, amplifying the place of Black queer ancestors in the Black freedom struggle challenged the perception that LGBTQ+ subjects and concerns were exogenous to Black political concerns.

Coalitions with prominent civil rights organizations provided another tangible connection to Black social movements past and present.[5] In a press release announcing the endorsement of the march by the National Association for the Advancement of Colored People (NAACP), Executive Director George Carter referenced their place "at the forefront in the struggle for equal rights," as part of the rationale for a resolution that called for the "end [of] discrimination against gay men and lesbian Americans in areas of American life where all citizens deserve equal protection and equal opportunity under the law."[6] However, these coalitional ties were not without detractors. Later that summer, as the nation's oldest civil rights organization prepared to stage its annual convention, a series of protests decried the NAACP's support for gay rights. Concerned Citizens for Traditional Family Values, an African American conservative group, objected to the group's pro-gay rights stance, characterizing it as immoral and illustrative of "the growing schism between the civil rights organization and the grassroots of the African American community."[7]

Wilson's meditation on historical continuities also extended to the adversaries of both movements. The activist reminded his audience that those who once opposed racial equality now mobilized against gays, lesbians, and people living with AIDS. "The Jesse Helms who discriminates against HIV-infected immigrants in 1993 is the same Jesse Helms who discriminated against Black schoolchildren in North Carolina in 1954," he declared. Helms, then the Republican senator for North Carolina, joined a vanguard of southern politicians who moved to the Republican Party in part as a response to the Democratic Party's support for desegregation and the protection of African American civil rights. In the 1980s, Helms opposed the passage of legislation to recognize Dr. King's birthday as a federal holiday and opposed funding for AIDS educational programs that he believed might promote homosexual behavior. Wilson also referenced the Republican senator from neighboring South Carolina: "The Strom Thurmond who tried to undermine the civil rights march in 1963 is the same Strom Thurmond who is trying to undermine lesbian and gay men in the military in 1993." In the days leading up to the 1963 March on Washington, Thurmond had denounced Rustin on the floor of the US Senate as a communist and criminal, infamously submitting into the Congressional Record evidence of the activist's 1953 morals charge conviction in Pasadena, California. In the early 1990s, the long-serving senator opposed repealing the ban on gay and lesbian military service. Wilson's genealogy of opposition to the empowerment of various marginalized communities not only exposed the shared terrain of white supremacy and homophobia, but framed them as co-constitutive. During a press conference before the march he asserted: "Oppression is of a whole cloth. We don't have the luxury of pretending that we can embrace a part of that cloth without accepting the whole of that cloth. The reality is that if we don't understand the connection certainly those people who are hatemongers do." In highlighting two antagonistic politicians to the civil rights and LGBTQ+ rights movements, Wilson articulated a view of these oppressive forces as mutually constitutive and compounding. His remarks evoke a longer history of the imbricated nature of the postwar Black freedom struggle, the gay and lesbian rights movement, and the challenges to both.[8]

· · · · · ·

By 1993, a kind of ambivalence marked the relationship between gay/lesbian and Black political identities. As Blackness became increasingly associated with heterosexuality and gay/lesbian political formations became racialized as white (a process deeply tied to local spatial contexts and organizational formations), these two constituencies became increasingly mutually referential in national political discourse. Some compared anti-Black racism and homophobia as similar forms of marginalization, suggesting that both groups pursue shared forms of redress, including antidiscrimination protections in housing and employment, hate crime legislation, policing reform, and the abolition of various laws that disproportionately criminalized both groups. Although these comparisons became most visible in early twenty-first-century debates over marriage equality, they have a longer history. Comparisons between gay/lesbian rights and Black civil rights grew during the last three decades of the twentieth century with the emergence of widespread political organizing among sexual and gender dissidents. These comparisons emerged in various places and spaces, including cities where African American elected officials forged important coalitions with gay and lesbian voters, at the national level as gay rights organizations sought admission to a broader coalition of civil rights groups in the late 1970s and 1980s, and in the halls of Congress as advocates pursued employment nondiscrimination legislation and the repeal of bans on gay, lesbian, and transgender military service.

However, there is another largely neglected origin point for these comparisons: the postwar Black freedom struggle and political challenges to it. *Ambivalent Affinities: A Political History of Blackness and Homosexuality after World War II* follows how ideas about same-sex intimacy and gender nonconformity (most often categorized as homosexuality) emerged within political contests over white supremacy and Black racial equality. In doing so, this monograph illuminates an important realm in which Blackness and homosexuality became simultaneously linked and distanced in the broader American political imaginary. I follow gay/lesbian activists, white supremacists, political conservatives, civil rights organizations, and Black municipal officials as they attempted to advance their political objectives by deploying varied conceptualizations of sexuality, gender, and race. Focusing on key moments of crisis, organizing, and discourse from World War II until the 1993 March on Washington for Lesbian, Gay, and Bi-Equal Rights and Liberation, I trace one branch of political history that would have important ramifications for late-twentieth- and early-twenty-first-century conversations about race and sexuality, reaching a crescendo around the movement for marriage equality in the 2000s and 2010s.

At its core, *Ambivalent Affinities* asserts that "Blackness" and "homosexuality" (later largely configured as "gay and lesbian" identification) should be understood as mutually constituted political formations emerging, in part, out of the modern civil rights movement and resistance to it. Such bidirectional referentiality, I argue, was rooted not in the language of shared or intersecting identities but rather in the rhetoric of similar and/or shared estrangements—that is, the processes through which certain individuals are marked by differentiation, subjected to policing, and excluded from social, political, and economic privileges. For gay and lesbian activists, African Americans' historical and contemporary marginalization formed a useful reference point for their own political subjectivities, even as some sought to extract themselves from categories of criminality and deviancy long racialized as Black and Brown. For some Black liberals, a sense of similar marginalization and shared adversaries nurtured alliances. However, tensions persisted as both groups had particular encounters with the state. Broadly, Black liberals adopted a pragmatic approach to sexual matters. Although this approach created opportunities to challenge homophobia reflected in law, policy, and politics, I argue that, in general, collective and individual action tended to align with the heteronormativity of society. This is due in part to the long-standing historic vulnerability of Black communities to narratives of sexual and gender deviance *and* in response to the heteronormativity of the state. Political conservatives and white supremacists also shaped this mutual referentiality, increasingly associating support for gay rights with support for racial equality, interracial sex, and Black political empowerment. By including white supremacists and political conservatives in the story, I attend to how shared grammars of deviancy facilitated these comparisons. I argue for an intersectional framing of postwar political histories that does not solely limit our understandings of Blackness and homosexuality as rooted in the realm of identification but also sees them as conceptual frames for non-normativity. This book deepens our understanding of how the homosexual-heterosexual binary (as it emerged as a political formation) continued to rely on a Black-white racial axis for articulation and conceptualization well into the post–World War II period.

· · · · · ·

This book constitutes a shoot, a branch of a large, deeply rooted genealogical tree of racial and sexual formations. Genealogies are filled with subversive and deconstructionist potential. The efforts to trace lineage, notes Michel Foucault, are less about documenting "an unbroken continuity" of descent than a way to "distur[b] what was thought unified; it shows the heterogeneity of what was imagined consistent with itself."[9] This work follows such provocative disruption in its efforts to contribute to scholarly interrogations of the shared lineages of racial and sexual formations.[10] At its core, this book offers one story about how homosexuality and Blackness are linked through shared estrangements and resistance to it. By estrangement, I refer to Nayan Shah's articulation of "an active process of forcible dislocation, removing people from 'an accustomed place or set of associations.' It sours the grounds of shared membership by sowing feelings of hostility, distrust, and 'unsympathetic and indifferent' regard." According to Shah, three key technologies can further these forms of differentiation: "colonial and imperial knowledge formation; state policing, incarceration and extralegal violence; subordination, exclusion, and normalization."[11] Each of these processes informs and is informed by various social formations, including class, gender, sexuality, and race. By resistance, I refer to varied ways of being and belonging that challenge political, ideological, economic, and material forms of estrangement.[12]

Taking inspiration from Shah's framework, *Ambivalent Affinities* interrogates how forms of estrangement on the basis of Black racial identification and queerness (with a particular focus on non-normative ways of being understood contemporarily as homosexuality) emerged within contests over Black racial equality. Here, Black estrangement is the process by which a group of people with sub-Saharan African ancestry in the United States experience(d) differentiation, marginalization, and exclusion across a number of social, political, cultural, and economic realms. Queer estrangement refers to the varied ways that acts, desires, subjectivities, and bodies associated with loosely defined ideas of gender and sexual nonconformity were (and in some instances are) criminalized, understood as deviant, and act as a bar to full citizenship. Across both categories, modes of instantiation include laws, policies, discourse, and both extralegal and institutional violence. To follow these forms of estrangement across postwar political history necessarily requires close attention to the construction of "normative" and "non-normative" categories. This book follows (non)normative categories of race, gender, and sexuality in ways that attend to two themes: grammars of deviance and state encounters.

Grammars of Deviance

Blackness and homosexuality have long been framed as deviant. For African-descended peoples, constructions of gender and sexual deviance have been crucial to varied manifestations of political, social, and economic subjugation. Conceptualizations of Black bodies as lewd and subhuman facilitated the material and ideological work of the transatlantic slave trade and the rise of chattel slavery in the Western Hemisphere. The racialization of slave and free status was intimately tied to sexuality and reproduction. As colonial governments banned interracial marriages and made enslaved status inheritable through the maternal line, slaveholders solidified their economic and political interests through the exploitation of enslaved women's (re)productive and sexual capacities. In the face of such degradation, enslaved people pursued bodily, familial, and erotic autonomy through a variety of means—means that proved consequential to the arrival of formal emancipation in the middle of the 1860s.[13] With freedom came the process of building and resuming interrupted lives—negotiating familial, marital, and romantic bonds and encountering the disciplining power of the state. While the newly emancipated often sought to have their marital bonds recognized, the state sought to regulate more fully their intimate lives.[14] Emancipation did not mark the end of sexual and gendered racial terror and exploitation; rather, it fomented its continuation, reconstitution, and reiteration. Through rioting, mob violence, lynching, and interpersonal sexual violence, African Americans experienced profound forms of racial terror that aimed to challenge their citizenship status within and beyond the former slaveholding states. Disfiguring discourses about Black sexualities, bodies, and ways of being legitimized legal and interpersonal violence.[15] As racial segregation and racially explicit forms of discrimination were being dismantled during the middle of the twentieth century, Black intimacies continued to be figured as deviant and dangerous. Journalists, politicians, and scholars continued to depict particular Black familial formations, intimacies, and behaviors as pathological, non-normative, and necessitating state regulation. Moreover, the centrality of heteronormativity within social welfare policy was and is used to police and punish Black domestic spaces and intimacies.[16] In the midst of such degradation, Black subjects continued to find joy, pleasure, and sustenance in their intimate lives, offering challenges to these marginalizing forces.

Beginning in the colonial era, formal and informal policing sought to curtail gender nonconformity and same-sex intimacy. Buggery and sodomy laws punished nonprocreative sexual activity and were disproportionately applied to those whose class, gender, and racial subjectivities rendered them less powerful. However, it was during the second half of the nineteenth century that same-sex intimacy and gender nonconformity were increasingly understood as deviant and subjected to state and institutional scrutiny. Responding in part to increasingly visible communities organized around sexual and gendered ways of being, Euro-American physicians, scientists, and knowledge producers created hierarchies and binaries of gender and sexuality. The Black-white binary provided a crucial set of reference points for hardening conceptualizations of heterosexuality and homosexuality in medical discourse and urban public space.[17] Cross-dressing laws were often deployed to police race, citizenship, and public space as well as gender expression. The end of Prohibition in the 1930s and the expansion of federal power during the New Deal era and World War II instituted a crucial shift in understandings of gender and sexual normativity. The ensuing concretization (however incomplete) of object-choice–based sexual identification and a hierarchy of heterosexuality and homosexuality resonated within the lives of gender and sexual transgressors in American life. Federal policies that made homosexuality grounds for termination from military and civilian employment, the proliferation of state sexual psychopath laws, police brutality and harassment, hostile medical and psychiatric practices, and denigrating public narratives all worked to deepen the political, social, and economic marginalization of queer persons. [18] However, these challenging years witnessed the growth of transgender, gay, and lesbian social spaces, organizations, and collectivities. The emergence of what Marc Stein characterizes as the gay and lesbian movement issued a multifaceted political challenge to these forms of material and epistemological violence.[19]

While various institutions, discourses, and political actors played a crucial role in shaping these narratives of deviancy, an array of individuals, collectivities, and organizations within the broad field of American conservatism also promulgated these ideas. As a robust historiography documents, race and space were central forces in the growth and articulation of modern conservatism. Crucial to these developments after World War II was the shift from nakedly racist appeals to ostensibly "color-blind" rhetoric that focused on the legitimacy of local autonomy in schooling, taxation, and suburban development, appeals that all worked to maintain segregation and racial inequality. Resistance to the civil rights movement occurred alongside an energized Protestant Christian electoral base alarmed by liberalizing sexual mores, reproductive rights, and gay rights organizing. These campaigns targeted some of the very initiatives that had seemed to be the most successful in advancing gay rights: antidiscrimination ordinances, sodomy law reforms, and coalitions with elected officials. In historiographies of both the Black freedom struggle and gay rights movement, racial and sexual conservatives are regularly cast as foils and foes—as those mobilizing profound opposition to the efforts and actions of those seeking liberation.[20] Fewer studies bring these historiographies together.[21] Those that have done so reveal an understudied strand of the history of conservatism in its profound imbrication of anti-Blackness with anti-queerness (both homophobia and more broadly).

This book joins this small but powerful literature to demonstrate how these particular strands are not only linked but reflective of an important shift. I argue that the centrality of sexual and gender deviance in white supremacist and radical right rhetoric organically facilitated increased attention to homosexuality as it became equated with sexual deviance after World War II. I document how white supremacists and radical right organizations increasingly linked Black political organizing (liberal and radical) to homosexuality as well as gay/lesbian political work. They did so, in part, because in the imaginaries of southern Democrats, radical right organizations (such as the American Nazi Party), and vanguard organizations of massive resistance (White Citizens' Councils and the United Klans of America), gender nonconformity and same-sex sex followed support for civil rights and/or Blackness.[22] Certainly, the homophobia at the heart of anti-communism and the sexual dimensions of anti-Blackness informed these efforts. However, as I note, the declining persuasiveness of anti-miscegenationist rhetoric prompted a discursive shift toward exploiting other signifiers of and references to sexual/gender nonconformity (including obscenity and homosexuality).

State Encounters, Resistance, and Ambivalent Affinities

If *Ambivalent Affinities* is an uneven story about three political constituencies, the state forms a fourth powerful presence. Specifically, the central actors in this book encounter the state in two ways. The first is as a criminalizing entity. Efforts to curtail the movement and empowerment of Black subjects in the aftermath of emancipation worked in tandem with the rise of social scientific data that deepened connections between Blackness and criminality during the second half of the nineteenth century and the first half of the twentieth century. The expansion of the carceral state continued after World War II as liberal and conservative politicians alike advanced laws and policies that expanded the net of criminalization. Across the liberal- conservative divide, law-and-order rhetoric cast people of color—and African Americans in particular—as threats to public safety and tranquility. Conservatives advanced a rhetoric of law and order that dovetailed with white fears of the Black freedom struggle and racial integration. Liberals, however, contributed to this apparatus by conceptualizing racial violence as individual and arbitrary, rather than systematic and structural, mobilizing "damage imagery" that cast forms of Black behavior as the fruits of white supremacy.[23] The militarization of law enforcement, differential policing and sentencing rates that accompanied the war on drugs, coupled with forms of surveillance associated with social welfare programs, wove a net of state containment and control that led to mass incarceration during the twentieth and early twenty-first centuries. Sexuality was a crucial arena of policing, as narratives about Black sexual depravity animated laws that targeted Black subjects for vagrancy, sex work, disorderly conduct, and morals charges. Moreover, practices of state surveillance associated with public assistance and housing placed the erotic and parental relationships of Black subjects under additional scrutiny.[24]

Queer Americans also experienced criminalization. Although statutes and practices that criminalized same-sex intimacy and gender nonconformity extend to the pre–Civil War era, these forms of policing intensified as a binary of sexual identity crystallized during the late nineteenth and first half of the twentieth centuries.[25] The removal of same-sex-desiring service members in the World War II–era military foretold an expansive shift in federal policy, or what Margot Canaday refers to as the homosexual-heterosexual binary in which individuals understood as the former were barred from naturalized citizenship, social welfare benefits, and military service. At the state and local levels, the proliferation of sexual psychopath laws (and policing of queer and transgender communities using vagrancy, immoral conduct, sodomy, and cross-dressing statutes) further criminalized sexual and gender nonconformity. In the 1970s, some gay liberals worked to distance themselves from other perceived social problems subject to policing (largely marked as urban and racialized as non-white), instead situating gay and lesbian citizens as needing protection from violence (regularly imagined as emanating from Black and Brown subjects). While these campaigns occurred at the national, state, and local level, they were most successful locally. However, often it was those members of LGBTQ+ communities who are the most normative presenting and privileged that were able to access shifts in policing, the decriminalization of private sexuality, and hate crime laws.[26] Even though this book is not an explicit study of criminalization, its imprint appears in almost every chapter. Rather than offer a novel argument, *Ambivalent Affinities* builds on work that shows how similar and disparate experiences with criminalization facilitated support for and tensions within Black-gay political coalitions.

Resistance to these forms of marginalization and inequity constitutes the second kind of state encounter detailed herein. Although the ideologies that animated both the gay and lesbian rights movement and the postwar Black freedom struggle are diverse and overlapping, this book most profoundly centers a group I frame as Black (or African American) liberals. This large collectivity articulated what political scientist Michael Dawson calls "radical egalitarianism" associated with a Black liberal tradition. According to Dawson, this vision entailed the "coupling [of] . . . a severe critique of racism in American society [with] an impassioned appeal for America to live up to the best of its values and support for a radical egalitarian view of a multiracial democratic society."[27] More specifically, I classify these actors as "Black liberals" because of two overriding characteristics: first, their commitment to the greater inclusion of Black Americans within the perceived benefits of capitalism (forms of inclusion that often disproportionately benefited middle-class and elite community members), and second, a prioritization of the governmental protections of civil and political rights as the a priori way to challenge and dismantle white supremacy.[28] Throughout the book, I also reference and pay attention to those in the Black radical tradition. I believe that a study that centers Black radicals is an essential counterpart to this work and will reveal different kinds of intersecting engagements between queerness and Blackness. However, I am interested in examining Black liberals given the powerful position they held within national politics by the end of the twentieth century and because of how they consistently pursued civil rights–based formal equality throughout the second half of the twentieth century. Of course, I do not mean to suggest that organizers and thinkers who formed a part of the Black radical tradition eschewed similar goals or that the individuals featured herein fit neatly into one or the other political traditions.[29]

This book concentrates on two different manifestations of Black liberal action: civil rights organizations (the NAACP, the National Urban League, and the Southern Christian Leadership Conference), which are my main focus, and in chapter 5, the actions of Maynard Jackson, the first Black mayor of Atlanta, and his administration.[30] In returning to Black liberal encounters with certain concepts of homosexuality, I argue that a kind of ambivalence marked their efforts. On the one hand, these individuals and organizations regularly prioritized specific objectives rather than embrace respectability (with its claims to sexual and gender normativity) for its own sake. These objectives were varied and included challenging heteronormative (and homophobic) law, policy, and custom, forging alliances with gay/lesbian political communities, and embracing a more expansive vision of Black intimate life beyond respectability. On the other hand, the power of normative gender/sexual definitions continued to influence Black liberal decision-making. I argue that Black liberals' keen understanding of the centrality of grammars of deviance to white supremacist articulations of anti-Blackness determined responses to anti-homosexual campaigns and battles over gay rights.

This book also examines the actions of organizations and individuals associated with the gay and lesbian rights movement (albeit to a much lesser extent).[31] This movement, like others, was diverse and included both radical and conservative branches. Given the book's focus on access to forms of state power, I largely prioritize analysis of gay and lesbian activists' reformist efforts (although not exclusively, as we will see in chapter 5). In general, these efforts emphasized visibility, or "coming out"; support for sodomy law reform; antidiscrimination statutes; and the cultivation of gay and lesbian voting blocs that might build strong working relationships with municipal elected officials (who in many places were increasingly African American but not exclusively so). Some within these movements tried to differentiate themselves from various kinds of urban criminality and deviancy, often associated with Black and Brown communities.[32] This book also seeks to be attentive to forms of organizing among gender variant communities, some of which aligned with gay and lesbian social movements and others of which sought out different political terrain. *Ambivalent Affinities* builds on this work, demonstrating how gay and lesbian liberals relied on comparisons between homophobia and anti-Black racism as well as their political organizing to the Black freedom struggle while simultaneously distancing themselves en masse from the concerns of those communities.

Methods

This book is an account of political estrangements after World War II. It amends the stories we tell about the postwar political landscape by following the intersecting mobilizations, discourses, and encounters between three overlapping but distinct groups: Black liberal activists and elected officials, largely white gay and lesbian radicals and liberals, and predominately white political conservatives who disliked the challenges issued by both of these groups. While the participants are varied, each chapter unfolds against the backdrop (and at times foreground) of African Americans (largely liberals) seeking political empowerment. These arenas include efforts for economic and political advancement during the early Cold War years, the modern civil rights movement, Black municipal governance, and the disproportionate impact of the AIDS crisis on communities of color. The story of postwar politics offered here seeks to answer Chandan Reddy's call to "retrieve different histories and accounts of power, ones that could prove to be crucial alternatives" to the vision of political life linked to the "liberal nation state."[33] *Ambivalent Affinities* offers a particular analysis of power, one in which the historical linkages between Blackness and queerness facilitated access to and a desire for channels of power among Black civil rights organizations, gay/lesbian activists, and conservatives.

While national in scope, this project shifts between various geographic and spatial registers, from national political discourse and organizing efforts to local municipal political battles. This sense of movement mirrors the varied places and ways gender and sexuality emerged within Black-white racial contests. Notably, a number of the moments registered here occur within the southern United States, suggesting the centrality of sex/sexuality to the region's racial politics. Temporally, my study is book-ended by two different years and moments. I begin in 1945, when the end of World War II overlaps with the continuing emergence of the homosexual-heterosexual binary within federal policy and a broader reinvigoration of Black political action. I end in 1993, when the NAACP's endorsement of the March on Washington for Lesbian, Gay and Bi-Equal Rights and Liberation signaled, to some, the shift of the gay and lesbian rights movement into the mainstream of civil rights organizations. In adopting this periodization, I do not mean to suggest an end to the continuing imbrication of racial and sexual categories. Rather, my focus on this period allows me to frame some of the consequences of these developments in the early twenty-first century.

This project is, first and foremost, a reflection of scattered and wide-ranging source material. My own approach to the archive was a peripatetic one. For almost a decade I scoured published sources, organizational records, personal manuscript collections, ephemera, public health documents, and legal, military, and bureaucratic records to locate points of intersections and dissonances. In so doing, I am able to present a story that functions more as a question than a definitive answer about the important ways ideas about homosexuality and Blackness remain profoundly imbricated yet distanced in the second half of the twentieth century. Numerous actors appear within these pages: career politicos, race men and women devoted to Black institutional life, individuals who fall outside of normative sexual and gender categories, white supremacist demagogues, policymakers, government officials, and more. This work thus draws from primary source material such as organizational records, constituent correspondence, white supremacist ephemera, newspapers, magazines, public health documents, legal and military records, and an oral history to tell a broad story.

As a work of Black feminist history, *Ambivalent Affinities* uses an intersectional framework in its consideration of post–World War II political power. Intersectionality attends to how social constructions of difference and the structures of domination that reinforce them are mutually constitutive, interlocking, and should not be analyzed in isolation. This framework accounts for the complex and potentially contradictory ways particular political communities experienced foreclosures and avenues for empowerment and strategizing.[34] My book thus remains attentive to how race, gender, sexuality, and, to a lesser extent, class informed the political action of different constituencies across nearly five decades. An intersectional framework also allows for a broadened consideration of how social categories can have contradictory and wide-ranging meanings. Evelyn Brooks Higginbotham identifies race as "double-voiced," as a force that could both unite but also fracture, facilitating homogenization and differentiation.[35] Sexuality operates in a similar vein: it is an experience, discourse, and ideological tool that has both unifying and severing force. I also employ methods central to Black feminist historical analyses, including speculation, reading against the grain, and close readings of sources.

This book is also a work of queer history in which "queer" functions as an analytic of power. "Queer" identifies a broad array of non-normative desires, sexual acts, familial formations, and gender formations that have been subjected to gender/sexual regulation beyond the frame of static identities. I offer an intersectional history of Blackness and queerness that is not limited to Black queer subjectivities. Rather, this work contributes to LGBT/queer history and African American history in two ways. First, it joins existing work arguing for how gay/lesbian political communities were explicitly and implicitly informed by and in conversation with Black social and political communities. In doing so, it joins what Christina Hanhardt identifies as the growing field of "queer political history," which calls for a broader analysis of power that shifts the subjects at the center of LGBT politics.[36] Second, this book understands Black Americans who articulated heterosexual identities and practiced some sexual/gender normativity in a world that sought to deny them both as queer subjects. I move beyond the assumption that heteronormative logics, including the politics of respectability, were the primary influence on Black political action. Rather, I demonstrate how, when, and why the binary of heterosexuality and homosexuality reverberated outward, informing Black liberal actors' choices and strategies. In particular, I join other scholars who examine how the legacy of sexual and gender non-normativity rooted in a history of chattel slavery and its aftermath continued to inform the actions of Black political actors, imaginaries, and subjectivities.[37]

Whereas the above understanding of queer incorporates an array of sexual and gender formations, this book focuses narrowly on homosexuality during the second half of the twentieth century. Indeed, it might seem as though this focus contradicts the expansive definition and method of queering articulated above. Limiting our view to concepts of homosexuality as they crossed paths with battles over Black racial empowerment, however, allows for a more precise understanding of the increasing power of heteronormativity during the second half of the twentieth century.[38] Moreover, conceptualizations of homosexuality, particularly as they emerged within political contestations over white supremacy, rarely were limited to a focus on same-sex intimacy and gender nonconformity. Rather, the appearance of homosexuality within political discourse acted as a fellow traveler to conceptions of kinship, extramarital sex, interracial and intraracial intimacy, and racialized space. This understanding underlies my main argument that homosexuality has been a constitutive node for conversations and contestations about Black liberal politics during the second half of the twentieth century.

Part 1 situates the complexity of Black liberal politics and its organizational forms within early Cold War–era homophobia and the uneven consolidation of a homosexual-heterosexual binary of sexual identity within American life. Chapter 1 examines the NAACP's encounter with anti-homosexual federal bureaucratic policy, excavating the organization's willingness, in the form of the Veterans' Affairs Bureau, to confront the discharge of Black service members for same-sex intimacies. In doing so, the NAACP facilitated a rare and fundamental challenge to the military's sexual exclusion as they sought to advance their vision of postwar racial equality. Chapter 2 tells an obverse story, as it moves from the broad, human rights activism of the immediate postwar years to the limiting influence of anti-communism on Black politics in the mid-1950s. When the National Urban League publicized the arrest and conviction of a segregationist on a same-sex intergenerational morals charge, they demonstrated how Black civil rights organizations used anti-gay moral panic for their own gain. Part 2 shifts from an inquiry into the sexual politics of Black liberal organizations to the use of sexual discourses by white supremacists and the radical right, whose narratives closely align support for civil rights and racial equality with sexual and gender non-normativity. Chapter 3 turns to the Alabama voting rights demonstrations of 1965. Alongside the racist rhetoric of Alabama public officials, who characterized the demonstrators as degenerates and criminals, rumors that the protestors engaged in lewd, public, same-sex sex reverberated within and outside of the state. This marked the beginning of a trend in which white supremacists and racial demagogues nationwide cast supporters of racial equality as queer. Chapter 4 surveys the propaganda of the American Nazi Party, the Citizens' Councils of America, and the United Klans of America which, across the 1960s and early 1970s, increasingly referenced gender nonconformity and same-sex desire alongside Blackness generally and Black political action in particular. Part 3 analyzes encounters between Black liberals and gay/lesbian activists (white and of color). Chapter 5 examines public battles over the 1976 mayoral resolution recognizing Gay Pride Day in Atlanta, Georgia and the resulting tumult from metropolitan area conservatives (largely white but also Black). This chapter analyzes how Mayor Maynard Jackson not only navigated the tensions of holding together a minoritarian liberal constituency but also encountered the racial animus of Citizens for a Decent Atlanta, who opposed the proclamation recognizing gay pride. It then turns briefly to the possibilities and foreclosures of Black-gay coalitions in 1980s Atlanta. Chapter 6 excavates the crucial work of the SCLC/WOMEN, the women's auxiliary of the Southern Christian Leadership Conference, which engaged in HIV/AIDS educational activism from 1986 to 1993. This chapter reveals how the tensions around the disease's (homo)sexual connotations and its increasingly disproportionate impact on Black communities resulted in ambivalent messaging, suggesting the continued pull of recuperative impulses around African American sexuality among some Black liberals. The epilogue is less a conclusion and more an offering of what I hope the book might proffer in the historical, historiographical, political, and material realms—all orbiting around my central claim that Black liberal political communities continue to turn to a redemptive heteronormative sexual politics, even as these efforts yield diminishing returns.

Ambivalent Affinities offers an analysis of post–World War II politics in which political understandings of (largely) gay and lesbian legal and social equality were tethered to contested conceptualizations of Black equality in similar realms. Although these linked articulations of Blackness and homosexuality emerged outside the realm of state action, they were profoundly undergirded by the anti-Blackness and heteronormativity of federal, state, and local laws and policies. This book, then, offers a crucial context for the continued imbrication of anti-Blackness, cisheteronormativity, and multifaceted challenges to both in the early twenty-first century.

Part I **Black Civil Rights Organizations and Sexual Exclusion in Early Cold War America**

. . . .

1 To Stand upon My Constitutional Rights

The NAACP Veterans' Affairs Bureau and
World War II–Era Sexual Exclusion, 1945–1950

....

On May 14, 1944, Lieutenant Lemuel S. Brown of the 398th Army Infantry composed a brief letter to Charles Hamilton Houston, an African American attorney and the architect of the National Association for the Advancement of Colored People's (NAACP) legal strategy to end de jure racial segregation. In the letter, the officer conveyed his decision "to stand upon my constitutional rights" and be tried via court-martial rather than voluntarily resign for "attempting to perpetrate an act of Homosexuality." His dilemma—to accept an undesirable discharge or potentially be convicted and incarcerated—mirrored that of thousands of people in the army and navy who encountered the military's intensified efforts to identify, punish, and expel same-sex-desiring persons from their ranks. Convicted and sentenced to five years confinement in a San Francisco, California, military prison, Brown implored Houston to "give this case your attention and advise me as to the best course to take if any."[1] As former dean of Howard University School of Law and special counsel to the NAACP, Houston was uniquely positioned to advocate on the soldier's behalf.[2] Concluding that Brown's five-year prison sentence was "more severe than usual," he promised that the veteran's situation would be "brought to the attention of the proper authorities."[3] Houston subsequently forwarded copies of this correspondence to Truman K. Gibson, an African American civilian aide in the War Department who addressed Black military personnel's complaints of racism.[4] Although the evidentiary record does not reveal whether Gibson intervened, the army freed Brown less than two years later.[5]

Freedom did not mark the conclusion of Brown's military-related hardships, however. In December 1946, Brown again solicited Houston for help. Writing from his lodging at the Saint Antoine Street YMCA in Detroit, Michigan, he recounted how "for the past two years mine has been the task of self-readjustment and rehabilitation with no assistance from those agencies or facilities provided by the Government."[6] Such "assistance" was readily available to millions of honorably discharged veterans in the pecuniary, educational, and employment benefits provisioned by the Servicemen's Readjustment Act of 1944. As Ira Katznelson notes, this landmark legislation—commonly referred to as the GI Bill of Rights (or simply the GI Bill)—was "the most wide-ranging set of social benefits ever offered by the federal government in a single, comprehensive initiative," helping to create "middle-class America."[7] Yet, because of his dishonorable discharge, this Black veteran was ineligible to receive these benefits. In his missive, Brown lamented the "mental anguish, the nervous strain, the embarrassment and the social ostracism I had been forced to endure." Such hardship emanated not only from his disgraceful removal from service but its alleged cause—homosexual conduct.[8]

Brown's appeal is an impactful testament to how certain American citizens endured not only entrenched anti-Blackness from the state but also deepening forms of homophobia. For African Americans, the racially discriminatory policies of the US military reflected profound inequities in American life, including employment discrimination, limited access to adequate education, and widespread disfranchisement in the South. In the army, for example, an implicit commitment to the dyadic notion of white superiority and Black inferiority institutionalized racial segregation, legitimized the detrimental provisioning, positioning, and promotion of Black GIs, and sanctioned the hostile actions of white comrades, superiors, and civilians.[9] While African Americans labored against these racial inequities, men and women suspected of engaging in same-sex sex (some of whom were also Black and people of color) experienced increasing forms of surveillance and punishment within the army and navy. Military officials routinely arrested, imprisoned, and hospitalized individuals suspected of same-sex intimacies, characterizing them as unfit for service. Notably, military officials used the same mechanism to enact racial and sexual discrimination: the undesirable or "blue" discharge. Such removals from service also reverberated in civilian life, acting as a bar to veterans' benefits and as a stigmatizing designation. Same-sex-desiring Black Americans, like Brown, experienced interlocking forms of racism and homophobia, compounding their marginalization.[10]

In response, a handful of veterans turned to the NAACP's short-lived auxiliary, the Veterans' Affairs Bureau, to improve their postwar fortunes by challenging their discharge status. This chapter analyzes the Veterans' Affairs Bureau's advocacy on behalf of several men removed from service for same-sex intimacies from 1944 to 1950. According to the extant documentation located within the NAACP records, eleven male veterans requested and received assistance in the amendment of their undesirable discharges for homosexuality-related offenses. Given the fragmentary nature of much of the discharge review correspondence, it is likely that additional veterans removed for same-sex intimacies sought assistance from this organization. I argue that such advocacy—limited though it was—should be understood as reflecting the Veterans' Affairs Bureau's desire to facilitate the flow of benefits to African Americans who already faced substantive barriers to postwar prosperity.[11] This pragmatic approach seemingly outweighed any potential reticence in offering aid to same-sex-desiring Black men due to sexual conservatism or the politics of respectability.[12] The NAACP's encounter with sexual exclusion in American citizenship policy was not isolated; rather, it foreshadowed how African American civil rights organizations increasingly encountered politicized concepts of homosexuality as they labored against discrimination and anti-Black racism. Finally, returning to these records offers glimpses into the community-building and resiliency practices of Black queer service members during the middle of the twentieth century.

Racial and Sexual Exclusion in World War II–Era Military and Veterans' Policy

In a January 31, 1942, letter to the *Pittsburgh Courier,* twenty-six-year-old James G. Thompson queried, "Should I sacrifice my life to live half [an] American? Would it be demanding too much to demand full citizenship rights in exchange for the sacrificing of my life?" These demands, he offered, constituted a Double V campaign, in which "the first V [stands] for victory over our enemies from without, the second V [stands] for victory over our enemies from within."[13] The popularity of this strategy within Black political and civic organizations reflected widespread outrage over racial inequities in civilian and military life. Officials consistently relegated African Americans to service details, limited opportunities for advancement and officer training, and distributed low-quality equipment to segregated units.[14] Army officials deployed narratives of Black racial inferiority and the possibility of interracial tensions to justify these actions.[15] Frequent hostility from white enlisted men, officers, and civilians in the form of racial epithets and threats of violence compounded feelings of shame and degradation among some Black soldiers, sailors, and airmen.[16] An anonymous soldier stationed near Sioux Falls, Iowa, testified to such abuse in a 1943 letter to the *Newark Afro-American,* asserting, "It is not a strange thing to hear a Lieutenant or major use the word N—r [*sic*]."[17] Such firsthand accounts highlight the profound disparities between the ideals of American democracy and the realities of Black military experiences.

Racial disparities also existed within the military's policing and judicial systems. For example, African Americans constituted 42 percent of all army personnel convicted of sexual crimes in the European theater of operations, despite the fact that they only represented 8 percent of all American forces in that region.[18] Military officials' deeply held assumptions of the sexual rapacity of African American men (especially toward white women) surely informed these outcomes.[19] Military officials also punished Black service members who complained of racial prejudice with burdensome labor assignments, imprisonment, and court-martial trials. Black service members received a disproportionate share of dishonorable (resulting from a court-martial conviction) and undesirable (or "blue") removals from service. Known as blue discharges in reference to the colored paper on which they were printed, undesirable removals from service targeted those accused of unfavorable behaviors, including alcoholism, drug addiction, chronic lying, and sexual psychopathy (including homosexuality).[20] According to a January 1946 memo from Major General Edward Witsell of the War Department, African Americans received 10,806 of the 48,603 blue discharges issued between December 1, 1941, and June 30, 1945. These statistics indicate the exceptionally discriminatory administration of these discharges, with African Americans constituting 22 percent of blue-discharge recipients despite comprising less than 10 percent of those serving in the armed forces.[21] Many Black service members and veterans shared the sentiments of one anonymous man who asserted that white officers issued these blue discharges to "intimidat[e] and descreminat[e] [*sic*] against Colored Soldiers."[22]

Despite the stigma associated with blue discharges, given their connotation of homosexual behavior, the military adopted this removal from service as a benevolent reform. Between the world wars, a coalition of military bureaucrats, psychiatrists, and prison wardens advocated for the use of undesirable discharges in lieu of a longer process of court-martials and imprisonment, which would result in a dishonorable discharge for those convicted of same-sex intimacies.[23] Army and navy administrators yielded to such calls in 1943 and 1944, respectively, when they adopted specific approaches to dealing with three defined classes of homosexuals: the violent offender, who would be court-martialed and dishonorably discharged; the "reclaimable offender," who would remain in service; and the mentally ill offender, who would leave the military with an undesirable discharge.[24] Despite this reformist impulse, the undesirable discharge process—which often included hospitalization or incarceration before a board of officers' hearing—was deliberately stigmatizing.[25] Most often, the board of officers expelled the accused from service, concluding that they "g[ave] evidence of traits of character other than those indicating discharge for mental or physical conditions . . . render[ing] conditions in the service undesirable."[26] According to Allan Bérubé's study of gay and lesbian service members in World War II, 4,000 sailors and 5,000 soldiers left the service with blue discharges—representing roughly 18 percent of the total number of such discharges issued.[27] Discharges continued after the end of hostilities, with 4,000 service members discharged between 1947 and 1950 for alleged homosexuality.[28]

The Veterans Administration (VA) extended the military's discrimination against racial and sexual minorities into civilian life, as it created substantive barriers to the receipt of aid provisioned by the GI Bill of Rights. This legislation bestowed an array of benefits to veterans and their families, including job training, subsidized life insurance, access to health care, and loans to attend college, create small businesses, and purchase homes or farms.[29] As chairman of the Committee on World War Veterans' Legislation, Mississippi Democratic congressman John Rankin successfully advocated for the decentralized administration of the bill to ensure that southern VA officials could freely deny benefits to African Americans, resulting in high denial rates.[30] Although the mechanisms that facilitated racial discrimination appeared within the very language of the bill, the VA adopted a specific policy to punish service members removed for alleged homosexuality. An April 1945 VA directive stipulated that "an undesirable discharge or blue discharge issued because of homosexual acts generally will be considered as under dishonorable conditions and a bar to entitlement."[31] This policy shift equated the consequences of discharges emanating from a court-martial conviction with that of an undesirable or blue discharge. Although there was no standard policy on how to treat the holders of blue discharges for non-sexual reasons, many veterans, such as Private Marion Hill, believed that the VA treated these discharges as dishonorable and sought to "ro[b] a man of his citizenship," by withholding veterans' benefits.[32] As Margot Canaday notes, the VA's racial and sexual exclusion at times worked at cross-purposes. Local VA administrators, with their autonomy to distribute benefits, could be slow to implement anti-homosexual directives emanating from central administrators. Ultimately, many racial and sexual minorities found themselves systemically denied benefits.[33]

Notably, perceptions of race and sexuality converged in public debates about the rationale and ramifications of blue discharges to same-sex-desiring and Black veterans. As Bérubé and Canaday note, an African American newspaper, the *Pittsburgh Courier*, joined a vanguard of journalists, civic organizations, and veterans' groups in questioning the efficacy and fairness of these removals from service. In an October 1945 article titled "Blue Discharges under Fire: GI's Denied Benefits," reporter John H. Young III questioned the rationale of denying financial and educational benefits to individuals deemed unfit for service, including those who exhibited traits of "inaptness and homo-sexuality." He professed an inability to "understand why the Army chooses to penalize these 'unfortunates' who seem most in need of the Army benefits and the opportunity to become better citizens under the educational provisions of the GI Bill of Rights."[34] In response to such public outcry and the recommendation of the House Committee on Military Affairs, the military granted honorable discharges to individuals accused of homosexuality rather than committing homosexual acts for a two-year period (1945–1947). After 1947, however, the military issued a "general" discharge for those deemed unsuitable for military service, marking those who received them with the same stigma of the blue discharge. Despite this short period of reform and the changed status of their removals, the VA continued to deny benefits to individuals discharged for same-sex intimacies.[35] The ignominy of blue discharges weighed heavily on veterans like Thurston Lane, who wrote to Gibson, the civilian aide to the Secretary of War in April 1947. Lane echoed the concerns of many veterans when he characterized his postwar fortunes as poor,:"[My] discharge is a hold on my future."[36]

It was for the betterment of those futures that hundreds of veterans turned to a premier Black civil rights organization—the NAACP.[37] Founded in 1909 in the aftermath of a devastating race riot in Springfield, Illinois, the organization emerged from the Niagara Movement of the early twentieth century in which an interracial cohort of intellectuals, journalists, and social reformers mobilized to challenge intensifying forms of discrimination and racial terror. Their efforts to combat racial oppression intensified during the 1930s and 1940s, as growing northern urban Black communities exercised increased political clout as one part of the New Deal coalition of Democratic Party voters. The NAACP built on this increasing electoral power by cultivating crucial relationships with President Franklin Delano Roosevelt's administration and members of the federal bureaucracy. Their efforts to combat racial discrimination continued after the war, when, as Martha Biondi argues, "a new rights consciousness among African Americans . . . permanently replaced a piecemeal or gradual approach to racial equality with a new immediacy and sweeping vision."[38] The dramatically increased membership rolls of the NAACP and its branches reflected this militancy at the grassroots level.[39] America's entry into World War II placed racial discrimination in the military, war industry production, and the experiences of returning veterans at the center of the organization's political agenda during the 1940s. The NAACP Legal Department—now under the helm of famed attorney and future Supreme Court Justice Thurgood Marshall—regularly contested the court-martial convictions of Black soldiers, some of them for actively protesting discrimination. Despite the organization's long-standing commitment to racial justice within the armed services, it was only with the passage of the GI Bill and the entreaties of returning Black veterans that the NAACP created a department solely dedicated to military affairs.[40]

The Veterans' Affairs Bureau and the Appeals of Black Veterans

The opening of the Veterans' Affairs Bureau in January 1945 institutionalized the NAACP's efforts to assist Black service personnel and veterans during World War II.[41] In creating this division, the board of directors responded to veterans' demands for "the establishment of a machinery to assure them justice and opportunity after the war." The national leadership charged the bureau with "handl[ing] all matters which might be referred to the Association to assure Negro veterans their full rights under the GI Bill of Rights and any other legislative and administrative machinery which may be established."[42] Additional responsibilities included investigating the racial climate of army camps and surrounding communities, promoting integration in the military and all "federally funded entities for veterans," and representing men removed from service with "other than honorable discharges."[43] Jesse O. Dedmon, the NAACP's secretary of veterans' affairs, largely guided the vision and success of the bureau (see fig. 1.1). An Oklahoma native, Dedmon attended Howard University for undergraduate and postgraduate legal study, graduating in 1932 and 1935, respectively. Serving as a trial judge advocate at Camp Claiborne, Louisiana, he received an honorable discharge for a disability in 1943. During the bureau's four years of official operation, Dedmon became an indefatigable advocate for military personnel past and present, traveling nationwide to organize local Veterans' Affairs Committees while attending to his duties in Washington, DC.[44] He and his staff responded to thousands of complaints of discrimination

FIGURE 1.1 Addison N. Scurlock, "Jesse O. Dedmon Jr. Attorney at Law 611 F Street, N.W. Washington, D.C. 20004," undated. Archival Records: Washington, DC, Photos Box 32. Courtesy of the Kautz Family YMCA Archives, University of Minnesota, Minneapolis.

and racism in the army and navy. They also helped individual veterans who sought access to medical care, GI benefits, and employment opportunities.

No other task consumed more of the staff's energy than assisting individuals burdened with blue discharges. Veterans consistently wrote to the bureau, local NAACP branches, and the national office in New York City requesting help in amending their discharges from undesirable to honorable. To amend a blue discharge, the military required veterans to file an appeal with the army and navy discharge review boards, which convened in Washington, DC and Saint Louis, Missouri. Although the review boards did not require veterans or their legal representatives to attend the hearings, many former servicemen labored to appear or have counsel present in hopes it would strengthen their appeal. These efforts did not necessarily lessen the barriers to amend a discharge, however.[45] Review boards required veterans to "show to the satisfaction of the Board . . . that the alleged entry or omission in the record was in error or unjust under directives, standards, administration, and practice either at the time, or subsequently changed in the petitioner's favor effective retroactively." This was to be done without "access to any classified papers or reports of investigation or papers related theretofore or any document received from the Federal Bureau of Investigation."[46] Given these obstacles, veterans rarely succeeded in amending their discharge status, even with the help of skilled NAACP attorneys.

In their correspondence to the bureau, Black veterans removed for sexual offenses made explicit appeals based on their rights as citizens and former service members. Such rhetoric reinforced fundamental connections between military service, citizenship, and access to social welfare benefits. Army private Leonard J. Johnson used such language in a March 1950 letter to the bureau. He requested a discharge review because he hoped "that my right[s] will not continue to be taken away from me" as a result of a discharge for "sexual psychopathy" (which could include homosexuality).[47] Similarly, New Orleans veteran Elon Bruce protested his treatment, declaring, "I am not given the same rights as other veterans since my discharge is blue" (emphasis original).[48] His decision to underline the word "blue" in dark pencil suggests his profound sense of stigma and dismay at such a separation from service and its attendant disqualification for veterans' benefits. Some servicemen who wrote to the NAACP defined their successful transition to civilian life beyond access to the GI Bill's provisions. Private Attar T. Gibson expressed frustration that he was unable to successfully transition to civilian life with such a mark on his record. He lamented his plight: "I find it difficult, if not impossible, to rehabilitate myself to useful civilian life in view of the [fact that the] discharge I now possess hinders my finding suitable employment."[49]

Many veterans framed their appeals in the language of rights and citizenship, but they responded to the validity of allegations of unsuitability for service or misconduct in varying ways. Of those who solicited assistance for homosexuality-related discharges, most refrained from commenting on the specific nature of the charges. Some, however, declared their innocence. In his letter to the bureau, army private Alfred Harrison claimed, "Just because I was talking to . . . [corporal] James Perkins, I was accused of committing an act of homo-sexology [sic], which I was falsely accused [of]." After their discharge from Fort Riley, Kansas, both men separately solicited assistance from the Veterans' Affairs Bureau, listing their addresses as a few blocks from each other in the Harlem neighborhood of New York City.[50] That the two wrote separately to the bureau but lived in close proximity suggests that some petitioners made strategic collective decisions about the submission, nature, and content of their appeals to the NAACP. Claims of innocence constitute a strategic action that acknowledged the limited sources of support for Black veterans removed for same-sex intimacy.

Although veterans of all backgrounds turned to social service and veterans' organizations for assistance, African Americans removed for homosexuality—like Army Private Henry Nord—likely encountered both racism and homophobia.[51] After his discharge, Nord turned to the American Legion for representation before the Army Discharge Review Board. A premier veterans' organization, the American Legion mirrored the white supremacist logics of the military and VA in its racially segregated chapters and a lack of African Americans in national leadership positions.[52] Initially, Nord received some assistance from a field representative, who agreed to gather further information about his removal from service. However, the circumstances of his discharge prompted a letter of reply from T. O. Kraabel, the organization's national secretary. Kraabel noted that during Nord's board of officers hearing, the veteran "admitted [to engaging in] homosexual practices, which is a very damaging statement in itself." Kraabel also alleged that the veteran was confined in Schick General Hospital for forty days and diagnosed with "sexual psychopathy, manifested by repeated episodes of homosexual activity both in civilian life and in military service." The American Legion's chief official asserted that "current army regulations and the policy of the President of the Army discharge review board will not grant a change of your discharge due to this testimony by yourself to the board." He ultimately refused to counsel the veteran concluding, "You would be wasting your time by asking for a rehearing of your case."[53] This response, in part, reflected the army's reluctance to amend the discharges of veterans removed for homosexual offenses.[54] However, Kraabel's refusal to assist Nord may have been racially motivated. The interlocking nature of racism and homophobia in military and civilian life rendered the NAACP's willingness to assist Black veterans removed for same-sex intimacies even more singular and important.

The Veterans' Affairs Bureau's visible advocacy for Black veterans ensured a steady flow of referrals and pleas for assistance.[55] Perhaps that is how J. E. Raynor, a United States Army captain and recruiter in the Harlem neighborhood of New York City became familiar with the bureau. On September 3, 1948, he wrote to Dedmon on behalf of William Carr, who had claimed to engage in sexual relationships with men in order to be removed from service. Raynor vouched for the veteran, stating, "He realizes his mistake and wishes to go straight from this point on." It is unclear whether Raynor used the word "straight" with knowledge of its sexual connotations. However, its usage does reflect Carr's desire to pass from an ostracized social status (homosexual) to an accepted one (heterosexual) and Raynor's belief that the bureau could help in the amendment of his discharge. Similarly, army personnel in Saint Louis, Missouri, directed veteran Henry Nord to the bureau after the Discharge Review Board rejected his appeal. In his letter to Dedmon, Nord disclosed that bureaucrats in the office suggested he "write to [the bureau] to see if there was some way [they] could assist [him] in reversing the decision of the reviewing board."[56] That this referral emanated from a person employed in the same office as the Army Discharge Review Board is notable. It suggests the profound visibility of Dedmon and his staff as advocates for Black men holding blue discharges. More fundamentally, the referral of veterans to the bureau for assistance indicates that some military personnel may have disapproved of the harsh treatment of blue-discharge holders. Such referrals echoed the assertion of a 1946 congressional report on blue discharges that the government "has no right to make the remainder of [undesirably discharged service members'] lives grievous" through the denial of benefits.[57]

Despite the willingness of NAACP officials in New York and Washington, DC to assist Black men discharged for same-sex desire, local branch officials and veterans did not always agree on the relationship between same-sex intimacy and the appropriate resolution of a blue-discharge amendment request. For example, in the spring of 1946, Daniel Byrd, the executive secretary of the New Orleans NAACP, wrote Dedmon about the blue discharge of army veteran Elon Bruce for homosexuality saying, "Bruce stated in conversation to me that he is a homo-sexual. He was born that way. The evidence proves he is that way, 'he even has dimples.'" Such an emphasis on the presumed corporeal nature of Bruce's sexuality reflected assumptions about homosexuality as an innate form of difference that was visibly inscribed on the body. Byrd's articulation of Bruce's same-sex desire guided his conclusion that "the Army should have never inducted this man" and his discharge should be annulled.[58] Byrd's actions mirrored those of other branch officials, who regularly forwarded veterans' requests for assistance to Dedmon and his staff. Such efforts reflected the NAACP's dramatic growth during and after the war, as well as the central place of municipal chapters in the national mission of the bureau.[59] Despite Byrd's conclusion, Bruce himself, in a subsequent communication to Dedmon, held a different understanding of the relationship between his military service and sexuality.

He asked "If there is a possibility of having [my discharge] changed. It's blue." He continued, "If so, I'd appreciate it very much. I am not given the same rights as the other veterans." Bruce's implication that his induction and service were legitimate undergirds his conviction that he should have access to veterans' benefits and be free of any stigma.[60]

The correspondence of Black veterans reflects the existence of different concepts of (homo)sexuality, biology, and gender. Whereas Bruce implicitly challenged the perceived incompatibility of homosexuality and honorable military service, Yeoman First Class Willis Austin, a former sailor, contested the notion that sex and eroticism between men made one a homosexual at all. In 1949, the Office of Naval Intelligence summoned Austin, who was stationed in Honolulu, Hawaii, to its office to address allegations he was "a sexual pervert." During a rigorous interrogation, military officials asked Austin if he "ever had any relations with a homosexual," to which he replied yes. He referenced encounters "when I was a kid just out of high school and on another occasion in San Diego since being in the service." This admission resulted in his prompt dismissal from the navy, despite a physician's subsequent determination that he did not exhibit "homosexual tendencies." A naval officer attending the hearing challenged the validity of Austin's discharge, asserting, "There is hardly a person living in or out of the navy that hasn't . . . participated in unnatural sex acts."[61] Austin's denial of being a "sexual pervert" and admission to having "relations with a homosexual" suggests that he understood his sexual partner only as being non-normative (perhaps based on gender nonconformity or his particular role during a sexual encounter).[62] In contrast, the military conceptualized sexual identity as primarily determined by object choice. Then, as now, not all men who engaged in sex with men considered themselves or were considered to be "homosexual." As Austin's experiences suggest, some men who had sex with men considered themselves to be "normal" or "heterosexual" based on their gender expression and sex role.[63] However, medical discourse, sexual psychopath laws, and popular culture increasingly advanced an understanding of homosexuality and heterosexuality as binary identities rooted in object choice.[64] Under this criterion, Bruce—whose confession of same-sex eroticism (not acts or an identity) to a chaplain precipitated his discharge—and Austin—who admitted to engaging in same-sex sex—were both considered homosexuals who should be removed from service.

Even as such definitions became dominant and led to more policing—thereby circumscribing service members' wartime experiences—it did not dominate their lives or even necessarily serve as reference points for self-definition. In fact, the military was in many respects a privileged locale of homosexuality: it provided crucial spaces for same-sex-desiring men and women to explore their identities, fall in love, and build community on bases, ships, and in the various cities that millions of service members passed through during the war years. Moreover, army, navy, and VA bureaucrats' preoccupation with identifying and punishing homosexuality—though clearly rooted in disciplinary and discriminatory intent—also served as a counter-discourse offering those named by its imposition of object choice–based definitions of sexuality and the identification of individuals as "homosexual" with opportunities for self-identification and self-understanding.[65] Perhaps Austin, who lived in San Francisco while appealing his discharge, participated in the growing queer community in that city. Similarly, Bruce, who resided in New Orleans after the war, may have (re) joined that city's Black queer community.[66]

After the end of World War II, same-sex-desiring African Americans continued to carve out spaces for community and self-expression in the military even as they faced intensified surveillance and policing. Although the board of officers' hearing transcript of Private William E. White is representative of the undesirable discharge process, these records are unique in their revelation of a vibrant queer world in the postwar Jim Crow South. To be sure, parsing reality from fiction in these records is difficult. However, the testimonies reveal that Black queer men found each other, forged friendships, fell in love, and endured the burdens of racism and homophobia together. During the board of officers hearing, Black servicemen and white officers at MacDill Air Force Base consistently cited White's feminine behavior as evidence that he was a homosexual. One witness claimed that White and his friends acted like "degraded women" and were seen "switching around" the base. Others testified that White and Staff Sergeant Johnson referred to each other as "bitches" and "girls."[67] The witnesses' reliance on feminine behavior as an indicator of same-sex eroticism suggests just how strongly such ideas continued to define homosexuality alongside object choice in the middle of the twentieth century.[68] Some embraced camp behavior as a way to challenge harassment, critique heteronormativity by transgressing gender norms, and boldly announce their sexuality.[69] That so many witnesses characterized White and Johnson as feminine suggests a visible and transgressive form of solidarity among queer persons on the base.[70] Indeed, this sense is supported by Sergeant Robert L. Tweed's allegation that in response to his threat to "report their doings at [White's] house [off-base]," Johnson retorted, "Well, they can't do anything to us, because <u>we</u> bitches run this base" (emphasis original).[71] Johnson's alleged comment suggests a tight-knit group that seemingly assessed their importance to the operation of the base as well as a perceived immunity from prosecution. The ultimate removals of White and Johnson indicate otherwise.

According to the transcript, Black same-sex-desiring and gender nonconforming men fellowshipped on and off the base alongside as well as apart from servicemen who identified as heterosexual. White and Johnson allegedly spent a great deal of time together, laughing and socializing in their respective work areas in front of peers. Members of White's circle also gathered at the Noncommissioned Officers Club, where their presence at times caused conflict with female civilians and other servicemen. During World War II, both Black and white individuals in same-sex relationships used designated military recreational spaces to fraternize and find romantic partners. However, on-base fraternizing came with some risk, including discovery and prosecution.[72] Socializing off-base in urban areas and private residences added an additional layer of protection, allowing momentary reprieves from the surveillance of military police, commanding officers, and potentially, civilian law enforcement authorities.[73] Get-togethers at White's home provided an opportunity for same-sex-desiring and gender nonconforming men to gather and provided a ready escape from the harsh oversight of military officials at MacDill. One witness reported hearing White declare, "The house of blue lights will rock tonight," in anticipation of a party later that evening. It was White's and Johnson's simultaneous request for leave to this off-base residence that prompted an investigation and their subsequent discharge, demonstrating the constant risks attendant with efforts to build community in the midst of intensifying military homophobia. Despite Dedmon's best efforts—which included gathering character statements from other servicemen and a hearing before the Army Discharge Review Board in Washington, DC—White retained his undesirable discharge status.

Challenging Sexual Exclusion and the Continuity of the NAACP's Activism

Despite evidence that the Veterans' Affairs Bureau challenged blue discharges for sexual offenses, staff members' thoughts on the legitimacy of policing same-sex-loving soldiers and sailors are not apparent in the archival record. Although discharge review requests within the NAACP records contain correspondence between staff members, veterans, and War Department bureaucrats, documentation referencing legal argumentation to amend discharges (like review board hearing transcripts) is absent. These lacunae are compounded by the destruction of the Army and Navy Discharge Review Boards' records in a 1973 fire at the Saint Louis National Archives facility, which rendered an invaluable source lost forever.[74] Bureau staffers (including Dedmon and an assistant attorney, Frank D. Reeves) did not deposit personal papers into any archival repositories like some of their more prominent colleagues who graduated from Howard University School of Law, foreclosing another potential source of information.[75] Although gaps in the historical record prevent greater analysis into the actions and views of bureau staff members, they also obscure the number of Black men removed for homosexuality who appealed to the NAACP for assistance. Many of the existing requests for discharge reviews in the bureau's records do not specify the reason for removal from service, suggesting that more men (and possibly some women) removed for alleged homosexuality requested assistance from the bureau than are analyzed here. Notably, Dedmon and his staff represented all but one of those accused of homosexual behavior who solicited their assistance, revealing a firm institutional commitment to challenging blue discharges no matter the alleged infraction.[76]

It is important to consider contemporary developments regarding racialized sexuality in order to understand the Veterans' Affairs Bureau's response to entreaties from men removed from service for alleged same-sex relationships. The organization had long confronted white anxieties over presumed Black hyper(hetero)sexuality, which often legitimized political and physical violence against African American communities and individuals. In addition, during the war, the renewed migration of African Americans to regions outside of the South and increasingly militant advocacy for racial equality heightened white fears that interracial sexual intimacy might accompany these broader changes. Such fears had profound and, at times, deadly ramifications. In Detroit, Michigan, rumors of Black men molesting white women incited a riot that left thirty-four people dead in 1943.[77] Similar anxieties over Black men's presumed rapacity is evident in the wartime work of the NAACP's Legal Department, which fielded numerous requests for representation in court-martial cases in which Black GIs faced allegations of raping white women. The 1940s also proved to be a critical moment in the NAACP's complicated and long-standing battle to combat miscegenation laws.[78] As Black GIs flooded the national office with requests to marry European women, the association facilitated what Peggy Pascoe characterizes as "geographies of evasion" in which they encouraged interracial couples to marry in a state where their union was legal, hoping the marriage might later be recognized in the couple's home state.[79] The NAACP's longstanding opposition on miscegenation laws derived from its conviction that such statutes rested on notions of Black inferiority. At the same time, the increasing rhetorical force of the nation's professed adherence to equality during the fight against a fascist white supremacist power abroad made miscegenation law less politically tenable for many Americans. The bureau's willingness to advocate on behalf of Black veterans accused of sexual crimes was more than likely influenced by an understanding of how lingering perceptions of Black bodies as lascivious made African Americans more susceptible to disproportionate and potentially unfair prosecution.

The NAACP's commitment to enhancing the economic opportunities available to African Americans also substantively shaped the bureau's commitment to challenging blue discharges. President Roosevelt's creation of the Fair Employment Practices Commission (FEPC)—which had limited authority to address complaints of racial segregation in defense-related and federally funded industries—did little to halt the rampant discrimination experienced by Black workers seeking employment in this sector. However, as Anthony S. Chen argues, the formation of this commission forged a liberal coalition that sought to expand and, strengthen its powers. Politically, these fights fostered a vision of postwar life in which the dismantling of employment discrimination on the basis of race, religion, or nationality was an important political goal. The NAACP occupied a central place in the campaign, lobbying congressional legislators, contributing testimony, and rallying their members to support various bills.[80] In a telegram to the Senate Appropriations Committee in June 1945, the NAACP attempted to persuade members to vote for a $585,000 appropriation for the FEPC, which represented a minuscule fraction of the government's $98 billion budget. "Surely the most intransigent Negrophobe cannot begrudge this pittance for maintenance of an agency to make industrial democracy slightly more of a reality," the NAACP statement read. The organization asserted that this commission was "almost alone . . . in giving hope to minorities, particularly the Negro, of assistance in obtaining employment in war plants."[81] In the end, however, such pleas were ignored as the dream of a federal FEPC withered in the Cold War climate.

Efforts to equitably administer the GI Bill of Rights sought to raise the fortunes of Black veterans and their families along with actively combating discrimination in public and private employment. As Katznelson observes in his discussion of the unequal administration of the GI Bill's benefits to southern Black veterans, the "combination of entrenched racism and willful exclusion . . . shunted them into second class standing and conditions." NAACP leaders recognized the damage that could be done to African American veterans if they were largely excluded from the benefits associated with the bill; they were especially suspicious of blue discharges, which they recognized as a fundamental mechanism of exclusion. In May 1945, less than a year after the bill passed, NAACP assistant secretary Roy Wilkins believed that "the armed forces [are] systematically giving Negroes blue discharges for the purpose of defeating their rights under GI Legislation."[82] The Veterans' Affairs Bureau mirrored its parent organization's desire to bolster the postwar fortunes of those who had served their country. In print and in person, Dedmon consistently encouraged veterans to pursue discharge reviews. In an address to the state convention of Maryland NAACP branches in the late spring of 1945, he emphasized the ability of veterans to "review and change the type and nature of any discharge except that ordered by a court-martial."[83] A Veterans' Affairs Bureau conference convened at Howard University on November 9–10, 1945, reveals the centrality of economic issues within the bureau's agenda. Employment concerns was the first subject on the conference program as well as one of the top five policy recommendations at its conclusion.[84] Dedmon also articulated the importance of challenging blue discharges to Veterans' Affairs committees, auxiliaries of the Veterans' Affairs Bureau within NAACP branches that assisted former service members. These groups were "urged to notify all veterans in their communities that they are entitled to have their blue discharges and other than honorable discharges reviewed."[85] Black newspaper editors echoed these calls, advising service members' families to encourage their loved ones "to do everything to avoid accepting or being given a Blue Discharge Certificate."[86]

The Red Scare, the Lavender Scare, and the Closure of the Veterans' Affairs Bureau

Black veterans' ability to contest their discharges using the NAACP's resources was short-lived as military affairs became less central to the organization's postwar agenda. By the end of 1948, the board of directors believed that the need for the Veterans' Affairs Bureau had effectively ended. In an August 10, 1948, letter, NAACP executive secretary Walter White informed Dedmon that "the question which has been raised on several occasions by members of the Board [is] whether or not the necessity of a Veterans' Bureau has not about ended."[87] Notably, White composed this letter several weeks after President Harry S. Truman signed Executive Order 9981, prohibiting racial discrimination and segregation in the military. Many African Americans saw Truman's order as fulfilling his promise to desegregate the armed forces, thereby achieving a key aspect of the NAACP's military-related agenda.[88] Dedmon strongly protested the board's suggestion that the bureau's work was over. In his reply, he asserted, "The need [for the bureau] is even greater now than at the time the Bureau was established." While he cited various reasons for its continued necessity, one of the most important was the "policy of the Veterans Administration to segregate and discriminate in employment and service." Dedmon also referenced the enduring popularity of the Veterans' Affairs Bureau among NAACP members. His suggestion that the proposal to close the bureau "should be brought to the attention of the annual conference in session" indicates his belief that the general membership would disapprove of the national leadership's plans. Ultimately, however, the national leadership closed the Veterans' Affairs Bureau, which suspended operations on January 1, 1949.[89] As NAACP-affiliated attorneys, Dedmon and Reeves continued to represent veterans before the Army and Navy Discharge Review Boards until the end of 1950.

Whereas the prospect of military desegregation was the immediate determining factor in closing the Veterans' Affairs Bureau, the narrowing parameters of the organization's political program ensured its demise. The rise of anti-communism in the postwar years prompted a split between the once-strong relationship between liberals and radicals committed to racial equality. Although the NAACP's national leadership initially criticized anti-communism as a tactic to silence dissenting voices on the left, the organization eventually embraced such rhetoric to ensure its survival during the Cold War. The NAACP dissolved its affiliation with radical leftist groups like the Civil Rights Congress, investigated the suspected communist affiliations of its members, and generally embraced the rising tide of pro-Americanism.[90] It also distanced itself from "fellow travelers" or anyone who might be associated with communist organizations or philosophies. The moderating influence of anti-communist sentiments within and outside of the NAACP, therefore, resulted in its espousal of anti-left rhetoric by the early 1950s. By the early 1950s, the NAACP abandoned human rights–based efforts that sought to ameliorate the plight of African Americans, including a failed attempt to use the newly formed United Nations to denounce various US human rights violations, including a sharp increase in racial violence after the war, the continued grip of Jim Crow segregation in the South, and limited educational and economic opportunities nationwide.

Although an overestimation of liberal white support and resistance from the US government stymied the NAACP's efforts in the United Nations, the rising influence of anti-communism in the late 1940s profoundly weakened the association's adherence to a broader human rights vision. This ideological shift may have contributed to the destruction of the Veterans' Affairs Bureau, which, in its own way, challenged both racial discrimination at the federal level and the military apparatus that carried it out. Although the costs of anti-communism did mean the marginalization of many leftist voices and perspectives in the late 1940s through the 1950s, such marginalization did not mean silence. Indeed, a vibrant vanguard of Black radical writing, organizing, and oration continued during these years. Organizers and intellectuals like Claudia Jones, Marvel Cooke, Audley Moore, W. E. B. Du Bois, Paul Robeson, and others continued to mobilize, sharpening their articulation of an "oppositional consciousness" that drew on their identities and experiences. They continued to assail colonialism, capitalist exploitation, white supremacy, and (to varying degrees) patriarchy, albeit under the surveillance and harassing force of the state.[91]

Along with the Red Scare, the onset of the Lavender Scare fundamentally circumscribed the already limited ability of the Veterans' Affairs Bureau to contest the discriminatory treatment of individuals accused of same-sex sex within the military. Federal bureaucratic concerns about sexual nonconformity extended into the civil service, as communism and homosexuality became increasingly linked in the public sphere. With antecedents in President Harry S. Truman's "Truman Loyalty Hearings," the federal government began to identify and fire federal civil employees accused of homosexuality. These purges resulted in the termination of 400 State Department employees between January 1947 and January 1953. These and other workers found themselves cast as "security risks" whose alleged sexuality made them vulnerable to blackmail and, thus, potential communist influence. Therefore, whereas anti-communism narrowed the scope of the NAACP's general political program, the Lavender Scare made individual challenges to the federal government's anti-homosexual policies untenable and, indeed, dangerous.[92]

Black Liberals and the Legacies of the Straight State

Despite the closure of the Veterans' Affairs Bureau, Black veterans like Watson Billy Marshall continued to seek assistance from social welfare groups, civil rights organizations, and elected officials to amend their discharge status well into the 1960s. A resident of Los Angeles, California, Marshall received a general discharge in 1963, secured through the advocacy of African American US representative Augustus F. Hawkins. In an interview with the *Los Angeles Sentinel*, Marshall celebrated his new status and shared two goals. The first was to return to his home state of Texas for the first time in eighteen years, suggesting that the stigma associated with this removal from service was so great that he felt unable to return home. Taking advantage of the newly accessible benefits, his second objective was to attend Howard University "to get a BA degree in music and teach piano." The article noted that Marshall wanted to take up "a position as a minister of music with some Baptist church."[93] Associations between queerness and African American organists, choir directors, and ministers of music had existed in the Black public sphere since the early twentieth century and were reinforced by coverage of the morals charge trials of various church musicians.[94] Therefore, Marshall's chosen profession, alongside the lingering associations between blue discharges and homosexuality, probably prompted some readers to make assumptions about his sexuality.

The experiences of veterans discussed in this chapter reveal three under analyzed aspects of Black life at mid-century. First, returning to the archival record offers crucial information about the lived experience of same-sex-desiring (and less often, gender nonconforming) African Americans. This subset of records demonstrates the tenacity of African American blue-discharge holders as they sought to challenge both racial and sexual discrimination. It also confirms that World War II was an important moment in the development of Black queer communities and sexualities, raising important questions about how individual and institutional understandings of sexual subjectivities continued to diverge. Second, at a broader, institutional level, their efforts, alongside those of the Veterans' Affairs Bureau officials who assisted them, illuminate a momentary alignment between political actions contesting racism and those contesting homophobia. That an auxiliary of the NAACP, the premier civil rights organization for much of the twentieth century, advocated on behalf of Black same-sex-desiring veterans challenges the class-based binary of tolerance and intolerance that structures some analyses of Black communal and political attitudes toward queer communities. The efforts of the Veterans' Affairs Bureau show that at least one African American political organization substantively based its strategy of engaging with same-sex-desiring individuals, as well as its engagement with broader discourses about such intimacies, in terms of the political imperatives of pursuing racial equality and amelioration. Its mandate to contest discrimination, particularly in employment, seems to have trumped concerns about sexual deviance. Certainly, this commitment, temporary as it was, does not suggest that African American political organizations were free of religious, medical, or socially motivated animus toward queer persons, or that these organizations did not prioritize heteronormative behavior and punish its perceived opposite (as the well-known marginalization of Bayard Rustin indicates). Instead, these actions demonstrate that the NAACP navigated, with some success, long-standing assumptions of Black heterosexual deviance alongside laws and policies that marginalized homosexual intimacies to protect the civil rights and economic welfare of Black Americans. Third and finally, excavating the history of the NAACP to include challenges to homophobic military law and policy alongside its more visible work to challenge miscegenation laws and the disproportionate prosecution of Black male veterans for sexual assault does not simply diversify the organization's actions. It raises a crucial set of questions about the particular ways that Black liberal civil rights organizations approached the consolidation of a sexual binary in American citizenship. That the federal government used the same apparatus—the blue discharge—to remove both African American and homosexual military personnel indicates how both groups were connected through a general framework of undesirability and potential deviance. As the next chapter demonstrates, civil rights organizations navigated the intensified homophobia of the Cold War years not simply by removing queer activists. At least one organization actually engaged in the prominent strategy of lavender baiting (or the implicit or explicit allegation of homosexual behavior) to undermine white supremacist attacks.

2 These Attempts of Our Enemies to Blacken My Character

The National Urban League and the
Political Uses of Homophobia, 1956–1957

. . . .

"For more than five years, the National Citizens Protective Association (NCPA) and its official publication, *The White Sentinel*, have maintained a constant fight for segregation and racial integrity." Thus began a mimeographed missive issued by John Wilson Hamilton in the fall of 1956. While the NCPA demonized various organizations it saw as arbiters of disorder, none were more dangerous than the National Urban League (NUL). Founded from the merger of two interracial Progressive Era organizations in New York City, the NUL prioritized economic and social welfare programs for growing Black urban populations. Despite the moderate nature of their political vision, Urban League chapters across the country found themselves assailed by NCPA-initiated attacks that accused the organization of harboring communist sympathies and promoting interracial sex. Hamilton's letter alleged that the National Urban League engineered his arrest for charges that were, in his words, "not only serious, they are dastardly and probably the worst possible charges that could be placed against me." He claimed that once they learned of the arrest "the negro press, both locally and nationally, went into ecstasies of glee." Facing conviction and incarceration, Hamilton requested "financial help to overcome these attempts of our enemies to blacken my character and destroy our organization."[1] Although the politically charged appeal is filled with falsehoods, two aspects of his account were true. The criminal charges against the rabid racist were, indeed, serious: engaging in a sexual act with a fifteen-year-old white male, and the NUL and the Black press enthusiastically publicized the charges, his arrest, and later, his conviction.

In contrast to chapter 1, which examined how a civil rights organization sought to support same-sex-desiring Black Americans in their challenges to the homophobic state, this chapter examines an obverse reaction: the deliberate use of homophobic rhetoric and the criminalization of same-sex sex to excoriate a racist leader. This chapter returns to the NUL's tactical dissemination of Hamilton's morals charge arrest and conviction to counter his campaign to defund local league chapters. Leveling a charge of sexual immorality at an anti-miscegenationist group dovetails with a long-standing strategy within anti-racist work: highlighting fundamental forms of hypocrisy among white supremacists. However, the same-sex nature of the charges gained additional traction during the intensely homophobic 1950s. Placing the actions of the NUL within the historical narrative of the civil rights movement expands scholarly understandings of how homophobia emerged within civil rights organizations by revealing that said groups were attuned to the efficacious nature of lavender baiting to undermine political opponents, a strategy commonly used in federal electoral politics. In describing the strategic use of lavender baiting, I do not seek to excuse or legitimize their homophobia or solely attribute its articulation to the larger Cold War political milieu. Rather, I seek to contextualize it within a political landscape in which charges of homosexuality could and did threaten the political and economic wellbeing not only of those accused but their close associates as well.

The National Citizens Protective Association's Campaign against the National Urban League

In the late summer of 1954, an anonymous person calling themselves "A Civic Informer" wrote to the *Saint Louis Post-Dispatch* about a troubling development: the growing prominence of the NCPA "a vicious anti-Negro organization," and its indefatigable leader, John Wilson Hamilton. A Boston, Massachusetts native, Hamilton became politicized as a teenager, allegedly joining the Communist Youth League. He later abandoned his leftist affiliations, becoming a devout follower of the anti-communist, racist, and radical right luminary Gerald L. K. Smith. Relocating to Saint Louis, Missouri, in 1947 to work full time for Smith's Christian Nationalist Crusade, Hamilton mounted a failed campaign for the US Senate as a part of the Christian Nationalist Party. It seems Hamilton's prominence (and tensions with Smith) increased after angry whites rioted in response to Black children swimming in the previously racially segregated Fairground Park pool in north Saint Louis. Hamilton founded the NCPA, which embraced an ideology of racial segregation and white racial purity, which its members saw as being increasingly under attack during the early Cold War years.

That Saint Louis emerged as a site for the Christian Nationalist Crusade and the NCPA reflects how residents in the Gate City had a long history of enacting imperial conquest, racial capitalism, and white supremacist action.[2] The infamous 1917 race riot in East Saint Louis on the bank of the Mississippi River—in which white residents beat and murdered their Black fellow citizens, ransacking their homes—prompted thousands to flee the city. In addition to racial terror, elected officials, policymakers, neighborhood associations, and individual white citizens helped to instantiate racial segregation into residential and public spaces. These efforts included a 1916 referendum in which voters barred the sale of residential property to anyone who did not match the racial background of 75 percent of inhabitants in a given area. When the law was rendered unconstitutional less than a year later, in *Buchanan v. Warley*, white residents then turned to racially restrictive covenants in housing deeds to prevent integration. Once again, it was a Saint Louis–based challenge to these exclusionary clauses that resulted in another Supreme Court decision invalidating such practices, the famous *Shelley v. Kraemer* case.[3] As Walter Johnson notes, Saint Louis emerged as a home for several right-wing organizations and leaders during the three decades after World War II, including Smith, who published the anti-communist publication *The Cross and the Flag*; Reverend John A. Stromer, an anti-communist and segregationist; Patrick Buchanan, a conservative who worked in the Nixon, Ford, and Reagan administrations and ran (unsuccessfully) for president three times; and Phyllis Schlafly, a conservative activist whose organization STOP ERA helped successfully block the ratification of the proposed constitutional amendment to guarantee equal rights regardless of sex.[4]

After forming the NCPA in 1951, Hamilton attracted more public attention when his organization unsuccessfully applied for a pro forma degree of incorporation as a nonprofit educational group from the Saint Louis city courts in April the following year. The *Saint Louis Post-Dispatch*'s editorial board praised the judge's decision in a searing editorial titled "Study in Animosity," asserting that "the kind of 'education' the association indulges in is strictly hate."[5] The NCPA's anti-Black rhetoric and involvement in local vandalism against synagogues during the early 1950s enhanced the group's notoriety.[6] However, Hamilton's successful election as a Republican to the Board of Election Commissioners suggests that some found his racist rhetoric appealing.[7] Although the NCPA had some local detractors, it does not appear that such opposition was strong enough to remove him from office or limit the NCPA's influence.

The far-right organization's decision to focus its ire on the NUL reflected its interracial origins and political vision. Founded in 1910, the NUL emerged from the amalgamation of three different organizations led by an inter-racial cadre of elites—the Committee for Improving Industrial Conditions of Negroes, the National League for the Protection of Colored Women, and the Committee on Urban Conditions Among Negroes. The NUL believed that assimilating working-class African Americans to the norms of industrial labor and urban living would be critical to the elimination of racial prejudice in other arenas. By the middle of the 1950s, the NUL had expanded its programmatic vision to include access to housing, health care, and other forms of material support. Moreover, its national leadership focused more prominently on the structural barriers that impacted employment and housing opportunities. Despite this broadened vision, the NUL continued to occupy a moderate place within Black liberal organizing after World War II. Under the leadership of Lester B. Granger, a Newport, Virginia, native and prominent social worker, the NUL mobilized data to mount campaigns of persuasion to combat racial discrimination, rooted in uplift, and good relationships with white elites.[8]

Whereas the national leadership stayed fairly constant in their approach to race relations, local chapters operated within the specificities of their municipal contexts and were financially reliant on general public goodwill. For example, in Detroit during the interwar years, the Urban League enacted a program of racial uplift that focused on the inculcation of attributes that northern employers would find attractive in southern migrants, including thrift, cleanliness, and sexual propriety. In Atlanta, Georgia, the Urban League chapter collaborated with other organizations to register thousands of African American voters during the 1940s. In Saint Louis, the Urban League largely focused its efforts on securing employment opportunities in the industrial, skilled, and professional sectors, as well as promoting the general health and wellbeing of local Black communities. These activities aligned their mission with other groups who received support from the Community Chest, an organization that facilitated fundraising campaigns to support local entities that provided welfare and social services. In Saint Louis, for example, groups like the Jewish Family Service Agency, the Girl Scouts of Greater Saint Louis, and the Saint Francis Girls Home constituted several of the dozen agencies that benefited from these philanthropic efforts. To determine eligibility, organizations were required to submit a projected budget for the upcoming year, which underwent a two-tier review process before being approved. The majority of those involved in the review process were unaffiliated with applying organizations while the remaining third were members of agencies eligible to receive funding.

After the fundraiser, Community Chest officials would distribute money on a monthly basis to ensure that agencies made appropriate expenditures. Nationally and locally, the Community Chest characterized such distribution as equitable and beneficial to the majority of residents. For example, a promotional pamphlet issued by the Greater Saint Louis Community Chest asserted that participating agencies "are not 'charities' but community services from which everybody benefits."[9] The Community Chests' dependence on public support made their campaigns (and by extension NUL chapters' financial viability) extremely vulnerable to public sentiment. Hamilton and his organization took advantage of this vulnerability in their campaign to undermine the NUL's influence.[10]

Of course, the Urban League was not the only organization committed to improving the social, economic, and political fortunes of Black residents of Saint Louis. Like other midwestern cities during the interwar years, scarcity of accessible housing, segregation in residential and commercial arenas, and low pay in the industrial and service sectors coexisted with a rich landscape of cultural, religious, and political institutions that supported racial uplift. Whereas liberal organizations like the NUL and NAACP sought increased access to public accommodations, decent housing, and improved employment in skilled trades and professions, a radical working-class movement offered an alternative vision that challenged the deep-seated inequities that marked Black life. As Keona Ervin documents, Black working-class women formed a vanguard of militant economic justice that built upon a rich history of socialist labor organizing in the late nineteenth and early twentieth centuries. In 1933, 500 Black women walked off the line of one the city's largest employers, the Funsten Nut Company, demanding a living wage and successfully organizing a campaign to join the Food Workers Industrial Union, a Communist Party–affiliated labor union. In 1937, Black women organized the Colored Clerks' Circle to force stores in predominantly Black communities to hire Black clerks, ultimately securing 200 positions. After the war, working-class and professional Black women continued to organize for fair wages, better working conditions, and access to housing.[11] This continued advocacy for equity and empowerment at work and home clashed with quotidian and organized white resistance in the Gateway City.

The NCPA's anti–Urban League propaganda exacerbated white southern fears that the NUL's civil rights advocacy was a communist-inspired plot to enact Black supremacy. A pamphlet titled "Where Does Your Money Go? 58 Chest-Funds Support Anti-White Urban League" is representative of the NCPA's general campaign against the organization. Incendiary headlines peppered the flyer including "[Urban League] incites Negroes to Violence against Whites," "Integrated Housing Another League Goal," and "Replace White Workers with Negroes Demands Urban League."[12] The *White Sentinel* featured similar characterizations of the NUL as a militant organization. "The Urban League is in many respects more vicious than the NAACP," declared the monthly newsletter. "The Urban League has been called 'the State Department' and the NAACP 'the War Department' of the racial integration movement."[13] Such statements cast the NUL as the diplomatic arm of the civil rights movement and more pernicious than the ever-vilified NAACP. A whisper campaign about the illegitimate use of philanthropic funds compounded this smear campaign. In a letter to the Saint Louis Community Chest president William Charles, M. Leo Bohanon, president of the Saint Louis Urban League, countered rumors that "the Urban League received $85,000 from the Community Chest which it uses to finance homes for Negroes who wish to purchase in all white neighborhoods." Bohanon asserted that these rumors were the work of those who "maliciously or otherwise are opposed to any improvement in the living conditions of Negroes."[14]

For the NCPA, however, the most dangerous aspect of Black civil rights organizing was its alleged promotion of interracial (hetero)sexual intimacy and mixed-race offspring. An NCPA flyer titled "The Kiss of Death" illustrates the anti-miscegenationist rhetoric ubiquitous in contemporary segregationist discourse (see fig. 2.1). The flyer depicts Caucasians as the bearers of "civilization, science," and "creative intelligence" while the "colored hordes" represent a return to savagery.[15] The publication portrayed interracial sex (especially between white women and Black men) as a threat to Western civilization and progress. Similar sexualized rhetoric characterized the NCPA's other propaganda against the NUL. Brochure headlines like "The Urban League Where Negro Men Can Romance White Women" were designed to stoke fears over interracial sexual contact.[16] Images of Black male and white female teenagers attending school together offered a suggestive visualization of the fraternization that might unfold within integrated spaces, facilitating interracial romances.[17] The NCPA also conflated interracial sex with other forms of sexual deviance. The article "[NUL] Holds Wild Inter-racial Orgies" claimed "Whites and social-climbing Negroes mix and mingle in every state of undress from formals and dinner jackets to fig leaves, bras and panties" at the annual NUL fundraiser ball in New York City.[18] In alluding to gender nonconforming behaviors and interracial fraternization, the article links interracial spaces with sexual debauchery (including same-sex sex).[19] Such references presaged what would become an

MORE CIVILIZATION — OR BACK TO THE JUNGLE FOREVER

SCIENCE

10% world — WHITE — *& 90% colored* — BLACK

CREATIVE INTELLIGENCE IS IN THE WHITE BLOOD--A MINORITY

SEGREGATE THE NEGRO OR LOSE THE WHITE BLOOD FOREVER

" THE KISS OF DEATH "

Remember India

The American mind is weakening. It is not as sound as 20 years ago. Selfishness, greed and easy living are doing the job.

We look frantically around for Russian spies, believing that Russia will attack us with armies. To us everything is material. In the meantime Russia is laughing. She has a more deadly weapon than the atomic bomb. She knows our strength is in our White stock and that when she has mixed our blood with negro that we are licked forever.

While Russia makes laws to protect herself, she continues to prod us to accept 16,000,000 negroes as social equals and we are doing everything possible to please her.

Radio announcers beg us to do this for strength and unity...Is India strong and united? She once had a White race. Every American who by word or deed helps Russia further this plan of race destruction is a traitor to kind and country.

Negro blood destroyed the civilization of Egypt, India, Phoenicia, Carthage, Greece and Rome. The Russians regard every negro in our midst as a weapon more deadly than the atomic bomb.

Segregation is the law of God, not man, and is observed thru the whole animal kingdom. It is the cornerstone of all civilization. It protects all life on our planet. It made America great. Break it down and you break down our society. Nature it was who gave the White man the brains to make the machine. If she had wanted the negro and Asiatic to enjoy this machine civilization as an equal she would have given him the intelligence to create the machine. Her method of control among animals is to curtail the intellect.

The Asiatic and negro are living on lend-lease civilization. Without the White support these people take their rightful place and are no longer a menace. Continue to rob the White race in order to bribe the Asiatic and negro and these people will overwhelm the White race and destroy all progress, religion, invention, art, and return us to the jungle. Preserve the White stock and you preserve the Christian way and the good life. Does a rose garden

scatter weed seeds in its bed because God made weed seeds? Maybe God wanted to see if we had sense enough to know what to do under the circumstances. Pressure creates mind. Nature's ways are not easy ways. Only the weak and decadent must have an easy solution. The solution of complete disappearance.

We should begin by getting our minds back. Tell the Russians we are White and intend to stay White and protect our civilization and our country. The Russians know what the negro is and that he is death to everything.

While negroes are multiplying by leaps and bounds, we are persecuting our White stock for trying to protect and preserve its White blood. We are accepting the most deadly thing about Communism, the negro, in order to fight Communism.

Our first move should be to quit sending American treasure to Asia or Africa or any colored race. Help all White people anywhere including the Germans who are our own kind. Help preserve the White blood which is a minority stock. If we would do this we would recover our sanity and lose our fear.

We still have time to save ourselves from Russian propaganda and the fate of India. Remember Christianty would not live 50 years among negroes and Chinese. Remember civilization would not survive if the White man is destroyed. Remember the White stock is the minority race and that the colored people far out-number and out breed the White man. Remember, mixing White children with negroes is a form of insanity. It takes the form of religion, democracy, brotherhood, etc. It is a pollution complex directed from Moscow. Remember discrimination is not a sin - . It is a sign of Mind of God working thru man to protect what is good. A discriminating person is an intelligent person. Remember the White man is making his last stand and that he has been overwhelmed by trash more than once and it is what you do and say as an individual that may determine his future forever, for even God cannot turn a negro into a White man again for God follows inevitable laws of kind making kind. In the meantime our courts, churches, newspapers, and radios are helping Russia in her deadly work of destroying America - or anything that is worth saving in America.

© W. Wolfe

Negro Blood Destroyed the Civilization of Egypt, India, Phoenicia, Carthage, Greece and Rome.

It will Destroy America!

5¢ per copy

National Citizens Protective Association
3154a S. Grand or P. O. Box 156, St. Louis, Mo.

50 for $1.00

FIGURE 2.1 National Citizens Protective Association, "Kiss of Death," 1956. Folder Hate Groups, 1957–1958, IB:33 National Urban League Records, Library of Congress, Washington, DC. Courtesy of Center for Local History, Arlington Public Libraries, Arlington, Virginia.

increasingly common white supremacist strategy during the 1960s and 1970s—associating support for racial equality with homosexuality.

This lurid propaganda resonated with white Americans alarmed by challenges to the existing racial order. "I won't give a penney [sic] to the Community Chest until the chest gives up the Urban League," declared one reader of Little Rock's *Arkansas Democrat*. He queried, "Why bring [economic ruin to other organizations that receive Chest funds] by supporting the Urban League which is trying to destroy the welfare of our future generations?"[20] In referencing the "welfare" of the next generation, this reader implied that the league threatened the imagined biological and social asset of whiteness through their promotion of racial equity. Another reader from El Dorado, Arkansas wrote, "There would be no campaign for money here if we were asked to support the Urban League."[21] In addition to voicing their displeasure in the press, sympathizers boycotted businesses that supported the inclusion of local Urban Leagues in Community Chest fundraisers and made threatening phone calls to Community Chest offices to advocate for the exclusion of Urban League chapters. Throughout the region, segregationist groups like the Citizens' Councils of America and the States' Rights Council of Georgia were important co-conspirators, circulating flyers and coordinating boycotts of fundraising campaigns.[22]

The consequences were immediate and acute. Five Community Chest campaigns barred local Urban League affiliates from receiving funds in 1956 and 1957. The Jacksonville, Florida, Community Chest withheld financial support from the local Urban League chapter because the group refused to distance itself from the national leadership's stand on integration.[23] In Norfolk, Virginia, Community Chest officials found themselves under intense pressure to drop the local Urban League. Bending to public opinion, they barred the chapter from receiving fundraising contributions, claiming there was not enough time for a thorough investigation of claims against the civil rights group.[24] The Richmond, Virginia, Urban League voluntarily withdrew from the annual fundraising campaign, stating that they were "not willing to see Richmond's most precious asset—its great Community Chest—seriously injured or destroyed by such hate groups."[25] Various southern communities and Urban League chapters weathered the NCPA's attacks, including Atlanta, Georgia; Saint Louis, Missouri; Tampa, Florida; Tulsa and Oklahoma City, Oklahoma; Memphis, Tennessee; and Louisville, Kentucky.[26] Although the NPCA-initiated campaign was the primary driver of ill feeling against the NUL, other factors made certain communities particularly fertile grounds for these attacks. Historically, the NUL struggled to establish and maintain chapters in many southern cities due to racial prejudice, mistrust from white locals, irregular leadership, and financial instability. Although white powerbrokers accepted many southern chapters by the mid-1950s, this longer history of adversity formed a crucial backdrop to the unfolding controversy. Faced with unprecedented opposition that threatened the livelihood of their organization across the country, the NUL moved to act.

The National Urban League Responds

By the fall of 1956, the NUL's executive council expressed grave concerns over the NCPA's attacks on the organization's work and their affiliates' financial well-being. Theodore Kheel, an executive committee member, characterized the attacks as "unprecedented regionally- federated and disturbingly effective campaigns waged by die-hard supporters of the radical status quo in the South."[27] The fervor and efficacy of this campaign prompted the NUL to respond. As one contemporary noted in the *New York Times*, "The league's decision to mount a counter-offensive represented a departure from its traditional avoidance of public controversy."[28] The national leadership adopted three tactics to counter these campaigns: working with national and local leadership of the United Community Funds and Councils of America (UCFCA), which oversaw local Community Chest divisions; generating local biracial support among leaders in targeted southern communities; and waging a public relations campaign to clarify the NUL's aims and discredit their opponents.

Cooperating with the UCFCA and its affiliates was a key aspect of the NUL's strategy to combat segregationist propaganda. Although national UCFCA officials like Lyman Ford (associate director) and Ralph Blanchard (executive director) were "cordial, understanding and cooperative" in their meetings and correspondence with NUL officials, considerable caution marked their responses. Although both men assured Maurice A. Moss, the NUL associate director, that they would present strategies to combat the segregationist campaign to the national board, "it was agreed that it should not be listed on the agenda as an item to be discussed nor included in any of 3c's releases."[29] Such reluctance to challenge the NCPA was evident in the national board's refusal to institute an official statement or policy about these attacks as late as 1957.[30] Yet this reluctance was not universal. Some local Community Chests publicly supported Urban League chapters and decried their detractors.[31] Despite the national leadership's general reticence to address the controversy, national and local Urban League leadership continued to communicate with UCFCA officials about strategies to counter these attacks.[32] Additionally, the NUL reached out to allies in the fields of social work and organized labor to mount an effective defense.[33]

The NUL also generated local African American support to counter these attacks. In a report about several southern communities with affiliate chapters, staff member Nelson C. Jackson noted "that Negro lay leadership" would be a key constituency in the fight against the NCPA. According to Jackson, local Black leaders could play a dual role in combating the white supremacists' campaign. As members of the community, Black leaders could directly appeal to Community Chest officials and local civic leaders in support of local chapters. Moreover, encouraging African American fraternal, lay, and religious organizations to participate in Community Chest fundraising efforts that included the Urban League demonstrated the financial power of Black residents. National officials adopted these strategies by reaching out to organizations (Black and white) and community figures to garner support.[34]

The NUL's public relations strategy was crucial. Writing to NUL executive director Granger in May 1956, Jackson suggested the "use of public relations media to positively tell the story of the local Urban League in an effort to offset lies and false propaganda by hate groups."[35] Like Jackson, Granger and several other NUL leaders believed that clarifying the organization's aims would effectively counter segregationist allegations.[36] Yet others advocated for a more aggressive approach. During a meeting between the executive committee and staff, R. Wood, an executive committee member, suggested that the NUL begin "smearing" segregationists that disseminated anti–Urban League materials. Wood argued that the NUL needed to assemble damaging information on white supremacist groups and forward it to Community Chests.[37] Although the NUL assembled a dossier on John Hamilton soon after, it did not include any salacious information.[38]

As the attacks continued during the late summer and early fall of 1956, members of the Urban League's national leadership once again advocated for the use of more damaging information against Hamilton and NCPA.[39] Harry Alston, the director of the NUL's southern field division, queried, "Would it be beyond the limits of the Urban League to have or give the time to someone to dig up even more than what we already have on the leaders of the opposition?" He suggested that the NUL "need[ed] to take the initiative" in countering the slanderous stories circulating throughout the South.[40] This comment suggests that a certain segment of the organization believed that simply refuting allegations against the NUL or clarifying their organizational aims was not enough. Instead, the NUL needed information on their opponents that was so damaging it would affect their legitimacy. Although the notion of "smearing" has a connotation with propagating falsehoods, it does not appear that the NUL fabricated information. Less than two weeks after Alston's suggestion, criminal allegations provided the NUL with the ammunition it needed to depict Hamilton as a sexual predator.

On the morning of October 13, 1956, Saint Louis police arrested an adolescent wandering the streets. After his arrest for loitering, the teenager volunteered that John Wilson Hamilton had solicited him for sex. According to the police report, Hamilton approached the unnamed minor on the street. Soon after, the two traveled to a nearby bar. Although it is unclear who initiated the invitation for sex, accounts indicate that the teenager agreed to perform oral sex for ten dollars. The two then traveled to the Saint Nicholas Hotel, purchasing some wine on the way. After the act took place, the youth followed Hamilton to the offices of the *White Sentinel*, which doubled as Hamilton's residence, to receive payment. Finding another individual in Hamilton's bed upon their arrival, the editor paid the youth two dollars and asked that he return the following morning for the remaining sum. It was on his return to Hamilton's residence the following morning that the youth was arrested. Police arrested Hamilton for "suspected sodomy [and] suspected . . . child molestation."[41] However, the latter charge was dropped.[42] Although Hamilton admitted to sharing a drink and a hotel room with his accuser, he denied that anything sexual had transpired.

Hamilton's arrest quickly came to the attention of Urban League president Bohanon, who forwarded news coverage about the event to the national office.[43] Titled "John W. Hamilton Arrested on Morals Charge," the short *Saint Louis Globe-Democrat* article recounts the basic events and identifies Hamilton as editor of the *White Sentinel*.[44] NUL officials were quick to use this information to their advantage. Three days later, Guichard Parris, the national director of public relations, forwarded the article to a number of newspaper editors. In a memo titled "A Suggested Subject for Editorial Treatment," Parris wrote, "This man, working with the White Citizens Councils, has been distributing millions of hate sheets throughout the South and elsewhere." Stating that the NUL was vulnerable to attack because of its financial relationship with Community Chests, Parris charged that the segregationist group was "determined to destroy every influence of interracial understanding and any programs directed toward integration."[45] Locally, the Saint Louis branch closely followed the events associated with Hamilton's arrest. During an October 18 board of directors meeting,

Bohanon "brought the board up to date on the attacks of the Urban League by the John Hamilton group and others." Relatedly, the executive director "alluded to the recent newspaper publicity concerning the questionable morals of John Hamilton." It appears, however, that the local branch did little independently to capitalize on the legal woes of its segregationist foe.[46]

The NUL informed its affiliates throughout the country, encouraging them to propagate knowledge of Hamilton's arrest. Nelson Jackson, an executive staff member, distributed a short memo to the executive secretaries of local league affiliates, which included a copy of the article. "You may use this material to the best advantage in the proper places—news-papers, Community Chest, etc.," he stated.[47] NUL officials also sent this article to the Community Chest national headquarters, hoping they would communicate the information to their affiliates throughout the South.[48] In addition, officials circulated a copy of the police report to southern League chapters to substantiate their claims.[49] NUL leaders issued only one public statement about Hamilton's arrest. Executive secretary Granger mentioned Hamilton's sexual as well as political misdeeds in his *New York Amsterdam News* column in November 1956. He characterized the charges as "impairing the morals of a male minor—sex perversion, to put it bluntly."[50]

The serendipitous nature of Hamilton's arrest raised questions about the local chapter's role in facilitating the scandal. Writing to Saint Louis Urban League leader Bohanon on October 19 regarding routine administrative matters, Jackson asked if he was "kidding when you indicated that rumor has started that the Urban League was behind Hamilton's activities and that this boy was a 'plant.'" "If that is true that's something that we will have to jump on in a hurry."[51] Scribbling notes in the margins of the letter that would later be articulated in a brief reply on October 22, Bohanon wrote, "There is positively no such rumor that the boy in the Hamilton case was a plant by the Urban League. Even our worst or perhaps our best enemies would not think that of us." It is unclear if Jackson misunderstood a joke by Bohanon or whether—as the latter joked in his reply—that the "telephone connections [sic] was bad" during their previous conversation, leading to a miscommunication.[52] However, the former's concern over rumors of the Urban League's involvement in Hamilton's arrest suggests that officials experienced some unease regarding their publicity efforts. Given that the NCPA's chief charge against the Urban League was sexual depravity, it might have been a short leap for individuals sympathetic to the NCPA's rhetoric to believe that the NUL might try to frame Hamilton on similar grounds.

The NUL's decision to publicize Hamilton's arrest complicates the nature of sexual politics associated with postwar race relations by calling scholarly attention away from narratives of illicit forms of heterosexual behavior. As discussed in the introduction, heterosexual intimacies, real and imagined, inter- and intraracial, were crucial to the maintenance of Jim Crow segregation as well as to African Americans' challenges to white supremacy generally.[53] Therefore, historians have consistently focused on African American engagements with popular conceptions of Black heterosexual licentiousness as well as white supremacist anxieties over illicit heterosexual interracial sex. This focus does not substantively address how Cold War anxieties over sexual and gender nonconformity influenced Black political communities, however.[54] Lavender baiting, or the ascription of homosexuality to an individual to disparage them in the public sphere, was a key political weapon during the 1950s. Both liberal and conservative anti-communists deployed such characterizations to undermine political opponents.[55] Even Republican Wisconsin senator Joseph McCarthy, a notorious anti-communist crusader, was susceptible to such charges. While he rose to the pinnacle of legislative power through sensational and unsubstantiated accusations that communists had infiltrated the federal government, bachelorhood and allegations that his close relationship with adviser Roy Cohn suggested homosexual desire ultimately facilitated the destruction of his political career.[56]

The NUL, then, did not simply publicize the arrest of an opponent for a sexual crime. Instead, the organization engaged in a contemporary, common, and highly effective offensive strategy used across the political spectrum. By circulating news of Hamilton's same-sex and intergenerational sexual liaison, NUL leaders engaged in lavender baiting to undermine his political legitimacy. In publicizing Hamilton's arrest, the NUL demonstrated a keen understanding of sexuality's prominence in Cold War domestic politics, wherein the allegedly sexually non-normative and predatory nature of various types of radicals (communists, anti-racists) could be deployed as a weapon. Aside from the political efficacy of this strategy, the NUL more than likely publicized Hamilton's arrest out of genuine moral censure. Since its formation, the national leadership of the Urban League embraced an assimilationist worldview that prioritized equitable opportunity and individual advancement, rather than a radical critique of structural, systemic inequities.[57] Adherence to bourgeois social and sexual norms was a fundamental aspect of their broader mission of racial uplift. Given the heightened anti-homosexual sentiment of the mid-twentieth century, it is unsurprising that the NUL would exhibit moral opprobrium toward same-sex-desiring persons.

Internal correspondence suggests the national leadership saw strategic gain in its decision to publicize Hamilton's arrest. However, it is unclear whether this publicization was spurred by pragmatism or preexisting homophobia. There is no explicit homophobic language nor disparaging remarks within the NUL's correspondence about the event. Many of these documents were noncirculating confidential memoranda, shielded from public scrutiny. Indeed, the most disparaging commentary on Hamilton's arrest came from Granger in his *New York Amsterdam News* column mentioned earlier.[58] Certainly, Granger's characterization of Hamilton's alleged actions as "sex perversion" combined with the national leadership's decision to publicize the charges, demonstrates that the NUL disapproved of same-sex intergenerational sex. However, the absence of additional homophobic language within the internal correspondence suggests that moral judgments, while likely present, may have been secondary to strategic political considerations. The pains the NUL took to spread news of Hamilton's arrest indicates a belief that the queer nature of the charges and the victim's age would engender opprobrium in white as well as Black communities, thus tarnishing the legitimacy of Hamilton, his organization, and their propaganda. However, it was the Black press that independently articulated the story, placing it in relation to three broad cultural narratives about homosexuals: the figure of the sexual psychopath, queer sex scandals of prominent public figures, and generally derogatory depictions of gay men and lesbians.

John W. Hamilton Enters the Black Sexual Public Sphere

Nationwide, the Black press reported Hamilton's arrest, trial, and ultimate conviction for sodomy. Headlines like "Hate Sheet Editor, Sex Deviate," "White Sentinel Editor Guilty of Perversion," and "Editor of Race-Baiting Paper Faces Morals Trial" typified Black newspaper reporting in Pittsburgh, Pennsylvania; Norfolk, Virginia; Baltimore, Maryland; and unsurprisingly, Saint Louis, Missouri.[59] The Black press's enthusiastic coverage of the story was stoked by several developments. Public familiarity with Hamilton, the NCPA, and its anti–Urban League campaign created a ready audience for the editor's public scandal. Furthermore, the lack of interest from regional and national mainstream newspapers gave the Black press unfettered access to and ownership of the story, allowing them to craft it without any opposing narratives.[60] The intergenerational and same-sex nature of Hamilton's offense profoundly shaped the coverage, as the two were often linked in the public imaginary.

Three journalistic contexts frame Black press coverage of the Hamilton scandal. First, it mirrored contemporary national discourses about sex crimes. During the 1930s and 1940s, a number of sexual crimes involving men and children captivated national attention and fueled fears over sexually predatory behaviors. Public interest in these crimes reflected heightened national anxieties over changing gender norms and weakening social controls over sexual behavior both before and after World War II. In response, many state legislatures and municipalities passed statutes that prosecuted various sexual offenses, including consensual same-sex sex between adults. Police departments and judges often targeted same-sex-desiring men in the enforcement of these statutes. The widespread tendency to conflate homosexuality and pedophilia also contributed to the disproportionate prosecution of same-sex-desiring men under sexual psychopath laws.[61] National press outlets often treated child molestation and homosexuality as inextricably linked or interchangeable, reflecting state and civilian perceptions of the sexual psychopath.[62]

Black communities were not immune from the hysteria over sexual psychopaths and sex crimes. During and after World War II African American press reports and editorials increasingly featured disparaging commentary and portrayals of homosexuality, which were associated with sexual criminality. This trend continued in the 1950s.[63] Headlines like "8-Year-Old Boy Attacked Near Home by Sex Maniac" and "Girls Feared Sex Victims" appeared in Black newspapers across the country.[64] In 1956, *Baltimore Afro-American* reporter Roger Maddox captured the general tone of this moral panic, proclaiming, "Sex crimes are seeping into the daily life of America like filth from a broken sewer." Giving various anecdotes of crimes against children, he exhorted parents "to warn children against these smooth-tongued and cunning beasts."[65]

Second, Black newspapers regularly featured reporting about sexual matters. As Kim Gallon notes in her work on Black newspapers during the interwar period, editors and journalists sought to attract readers through their coverage of an array of sexual topics, including divorces, sex scandals, homosexuality, interracial sex, and the erotic appeal of Black women's bodies. These depictions, Gallon argues, "filled the interstices between anti-black sexual stereotypes and respectability politics" creating various "black sexual public spheres" in the process.[66] In particular, Black newspapers characterized homosexuality (almost always between people understood to be male) in more benign ways.[67] These depictions seemed to have shifted in some places, as national press coverage became more homophobic.[68] For example, the notable sex scandal of Pentecostal minister Prophet James Frances Jones (also known as Prophet Jones) provided a crucial context for coverage of Hamilton's case. Jones, a native of Birmingham, Alabama, migrated to Detroit in 1938 to begin a ministry under the fledgling denomination Triumph the Church and Kingdom of God in Christ. He quickly rose to local and national prominence, as much for his ostentatious flamboyance as for his professed ability to bless his parishioners. In February 1956, he was arrested for attempting to fellate an undercover vice officer. In the eyes of law enforcement, the allegations appeared to be confirmed when, upon arresting Jones at his home, police officers found him alone with two teenage boys dressed in his pajamas.[69] As Tim Retzloff documents, the Black press widely publicized his morals charge arrest, trial, and ultimate acquittal. However, the damage to Jones's reputation was irreparable. Narratives about sexual psychopathy, queer sex scandals (like that of Prophet Jones), and generally derogatory press coverage of homosexuality clearly informed the broader Black public imaginary that consumed news of Hamilton's arrest on a morals charge at the end of 1956.[70]

National Black press coverage of Hamilton's offense used the sensational language associated with sexual psychopath stories, including the equation of homosexuality and child molestation. Notably, reporters did not depict the white youth as a victim. Knowledge about the commercial nature of the sexual encounter as well as the teenager's subsequent delinquency charge "by reason of a morals offense" suggests that he may have participated in the informal economy of male youth sex work that existed in many cities.[71] Oftentimes, male youths who engaged in sex work occupied the same urban spaces as female sex workers and were treated similarly by law enforcement and judicial authorities. And, as was true for female sex work, their participation ranged from infrequent to regular and included an array of remuneration standards, financial and material.[72] In the trial testimony, the white teenager readily admitted he was trying to earn money and solicited Hamilton for sex.[73] Such information may have substantively shaped press coverage. And it was certainly the case that the national Black press emphasized the intergenerational and same-sex nature of the encounter to denigrate Hamilton.

Third and finally, coverage of Hamilton's sex scandal occurred during a moment in which commercial Black newspapers were narrowing the scope of their political commentary and reporting. As Fred Carroll recounts, by the end of World War II, progressive and radical voices were firmly ensconced in commercial Black press outlets, a process aided by the expansion of circulation and deepening radicalization among Black Americans. Mirroring many Black liberal organizations, commercial newspapers marginalized or fired those with any historical ties to communism or with progressive views in the years after the end of the war. Carroll asserts that pressure from the federal government, white newspapers, and anticommunists forced the commercial Black press to narrow its political vision. Supporting the Urban League—the most moderate of civil rights organizations at the time—with such coverage positioned commercial Black newspapers not as dens of subversive radicals but patriotic challengers of white supremacy. Finally, it should be noted that media scrutiny of Hamilton and the NUL occurred during a time when mainstream white newspapers had not yet turned a consistent eye toward race relations in the South and the civil rights movement. Not only did this translate into Black press outlets having unfettered access to the story, but it also might explain in part the general dearth of coverage in the mainstream white press.[74]

The *Saint Louis Argus* was one of the few Black newspapers to feature sensational reporting that characterized the youth as a victim and Hamilton as a predator. Certainly, the *Argus*'s coverage was affected by its proximity to the NCPA, ensuring a great familiarity with and disdain for Hamilton and his racist ideologies. Another event may have also influenced the tenor of the coverage. A week prior to Hamilton's arrest, two white men attempted to abduct and sexually assault a Black child working as a shoeshine.[75] Saint Louis's Black community was thus already aware of—and more than likely extremely sensitive to—sexual crimes involving minors. Stories that highlighted the intergenerational nature of the encounter reflected this sensitivity. Headlines like "John Hamilton Is Guilty//Given 2 Yrs. [*sic*] Charge with Boy" and captions such as "Alone in 311 with a boy of tender years" all drew attention to the adolescent's age.[76] Additionally, *Saint Louis Argus* reporting linked Hamilton's political philosophies and sexual desires to his appearance. In "Portrait of a White Supremacist," *Argus* editor Howard B. Woods characterized the segregationist as "balding, stockily [*sic*] built" and possessing a chin that "melts away into a fat thick neck which is in no way associated with persons of strong character."[77] Similarly, all but one of the *Saint Louis Argus* articles included an unflattering picture

CONFUSIN' AIN'T IT?

FIGURE 2.2 "Confusin' Ain't It," *Saint Louis Argus,* October 19,1956. Image courtesy of the State Historical Society of Missouri, Columbia.

of Hamilton. Captions like "His fitness questioned," "Did he or did he not?" and "In rendezvous at St. Nicholas" accompanied images of the segregationist. These images, like Woods's editorial writing, made Hamilton appear if not sinister, then surely untrustworthy.[78]

Alongside their denigration of same-sex intimacy, Black press coverage emphasized the hypocrisy of an advocate for white racial purity engaging in sexual misconduct. This tactic was evident in a *Saint Louis Argus* editorial titled "Room 311." Recounting the circumstances of Hamilton's arrest, the editorial writer observed that "to he who shouts the cry of 'racial purity, mongrelization and white supremacy,' the set of circumstances surrounding the matter seem odd, indeed."[79] The editorial also suggested that Hamilton's crime was not a singular incident. The anonymous author encouraged law enforcement officials to investigate Hamilton's exploits in Boston to "clear up the mysterious two hours Hamilton spent with a lad in the St. Nicholas hotel's now notorious room 311." The adjacent cartoon illustrated this hypocrisy in stark terms (see fig. 2.2). In the drawing, an African American man holds two newspapers: the *White Sentinel* and the *Saint Louis Globe-Dispatch*.[80] The segregationist *White Sentinel* headline "Protect White Womanhood" is contrasted with the imaginary daily newspaper's headline "Racist Charged with Molesting Boy." The figure holding the papers is the embodiment of puzzlement, with wide eyes and raised eyebrows. The caption reads, "Confusin' Ain't It?" This image graphically illustrates the primary political force of the Hamilton scandal: the hypocrisy of segregationists who characterized Black men as sexual predators while engaging in (or excusing) predatory sexual behavior among their ilk. Together, these editorials demonstrate that African Americans, often the targets of derisive characterizations of their sexuality, were willing to articulate similar commentary about their opponents in the public sphere.[81]

Yet not all African Americans supported the extensive reporting on Hamilton's legal troubles. *Baltimore Afro-American* reader Richard Howell declared, "If I wanted to read men's rooms [sic] stories like the AFRO carried on John Wilson Hamilton, the *White Citizens* editor, I'll buy one of those peep-hole magazines, not a decent newspaper." Castigating the *Baltimore Afro-American* for lowering its journalistic standards by publicizing the story, Howell concluded, "He is not worth all the attention you gave him."[82] Saint Louis teacher Dorothy Lemmons agreed. In a letter to the editor titled "Shocked," she lamented that the *Saint Louis Argus* "had degenerated into a sensational smut-sheet." She wondered whether newspapers were so anxious to make a profit "that they turn their backs once and for all on respectability ?"[83] Readers like Lemmons and Howell believed that such press coverage reflected the character of the African American community and should, therefore, maintain decorum by not addressing certain subjects. However, Black editors incorporated articles about sexuality in their newspapers, responding to a desire for stories about divorce scandals, interracial marriages, homosexuality, and female impersonation.[84] Clearly, for readers like Lemmons and Howell, such coverage was not warranted despite the potential damage to Hamilton and his cause. These glimpses of African American reader opinions suggest the contested nature of sexual matters within the Black public sphere in the postwar period.

Other readers applauded the reporting and were keenly aware of the political efficacy of publicizing Hamilton's actions. A. R. Royal, a *Saint Louis Argus* reader, commended the press coverage and attributed Hamilton's conviction to the negative publicity. Mrs. Joyce Caldwell encouraged the *Saint Louis Argus* staff to continue their coverage of the trial, stating, "I'm behind you a hundred per cent [sic] as every one of your readers should be." She suggested that some of the NCPA's followers might disavow the "white supremacy campaign" if they knew of Hamilton's sexual conduct, and she lamented the limited reporting in the city's two leading newspapers, the *Post-Dispatch* and the *Globe-Democrat*. She expressed her "wish [that] all the dailies had done as good a job" as the *Argus*.[85] The unwillingness of white dailies to devote much space to the story was not limited to Saint Louis. *Baltimore Afro-American* reader Beulah Parks also mentioned the limited reporting in mainstream newspapers in her area. Questioning the decision of "white newspapers" and "wire services" to not pick up the story, Parks wondered whether they were "ashamed of this man who had made a career out of racial bigotry."[86]

While Parks may have overestimated the conscience of white journalists, her observation of the lack of reporting on Hamilton's arrest and conviction was accurate. There were a few notable exceptions, however. Two major Saint Louis newspapers, the *Post-Dispatch* and the *Globe-Democrat*, offered limited coverage of Hamilton's arrest and conviction (three brief articles). All were located on the inside pages of the newspaper, were not prominently displayed, and lacked any editorial commentary.[87] No other surveyed southern newspaper reported the incident.[88] Nationally, coverage was equally scant. The *Washington Post* featured a short matter-of-fact article about the arrest.[89] Gossip columnist Walter Winchell gave the most extensive commentary of any national mainstream reporter in his syndicated column. Briefly referencing the conviction, Winchell ridiculed the NCPA's ideology with the witticism that Hamilton "couldn't segregate that news. It's there in black and white."[90]

Although Winchell's wordplay on segregation and the color of newsprint may have amused some readers, the reality was that national press coverage was largely segregated along racial and regional lines. After World War II, newspapers and television news bureaus had their own political and bureaucratic rationales for the degree of attention they gave African American politics and early civil rights activism. For the northern and national press, long-standing biases toward local events obscured the portentous mobilizations fomenting below the Mason-Dixon Line. Although wire services and some dailies covered early conflagrations like the Emmett Till murder trial in 1955 and the Montgomery bus boycott in 1955 and 1956, it was not until the clash over racial integration at Little Rock (Arkansas) High School in September 1957 that national attention truly began to focus on civil rights campaigns. Excluding a handful of moderate and liberal southern editors, most newspapers in the old Confederacy supported resistance to desegregation through editorial endorsement or silence. This early neglect ensured that the Black press monopolized coverage of the modern civil rights movement during the early years.[91] These realities substantively affected the NUL's attempts to publicize Hamilton's arrest. Their press releases more than likely fell on disinterested ears at many mainstream newspapers, ears that had not yet been forced to heed Black voices, let alone those pressing for racial equality and civil rights.

Although Hamilton's conviction may have been on the periphery of the national mainstream press, there is evidence that knowledge of Hamilton's arrest circulated within radical right circles. Before the scandal, the anticommunist publication the *American Nationalist* commended Hamilton and the NCPA for their "especially fine job in combating the activities of the [NAACP]."[92] Yet this praise ended abruptly after Hamilton's conviction. In March 1957 the *American Nationalist* briefly noted that Hamilton was convicted for "homosexual activity" including "a sodomy offense against a 15-year-old boy." Most telling was the article's designation of Hamilton as "a self-professed former Communist." Whereas the Black press linked Hamilton's racist political ideologies to his sexual behavior, this conservative periodical insinuated that his sexual behavior was intimately tied to his communist past.[93]

The Political Uses of Homophobia

Explicating the story of the NUL's publicization of John W. Hamilton's arrest and conviction on a morals charge brings into sharp relief the place of sexuality in civil rights liberal politics and the Black public sphere. The Black press's ability and willingness to publicize the scandal affirms the importance of sexuality within the Black public sphere and the importance of Black newspapers in conveying particular ideas about homosexuality for its readers. The NUL's willingness to mobilize lavender baiting to undermine a segregationist foe complicates the scholarship about sexuality within the modern civil rights movement. It illustrates the multifaceted nature of Black liberal homophobia during this period as an ideology that circumscribed the experiences of activists, informed coalitions, and could be mobilized as one weapon within a broader arsenal. More consequentially, the events at the heart of the first two chapters indicate not only how the consolidation of a homosexual-heterosexual binary within American citizenship reverberated in the experiences of same-sex-desiring and gender nonconforming African Americans. They also show how Black political communities had to navigate these shifts as they sought to access and transform notions of citizenship. This occurred, in part, because of the long-standing associations between Blackness and sexual/gender variance. As the next section will illuminate, these associations would take on new meanings among white supremacists as they began to more forcefully link homosexuality, communism, and support for Black racial equality, and Blackness in efforts to preserve a racial regime under increasing national and local assault.

Part II **The Sexual Deployments of White Supremacists**

. . . .

Freedom March Makes Queers Bed Fellows

Sexual Rumors and the 1965 Alabama
Voting Rights Demonstrations

· ·

"I'm sorry you can't win cause the devil is fighting you," wrote New York City resident Joe Doherty to Alabama governor and ardent segregationist George C. Wallace on March 22, 1965. Doherty joined millions of Americans who were captivated by the unfolding clash between interracial civil rights demonstrators and Alabama state officials, local law enforcement, and white civilians. The violent response to nonviolent civil rights demonstrations enhanced public sympathy for the civil rights movement and prompted a groundswell of support for the Voting Rights Act of 1965, passed by Congress later that year.[1] But for some, like Doherty, it was not the violence in Selma, Alabama or the murders of three supporters of racial equality that spring that caused alarm. Rather, it was the nonviolent demonstrators, who represented a subversive, immoral threat to gender, sexual, and racial norms. It was this threat that Doherty sought to amplify by including a scurrilous rumor about "three in the ranks of to-day['s] [march] from Selma to Montgomery: A Rabbi, A Rights Leader, and [a] NYC Politico." According to the letter, when the three men were "schoolmates," they engaged in sodomy—the "Rabbi" with the "Rights Leader" and the "NYC Politico" with a "buck negro." It was this past association, he wrote, that made these figures "friends marching arm in arm in the 'Freedom March.'" He concluded that "politics makes strange bed fellows, and 'Freedom March' makes 'Queers' bed fellows."[2] In mobilizing the term "politics makes strange bedfellows," Doherty drew upon the prevailing wisdom that individuals or constituencies might align momentarily over key issues, even if they appeared to have divergent commitments or, indeed, conflicts with one another. But the second phrase, "Freedom March makes Queers bed fellows," suggests that coalitions between white liberals, Black civil rights organizers, and white religious leaders were rooted not solely in a shared commitment to desegregation or even racial equality. Rather, a desire for illicit sex—and indeed same-sex sex—motivated these interracial political alliances.

As we have seen, this concept—that those who supported racial desegregation and/or equality were susceptible to non-normative sexual and gender behavior—has a long history. However, the discursive connections between same-sex intimacy and support for racial equality, if not new, became increasingly prominent during the postwar period. One well-known moment in which anti-Blackness and homophobia converged is in the work of the Florida Legislative Investigation Committee, also known as the Johns Committee after its chairperson Charley Johns. The state legislature created the bicameral committee in 1956 as a part of the South's region-wide response to civil rights organizing and the *Brown v. Board of Education* Supreme Court ruling mandating desegregation of public educational facilities.[3] Initially, the Johns Committee harassed and prosecuted civil rights organizations and activists for alleged communist sympathies and/or criminal activity. After failing to substantively stymie Black Floridians' mobilizations for equal rights, the committee turned to another alleged menace: gay and lesbian educators in public schools and universities. Whereas some histories treat these two phases as unrelated iterations of the committee's work, others reveal how their staunch anti-communism acted as a crucial bridge between their anti-Black and homophobic crusades.[4] Whereas the Johns Committee articulated its own hazy associations between Blackness and homosexuality, more explicit connections between effeminacy, same-sex intimacy, and support for racial equality are evident in postwar Mississippi. As John Howard argues, characterizations of interracial cadres of civil rights activists as "racial perverts" and "libertines," as well as feminized depictions of white male activists "implied . . . that the proponents of racial justice harbored deviant sexual practices that went beyond interracial heterosexual intercourse to include interracial homosexual intercourse."[5] This rhetoric was especially powerful during and after the Freedom Summer campaigns of 1964, a coalitional effort between several civil rights organizations to extend the long-denied franchise to Black Mississippians.

Such rhetoric was not limited to Mississippi, however. Beginning in late March 1965, white supremacists charged that interracial participants in the Alabama voting rights demonstrations had engaged in public intoxication, sex orgies, interracial heterosexual couplings, and homosexual trysts.[6] This chapter analyzes the emergence, articulation of, and national response to allegations that voting rights demonstrators engaged in queer (or nonnormative) sexual behavior. In adopting this scope, I agree with Jared Leighton's assertion that "there is no other comparable [civil rights campaign] where claims of 'sex perversion' were so widespread."[7] I build on his analysis to argue that placing references to homosexuality in the broader context of two cultural developments regarding sexuality reveals the impetus for its increasing prominence within white supremacist literature during the ensuing ten years: (1) the declining power of references to miscegenation and Black hyper(hetero)sexuality to mobilize non-southern white support for racial segregation and (2) heightened anxieties over the increasing visibility of gay men and lesbians as well as transgender communities. This particular mass mobilization marked a watershed moment for this set of racial-sexual configurations in white supremacist discourse, signaling the increasing centrality of homophobia within such propaganda for the remainder of the 1960s and early 1970s.[8] This chapter analyzes the national outcry over Alabama Congressman William L. Dickinson's public accusations of sexual debauchery among demonstrators. I assert that these allegations were nurtured by long-standing associations between civil rights advocacy and interracial sex as well as contemporary media representations of sympathetic whites as irreligious counterculturalists. Whereas regional press outlets framed the marchers as social deviants, pamphlets, recorded speeches and private correspondence consistently aligned homosexuality with civil rights organizing in ways that would reverberate into the next decade.

Rumors and Racial Unrest in the Alabama Voting Rights Demonstrations

When US representative William L. Dickinson gave remarks on the floor of Congress in March 1965, he surely believed that he was alerting the nation to a growing menace. A native of Opelika, Alabama, World War II veteran, and Republican representing the state's Second District, Dickinson owed his electoral victory, in part, to the long coattails of Barry Goldwater, whose brand of anti-communism and small government conservatism had energized political conservatives the previous year. Dickinson was only weeks into his term as a freshman congressman when he alleged that participants in the voting rights demonstrations were immoral subversives. In his address, he presented a taxonomy of the protesters, dividing them into four groups. The first two—"the Alabama Negro" and "the do-gooders" from outside of the state—formed "only a small part of the total [protest] effort." The more prominent group were what he described as "human flotsam: adventurers, beatniks, prostitutes, and similar rabble," who found their way to Alabama for personal gain and pleasure. Dickinson alleged that "they are promised $10 per day, free room and board and all of the sex they want from opposite members of either race." He charged, "Only by the ultimate sex act with one of another color can they demonstrate they have no prejudice." Interracial sex between marchers was not the only transgressive behavior that allegedly took place. "Drunkenness and sex orgies were the order of the day in Selma, on the road to Montgomery and in Montgomery," the congressman reported. He also claimed that "an all-night session of debauchery [took place] within [a Negro church] itself." Dickinson characterized the protesters as "a bunch of godless riffraff out for kicks and self-gratification that have left every campsite between Selma and Montgomery littered with whisky bottles, beer cans and used contraceptives." He devoted the remainder of his speech to exposing the real organizers of the march and, indeed, the entire civil rights movement: the Communist Party.[9] Dickinson's account of the mobilization challenged national media coverage that depicted demonstrators as respectable and God-fearing. Equally important, his framing of demonstrators as invading hordes recast the forceful and, at times, violent responses of white Alabamians as warranted.

Indeed, it was the very likelihood of violence that made Selma, Alabama, an ideal place to launch a voting rights campaign. As in many parts of the Deep South, the Dallas County voter registration rolls reflected the pervasiveness of voter suppression and intimidation as a tactic to maintain white political power. For example, of the 15,000 African American residents comprising half of the county's voting age population in 1961, only 156 were registered to vote. In 1963, these inequities prompted the Student Nonviolent Coordinating Committee (SNCC) to initiate a voter registration campaign. However, the violent response of Dallas County Sheriff James G. Clark Jr. and state circuit judge James A. Hare inhibited movement building during the latter part of 1964. This intransigence drew the attention of Martin Luther King Jr. and the Southern Christian Leadership Conference (SCLC). Selma's gross inequities, as well as local and state officials' history of resistance to Black political assertiveness, made this Black Belt county an attractive place to launch a drive for electoral empowerment.[10] As David J. Garrow notes, the failure of the 1962 Albany, Georgia, campaign (in which the Police Chief Laurie Pritchett arrested demonstrators largely without incident) and the success of the 1963 Birmingham, Alabama, demonstrations (in which Police Chief Eugene "Bull" Connor violently attacked protesters with firehoses and dogs) cemented the SCLC's embrace of "nonviolent coercion" over "nonviolent persuasion."[11] The latter tactic focused on changing the minds and hearts of white opponents of integration, a task that often proved incredibly difficult. "Nonviolent coercion," on the other hand, forced their opponents to acquiesce to federal legislation, often by stirring the national consciousness through violent clashes with local law enforcement. One of the chief aims of the Selma campaign was to encourage "Americans of conscience in the name of decency [to] demand federal intervention and legislation" to protect the African American franchise.[12]

A series of public protests during the first three months of 1965 evoked white resistance that, at times, manifest in naked violence by law enforcement and white citizens.[13] In an effort to prevent a clash between local law enforcement and protesters, Selma mayor Joseph T. Smitherman appointed former county sheriff Wilson Baker as director of public safety.[14] This attempt to undermine Clark's authority failed, however, when violence unfolded in front of the Selma courthouse in January and February. On February 19, the murder of Jimmie Lee Jackson, a young African American protester, by a state trooper in nearby Marion affirmed for many activists the storied violence of state and local law enforcement.[15] Jackson's death prompted the boldest action of the campaign thus far: a proposed fifty-nine-mile march by Selma's Black residents and visiting activists to the state capital of Montgomery. They did so in direct violation of Governor Wallace's order to cease and desist their procession on US Highway 80. On March 7, Alabama state troopers confronted demonstrators as they attempted to cross the Edmund Pettus Bridge. After a tense standoff in which marchers refused to retreat, state troopers forced them back across the bridge, using tear gas and nightsticks. Photographic and television coverage of the violence shocked many Americans. The American Broadcast Corporation interrupted the Sunday evening film *Judgment at Nuremberg* with live coverage of the assault; the parallels between the persecution of European Jews and the violent repulsion of largely Black marchers were brutally clear. The events of "Bloody Sunday," as it became known, prompted hundreds of Americans to make a pilgrimage to Selma to protest the violence they believed violated their Judeo-Christian and democratic values.[16]

The presence of new demonstrators only intensified the intransigence of many local white residents, provoking new episodes of violence that had tangible ramifications for national attitudes on voting rights legislation. The March 11 death of Washington, DC Unitarian Minister James Reeb from an attack by white Selma residents galvanized more people to join the protests, including large numbers of ministers, priests, and nuns. Together, the demonstrators, whose ranks swelled to 25,000, completed the march from

Selma to Montgomery on March 25, protected by federally deputized state troopers. This moment of triumph was short-lived. Enraged local Ku Klux Klan members shot and killed Viola Liuzzo, a white SCLC volunteer and housewife from Detroit, Michigan, as she was transporting a young Black activist back to Selma. The contrast between these acts of violence and the nonviolent interracial, interfaith demonstrators was powerful, prompting a shift in public and political opinion in favor of national voting rights legislation. President Lyndon Baines Johnson and his administration accelerated their efforts, facilitating the passage of a sweeping piece of landmark legislation in August 1965.[17]

National press coverage of direct-action protests and civil rights activism was not inevitable. As chapter 2 noted, major national press outlets largely ignored the South (and especially Black southern communities) during the first half of the twentieth century. This myopia left the early skirmishes of the civil rights movement within the province of the Black press. After the 1957 Little Rock high school integration crisis, northern news outlets assigned more reporters to covering clashes between civil rights advocates and southern officials. However, it was the mass direct-action campaigns of the early 1960s that ensured national news outlets like the *New York Times*, the *Washington Post*, and the Associated Press would assign reporters, television crews, and photojournalists to "the race beat."[18] Television reporting of civil rights clashes also increased during this period. However, as Aniko Bodroghkozy argues, news reporting relied on a set of standard tropes that prioritized white southern moderates and cast African Americans as objects, rather than subjects, in the unfolding drama.[19] Such coverage nonetheless facilitated movement aims. Reflecting on the civil rights movement years later, SNCC leader (and later congressman) John Lewis asserted, "If it hadn't been for the media . . . the civil rights movement would have been like a bird without wings, a choir without a song."[20] Segregationists understood this as well, and during the 1950s and 1960s, many white southerners became extremely distrustful of northern journalists. They perceived the coverage as, at best, unflattering and, at worst, outright libel. And although some advocates of segregation attempted to use national television news outlets to advocate for racial separation, many distrusted the medium's ability to accurately portray their beliefs and actions. Such perceptions fueled hostility toward out-of-town reporters traveling in the region. White southerners harassed, intimidated, and sometimes attacked journalists as they endeavored to cover direct-action campaigns. These dangers were even more pronounced for Black reporters, whose susceptibility to violent attacks by white supremacists in the early 1960s forced them to abdicate their hold over civil rights coverage.[21]

For southern elected officials, editors, and journalists alike, controlling the national narrative about southern race relations was critical. State governments created print and television propaganda that presented alternative narratives of southern race relations. In 1963, for example, state officials created the Alabama Legislative Commission to Preserve the Peace (ALCPP), modeled on the House Un-American Activities Committee, which was created to investigate political dissidence and disloyalty among individual citizens and institutions in 1948. Like other state publicity and surveillance organizations, the ALCPP sought to undermine civil rights activism by characterizing it as communist inspired and linking northern racial integration with increases in violent crime.[22] Southern newspaper editors—who had long published stories about Black political subversion and criminality—were active participants in local politics and massive resistance efforts. As Sid Bedingfield documents, journalists at the *Charleston News and Courier* (especially editor Thomas R. Waring Jr. and correspondent William D. Workman) used the paper as one of many vehicles to advance their particular vision of massive resistance.[23] For editors more resistant to join the fray, public pressure through falling subscriptions or threats of physical violence were a powerful incentive. With the exception of a small number of newspaper editors and journalists with moderate views on race relations, the southern press staunchly supported the racial status quo.[24] In addition, Alabama state and municipal officials went to extraordinary lengths to undermine northern reporters' ability to cover the movement. In 1960, officials in Montgomery and Birmingham filed failed libel suits against the *New York Times* and reporter Harrison Salisbury.[25] These efforts, however, did little to lessen the number of reporters, photojournalists, and television crews covering the unfolding demonstrations.[26]

It was within this broader context that newspapers across the state reported various events associated with the 1965 Alabama voting rights demonstrations. Much of this coverage reiterated stereotypes about movement activists and sympathizers.[27] A March 27 *Birmingham News* titled "Pink-Hued Smoke Hangs Over Integration Drive," is a typical example. In it, staff writer Ted Pearson claimed, "Much of the tactical and strategical [*sic*] aspects of the integration movement so closely parallels the teachings of communism's luminaries that they could have come right out of the Red handbook."[28] With this red-baiting, Pearson highlighted what many southerners believed was the subversive source of racial unrest. Similarly, a

March 26 editorial in the *Montgomery Advertiser* aligned civil rights protest with communist influence, asserting that "communism has become a compass and driveshaft in the [Negro] revolt."[29]

Regional newspapers also cast civil rights activists as mentally disturbed social misfits. The March 18 *Richmond Times-Dispatch* editorial "Why They Lose Their Heads" dissected the presumed damaged psyche of the demonstrators,[30] characterizing the protesters as "unstable," "publicity seekers," and desirous of "possible martyrdom."[31] Southern papers also published letters to the editor espousing such views. Writing to the *Montgomery Advertiser* on March 21, resident J. J. Mallory characterized the marchers as "goons" who were "masquerading under the general category of Christians."[32] He accused the participants of "fan[ning] anew the flames of hatred of the Reconstruction Era," referencing convictions that "outside agitators" consistently sought to foment discontent around race issues. These claims were nurtured by the erroneous assumptions that most Black southerners were satisfied with the racial status quo until northern civil rights activists arrived, fomenting discontent.[33] Mallory's reference to the sectionalism of Reconstruction-era politics also suggests that some southerners saw similarities between contemporary federal protections for civil rights activists and federal provisions for newly freed African Americans enacted almost a century earlier.[34]

Perhaps no figure embodied the presumed deviance of white demonstrators more than the caricature of the beatnik. The beatnik stereotype was based on the Beats, a small coterie of writers and artists concentrated in New York City and San Francisco. This primarily male group embraced sexual nonconformity, interracial fraternization, drug use, and personal exploration of Eastern religions. Some of their most prolific members, like Allen Ginsberg, were same-sex-desiring and explored such themes in their writings. Moreover, many Beat institutions and social spaces overlapped with the growing urban enclaves of queer denizens in both cities.[35] The beatniks of popular imagination, therefore, represented more than social and political forms of deviance. The (always white) beatnik exemplified the gender and sexual nonconformity that challenged mid-century standards of respectability. White activists involved in direct mass-action campaigns of the early 1960s were regularly characterized as beatniks. As John Howard argues, some white southerners believed that white civil rights demonstrators' visible disregard for racial etiquette indicated their lack of adherence to gender and sexual norms.[36] These assumptions were evident in Mississippi press coverage of the 1961 Freedom Rides and the 1964 Freedom Summer campaign in which white teenagers and young adults poured into the state to challenge the existing racial regime.[37] Similar articulations were put forth by white supremacists across the South, as they saw increasing numbers of white non-southerners aiding Black southerners in their efforts to achieve racial equality.

A *Birmingham News* piece called "Hep-Talking Beatniks Dig Demonstrations in Alabama" is a representative account. Reporter Tom Lankford characterized the "beatniks" as "dress[ing] shabbily, wear[ing] long beards, and hav[ing] long unkempt hair." He asserted that "such beatnik terms as fuzz (police) and ribble (hassle) are becoming common currency in Selma, imported by persons from all over the nation who have swarmed here in the last three weeks."[38] A more explicit formulation of the "beatnik nonconforming libertine" narrative appeared in a stand-alone photograph in the March 12 *Montgomery Advertiser.* It featured an image of an alleged Canadian demonstrator who, according to the caption, had "stripped to his shorts and socks, picked up his briefcase and tore off down the street" in the frigid February Toronto weather. The image of the almost nude demonstrator and caption implied that those eager to participate in the protests were mentally unbalanced and publicly indecent.[39]

If the figure of the beatnik embodied perceptions of young white civil rights activists as sexual libertines, the figure of the "false cleric" represented the perceived moral bankruptcy and corruption associated with support for racial equality. The participation of numerous clergy and members of religious orders in the 1965 Alabama voting rights demonstrations was a high point of liberal religious political activism during the 1960s. Although clerical activism was not novel in the twentieth century, the conservative climate of the 1950s and fears of red-baiting inhibited many from embracing progressive political protest. In the 1960s, however, many white ministers, priests, nuns, and rabbis were questioning racial segregation in religious institutions and inequality in American life. They often did so despite significant lay and, at times, denominational disapproval.[40] Although some white clerics and members of religious orders had engaged in earlier civil rights campaigns, Selma was a watershed moment. In response to the Bloody Sunday incident, a small number of ministers heeded Martin Luther King Jr.'s call to travel to Selma to protest, engaging in interfaith cooperation. Reverend Reeb's shocking death on March 11 encouraged even more clergy and members of religious orders to join the demonstrations in Selma and Montgomery.[41]

Southern press coverage consistently questioned the motives of the religiously affiliated people who traveled to Alabama to support civil and voting rights legislation. Such skepticism reflected opprobrium over clerical activism as well as a deep-seated anticlerical sentiment within segregationist rhetoric. Antipathy toward northern ministers associated with mainline denominations emerged in the early days of massive resistance to desegregation. In general, denominationally affiliated ministers (from the North and the South) supported amicable race relations and compliance with federal desegregation mandates. Ministerial unwillingness to mobilize scripture to sanction segregation revealed a severe disjuncture between southern religious leaders, politicians, and parishioners.[42] This disdain for clerical march participants was evident in state and regional press coverage of the Alabama voting rights demonstrations. In a letter to the *Montgomery Advertiser*, M. H. Smith of Prattville suggested that members of religious orders participating in the demonstrations were not legitimate. He quipped, "The costume rental business must be a profitable one these days because there are great numbers of phony clerics parading around." He further asserted that any "real ministers" present should "try to teach their flock some morals in view of the obscenities which go on in the streets as night falls, which has yet to reach the public thru mass media."[43] Later that year, the Alabama State Legislature echoed these allegations when they enacted a provision to "outlaw impersonation of members of the clergy and religious orders."[44] White supremacists clearly sought to undermine the legitimacy of the Judeo-Christian rhetoric of the civil rights movement. As Jane Dailey notes, religious defenses of segregation within Protestantism were, in part, a struggle over "competing claims to Christian orthodoxy" that either prioritized forms of difference or believed such differences could be made irrelevant through Christian belief. Therefore, the ministers who participated in these demonstrations were cast not only as racial agitators but as violators of Christian dogma.[45]

As Smith's letter to the *Montgomery Advertiser* suggests, the national media was the third member of the deviant trio associated with voting rights campaigns. In "Making the Best of the Bad," the editorial board of that same newspaper excoriated the northern press for what they believed was far from objective coverage of the mobilizations.[46] More than likely written by editor Grover Hall, the editorial asserted that "a large element of the press and television" media were "generator[s] of evil." Referencing the "incorrigible performance" of the national press during the unfolding demonstrations, Hall said "the world has been made to believe that Selma is a crimson jungle and that its hospitals remain full of the clubbed and bullwhipped." However, he noted, "the word is getting around [about the character of the demonstrations] even in the case of liberal cuties like the syndicated columnists Rowland Evans and Robert Novak."[47] Editorials like this sought to shore up white supremacy by questioning the integrity of mainstream news outlets, whose coverage of political battles over racial equality were seen as antagonistic to southern whites.[48] It was the allegedly derelict coverage of the national news media, alongside the perceptions of deviant beatniks and immoral ministers, that fueled rumors of sexual impropriety at the demonstrations.

By the end of March, Alabama elected officials, including the governor, quickly publicized a number of salacious rumors. The rumors generally asserted that interracial sexual orgies, public urination, and drinking had occurred on the evening of March 10—the same night in which demonstrators held a vigil for the critically wounded Rev. Reeb.[49] The first reference to such rumors appeared in Leslie Carpenter's nationally syndicated column on March 21. He reported that "well-meaning people who have returned from Selma have expressed horror over the behavior of some of the hoodlums who have joined demonstrations in the Alabama town." He added, "There have been sex orgies involving some of them, it's said."[50] A widely circulated news story titled "Lovemaking in Open Definitely Occurred in Selma Prayer Vigil" appeared in the *Birmingham News* on March 28. Not quite an exposé, the report sought to verify and debunk various widely circulating rumors about the marchers' behavior. For example, the article dismissed the allegation that "as many as 40 negro attacks on a white female demonstrator resulted in her death." However, the article substantiated rumors of public urination and sexual activity. In the article's sole interview, public safety director Wilson Baker confirmed that demonstrators were "very definitely open in kissing and loving and drinking."[51] The wide circulation of this article and its allegations fueled already rampant rumors of the sexual nature of the marches.[52]

On March 23, an Alabama State Legislative resolution transformed the rumors into government-sanctioned allegations condemning the alleged impropriety of the demonstrators. Legislators accused the "so-called preachers" of "drinking strong drink promiscuously" and "using the most vulgar and profane language on the streets of Montgomery." The legislature also asserted that "there is evidence of much fornication, and young women are returning to their respective states apparently as unwed expectant mothers." The reference to rampant heterosexual couplings reinforced the assumed sexual promiscuity of civil rights activists while also implying that these trysts may have been interracial. Notably, the legislators attempted to counter the march's moral legitimacy by identifying ministers, priests, and rabbis who had allegedly "spoken out against such acts." The resolution "encourage[d] our religious leaders to continue diligently to ask the people to refrain from any future ungodly demonstrations, and that each leader insist upon the revelation of the true identity of outside invaders into our state and our respective religious orders."[53] This story, national wire services also reported, was part of the state's official response to the demonstrations, as it attempted to shore up Alabama's reputation.[54] However, it was the public accusations from Congressman Dickinson that further maligned the state in the eyes of many Americans while affirming for others the obscene nature of civil rights activism.

National press coverage largely focused on the sexual dimensions of Dickinson's allegations while simultaneously questioning their veracity. Sensational headlines like "Selma Orgies Charged by Alabama Lawmaker," "House Told Drunkenness, Sex Orgies Marked Part of Selma Rights March," and "Selma March Said Marked by Sex Orgies" were rampant.[55] The first *Washington Post* article on the address noted that its reporters who covered the demonstrations in Selma and Montgomery "had seen no evidence of Dickinson's charges."[56] Early coverage in the *Los Angeles Times* featured the refutations of SCLC program director Charles Blackwell in the secondary headline, which read "Statements Hit as 'Garbage.'"[57] With each passing day, national press coverage became increasingly critical and derisive. Art Buchwald, a humorist and syndicated columnist, mocked Dickinson's attempts to incite indignation at the march through such scurrilous allegations. "After Mr. Dickinson's speech, I predict thousands of students will change their plans and go to Alabama instead of Florida," Buchwald stated. He flippantly concluded, "When you add sex to civil rights, you've got an unbeatable combination."[58] Such criticisms were not limited to northern press outlets. The *Tuscaloosa News*, whose editor Buford Boone had taken a strong stance against the threat of mob violence during the integration of the University of Alabama in 1963, also questioned the veracity of the charges. "Many people are asking . . . why the newspapers have not carried stories about certain horrible happenings that are supposed to have occurred in Selma," Boone wrote. He stated bluntly, "The answer is that the events did not occur."[59] However, such denunciations were rare among southern editorialists.

A more consequential refutation of the charges of sexual impropriety was a much-publicized speech by Bob Craig, managing editor of the *Spartanburg* (SC) *Journal*, to the annual meeting of Sigma Delta Chi, now known as the Society of Professional Journalists. In his address, Craig recounted how he traveled to Alabama hoping to document the alleged public indecency of the marchers. However, not only was he unable to find any sexual activity, he could not find anyone able to provide the lurid images he sought. Instead, he encountered some young march participants "having a good time talking about the march and college and a lot of things."[60] This article did more than simply add several more inches to the mounting number of news reports claiming Dickinson's allegations were unfounded. It suggests that some in the press corps implicitly rallied to demonstrate the false nature of these charges to protect their own journalistic integrity. Northern news bureaus may have facilitated the deluge of critical coverage as a response to Dickinson's challenge to their objectivity. More fundamentally, however, these stories insulated the national press from charges that they were selectively reporting events associated with civil rights mobilizations.

Not surprisingly, civil rights activists were some of the first to denounce Dickinson's scurrilous charges. They framed their criticisms through historically informed narratives of sexual violence and the sexual hypocrisy of white supremacists. As mentioned previously, SCLC official Charles Blackwell called the congressman's remarks "garbage," asserting, "no man of any degree of sobriety would make any such a charge as that because we had the most distinguished intellectuals in the country and numerous high church people . . . participating in the march." Blackwell said he "regard[ed] the comments from the representative as being the kind of garbage that men of his general geographical area are too often identified with."[61] In referencing segregationists' ubiquitous contentions that African Americans and civil rights advocates were licentious miscreants, Blackwell recast the allegations as perverse fantasies. James Bevel, SCLC director of direct action, also referenced the sexual preoccupations of some white southerners in his denunciation. At a mass meeting, he extolled his audience to "look out around you and you'll see there's not a full-blooded Negro in the House." He declared, "The whole Negro race has been mongrelized by white folks." Bevel's allusion to the sexual assault of Black women by white men during and after legalized slavery was intended to expose it as a mechanism of intimidation and amplify the hypocrisy of supporters of segregation. His use of the word "mongrelize" explicitly appropriated the language of segregationists and white racial purity advocates, who asserted that Black men's unbridled lust for white women would result in the dissolution of the white race through intermarriage as well as sexual assault. Bevel alleged, conversely, that it was the lustful impulses of white men that facilitated race mixing. Bevel concluded, "White men are the meanest men in the world. They have all these negro half children and then they never take care of them. They don't even care if those children live in slavery."[62] This incisive statement deftly condemns the long-standing reality of Black-white familial relations by locating their existence during both the era of legal enslavement and the contemporary denigration of Black personhood under Jim Crow segregation.

The willingness of civil rights advocates to pejoratively reference the sexual behavior of white southerners indicates the importance of sex in political struggles over white supremacy. As Danielle McGuire explicates, African Americans after World War II were increasingly willing to highlight and organize against the assault of Black women by white men as a part of their campaigns for racial empowerment. And as chapters 1 and 2 reveal, African American civil rights organizations were also adept at engaging with and mobilizing sexual political narratives to suit their needs. In the wake of the Alabama voting rights demonstrations, segregationists, increasingly cast in the nation's eye as violent reactionaries, were more vulnerable to allegations that it was their sexual behavior that was immoral. Even in the South, the sexual regimes undergirding white supremacy were under assault. This was reflected, in part, by the increasing willingness of southern municipal and local governments to prosecute white men for sexually assaulting Black women. As McGuire argues, Black women's decades-long campaign to force the legal system to recognize and protect their bodily integrity was beginning to yield results. The November 1965 conviction of Hattiesburg, Mississippi, resident Norman Cannon, a white man, for the rape of Rosa Lee Coates, an African American teenager, was an important moment in the dismantling of white supremacist sexual terrorism.[63] Civil rights activists' denunciations of the rumors of sexual impropriety in their movement, then, reflected African Americans' general willingness to strike against the sexual dimensions of white supremacist thought and action.

Whereas civil rights activists registered their objections in the public sphere, everyday citizens expressed their outrage over the allegations in private letters to Representative Dickinson. A postcard signed "An American Citizen (Not a Negro by the Way)" dared Dickinson to "be a man and repeat these lies off the floor of the House, or does the cloak of immunity give courage to the Southern Gentlemen?"[64] Another letter, from C. R. Rowan of Laguna Beach, California, agreed with the congressman's motivations but questioned his strategy. "You bastard," Rowan declared, "why would you do all this without positive proof in your hands?" He declared, "You are a big Liar!!" and "I am ashamed to be white like you!"[65] Alabama residents also registered their disgust with the allegations. Sara C. Mayberry wrote from an unspecified address, "Shame on you for the evil lies you are telling about the Selma March."[66] Wesley Crowe of Mobile proclaimed, "It's not the Negro man who is obsessed by wanting to have sexual relations with whites; it's the white man for the Negro Woman, which accounts for all the half-breeds in Alabama now who are your unacknowledged cousins."[67] Crowe's use of the same historical narrative of white male sexual hypocrisy wielded by civil rights activists suggests how narratives of African American hyper(hetero)sexual depravity were losing some of their legitimacy in the national public sphere.

As criticism mounted during the first two weeks of April, Dickinson frantically searched for evidence to substantiate his claims. He assembled thirty individual affidavits—mostly from members of local law enforcement and military agencies—documenting the marchers' alleged public urination, indecent exposure, drunkenness, and interracial heterosexual couplings.[68] He also obtained a copy of Bayard Rustin's 1953 morals charge arrest record and a flyer allegedly circulated by the SCLC that promised sex and alcohol to participants.[69] His search for photographs, the most impactful form of documentation, was futile, however. Of the ten people he contacted to acquire such evidence, only two were able to provide them. The photographs he did obtain were seemingly of little value, as they did not appear in his personal papers or published statements.[70]

Increasingly desperate to substantiate his claims, Dickinson wrote to J. Edgar Hoover, the director of the Federal Bureau of Investigation (FBI), for assistance. Rather than seek information about the protesters alleged immorality, he inquired about the presumed communist affiliations of movement leaders and organizations. Dickinson asked Hoover for "whatever information your agency has in its files on Dr. Martin Luther King and particularly that information that pertains to Dr. King's affiliations with Communist and Communist-front organizations" as well as the SCLC and the Southern Conference Education Fund.[71] Replying four days later, Hoover stated, "I readily understand your desire to obtain data from FBI files on the individual and organizations you mentioned," but that "information in our files must be maintained as confidential pursuant regulations of the Department of Justice."[72] Given Hoover's infamous desire to undermine Dr. King and other civil rights activists through inquiries into and surveillance of their intimate lives, it seems that the FBI director considered the rumors to be without merit.[73]

Armed with over two dozen affidavits, Dickinson addressed Congress once more on April 27. He opened his remarks with an acknowledgment that "I have been challenged by a few persons to make good on my offer of proof of the speech I made on this floor 4 weeks ago. . . . I am here to offer it in black and white from eyewitnesses and ready to substantiate every statement that I made, and more, in order that the house might be apprised of [the] situation as it existed." However, as he attempted to read the signed affidavits, two other representatives (a Democrat and a Republican) interrupted his testimony with questions about the reliability of the statements. After the Speaker of the House was able to regain control, Dickinson was allowed to read several statements, including that of Ed Strickland, the staff director of the ALCPP. He claimed to have access to films that would "substantiate every fact in my speech, which would be made available to the proper committee of this house." Dickinson then noted, "I have no reason to doubt the statements of this official."[74] This action shifted the responsibility of producing visual proof to this state-level investigatory agency while suggesting that the evidence would only be shared with government officials.

In response, several congresspeople read statements from ministers, priests, nuns, and laypeople of religious conviction who were deeply offended by the allegations.[75] Monsignor. John J. Ev. Egan of Chicago, Illinois, proclaimed, "The charges against the Selma-Montgomery march are preposterous and a disgrace to Congress." Mrs. John E. Jennings of Saint Louis, Missouri, who had traveled to Selma with a group of young people, denied the charges and, like others, highlighted the sexual behavior of segregationists, noting "accusations ridiculous; however, would like to protest the lewd gestures made by [white] Montgomery bystanders." Finally, Rev. Frederick Guthrie of Boston, Massachusetts, simply wrote, "Orgy, my foot. We have deeper lessons to march for." These statements offer a glimpse of the intense criticism and scorn emanating from clergy supporting the protests.

Faith leaders registered their disgust with the allegations in the public press as well. One notable example was an April 27 press conference held by two ministers and a nun immediately following Dickinson's speech. Concerned over the allegations, they recounted meeting with the congressman to see his purported evidence and leaving unsatisfied. Kansas City, Missouri, resident Sister Mary Leoline of the order Sisters of Charity of the Blessed Virgin Mary stated that Dickinson's photographs revealed nothing offensive. "If it hadn't been a racially mixed group . . . and if they were not engaged in civil rights activities no one would pay attention to the pictures," she asserted.[76] Episcopal priest Don Orsini, of Pittsburgh, Pennsylvania, asserted that Dickinson "cries proof-proof-but he has no proof." He also character-ized the congressman as "a sort of little Joe McCarthyism [*sic*]." This allu-sion to the Republican Wisconsin senator who rose to prominence as the head of the House Un-American Activities Committee in the early 1950s im-plies that the Alabama congressman also hurled false accusations to bol-ster his own fame. Moreover, given the very public lavender baiting of McCarthy that facilitated his declining prominence, the remark may have been a snide allusion to Dickinson's intimate life.[77]

This reference to McCarthy raises an important question: Why would Dick-inson level such grave charges without substantive proof? A testy written ex-change between Dickinson and Strickland suggests that the congressman acted on the assumption that state officials would provide photographic evi-dence. The day after his speech, Strickland responded to the congressman's public remarks about the ALCPP, seeking to clarify their earlier conversations about the existence of visual evidence. According to Strickland, Dickinson contacted him between March 21 and 31 to ask if the official "had or knew of any pictures that showed indecent acts on the part of the marchers." Strick-land asserted that he had told Dickinson that much of the footage either did not show demonstrators engaging in obscene acts or was of such poor quality that no lewd activity could be discerned. He further noted that he "was merely working on the march film . . . [but] did not own or control it." The ALCPP "had been interested in proving or attempting to prove that the march was communist-inspired or dominated . . . [and] considered this of far greater im-portance than any immoral acts which occurred." Throughout the letter, the director seemed genuinely baffled by Dickinson's public statements, yet also supportive of his efforts to undermine the demonstrations.[78]

The congressman's immediate reply offered an alternative sequence of events and fundamentally revealed his intense embarrassment over the pub-lic backlash. Dickinson alleged that Strickland repeatedly told him that the "immorality of the march, as well as Communistic aspects, were all cov-ered with photographs." Dickinson also alleged that Strickland claimed to know "of several other sources of photos of the immoral or lewd kind which [Strickland] would get or help me get." Dickinson confided in the letter that he had "really gotten out on a limb depending on what [Strickland] had said" in his first address. He continued in this vein, harping on Strickland's repeated assurances that the state would provide visual documentation of the marchers' sexual immorality. Dickinson closed with this allegation and request: "It appears, you have lied to me, Ed. I hope you will not make it public that you have no pictures."[79] Dickinson's private exchange with

Strickland suggests the depth of his humiliation and anger at being publicly castigated (largely in isolation). His inability to produce photographic evidence was a fatal error in his decision to publicize the scurrilous rumors of salacious behavior. Nonetheless, his accusations reverberated widely among another segment of Americans for whom the rumors confirmed their worst fears about the sexual behavior that accompanied civil rights protests.

Queering Selma in the White Supremacist Imaginary

Whereas Dickinson's allegations were met with derision and disbelief in the national public sphere, many Americans not only believed the charges but continued to reference them as evidence of the debauched nature of civil rights activism. In the weeks and months following the demonstrations, a flurry of texts reiterating the charges emerged. Although many of these pamphlets, tracts, and books were created in Alabama, Americans nation-wide felt compelled to repeat, rearticulate, and amend the rumors. Although most of these texts focused on interracial heterosexual trysts, public drinking, urination, and indecent exposure, explicit and implicit references to homosexuality appeared with notable frequency. Allegations of sexual orgies and perceived gender variance fueled perceptions that protesters violated racial, gender, and sexual norms.

Increasing references to homosexuality in civil rights activism reflected, in part, the greater visibility of same-sex intimacy and gender nonconformity within the nation as a whole. By 1965, Americans were experiencing a marked increase in print and television presentations of homosexuality due, in part, to the weakening of obscenity law, which had disproportionately censored depictions of such behavior in literature, theater plays, film, and publications.[80] In 1957, the Supreme Court struck down the Hicklin test, a British standard for obscenity adopted in *Rosen v. United States* (1896). In the decision for *Roth v. United States*, Justice William Brennan delimited the criteria for obscenity as being defined by "whether to the average person, applying contemporary standards," the material would be deemed indecent.[81] Although explorations of homosexuality in the popular media were not new, the sheer number, as well as the tenor, of these stories during the postwar years and the early 1960s especially were novel. From social scientific interrogations like Alfred Kinsey's *Sexual Behavior in the Human Male* (1948), Jess Stearn's *The Sixth Man* (1961), and Robert E. L. Masters's *The Homosexual Revolution* (1964) to photojournalist presentations like the *Life* magazine feature "Homosexuality in America" (1964), millions of Americans were confronted with more and varied (although still largely stigmatizing) characterizations of gay men and lesbians.[82] The visibility of transsexual and transgender persons also increased during the Cold War period. As Martin Meeker argues, these publications "became the lens through which the American public learned about homosexuality as well as the lens through which individuals exploring their sexuality came to understand themselves."[83] If media coverage facilitated personal understanding and collective empowerment for some whose sexualities and genders fell outside normative boundaries, it also heightened the anxieties of many more Americans that the incidence of homosexuality was increasing. Visibility did little to counter public opprobrium of sexual and gender minorities in most segments of society. In a 1965 survey of 180 people, most respondents answered the question "What is a deviant?" with "homosexuals." That participants responded less often with "drug addicts," "alcoholics," "prostitutes," or "murderers" suggests just how closely notions of deviance and homosexuality were joined together.[84] For some Americans, then, the increasing visibility of homosexuality, alongside continuing battles over racial equality, created an environment in which imbricated anxieties over race, sex, and gender flourished.

Alongside these generally heightened concerns over gay men and lesbians, four queer sex scandals involving political figures concretized ideological links between liberal support for civil rights and same-sex desire. That these scandals occurred in such a short window of time (between the spring of 1962 and the fall of 1964) created a cumulative effect, fusing together civil rights advocacy and homosexual behavior. The first was the public disclosure of the 1953 morals charge conviction of Bayard Rustin, deputy director of the 1963 March on Washington for Jobs and Freedom. In a congressional speech, South Carolina senator Strom Thurmond exposed Rustin's arrest and conviction in an effort to undermine the march and civil rights movement. The second involved Aaron Henry, president of the Mississippi State NAACP, who was convicted of soliciting an eighteen-year-old white male transient for sex in March 1962. Henry's public allegation that the arrest was a "diablolical plot" orchestrated by local Mississippi officials resulted in a high-profile libel case brought by Ben Collins the Clarksdale Chief of Police and the Coahoma County prosecutor Thomas "Babe" Pearson. Although the libel case was ultimately overturned, Henry's morals charge conviction stood. [85] The two other scandals were associated with President Johnson, who signed the Civil Rights Act in 1964. The first was the morals charge arrest of Walter Jenkins, a close adviser to President Johnson for engaging in a same-sex sexual act in a Washington, DC YMCA restroom. Knowledge of Jenkin's arrest circulated widely in the weeks leading up to the presidential contest between Johnson, a Democrat, and Republican nominee Goldwater. For many Americans, Jenkins epitomized the moral bankruptcy of the Johnson administration and liberal Democrats more generally.[86] A second scandal involved US senator Thomas Kuchel, a moderate Republican from California, who actively supported federal civil rights and voting rights legislation. Kuchel endorsed Nelson Rockefeller, a moderate senator from New York, for the 1964 Republication presidential nomination over the conservative Barry Goldwater. Kuchel's endorsement inspired four political conservatives to fabricate a claim that the senator was arrested on a morals charge in 1950. This fraudulent affidavit circulated widely among congresspeople, conservative groups, and journalists. Seeking to salvage his reputation, Kuchel filed a defamation suit in February 1965, forcing a retraction from the four accusers. However, many conservatives continued to believe the rumors.[87] Together, these sex scandals reinforced already existing connections between support for civil rights, male sexual libertinism, and criminality.

It was within this general milieu of heightened exposure to (and anxieties over) homosexuality that references to same-sex desire and gender nonconformity appeared in published exposés and commentaries on the Alabama voting rights demonstrations. Albert C. Persons's *The True Selma Story: Sex and Civil Rights*, published in 1965, was one of the most widely circulating tracts. A journalist and outspoken opponent of civil rights and voting rights legislation, Persons presented his text as a thorough and objective investigation of the demonstrations.[88] Based on "scores of interviews," the tract luridly alleged that demonstrators engaged in "open, promiscuous, degenerate activity," including interracial orgies and obscene public behavior.[89] Persons's exposé also addressed nonsexual issues, like the influence of communism on the demonstrations and the doctoring of news photos to obscure the activists' violent behavior. Although Persons emphasized displays of heterosexual misconduct, his account also depicted homosexuality.

Unsurprisingly, Rustin figured prominently in the text, with Persons framing the pacifist organizer as the embodiment of sexual criminality among civil rights activists. The enclosed article "Bayard and Ralph, Just a Couple of the Boys" recounted the former's 1953 morals charge conviction as well as SCLC Reverend Ralph Abernathy's alleged seduction of a fifteen-year-old female parishioner in 1958. Persons characterized Rustin as "a homosexual who solicits on city streets, whose life's work is the subversion of the moral fiber of the youth of America." Deploying the pervasive assumption that homosexuals were predatory, Persons linked such predation to subversive civil rights advocacy. Later in the article, Persons emphasized Rustin's alleged lack of public decency as the damning aspect of his character, rather than the object of his sexual desire. "In this enlightened age," Persons wrote, "we are neither surprised nor concerned with a person's private sex practices. When they cease to be private however, they become offensive and call into question a person's mental balance and standards [sic] of values." This emphasis on public immorality not only advanced the stigmatizing notion of the closet but also referenced broader rumors of public sexual orgies. Implicitly linking Rustin's conviction with the latest charge against civil rights activists, Persons later made such connections explicit when he concluded, "Small wonder—if Rustin's influence can be seen here [in Selma]."

Same-sex intimacy and gender nonconformity were also evident in the imagery used in the pamphlet, which depicted beatniks, who, as we have seen, were often interpreted as same-sex desiring and gender nonconforming. One photograph explicitly suggested the allure and dangers of interracial and same-sex fraternization (see fig. 3.1). It depicts three youths—two Black, one white—laying on the pavement, presumably resting during the long march to Montgomery from Selma. Flanked by his Black counterparts, the faceless white youth appears to be in the midst of a tug-of-war, each arm embraced by his fellow marchers. The white marcher's right hand appears to be thrust between the legs of one of the Black marchers—whose attention seems to be riveted on it. Judging from the awkward angle of the white demonstrator, he may be in motion or attempting to stand up. Regardless, the photograph could be interpreted as having homoerotic undertones. Three question marks serve as the caption. This caption (or lack thereof) indicates the author's confusion about the youths' actions as well as the perceived perversity of the display (perhaps so perverse that words cannot capture what is taking place).[90]

The pamphlet's cover implicitly references sexuality. The illustration is a crude copy of James Karales's iconic black-and-white photograph of the march from Selma to Montgomery, taken as a part of his assignment for *Look* magazine (see fig. 3.2). The use of bright red, black, and small amounts of white to illustrate the famous procession conveys a central theme of the exposé: that the demonstrations were communist-inspired. All of the figures' faces and hands are Black, suggesting that an association

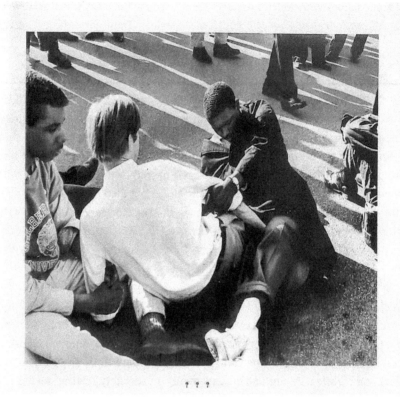

FIGURE 3.1 Photograph in Albert C. Persons, *The True Selma Story: Sex and Civil Rights*, 1965. Courtesy of Joseph A. Labadie Collection, Special Collections Research Center, University of Michigan, Ann Arbor.

with African Americans tainted whites who engaged in civil rights advocacy. At first glance, there is nothing about the image that appears sexual. However, two groups of figures imply that the sexual deviance of demonstrators is evident for those attentive to its manifestations. The first group consists of a trio of marchers at the front of the group, two men and one woman. Although their race is not explicitly discernable, the pamphlet's text could lead many readers to believe that the female figure is white and the two men are Black.

These three figures appear in the original photograph, although their race is not easily discernable. Another trio featured in the middle of the procession, in contrast, was radically altered. They are a priest, a figure in a white shirt with an American flag protruding somewhat inexplicably from his shoulder or back, and a man wearing a jacket. The latter two figures are depicted in the

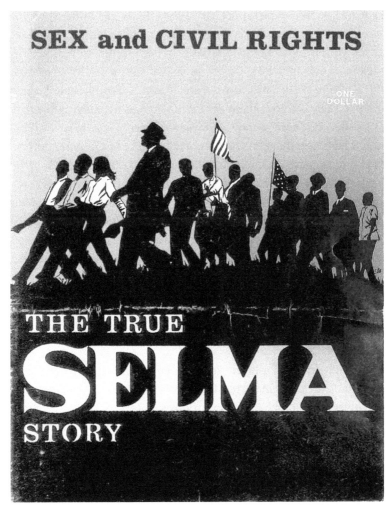

FIGURE 3.2 Albert C. Persons, cover illustration of *The True Selma Story: Sex and Civil Rights*, 1965. Courtesy of Joseph A. Labadie Collection, Special Collections Research Center, University of Michigan, Ann Arbor.

original photograph but are not adjacent to each other. The figure in the white shirt, somewhat hunched over, has been placed immediately in front of the other figure in a position that seems to suggest anal sex. The priest, while apparent in the original photograph, has been fundamentally altered. On the cover, the priest stands arms somewhat akimbo, his left leg bent inward toward his right knee. Although his hands are not visible, his posture references the figure of the swish, or a caricature of gay male effeminacy that circulated widely during the 1930s, and beyond.[91]

The radically altered depiction of the priest reflects just how important rumors of clerical sexual misdeeds were in white supremacist rhetoric about the Alabama voting rights demonstrations. In her examination of the rumors of sexual orgies in Selma, Dailey notes that the centrality of priests, nuns, and ministers in such narratives were attempts to counter civil rights advocates' portrayals of nonviolent demonstrations as embodying the true spirit of Christianity. Segregationist efforts to cast religious figures as seekers of interracial heterosexual trysts sought to undermine the moral authority of interfaith cooperation that marked the demonstrations.[92] In *The True Selma Story*, the cover illustration adds homosexuality and gender variance to the perceived deviance associated with clerical participation. Even though references to interracial heterosexual trysts between white clerics and African Americans was sure to deeply offend Christians who believed miscegenation was sinful, the ascription of homosexuality to ministers may have reverberated more broadly—even disturbing nonbelievers who found same-sex attraction abhorrent. The placement of these figures together in the midst of an otherwise faithful reproduction of Karales's photograph was clearly meant to align homosexuality with interracial heterosexuality and communist subversion.

A similar photograph of alleged same-sex eroticism appears in a much longer text simply titled *Selma*. The almost 280-page monograph, commissioned by Governor Wallace's office, purported to be an exhaustive study of the demonstrations and the modern civil rights movement.[93] Its author, Robert Mikell, was an Alabama writer who published a biography of Robert Shelton, grand wizard of the United Klans of America. Characterizing the book as "a collection of numerous miles of legwork" and "evaluating non-fiction facts from fiction," Mikell largely replicated Congressman Dickinson's allegations, focusing primarily on interracial heterosexual sex. One image, however, suggested same-sex intimacies among civil rights activists.[94] The photograph depicted SNCC activist James Forman lying on a street corner between two other African American men. The figure on his right is resting on the ground, while the figure on his left appears to be sitting or rising to his feet. The caption reads, "James Forman, a leading civil rights leader (center) nests with his aids [*sic*], before attempting another demonstration in Montgomery." The word "nests" suggests erotic intimacy between the men. However, two adjacent photographs betray the image's true context. Forman and the two other men were forced to the ground by city police on a street corner near the Dexter Avenue Baptist Church in Montgomery. The photograph in question was taken as the three men attempted to recover from this assault. The presence of this image in a book commissioned by the governor's office and produced in collusion with Sheriff Clark and Al Lingo, the head of the Alabama state troopers, affirms the role of elected officials and law enforcement in propagating allegations of same-sex intimacy among civil rights demonstrators.[95]

Three pieces of amateur propaganda about the demonstrations also reference homosexuality. The first is Reverend Bob Marsh's reprinted sermon, *The Sorrow of Selma*, which largely fixated on the alleged communist nature of civil rights advocacy. Delivered on March 28 in a radio broadcast, the Andalusia, Alabama, minister's sermon was so popular that it was printed and widely circulated throughout the state. Marsh asserted, "There is no way to dodge the fact that the 'Sorrow of Selma' clearly reveals an undercurrent of communist activity." The *Sorrow of Selma* is a capacious designation, referencing the Alabama voting rights demonstrations as well as the alleged sexual behavior associated with them. Marsh asserted that the Communist Party sought to "eliminate laws governing obscenity by calling them censorship and eliminate laws against homosexuality, degeneracy, and promiscuity," referencing white supremacists' contention that communist agents sought to undermine not only the political system of the United States but its moral and social fabric as well.[96] Because civil rights advocacy was (to his mind) communist inspired, it was logically correlated with defying sexual norms. A similar refrain appeared in a second piece of propaganda by Dr. Charles Bishop of Bainbridge, Georgia. Titled *A True Picture of the Alabama Story*, the circular characterized the marchers as "rebellious Negro trash, homosexuals, beatniks, thieves, dope peddlers, addicts, and paid professional agitators." Asserting that "about 1/3 were estimated to be white, many with a foreign look . . . about 1/3 were women, mostly teens,"[97] Bishop's composition of the demonstrators fused anxieties over same-sex desire, criminals, interracial sexuality, and immigrants.

A third piece of propaganda is the 1965 pamphlet *Martin Luther King and His Civil Rights Urinators*, by the Cinema Educational Guild in Hollywood, California. The organization's founder, Myron C. Fagan, a virulent anti-communist and former motion picture screenwriter, more than likely wrote the pamphlet.[98] According to the author, the interracial protestors at Selma committed "Negro-Communist atrocities" such as public nudity, interracial sex, and public urination. Like Dickinson, Fagan roundly criticized the national media, which, he believed, failed to report these behaviors out of profound sympathy for the demonstrators. In doing so, Fagan asserted, they actually encouraged such publicly indecent behavior and obscured the fact that it was "sex-craved African savages, beatniks, prostitutes, sex-perverts, [and] homosexuals who are screaming for 'Civil Rights' and 'Equality' for Negroes—and are encouraged and protected by our president." He continued, "But that should not be so astonishing—after all Johnson's palsy—walsies [sic] throughout his career are known crooks, swindlers, congenital liars, political charlatans, homosexuals, etc."[99]

While references to same-sex desire surfaced in published propaganda, they were even more prominently expressed by everyday Americans disturbed by the demonstrations. In March and April 1965, thousands of letters poured into the offices of Governor Wallace, Representative Dickinson, and Alabama Democratic senators John Sparkman and Lister Hill. Outrage over the goals of the protests was interwoven with utter disgust over the alleged sexual behaviors of the demonstrators. The rumors confirmed many white Americans' worst fears that the civil rights movement posed a fundamental threat to the sexual and gender norms that structured southern (and indeed, national) social and cultural life. Writers repeatedly identified homosexuality as a key threat to their way of life. A central question haunts these letters—were these individuals simply repeating narratives they had read, or were they formulating independent connections between homosexuality and civil rights advocacy? Determining this is extremely difficult. As I have noted, in the early 1960s, some white supremacist and radical right groups articulated connections between civil rights advocacy, communism, and homosexuality. A wide array of radical-right organizations, representing anti-communists, libertarians, segregationists, fascists, and anti-Semites, often invoked the alleged threat of homosexuality in their anti-civil rights sentiments. It is possible that some of the individuals writing to Alabama officials were simply reiterating homophobic narratives gleaned elsewhere. However, in the early 1960s, narratives linking homosexuality with civil rights advocacy nationally were not particularly prominent. Nor would many of the correspondents have seen propaganda explicitly linking homosexuality to the Alabama voting rights demonstrations in March and April 1965, when most of these letters were composed. Instead, many of the writers were probably responding to the swirling rumors of sexual debauchery as well as the increased visibility of homosexuality in the public sphere.

Although the specific context in which each individual composed their letter is unclear, two trends are worth noting. The first is the geographic diversity of the correspondence. While many letter writers are Alabamians or southerners, a significant number lived in other parts of the country. Some of the letters came from hotbeds of conservative activism like California's Orange County. However, as Joe Doherty's letter quoted at the beginning of this chapter, attests, others came from urban areas not strongly associated with political conservatism or an active white supremacist movement. Such geographic diversity reflects the ubiquity of white supremacist views and antipathy toward civil rights mobilizations.[100] The second trend is that it appears that many of the letter writers were women. As a corrective to the largely male-dominated world of white supremacist publishing, the personal correspondence of conservative women provides an important window into the perceived relationship between sexuality and Black racial advancement among this constituency.[101] Conservative women often organized letter-writing campaigns to elected officials as a way to register their protest. It is particularly interesting that gender does not seem to have substantively shaped the manner in which individuals referenced homosexuality; women were as concerned as men about the threat of such presumed sexual disorder to American life.

Not surprisingly, many individuals wrote directly to Representative Dickinson. In the weeks following his speech, his office received over 1,000 letters a day. Facing incessant demand for reprints of the speech, his congressional staff disseminated a limited number of copies.[102] Other correspondents requested visual evidence of demonstrators' sexual behavior. Some of the requests came from representatives of segregationist organizations who sought to circulate such copies to their members. George Burruss Jr. of the Richmond, Virginia, chapter of the Defenders of State Sovereignty and Individual Liberties was "anxious to obtain a 16mm movie tape of the 'Selma March' if there is any available." He divulged, "We would like to show it at our next chapter meeting on June 23rd."[103] Segregationists had long used salacious images of interracial heterosexual couples to broadcast the dangers of racial integration and engender support among otherwise apathetic whites. A desire for such cinematic evidence adhered to this strategy of eliciting moral outrage. Other requests suggested that more than purely political interest motivated the desire to see the reputed photographs and films. Kirby Walker, an engineer living in Forest Park, Illinois, requested copies of any relevant photographs "for my own private records." He assured the congressman the images would be "seen by adults only and would not be published."[104] Rustburg, Virginia high school student Paul J. Wilson Jr. expressed interest in "know[ing] more about" alleged deeds of protesters. Writing from his sixth period American history class, he requested "any material or photographs you could send me."[105] We can surmise that some of the requests for visual evidence of interracial and same-sex intimacy were for pornographic purposes, wherein disgust and voyeuristic fascination over taboo sexual behavior coexisted.

Whereas requests for visual evidence may have been limited to Congressman Dickinson, letters to a number of elected officials consistently enumerated and asked about the alleged behaviors and characteristics of the demonstrators. While correspondents assumed that homosexual behavior took place at the demonstrations, the nomenclature used to reference it was fairly diverse. Harold J. Olson of Milwaukee, Wisconsin, requested "a copy of your speech on the immorality, debauchery and sex mixing and homosexual practices which took place in the recent Alabama march."[106] R. James Robinson of Shreveport, Louisiana, used explicitly clinical language, stating that "The march provided an opportunity for nymphomaniacs, masochists, sadists and sundry sexual psychopaths to exercise their anomalies with license."[107] Others used colloquial terms, such as William H. Mangan of Pittsburgh, Pennsylvania, who referenced the "beatniks, riff raff, and sex perverts" who allegedly participated in the marches. Atmore, Alabama, resident G. W. Swift Sr. simply referenced the "perverts, degenerates, liars, and crooks, *male and female*, from those who participated in the orgies you have exposed" (emphasis original).[108]

The terms degenerate and sex perversion are significant in that they historically have been used to refer to same-sex acts as well as heterosexual interracial relationships. For example, Albert Persons's *The True Selma Story* uses the phrase "sex pervert" to describe Bayard Rustin—here a clear reference to homosexuality. However, in the pamphlet *Martin Luther King, Jr. and His Civil Rights Urinators*, Fagan described sexual perverts and homosexuals separately, suggesting two different groups of individuals and (presumably) behaviors. In many of the letters only one term is used, obscuring the writer's intended reference point. The use of "degenerate" and "sex perverts" suggests two important possibilities. The first is that correspondents articulated long-standing associations between non-normative sexual expression and racial difference. As the introduction referenced, turn-of-the-twentieth-century medical discourse used understandings of racial hierarchies of development to guide their conceptualizations of homosexuals.[109] These realities were reinscribed in the early-twentieth-century urban landscape, where sexual and racial others were strongly correlated as occupying spaces of degeneracy.[110] Therefore, the persistence of these disparate terms suggests how understandings of racial difference continued to be a reference point for homosexuality well into the middle of the twentieth century. A second possibility is that correspondents mixed and mingled terms in ways that conflated civil rights protesters and homosexuals. In doing so, they expressed profound anxieties regarding the interlocking nature of race and sex.

Alongside these general references to homosexuality, some writers identified specific people as prone to same-sex attractions. Rustin was the most commonly referenced individual suggesting how widely news of his morals charge conviction traveled in the conservative American imaginary. In a lengthy missive about "the racial turmoil in the South [which was] a result of communist plans," Helen Coolidge of Los Angeles described him as a "draft dodger [who] has been convicted of sex perversion."[111] Mrs. Edwin Pierce referenced her distaste with "such trash as King, you know MARTIN LUTHER, with his CONVICTED HOMOSEXUAL, long time secretary called by some MARTIN LUTHERS [sic] QUEEN; and all of us know he is a COMENIST [sic]."[112] In his letter to Dickinson, Major Olenius Olson Jr. of Chicago included a report on Rustin. Olson noted, "The report of Rustin is very interesting since he is the one sex pervert having importance to the president that has not been exposed in the press."[113] Olson sought to denigrate President Johnson's political legitimacy by exposing other known homosexuals in his confidence.

Correspondents also accused Dr. Martin Luther King Jr. of homosexual behavior. In his letter to Congressman Dickinson, C. T. Clarke of Birmingham, Alabama, articulated his hope that Dickinson would present photographic evidence of the marchers' behavior to the American public, then stated, "There is a record in the Juvenile Court in Birmingham on Martin Luther King for sex perversion."[114] Whereas Clarke referenced an alleged court document, Arthur A. Hansel of Phoenix, Arizona, simply stated, "KING as Insurrectionist—homosexual and sex pervert."[115] For Hansel, same-sex desire and racial minority status were closely linked deviances that could be used to mark anyone who engaged in politically transgressive behavior. In his letter to Governor Wallace, Hansel identified a number of white people who supported Black civil rights as "Nigger Queers." William Gowan of Savannah, Georgia, shared a rumor that had appeared in a white supremacist publication less than two years earlier.[116] He asserted that "a group of demonstrators all of them male who were locked up in jail here for about 20 days, practically all of them came down with Gonorrhea after so many days that it would have been impossible for any of them to have caught [it] before they were jailed."[117] All of these references imply that those who engaged in civil rights activism also engaged in same-sex sex.

These letter writers also cast political liberals, elected officials, and government employees as queer. Given Cold War–era paranoia about the presence of gay men and lesbians in military and civilian federal employment (discussed in chapter 1), it is not surprising that a number of correspondents made these connections. The sex scandals of Walter Jenkins and Thomas Kuchel built on these connections by placing same-sex-desiring men in the White House and the Senate, and they were, indeed, referenced in the correspondence. W. Pearl B. Phinney of New York City referenced Jenkins in her assertion that Johnson was a "corrupting influence."[118] In a sarcastic letter to Dickinson, E. L. Smelser of Lake Geneva, Wisconsin, asked, "What other administration has given us a President (if you can call him that), a dusky emperor and a Prince Charming?" Whereas the first two were obvious references to President Johnson and Dr. King, Smelser clarified the identity of the final person as "Walter J. none other" (that is Jenkins). Allegations of Kuchel's homosexuality also emerged in the correspondence. Mrs. Arden Porter of Saginaw, Michigan, believed "the homosexual scandal in California was obscured by the new outbreak of violence in the South."[119] Similarly, Bill Eaton of Arcadia, California, suggested that Congressman Dickinson should "expose the homosexual orgies of the civil rights congressmen, such as Senator Kuchel."[120] Both correspondents believed that this scandal deserved greater publicity to reveal the nature of liberal whites who supported racial equality and national civil rights legislation.

Correspondents protested the federal protection of civil rights activists, casting it as characteristic of the illegitimate growth of federal power. George Warren of Lakewood, Colorado, applauded Governor Wallace's refusal to provide protection for the marchers, instead "let[ting] 'big crook' [Johnson] provide his own security for the move of perverts [sic] that are marching on your state capital."[121] Alexander City, Alabama, resident John A. Darden stated, "I never would have dreamed that a horde of beatniks, sex perverts, dope addicts, so-called ministers, do-gooders, left-wingers . . . could have received the protection of our armed forces on a fifty-mile march on a heavily traveled highway."[122] Such attitudes reflected general concerns over the extension of federal protections to racial minorities at the expense of white taxpayers and gestures toward the concern that other types of individuals (and their ways of being) might be protected as well.

The Rhetorical Legacies of Selma

Although Dickinson received thousands of supportive letters during the spring of 1965, one missive included a piece of ephemera that embodied the past and future of white supremacist thought. The broadside, created by the Georgia Commission for Education, a state-sponsored segregationist group, features four different articles or images. One was a photograph of Dr. King at the Highlander Folk School, described as a "communist training school." The other side features an editorial by David Lawrence, of the *New York Tribune*, critiquing federal voting rights legislation as a violation of state sovereignty. Next to it appears a photograph and caption that claims to depict President Johnson dancing with a Black woman. Together, these items reflect three pillars of Cold War white supremacist thought: that civil rights advocacy was communist-inspired; that such advocacy was deeply connected to a desire for interracial heterosexual intimacies; and that federal intervention into state and regional racial affairs was unconstitutional. The fourth image, however, represents what was at that time a novel set of discursive associations. It depicts a group of men standing together under the headline "Civil Rights Ministers Sponsor Homosexual Dance." One of the ministers is Black and the other three white, and all are associated with the Council on Religion and the Homosexual in San Francisco, California. This organization, founded in 1964, brought together liberal Protestant religious leaders and local queer communities for dialogue. The image depicts a press conference held by the ministers in response to the police raid of a sponsored 1965 New Year's Day dance attended by members of the city's sexual and gender dissidents, an event that galvanized queer organizing in the city against police harassment.[123] However, an accompanying caption recast the image as a fundraiser for the civil rights movement. It read, "Did the rest of King's vanguards—the other 'men of God,' the priests and rabbis . . . the virtuous little nuns, the liberal senator's cultured wife and her comrades-in-arms, the Ruskin [*sic*] pervert, demonstration leader . . . attend the Civil Rights homosexual ball (was it a get-together to further protest voter registration?) sponsored by the mighty King's homo brethren?" It then sarcastically concluded, "The SAINTS come marching in!!!"[124]

Placing this image and caption alongside President Johnson's dancing with a Black woman indicates both the durability of certain white supremacist sexual narratives and the development of new tactics suited to the contemporary moment. Narratives of interracial heterosexual deviance continued to dominate anti–civil rights propaganda. However, anxieties over same-sex intimacies became increasingly visible among white supremacist groups and their supporters, and allegations of such "perversion" were explicitly connected to groups believed to support civil rights. The Alabama voting rights demonstrations represented the most prominent and explicit articulation of these connections. That homosexuality became the preferred form of sexual deviancy associated with the Black freedom struggle reflected the declining efficacy of interracial heterosexual and Black hyper(hetero)sexual narratives in mobilizing white Americans to support the maintenance of racial segregation. Depictions linking homosexuality to civil rights activism would continue to animate white supremacist literature during the late 1960s: as the imagined coterie of civil rights allies at the "Civil Rights homosexual ball" suggests, gay, lesbian, and transgender Americans would be positioned not only alongside civil rights and Black Power activists but would become conflated with them and, indeed, would serve as their most abject public face.

4 Nobody Has the Right to Turn Us into a Nation of Queers

Race and Homosexuality in White Supremacist Propaganda, 1961–1975

"A stabbing at a local air force base in Marietta, Georgia has received the typical whitewash," declared a small article in the White Citizens' Council organ *The Citizens' Council* in the fall of 1956. Titled "Fruits of Mixing," the news notice recounted a melee that erupted between Black and white servicemen at a dance at Dobbins Air Force Base. Expressing concern over the possibility of Black men dancing with white women, the author joked, "It was hardly likely that the Negro [serviceman] was there dancing with white *MEN*" (emphasis original). This sarcastic statement about dancing and the title "Fruits of Mixing" raised two possible consequences of racial integration—interracial heterosexual and homosexual intimacy.[1] The spectre of homosexuality in integrated military spaces emerged again in 1973, when the same publication, now titled *The Citizen*, featured the interracial same-sex wedding of two Women's Army Corps (WAC) members. According to the article, the two WACs, who were stationed at Fort Ord Army Base in Monterey Bay, California, "turned to homosexuality" during basic training like "'a lot of [other] WACS.'"[2] The report said that the couple persuaded an Episcopalian minister to perform a marriage ceremony, which, in turn, led to their "honorable discharges" and subsequent media celebrity.[3] When asked by a reporter if "their black-white all-girl marriage would last," they replied, "'We certainly hope so.'" By ending with the couple's hopes, *The Citizen* intimated that their union might survive in a society where a same-sex marriage might one day be socially accepted and legally recognized.

Separated by almost two decades, these references to same-sex intimacies suggest change and continuity within white supremacist rhetoric that racial integration and homosexuality were connected. As chapter 3 demonstrated, white supremacists increasingly linked homosexuality to civil rights advocacy and liberal politics. The sexual panic around the Alabama voting rights demonstrations illustrates how these ideas surfaced in state action and public discourse about civil rights activism during the first half of the 1960s. Increasingly during the 1960s and 1970s, white supremacist writers and publishers began to reference homosexuality (which included both same-sex sex and gender nonconformity) more broadly, casting it as an antecedent to, corollary of, and consequence of support for Black civil rights and racial equality. Within white supremacist literature, references to same-sex intimacies and gender nonconformity suggest two important developments within discursive defenses of racial segregation. As we began to see in chapter 3, white supremacists witnessed the declining political efficacy of narratives of interracial heterosexual relationships and Black sexual depravity to mobilize public support for racial segregation. At the same time, white supremacists began to explicitly reference gay, lesbian, and transgender communities alongside African American communities and pursuits of Black political empowerment.

This chapter builds on existing scholarship that identifies the deeply imbricated roots of homophobic and anti-Black racist ideologies within American conservatism by turning to the publications of three white supremacist groups, each of whom represents distinct but overlapping constituencies associated with massive resistance to civil rights activism: the American Nazi Party (ANP), the United Klans of America (UKA), and the Citizens' Councils of America (CCA). The ANP was a white racial militant group that operated on the fringes of acceptable regional and national sentiments regarding race. The UKA, the most powerful Ku Klux Klan (KKK) organization of the 1960s and early 1970s, found itself increasingly marginalized due to its member-incited violence against civil rights workers and African Americans. Finally, the CCA emerged from the ferment of the first phase of massive resistance and represented mainstream (white) southern thought on race relations during the late 1950s and 1960s. Yet it, too, waned in influence as the legislative and legal civil rights victories of the 1960s blunted the willingness of many white Americans to support resistance to desegregation by any and all means. My analysis of the rhetoric deployed by these organizations reveals how and why white supremacists increasingly articulated connections between homosexuality and racial liberalism as they struggled to fight the tide of racial change; it also uncovers important differences in how they viewed homosexuality in relationship to other putative forms of "deviance."

The American Nazi Party

"Millions of Americans are wise to the Communists and Jews, and are sick to death of Kikes, Communists, Coons and Queers," declared ANP founder

George Lincoln Rockwell in the inaugural issue of the party's organ, the *Rockwell Report*, in October 1961.[4] For Rockwell and his supporters, these groups constituted an adversarial vanguard that sought to undermine the purity of the white race. Rockwell's early political experiences are a virtual guidebook through the conservative ideological landscape of the 1950s.[5] During his time in the navy, he became a virulent anti-communist, admiring Senator Joseph McCarthy and anti-Semitic Cold War warrior Gerald L. K. Smith. Civilian life presented a number of professional and political disappointments, including a failed career as a newspaper and magazine publisher, a brief affiliation with leading conservative intellectual William F. Buckley Jr., and fleeting associations with segregationist and National States Rights Party leaders John Kasper and J. B. Stoner. Disillusioned, Rockwell finally embraced the rhetoric of Adolf Hitler and Nazi fascism, founding the ANP in 1958.[6]

The ANP was one of many white racial militant groups that formed a crucial segment of white resistance to federally mandated desegregation and the civil rights movement. Groups like the National States Rights Party, based in Tennessee, and the National Association for the Advancement of White People, based in Delaware, offered a stark contrast to the lawful resistance advocated by southern elites, government officials, and business conservatives. Yet white racial militant groups, with their charismatic leaders, advocacy of violent resistance, and affinity for fascist and anti-Semitic rhetoric, were highly successful in energizing middle- and working-class whites throughout the South (and beyond).[7] Rockwell's magnetic personality, forceful rhetoric, and colorful demonstrations catapulted the Arlington, Virginia–based group into the nation's consciousness, despite the fact that the ANP never had more than a hundred members nationally at any given time.[8] His political odysseys through Cold War radical-right circles informed his broad political philosophy, which touched on many of the hallmarks of modern conservative thought, including sexual conservatism, antipathy to the civil rights movement, and anti-communism.[9] Rockwell wrote most of the publication's content, which often read as diatribes against any number of constituencies that the fascist organization counted among its adversaries. Through this publication and other venues, homophobia joined anti-communism, anti-Semitism, and anti-Black racism as a core ideological tenet. In a sense, the ANP built upon general Cold War–era characterizations of political subversives as prone to homosexual behavior.[10]

Curiously, rumors of same-sex intimacy among its members haunted the ANP and act as a crucial context for the organization's homophobia.

Several members, including Matt Koehl, the ANP's second-in-command, and Leonard Holstein, leader of the West Coast chapter, were rumored to have engaged in sexual liaisons with men.[11] These rumors were so widespread that they were raised in a 1966 *Playboy* magazine interview with Rockwell conducted by African American journalist and author Alex Haley. After Rockwell declared that homosexuals were the "ultimate symbol of a decaying society," Haley asked about the rumored presence of queer men within the ANP's ranks. After giving several evasive answers, Rockwell admitted that he had encountered "quite a few [homosexuals]" in the organization, whom he promptly expelled. He explained their presence in the all-male ANP was "as tempting [to a homosexual] as a girls' school would be to me."[12] Centering his own heterosexual desire, the Nazi leader sought to distance the organization from implications of homosexuality while also gesturing toward his own (hetero)sexual virility.

It is within this context that ANP writings denounced homophile organizations and publications. Although it is unclear how Rockwell and his followers discovered these groups, it is likely that they encountered gay publications like the *Mattachine Review* and *One Magazine* at bookstores and newsstands. In the early 1960s, the weakening of obscenity laws facilitated the circulation of publications that catered to gay men and lesbians, including those of homophile organizations. Exposés of gay life that proliferated in postwar popular media may also have informed ANP members of the presence of homophile organizations, some of which were referenced in mainstream articles.[13] Moreover, the presence of a militant homophile organization in the nation's capital also contributed to the ANP's knowledge of gay rights organizations. In 1961, Frank Kameny, an astronomer terminated by the federal government as a result of the Lavender Scare, founded the District of Columbia branch of the Mattachine Society, a gay rights organization. Radicalized by this discriminatory experience, Kameny embodied a new generation of activists who embraced publicly visible social protest. Such visibility increased in 1962 when the group received a municipal license to fundraise in the District of Columbia. This action attracted the attention of John Dowdy, a Democratic congressman from Texas and chair of the House Committee on the District of Columbia. Dowdy introduced a bill that severely restricted the grounds of eligibility for the municipal license in an attempt to undermine the fledging group. During congressional hearings to investigate the Mattachine Society, Kameny impressed many people with his witty and incisive testimony. Although the city eventually revoked the group's license, the hearings gave the Mattachine Society unprecedented publicity.[14]

The June 1962 edition of the *Rockwell Report* featured a sensational cover with a reproduced article from *One Magazine*, the organ of One, Inc.[15] The word "SHAME!" is emblazoned on the cover of the reproduced publication, and below it, a headline screams, "Only a Nazi Reformation Can Destroy This Filthy Cancer."[16] Rockwell excoriated the homophile organization, characterizing it as promoting the legalization of pedophilia and "a stop to motherhood and normal relations between the sexes!!!" Featured images of (semi)nude men and minors characterized the publication as pornographic. Rockwell asserted, "Nobody has a 'right' to turn us into a nation of queers."[17] This statement echoed the widespread belief that gay men were predatory and sought to promote homosexuality. Moreover, the use of the word "right" explicitly links homophile organizing to other forms of social protest to access federal protections and/or the full benefits of citizenship. Such implicit associations between homophile organizing and the civil rights movement increasingly cast both as attempts to subvert American democracy and constitutional law.

The ANP viewed any information about queer sociality as a threat to its values. Three years after the critique of homophile magazines, the *Rockwell Report* featured a brief exposé of a guide to San Francisco's gay bars, homophile organizations, temporary housing, popular cruising spots, and even local lexicon. Rockwell railed against the pamphlet, characterizing it as a "brazen and filthy sheet [that] openly advises queers where they can get together for their unspeakable orgies." He blamed "our Judaized and liberal administrations" for the proliferation of such documents, claiming officials were "too chicken to apply our own laws and close these dens of degeneracy."[18] This critique placed the responsibility to police the public sphere squarely at the feet of the American government, which, Rockwell believed, abrogated its duties to enforce obscenity laws.

The ANP was not alone in its concern over the increasing visibility of gay political organizing across the United States. During the 1960s, other conservative groups also decried what they deemed to be the immoral proliferation of sexual, reproductive, and gendered behaviors that violated heteronormative standards.[19] In 1965, the Liberty League, an anti-communist organization headquartered in Los Angeles, California, launched a public campaign against the Mattachine Society of Washington, DC and its San Francisco–based lesbian counterpart, Daughters of Bilitis. In the Liberty League's publication *Common Sense*, its leader, Connie Clare Chandler, denounced both organizations as "aligned with communists and . . . following a Moscow directive to undermine the sexual laws and moral codes of the United States." She asserted that they sought to "promote pornography, sexual promiscuity and obscene books to corrupt and infest youth."[20] Chandler mirrored a vibrant network of conservative women who organized against perceived menaces like communism, racial integration, and sex education.[21] The Liberty League and the ANP shared a conviction that gay and lesbian rights organizations constituted a fundamental moral and political threat to the nation's well-being. Moreover, the appearance of Liberty League material in the personal papers of James A. Hare, a segregationist judge in Selma, Alabama, suggests that a network of political conservatives crisscrossed the nation, sharing knowledge and tactics.[22]

ANP rhetoric consistently characterized Jewish Americans as promoting homosexual behavior as part of a larger mission to subvert American democracy and morality. The ANP's anti-Semitism is unsurprising given its adherence to the fascist philosophies of Adolf Hitler, which were notoriously rooted in an intense hatred of Jews and an ardent belief in white Aryan (Christian) racial superiority. In one tirade, Rockwell charged that "Jewish psychiatrists have made it 'forgivable' for men to want to crawl in bed with other men to make 'love'—not to mention 'queer' women."[23] Although homophobic references to Jewish communities are scattered across the group's rhetoric, two cartoons published in the *Rockwell Report* are especially (and literally) illustrative. The first image depicts two Nordic figures, representing white Americans, flinging pails of mud at each other (see fig. 4.1). In the foreground, two stereotypical figures, wearing the Star of David and the hammer and sickle of the Communist Party, act as enablers, filling buckets with various sentiments abhorrent to the ANP: "hate Germany," "race mixing," and "lies." One bucket labeled "sex perversion" is tossed aside, suggesting that Jewish communists promoted lavender baiting and/or sexual non-normativity to divide members of the white race.[24]

In the second image, labeled "Portrait of the Enemy!," Rockwell identifies five figures he believed threatened the well-being of white Americans: "the 'Great' Liberal," "the Communist Leader," "the Culture Distorter," "the Capitalist-Zionist," and "the Devil." Each is depicted as a racist caricature, surrounded by words and images associated with his aims and activities. The text identifies the "Culture Distorter" as a publisher, university professor, and book reviewer who promotes interracial sex. Cast as little more than a smut peddler, the bedraggled figure is surrounded by representations of television, fine art, film, and publications. Words on the cover of the publi-

FIGURE 4.1 "Jews Use White Morality," *Rockwell Report*, 1962. Courtesy of Stephen O. Murray and Keelung Hong Special Collections Library, Michigan State University, East Lansing.

cations ("eros" and "gay") as well as the free-floating words "filth," "queers," and "sex perversion" identify the content of materials that the "Culture Distorter" allegedly propagated.[25] Such rhetoric referenced broader anti-Semitic narratives that Jewish Americans controlled newspapers, television stations, film studios, and other media outlets. It also drew upon conservative fears that media outlets acted as conduits to promote nonheteronormative gender and sexual behaviors.

The ANP's rhetoric also associated homosexual behavior with federal government employees, consistently characterizing foreign service and intelligence spaces as dens of sexual iniquity. In the March 1962 issue of the *Rockwell Report*, one article reported that "disgusting 'queer' men who fondle each other and put each other in high positions in our Government and

State Department [are depicted] as 'nice guys' and 'diplomats.'"[26] This phrase referenced the famous disclosure, in 1950, from former Deputy Secretary of the State Department John Peurifoy that this agency had removed ninety-one homosexuals from federal employment.[27] Like other white supremacists, the ANP fused anti-federal and anti-liberal sentiments in their commentary on the Walter Jenkins sex scandal of October 1964. As chapter 3 noted, news of Jenkins's arrest circulated widely in conservative circles. Although Republican presidential candidate Barry Goldwater refused to publicize the arrest during his contest against Lyndon B. Johnson for the US presidency, far-right organizations like the ANP had no such hesitations. ANP members in Dallas, Texas, protested in front of Jenkins's home, while affiliates in the nation's capital demonstrated at the White House. Marching in front of the gated lawn of the former, ANP members wielded placards stating, "Is LBJ Queer?" in an attempt to link the president with his colleague's misconduct.[28] Oblique references to Jenkins appeared in ANP published propaganda as well. In "Poem to a Wild Pansy," which appeared in the November 1964 edition of the *Rockwell Report*, the first-person narrator fuses aspects of the "security risk" narrative of Cold War politics with details of the Jenkins scandal: "My clearance is 'q' / And from much overwork / Though my loyalty's true / I've developed a quirk / When it's time to retire / At the end of the day / I've the queerest desire / For the YMCA."[29] The words "loyalty" and "security clearance" identified the narrator as a member of the intelligence community. The reference to the YMCA allude to the institution's longstanding role as a meeting place for same-sex-desiring men as well as the location of Jenkins's arrest.[30] The inclusion of "queerest" referenced a derogatory term for same-sex-desiring men. Indeed, the quip "My clearance is 'q'" implies that queerness was not only normative within the federal intelligence community but, indeed, a credential that could facilitate access to confidential information.

Links between federal employment and queerness also appeared in a March 1966 ANP feature characterizing "anti-Nazis" in Washington, DC as effeminate sexual nonconformists. The protagonist of the piece—Clarence Fauntroy Pansy—is a youth who "was often caught playing hookey to hang around the YMCA men's room near the White House where he fell in with other anti-Nazi types . . . a gang of liberals called the 'Loverboys.'" Whereas the text reiterated well-worn narratives about gay men in federal employment, John Patler's accompanying illustration was a satirical conglomeration of various figures despised by the Nazis. Clarence Fauntroy Pansy was dressed in sandals, tattered clothing, and long hair—countercultural and youthful fashions that blurred gender distinctions. Clarence also held a flower, perhaps a pansy, given his name, a reference to effeminate gay men.[31] Such discursive and visual characterizations of liberals as feminine and sexually non-normative not only denigrated their masculinity but also fundamentally raised questions about their fitness for federal employment. The hypermasculine presentation of the ANP, articulated in both prose and imagery, offered a sharp contrast.

Although ANP writings also cast African Americans as prone to same-sex desire, such depictions occurred less frequently, in large measure because of the centrality of anti-Semitism to the ANP philosophy.[32] ANP publications consistently depicted African Americans as grotesque, lascivious beings, pawns in the service of Jewish communist machinations. Rockwell expressed such beliefs in his 1962 fabricated exposé of homophile organizations when he charged that "black homosexuals by order of the Jew terrorists" sexually assaulted imprisoned ANP members.[33] As we shall see, carceral spaces would emerge more consistently during the late 1960s and 1970s in the white supremacist imaginary as spaces of interracial violence and same-sex assault." "Black homosexuals" appeared again in a brief article excoriating civil rights activists' calls for the passage of civil rights legislation. There, Rockwell made reference to a "black *FAIREY* [sic]—the *WORST* sight I have *EVER* seen" (emphases original).[34] To Rockwell, the combination of racial difference, and sexual/ gender nonconformity (as embodied by the Black, feminine, male-identified, same-sex-desiring body) represented a grotesque amalgamation of deviant identities, undeserving of equality.

Not surprisingly, Bayard Rustin emerged within ANP propaganda as a "sexual pervert" and a "red nigger queer."[35] In an account of the 1963 March on Washington for Jobs and Freedom, Rockwell asserted that "Bayard Rustin, stood on the steps of the Lincoln Memorial and was *cheered* by the black ocean of niggers, and by the communists, queers, kikes and cannibals from the new 'states' of Africa."[36] Almost two years later, Rockwell argued that "the Homosexuals, like Communists and niggers (in many cases the same people) continue to become more arrogant, aggressive, and obnoxious."[37] In a later article, he called political liberals "homosexual liberal lovers of the inferior races," linked perceived political and sexual transgressions.[38] Although Rockwell was the most consistent articulator of these connections between Blackness, homosexuality, civil rights, and communism, these associations appeared in other ANP publications. In the September/ October 1963 edition of *The Stormtrooper*, another ANP publication, Captain Seth D. Ryan alleged that incarcerated African American civil rights demonstrators transmitted venereal disease to one another "through homosexual activity" in a Savannah, Georgia, jail. Mocking the moral tenor of movement rhetoric, Ryan concluded, "That's really taking Brotherhood literally."[39]

Even though racist derision of the civil rights movement was not new, the association between same-sex sex and civil rights advocacy played an increasingly prominent role in segregationist and New Right circles. For the ANP, anxieties over homosexuality were deeply rooted in a Cold War political culture that cast homosexuality and communism as bedfellows. The increased visibility of gay men and lesbians, as well as the juggernaut of the civil rights movement, heightened white supremacist fears of the proliferation of sexual and political deviance. Rockwell would not live to see the full flowering of this rhetoric, however; he was killed in 1967 by a disgruntled ex-disciple. The ANP, bereft of its charismatic leader and torn asunder by infighting, faded into obscurity. Yet its homophobic rhetoric would find a fuller articulation by an older prominent white supremacist organization.

The United Klans of America

The United Klans of America (UKA) also formulated connections between Black political movements, white liberal support for civil rights, and homosexuality. This organization was one faction of the Ku Klux Klan (KKK), arguably the most infamous racial terrorist organization in American history. Formed in 1866 by Confederate army veterans in Pulaski, Tennessee, the KKK quickly spread to other southern communities, violently policing the actions of newly freed African Americans. Although the Klan virtually disappeared as Jim Crow laws and social customs ensured the political, social, and economic marginalization of African Americans, it reemerged nationwide with the cinematic spectacle of D. W. Griffith's *Birth of a Nation* in 1915, which lauded the vigilante group's terrorism against formerly enslaved African Americans. Although their national popularity peaked in the 1920s, Klan groups persisted in their program of racial terror through the Great Depression, World War II, and the early Cold War years. Finding new viability at the height of massive resistance to the civil rights movement in the mid- to late 1950s, the US Klans, led by Eldon Lee, emerged as the preeminent Klan organization. After Lee's death in 1960, the UKA, led by Tuscaloosa, Alabama, native Robert Shelton, emerged as its successor.

Although numerous klaverns thrived in states like North Carolina and Alabama, the national organization increasingly found itself politically marginalized. During the 1960s and early 1970s, conservative rhetoric that emphasized selective concessions and coded language that referenced freedom of association and personal rights eclipsed the Klan's virulent, blatant, and unyielding rhetoric of resistance to desegregation. The Klan also found itself increasingly harassed by the Federal Bureau of Investigation (FBI), which sought to enervate the organization through its COINTELPRO-White Hate program. Moreover, the consistent involvement of Klan members in violent reprisals against civil rights activists and Black communities reinforced perceptions of UKA members as violent, backward reactionaries. The 1963 and 1964 murders of civil rights activist Medgar Evers in Jackson, Mississippi; four Black children in the bombing of Birmingham, Alabama's 16th Street Baptist Church; and civil rights activists James Chaney, Andrew Goodman, and Michael Schwerner in Philadelphia, Mississippi, increasingly placed the Klan far outside of the boundaries of acceptable dissent to civil rights activism.[40]

The murder of Viola Liuzzo in March 1965 was the capstone to a crescendo of Klan-associated violence. As noted chapter 3, Luizzo's death sparked international outrage and was a key event in the passage of the 1965 Voting Rights Act. Her grief-stricken husband, Anthony Liuzzo, forcefully condemned their violence, declaring that the federal government should build "a 90-foot fence around the state of Alabama and let those segregationists live with themselves." In response, UKA leader Shelton quipped, "The only necessity of putting a fence around Alabama is to keep some of the misfits and sex perverts out."[41] Unlike the ANP, which most consistently correlated homosexuality with Jewish subversives, the UKA consistently associated homosexuality with Blackness and advocacy for racial equality. This reflected the centrality of anti-Blackness within the Klan's ideology— framing people of African descent as criminal, intellectually inferior, and sexually deviant. During the 1960s and 1970s, UKA propaganda linked homosexuality to inter- and intraracial heterosexual intimacies.[42]

Notably, biblical scripture and Protestant dogma appeared more consistently in UKA rhetorical opposition to homosexuality (and racial equality) than in that of the ANP or, as we will see, the CCA.[43] The wide circulation of tracts like Pastor Carey Daniel's "God: The Original Segregationist" demonstrates that many southerners turned to the Bible as an authoritative source in their battles to preserve white supremacy. More fundamentally, as Jane Dailey has argued, racial integration and the threat of miscegenation cast the maintenance of segregation as a spiritual battle, one in which organized southern Christian life was at stake.[44] This was especially true for more militant segregationist groups like the Klan. By the mid-1960s, white supremacists increasingly referenced scripture to oppose civil rights activists who claimed that interfaith and interracial cooperation embodied the true spirit of Christianity.

Klan writings mobilized the "curse of Ham" narrative, linking homosexuality with Blackness. According to biblical scripture, when Noah was drunk, his middle son saw his father's nakedness. Ham told his brothers, who immediately covered their unconscious father's body. Upon learning of his son's transgression, Noah issued a curse against Ham's son Canaan, stating, "The lowest of the slaves will he be to his brothers."[45] Since the Middle Ages, Europeans (and later Americans) have interpreted this event as the cause of darker skin tones among people of sub-Saharan African descent. The story achieved greater prominence in the late sixteenth and early seventeenth centuries as European participation in the Atlantic slave trade became a lucrative economic activity. The "curse of Ham" was used to justify the social control of people of African descent by naturalizing their servile status and sexual depravity and placing both within a Judeo-Christian divine order.[46] However, it was later superseded by the use of other biblical passages about the cohabitation of the races to justify segregation.[47]

UKA rhetoric mobilized and amended this tale. In the 1967 pamphlet *God Is the Author of Segregation*, the author charged Ham with "commit[ting] a heinous and bestial crime against his father, the deprayed [*sic*] and degenerate sin of sodomy." Anticipating readers' skepticism, the author asserts, "Bible scholars are in agreement that such a sinful act was perpetrated by Ham."[48] Returning to the subject of homosexuality later in the pamphlet, the author claims, "The Bible has much to say about sex perversion; and God Almighty Condemns it. Read Your Bible."[49] The revised story of Ham appeared two years later in a November 1969 *The Fiery Cross* article "Genesis Nine." Here, an anonymous author asserts that Ham "was found guilty of sodomy resulting in a curse and the state of perpetual servitude upon his fourth son Canaan." In addition to "perpetual servitude," Ham's progeny created "voodoism," "conjuring arts," and "the aggregate of abominable forms of worship." These deviant forms of religious behavior were allegedly "practiced in the tribes of Africa and affected any integrated society amalgamated with the cursed line of Canaan."[50] Both revisions of biblical scripture sought to expand the boundaries of Black sexual degeneracy to include homosexuality while placing such sexual desires at the root of a people's divinely dictated subservient status. More pointedly, they served as a warning to all who considered integration innocuous that, in fact, close interracial contact would risk exposure not only to non-normative sexual desires but to non-normative religious practices as well. The apparent need to amend biblical scripture to justify racial segregation reflects, in part, the ambivalent role of Christianity in segregationist defenses of white supremacy.[51]

Klan rhetoric also linked homosexual behavior with ministers and priests. As noted in chapter 3, supporters of racial segregation incorporated clerics into the rumors of sexual debauchery during the Alabama voting rights demonstrations, exemplifying a degree of anticlericalism that was already a significant aspect of massive resistance rhetoric.[52] UKA rhetoric built on these narratives by criticizing religious figures and institutions that sought to build community with sexual minorities. In "Liberals Approve of the Third Sex," an anonymous author recounted a *New York Times* article on an Episcopalian clerical forum that considered softening the denomination's views on homosexuality.[53] The article mischaracterized the ministers' views on the subject, claiming that the majority of the participants believed that same-sex attractions could "be judged *right* if the participants were expressing genuine love" (emphasis original). "Sensible voices," the author asserted, "always seem to be drowned out by the cries of the emotional majority, many of whom have private reasons for their feelings on homosexuality." The author strongly implied that moderate views on same-sex partnerships were motivated by the ministers' sexual desires.[54] This tactic reflected white supremacist claims that ministers and nuns who supported civil rights activism actually sought to facilitate their own access to interracial heterosexual—and, in this article, homosexual—relationships.

Connections between liberal clerics' support for civil rights and tolerance for sexual minorities emerged more forcefully in the rhetoric of the Circuit Riders. Based in Cincinnati, Ohio, this group of conservative Methodists organized in the early 1950s to "oppos[e] all socialistic, communist, and 'anti-American' teachings within the Methodist church" and later broadened its mission to investigate communist influence in the civil rights movement, churches, and the government.[55] As mentioned in chapter 3, the Circuit Riders publicized the police raid of a dance held by the San Francisco–based Council on Religion and the Homosexual in January 1965. Consisting of clergymen from the Episcopalian, Methodist, and Lutheran denominations, the council sought to foster "a dialogue" between the church and the growing population of queer youth in the city.[56] The Circuit Riders also reproduced a review of James Baldwin's *The Fire Next Time* and *Another Country* originally published in *Hi-Way*, a United Presbyterian Church periodical for teenagers. In sprawling cursive on the margins of the article, a Circuit Rider member queries, "Is sex deviation obscenity an acceptable church program for Presbyterian High School Youth?" The comment was as much a reflection of the subject of Baldwin's writing as it was a reference to Baldwin's identity as a gay man. Together, the Circuit Riders and the UKA dovetailed with broader conservative critiques of the place of religious authorities in conflicts over racial segregation and changing sexual mores.

UKA propaganda also characterized participants in countercultural and leftist movements as prone to homosexuality. Beatniks, so prominent in white supremacist coverage of the Alabama voting rights demonstrations in 1965, now appeared alongside anti-war protesters, the radical left, and hippies in *The Fiery Cross* stories of the late 1960s and early 1970s.[57] The white supremacist magazine identified homosexuality as a key characteristic of these groups: "An unusually large number of leaders and members of the New Revolutionary Left are sex perverts, either homosexuals or lesbians," declared a 1971 news story.[58] Certainly, gay men and lesbians participated in liberal and leftist social movements before and after World War II. As Aaron Lecklider has shown, sexual dissidents found opportunities for love and organizing in leftist spaces during the first half of the twentieth century.[59] Indeed, the founders of the first iteration of the Mattachine Society were members of the Communist Party and modeled the organization on the party's cell structure. Many gay liberationists were socialists and saw the struggle against homophobia and transphobia as intimately connected to struggles against imperialism, capitalism, racism, and patriarchy (and indeed participated in other social movements).[60] The UKA and other white supremacists, however, magnified the presence of gay men and lesbians in the New Left to malign their political legitimacy. This tactic adhered to a more general tendency among political conservatives, not just white supremacists, to cast liberals and radicals as sexual libertines.[61] This libertinism, which Shelton called "the New Morality," included the sale and distribution of pornography, public obscenity, interracial marriage, gender nonconformity, and homosexuality.

In the UKA imaginary, political liberals ensconced in federal institutions and positions of power also facilitated same-sex intimacies. That the Klan fixated on the Supreme Court, under the leadership of Chief Justice Earl Warren, is unsurprising given the court's role in dismantling key aspects of racial segregation and white supremacy.[62] However, the weakening of obscenity laws in the 1950s and 1960s also earned the Supreme Court the enmity of social conservatives, who mobilized against pornography and other materials deemed obscene.[63] UKA rhetoric reflected this outrage. In the April 1969 edition of *The Fiery Cross*, Melvin Sexton, executive administrator of the UKA, proclaimed, "The nine sickle buzzards on the Supreme Court of the United States has [*sic*] given the green light to rapists, bank robbers, arsonists, sex deviates, and yes even traitors to our beloved country by turning them loose to prey on the helpless public again."[64] Criticism of the expansionist vision of the federal judiciary was reinforced in Carl F. Lyons's four-page article "The New Morality," which equated sexual liberalism with libertinism. Lyons asserted, "All federal and state laws prohibiting and relating to . . . obscene practices, including homosexualism [*sic*], transvestism [*sic*], and the entire gamut of sexual deviations included under laws pertaining to sodomy are now being questioned."[65] Lyons's and Sexton's critiques occurred alongside the New Right's outcry over the nomination of Abe Fortas as chief justice of the Supreme Court in 1968. In their campaign to block his appointment, congressional conservatives characterized Fortas as encouraging the circulation of pornography by emphasizing cases where he overturned obscenity convictions.[66] That some of the most virulent segregationists in Congress were at the forefront of these attacks reflects the importance of morality-related issues in bolstering the power of southern politicians.

Like the ANP, UKA rhetoric also cast the federal government as a hotbed of homosexuality. Their attacks continued to build on Cold War–era fears that the intelligence and foreign service sectors were enclaves for same-sex-desiring men who constituted potential security risks.[67] A 1968 article titled "LBJ's Homo Haven" nakedly characterized the State Department as a safe space for queer men (see fig. 4.2). An accompanying cartoon depicted two men, one seated behind a desk with the presidential seal and another standing nearby who points to the curtained window behind the seated figure and declares: "Will you tell the foreign officer to stop going around putting up pink drapes!" In addition to playing on stereotypes of gay men as effeminate, the article charged that the State Department "recruit[ed] homosexuals, prostitutes, and gigolos to provide entertainment for African and Oriental diplomats" and make intelligence contacts with "others like them" abroad.[68] In asserting that queer men would be able to gain confidential information by associating with "others like them," the article obliquely suggested that foreign service officers' sexuality not only created the potential for security breaches but was, in fact, central to the execution of intelligence objectives. Characterizations of diplomacy as facilitating access to sexual encounters reified assumptions of developing nations as dens of

FIGURE 4.2 "LBJ's Homo Haven," *The Fiery Cross*, 1968. Image courtesy of Joseph A. Labadie Collection, Special Collections Research Center, University of Michigan, Ann Arbor.

immorality while disparaging federal attempts to gain the respect of these emerging independent states in the global Cold War.

Although the UKA's homophobic animus was directed toward a number of constituencies associated with racial and liberal thought, the group most often linked same-sex desire with African Americans, civil rights and Black Power activists, and racial integration. Such caricatures aligned with the general white supremacist strategy of denigrating supporters of racial equality as social misfits, pleasure seekers, and violators of law and order. UKA grand wizard Robert Shelton's characterization of the Poor People's Campaign in the summer of 1968 exemplifies this trend. Originally conceived by Dr. Martin Luther King Jr., the Southern Christian Leadership Conference's (SCLC's) nonviolent demonstrations in the nation's capital advocated greater funding for anti-poverty legislation and full employment initiatives. In the wake of Dr. King's assassination on April 4, 1968, Reverend Ralph Abernathy, the new executive director of the SCLC, continued the campaign. The protest culminated in nonviolent civil disobedience and the erection of a 3,000-resident tent city on the National Mall. Reflecting on the event in May, Shelton charged Abernathy with recruiting "the so-called 'poor' negroes, prostitutes, perverts, beatniks, hippies, and whatever other element in our society that would go along for the walk, free food, lodging and a grab-bag of unnatural sexual assortments from miscegenation to homosexuality." Shelton cast the march as a "nameless perversion of democracy that Mr. Abernathy and his communist comrades call the American dream [that was] nothing short of treason, blatant *treason!*"[69] His characterization of this campaign as a "perversion of democracy" reinforced white supremacist claims that civil rights activism was anti-American (and perhaps communist- inspired) as well as an avenue for participants to satiate their material and sexual needs. Echoing rhetoric surrounding the 1965 Alabama voting rights demonstrations, such constructions also built on New Right beliefs that liberals and leftists were seeking government assistance and pursuing their own aberrant pleasures.

Unsurprisingly, rhetoric about non-normative sexuality was closely associated with ideas about gender. The UKA argued that white southern acceptance of federal desegregation efforts could have deleterious effects on white manhood. For example, in the comics section of *The Fiery Cross*, a hypermasculine figure holding a piece of paper emblazoned with "School Guide Lines [*sic*]" faces three absurd-looking caricatures of federal officials (see fig. 4.3). One is a man with a large paunch. The middle figure is a naive sap willing to trust federal plans to implement desegregation. The third is an effete, pointy-headed bald man wearing pince-nez glasses and smoking a cigarette. The masculine figure states, "Now if You Three Federal Officials Are What 'Integration Guidelines' Can Do to Southerners . . . Then We Reject Them."[70]

The stark contrast between the three federal officials and the presumed Klan member is reiterated in another cartoon in the same edition that depicts two white men, with strong masculine features, dressed in suits who are observing another man walking some distance away (see fig. 4.4). A stereotypical young liberal or leftist, the moving figure has long hair and wears thick-rimmed glasses, and a turtleneck. An elongated face and a self-contented smile complement his distended stomach. The two observers declare, "It's Either a Civil Rights Worker or a 'Female' Communist."[71] Images like these reflect the centrality of masculinity and gender more broadly in battles over the dismantling of segregation. Civil rights mobilizations offered another fundamental challenge to normative white male masculinity. In the South, the social logic of Jim Crow placed white men (and especially those of means) at the apex of society, with sexual access to both white and Black women as well as social control of Black men. The dissolution of Jim Crow segregation threatened that hegemony. In response, segregationist

FIGURE 4.3 "Comics Section," *The Fiery Cross*, 1967. Image courtesy of the Archives Division of the Auburn Avenue Research Library, Atlanta, Georgia.

rhetoric called on white men to protect white women from alleged Black male predations as part of preserving their own privilege. Of course, segregation was a national phenomenon, and narratives about protecting white women and children's virtue from Black predation also existed in the North, where some of the most violent racial clashes during the early and middle twentieth centuries were rooted in fears of Black men's lasciviousness.[72] Moreover, anxieties over masculinity had consumed political and popular discourse during the late 1940s and 1950s, as concerns around suburbanization, communism, and even militarization stoked fears that white American masculinity was being enervated. These cartoons attempted to defend racial segregation by demonstrating how compliance with desegregation mandates might enfeeble and effeminate southern white men and possibly white men nationwide.[73]

FIGURE 4.4 "Comics Section," *The Fiery Cross*, 1967. Image courtesy of the Archives Division of the Auburn Avenue Research Library, Atlanta, Georgia.

Even though Klan rhetoric cast some white men as sexual and gender nonconformists, UKA discourse tended to associate Black Americans (and Blackness) with same-sex desire and gender nonconformity. Most often, these stories and images appeared in the "Along the Black Front" section of *The Fiery Cross*. Running from two to four pages each issue, the section often featured images and stories about interracial sex, civil rights activism, or (more often than not in the Klan imaginary) both. Two potential motivations for regular representations of Black sexualities and genders are apparent. First, stories that depicted African American sexuality as uncontrollable, predatory, and perverse reinforced the need for social separation and political subordination. Second, this fear coexisted with a voyeuristic fascination with Black sexualities and genders as both taboo and exotic.[74] For example, taboos on both interracial heterosexual encounters and homosexuality appeared in a brief 1968 notice about a theatrical production called *Black Cleopatra* in which the Egyptian queen is in love with her "female nurse" prior to her romantic entanglement with Mark Anthony, "her first white man."[75] Significantly, photographs accompanied the vast majority of the articles. The November 1970 "Along the Black Front" featured a photograph of several nude Black men, their backsides exposed as they were strip-searched. Featuring alleged members of the Philadelphia, Pennsylvania, chapter of the Black Panther Party, this image may have appealed to readers' voyeuristic proclivities. The Panther members, who were suspects in a murder investigation, "claim[ed] to be the brunt of unfair harassment." Black Power organizations including the Black Panther Party were subject to intense state scrutiny, notably coordinated through COINTELPRO, an FBI program that sought to undermine Black Power and civil rights organizations by exacerbating internal tensions and fomenting law enforcement harassment. Visually, the photo emasculated the Black Panthers, literally stripping them of the most visible and potent symbols of their politicized masculinity: the black clothing, sunglasses, and berets that constituted the organization's uniform. More fundamentally, the image fed into white prurient fascination with Black bodies.[76]

"Along the Black Front" also featured gender variant individuals and communities. Although depictions of transgender, transsexual, and gender-nonconforming people had long circulated within the American press, media coverage of Christine Jorgenson and her gender affirming surgery in the 1950s increased national fascination with those who traversed gender and sex categories. Local newspapers continued to cover drag balls and female impersonator troupes in various cities—but not to the same degree as before World War II. Moreover, growing activism among gender-variant persons—both as a part of gay liberation movements and as separate forms of organizing—enhanced visibility.[77] The UKA referenced this visibility in its denigrating depictions of gender-variant people who belonged to or were connected with Black communities. For example, *The Fiery Cross* ridiculed a Chicago, Illinois, drag ball featuring Black drag kings and queens.[78] Another news brief created a violent spectacle of the death of two Black feminine presenting people, allegedly from breast cancer caused by "a disease carried only by Negroes, commonly known as 'sickle cell anemia.'"[79] The UKA's derision of Black gender nonconforming subjects mirrors the ways in which, according to Emily Skidmore, whiteness mediated the "authentic" transsexual subject during the middle of the twentieth century. Therefore, it was their racial identification as well as their gender identities/expressions that made these particular individuals worthy of ridicule in this white supremacist publication.[80]

"Along the Black Front" coverage of Dawn Langley Hall, a white British writer who immigrated to Charleston, South Carolina, in 1968, illustrates how the UKA linked gender, sexual, and racial transgression. Hall came to public prominence after marrying John Paul Simmons, an African American laborer. *The Fiery Cross*'s coverage, which always included a photograph of the couple, emphasized Hall's transgender identity as well as the couple's interracial union.[81] Editorial disdain for the duo is clear in the caption accompanying the second article: "The sex change bride . . . tells of racist terrors confronting *it*, and *its mate* in Charleston, South Carolina" (emphases added). Both the pronoun "it" and the term "mate" dehumanized Hall and Simmons, casting their relationship as a bizarre spectacle. Coverage of this union more than likely mobilized concerns about interracial marriage as a gateway for other kinds of illicit unions, including those that departed from cisgender heterosexual norms.

The Fiery Cross also reported on same-sex marriages between 1968 and 1971.[82] One article reported the marriage of two Black women who "liberated themselves from a tradition that joins only those of the opposite sex." The term "liberated" is a sarcastic reference to any number of contemporary political movements for gender, racial, or sexual equality.[83] Another article featured the marriage of "two negro men," asserting that same-sex matrimony "has been the going thing among male negroes and female negroes." The accompanying photograph depicted a Black man passionately kissing a phenotypically white individual (implied in the text to be male) dressed in a bridal gown. The image sought to stoke fears of interracial marriage as well as same-sex desire.[84]

An additional article recounted the successful lawsuit of James McConnell, a librarian whose offer of employment from the University of Minnesota was withdrawn in 1970 after he and his partner, law student James Baker, applied for a marriage license.[85] Although the brief reference to McConnell is limited to his successful lawsuit to renew the university's offer of employment, the couple's failed attempt to sue for legal recognition of their marriage was an important early legal effort for same-sex marriage. A small number of gay men and lesbians pursued same-sex marriage as an important goal during the gay liberation struggles of the 1970s.[86] In *Baker v. Nelson*, the Minnesota Supreme Court rejected the argument that the 1967 *Loving v. Virginia* decision, which invalidated miscegenation laws, could be extended to same-sex unions. By featuring this case, the UKA articulated their fears that desegregation would lead to the dissolution of an array of racial, gender, and sexual prescriptions. Whereas images of Black couples reinforced notions of Black sexual and gender non-normativity, images of two white men seeking a marriage license sought to stoke concerns over changing sexual and gender norms.[87] As referenced in the introduction, the Black-white racial binary informed a binary of sexual identity that posed heterosexuality and homosexuality as oppositional. Indeed, gay men and lesbians used references to racial difference as powerful analogies to press for equality and collective identity in the late 1960s and early 1970s.[88] Homophile activist Frank Kameny referenced the civil rights movement and anti-Black racism as a frame through which to understand gay and lesbian political organizing and homophobia during the 1960s.[89] In addition to drawing these connections themselves, then, white supremacists may have been attuned to gay men and lesbians' articulation of their minority status through the historical example of Black racial difference. Moreover, the temporal overlap of gay/lesbian and African American political organizing likely bolstered these associations in the minds of the Klansmen and others.

The ANP and UKA share points of continuity in their propaganda: liberal ministers, federal government employees, and radical activists were all cast as prone to homosexual behavior. However, the Klan more consistently linked civil rights advocacy—and the Black communities it sought to empower—with queerness. That Klan rhetoric increasingly embraced these narratives after 1967, the year the Supreme Court invalidated laws prohibiting interracial marriage in *Loving v. Virginia*, suggests that its propagandists sought to move beyond miscegenationist narratives to buoy support for segregation. The sharp increase in references to homosexuality around 1967 (rather than, as we might expect, after the 1969 Stonewall uprising, or organic protests in response to raid on the Stonewall Inn, a New York City bar frequented by queer patrons) indicates the potency of crumbling legal and, to a certain degree, social sanctions against interracial marriage in reorienting white supremacist tactics. More broadly, ardent opponents of desegregation realized that they had to broaden their appeals beyond traditional narratives of interracial and Black heterosexual behavior to include other forms of perceived deviance. Homophile politics and gay liberation provided a rallying point for white Americans worried about challenges to sexual, gender, and racial norms. The Klan's focus on same-sex marriage foreshadowed profound fears that the end of racial segregation could fundamentally challenge categories of acceptable sexual behavior, gender expression, and conceptualizations of family.

The Citizens' Councils of America

While ANP and UKA rhetoric suggest that homophobia was increasingly central to radical white supremacist strategies, an examination of one of the most tactically moderate and rhetorically conservative segregationist groups reinforces this view. The White Citizens' Councils (later known simply as Citizens' Councils) were one of the most well-known massive resistance organization of the 1950s. Founded in Indianola, Mississippi, in reaction to the 1954 *Brown v. Board of Education* decision, council-like organizations quickly spread throughout the South. Often led by local elites, Citizens' Councils mobilized anger and fears over racial desegregation into action. As the movement spread, the CCA emerged to coordinate the efforts of various councils to promote their aims nationally.[90] Although the organization reached the height of its political power in 1957, with a membership of 250,000, the CCA never exerted complete control over local branches.[91] Headquartered in Jackson, Mississippi, the CCA became, in the words of Neil McMillen, "a systemized and business-like operation, skillfully managed by a staff of professionals who had pursued careers in the defense of white supremacy."[92] Central to this "operation" was the dissemination of propaganda to rally white Americans nationwide.[93] Even as pamphlets, flyers, periodicals, and films streamed from headquarters, *The Citizens' Council* newsletter (renamed *The Citizen* in 1961) became one of the most potent tools in battles against desegregation.[94] Reaching a circulation high of 50,000 in 1960, *The Citizen* sought to justify racial segregation with broad-based appeals to state sovereignty and political conservatism.[95] In an effort to distance itself from more extreme groups like the KKK, the CCA eschewed violence and anti-Semitism.[96]

References to homosexuality appeared more consistently in the group's rhetoric in the late 1960s, aligning with national outrage among political conservatives over a number of social issues. Whereas the ANP and UKA referenced the increasing visibility of pornography and other materials considered obscene, the CCA joined national battles against reforming sexual education in public schools. In 1968 and 1969, conservative parent groups rallied to diminish the influence of the Sex Information and Education Council of the United States (SIECUS), a national organization formed in 1964 to provide candid information on contraception, sexual development, and sexuality.[97] Ensuing debates over sex education in public schools caught the attention of *The Citizen* editor Medford Evans.[98] In his June 1969 exposé, "Tree of Knowledge? Sex Education in Integrated Schools," Evans charged SIECUS with undermining traditional sex education and promoting taboo sexual behavior, including interracial sex and homosexuality.[99] In discussing the alleged lesson plans, Evans claimed that parents who objected would be branded "bigots," prefiguring contemporary conservative critique of political correctness. "Homosexuality is perhaps controversial," he continued in a mocking tone, "perhaps you can argue against it, or at least say you'd rather not. But black and white together? That goes without saying!" By comparing the taboo nature of homosexuality and interracial heterosexuality, Evans implied that permissiveness around the latter might, at some point in the future, facilitate social acceptance of the former.

An article in the September 1972 issue of *The Citizen* fused together anticlericalism, anti-miscegenation, and homophobia. Titled "Methodist Sex Films," the reporting alleged that members of the "National Sex Forum, a division of the Methodist Glide Urban Center in San Francisco" showed films that "endors[ed] such practices as promiscuity, homosexuality and male and female masturbation" in Honolulu, Hawaii.[100] According to the article, a select group of 1,500 viewed the film, including "physicians . . . social workers, educators, attorneys, clergy, psychiatrists . . . university faculty and students." Allegedly, Honolulu was chosen because of its "heterogeneous racial makeup" and, presumably, the great ease with which people of different races could intermingle.[101] This article implied that these films endorsed deviant sexual behaviors by indoctrinating individuals already regularly associated with liberalism (university professors, students, liberal ministers, etc.) and those who held positions of influence.[102]

CCA rhetoric referenced growing anxieties over prisons as sites of Black violence and rampant interracial sexual violence. The late 1960s and early 1970s witnessed several highly publicized prison uprisings in response to overcrowding and violence from guards, including two at California's Folsom Prison in 1968 and 1971 and one at New York's Attica Prison that left forty-three people dead. Enhanced tensions between prisoners also resulted in violence with racial overtones.[103] As Regina Kunzel argues, male carceral sexual violence became increasingly viewed through a largely racialized frame in which Black prisoners allegedly sexually assaulted their white counterparts as a form of political retaliation. This new iteration of the Black male rapist trope proved especially attractive to advocates of racial segregation and white supremacy insofar as it melded older notions of Black sexual violence against white women with more recent anxieties over same-sex desire and white male vulnerability.[104] *The Citizen* featured two articles reporting alleged interracial sexual assault. One relayed a lawsuit from sixty-two white inmates at a Missouri prison who alleged that prison guards had deliberately placed them with Black inmates knowing they would be assaulted.[105] Another mentioned the alleged abuse of four white men in a Saint Louis, Missouri, city jail.[106] These articles almost certainly bolstered concerns about empowered Black citizens and Black men as dangerous criminals, unfit for citizenship and equality.

Similar stories appeared in local CCA chapter publications. *The Citizens' Tri-State Informer*, an Overland, Missouri–based publication, carried two articles about the figure of the Black male prison rapist, focusing on the same facilities featured in *The Citizen*.[107] Another brief article titled "Prison Furloughs" mocked a state policy that "furloughed" inmates who agreed not to take drugs, drink alcohol, or "engage in sexual activities with members of the opposite sex" (such policies were common during the 1970s and were mirrored in federal law with the passage of the Federal Prisoners Rehabilitation Act of 1965). The writer sarcastically asserted that the legislators "figure[d] the black male inmate who raped a *male* bus passenger while on furlough did not violate his promise [to abstain from sexual activity with women]" (emphasis original).[108] In this reporting, the unleashed rapacity of the furloughed Black inmate is seemingly facilitated by the state legislature. The anonymous writer's derisive depiction of the state legislators as lenient toward Black prisoners somewhat mirrors what would become an infamous strategy in the 1988 presidential election in which Republican candidate George H. W. Bush released an infamous television attack ad accusing his opponent Michael Dukakis, of being at fault when a Massachusetts inmate named Willie Horton, who was furloughed in 1986, sexually assaulted and injured a woman after absconding from custody.[109] Although all of these accounts demarcate the prison as a chaotic and dangerous space, this article suggested that such aggressive behavior might continue after the offender's release.

Unsurprisingly, CCA chapter newspapers and circulars commonly associated homosexuality with political and racial liberals.[110] *The Citizens' Report*, a publication of the Southern Louisiana Citizens' Council, reprinted an article from the *Christian Crusade* linking same-sex desire to moral decline. Writer Terry McGinnity fretted that "homosexuality is rampant—both male and female—and is celebrated in theater, film and novel," and called for a return to "natural things," among them, "winning wars . . . putting smart aleck kids in their place, discouraging sexual perversion . . . arresting or deporting revolutionaries and getting rid of judges who can't define pornography."[111] *The Councilor*, another Louisiana-based chapter publication, resurfaced the arrest of President Lyndon B. Johnson's adviser Walter Jenkins six years earlier, linking liberal politicians with perceived sexual deviance. Titled "Skinny Dippers," the article cited a *Washington Observer* report that the Pentagon swimming pools reserved chairs for individuals who made $11,900 a year and that "skinny dipping" was popular "in the days of LBJ–Walter Jenkins era."[112]

CCA publications also reported on gay and lesbian political organizing. In September 1970, *The Councilor* noted the formation of a gay student alliance at the University of Wisconsin, characterizing it as "an association admitting only sex perverts as members."[113] A longer article in *The Citizens' Tri-State Informer* announced the declassification of homosexuality as a mental disorder in 1973 by the American Psychiatric Association (APA). The anonymous author noted that "homosexual organizations and liberal organizations" had successfully pressured the APA for the change. Claiming that conservatives "reacted with disbelief" at the professional organization's decision, the author concluded that "it demonstrates how influential and persuasive the liberals are in the US today."[114]

Blackness and Queerness in the Radical-Right Imaginary

The October 1976 edition of *The Thunderbolt*, a Klan-affiliated Georgia publication, reported on Gay Pride celebrations in Philadelphia, Atlanta, and Los Angeles. In "Negro and Jewish Politicians Honor Queer Perverts," the anonymous author claimed that political recognition of gay and lesbian communities within these municipalities was part of a grand scheme to further demoralize America. The writer asserted, "It seems as though the leftists are trying to get every type of odd ball 'minority group' in existence together against the White Christian majority." This antigay article predated the infamous Save Our Children campaign of 1977, which used the rhetoric of child protection to encourage voters to repeal a Miami-Dade County antidiscrimination ordinance.[115] Identifying a burgeoning coalition bringing together Black and white liberals with gay and lesbian communities, this article was part of a general white supremacist trend that associated civil rights advocacy and support for racial equality with same-sex desire and gay political organizing.[116] Moreover, the public visibility of gay and lesbian organizing facilitated increasing tolerance among certain Americans—and increased the anxieties and intolerance of others. What is crucial, however, is that sexual and gender dissidents emerged as an additional target for white supremacists, one that indexed for some the general moral decline of the nation. As the next chapter elucidates, the relationship between anti-Black and antigay mobilizations informed the at times tense coalitions between African American public officials and gay political communities that increasingly sought a place in municipal governance.

Part III **Gay Political Visions and the Politics of Estrangement**

· ·

5 Civil Rights and Moral Wrongs

The Politics of Gay Visibility in Atlanta, 1976–1989

· ·

As 500 people gathered on Saturday, June 26, 1976, to celebrate the city's fifth annual Gay Pride Day, they probably encountered stares, cheers, and some jeers. At various points along the Peachtree Street route, demonstrators held hands, embraced, and encouraged others to "Smash Gay Oppression." A few dozen marchers chanted, "Gay, Straight, Black, White—Same Struggle, Same Fight." The march ended at Piedmont Park in the Midtown neighborhood, an area increasingly associated with gay and lesbian political and social life. Arrayed on a grassy knoll in front of a small stage, attendees burst into a round of "We Shall Overcome," a famous anthem associated with the postwar Black freedom struggle. These audible connections between Black and gay political identities were amplified by a crucial development: earlier that week Maynard Jackson, the city's first African American mayor, had issued a proclamation formally recognizing Gay Pride Day. When one of the speakers mentioned the mayor, cheers of jubilation erupted from the crowd. Moments later, a similar cheer celebrated the defeat of an adversary—the antigay rights group Citizens for a Decent Atlanta. The previous day, this semi-anonymous group of metropolitan residents failed to secure a court injunction to reverse the mayoral proclamation. Noting this controversy, a speaker queried, "I wonder if people are trying to use [mayoral recognition of gay pride] to get rid of a Black mayor?" This statement proved prescient. The following week, Citizens for a Decent Atlanta and some of the city's most powerful white Protestant ministers called for Jackson's resignation if he refused to rescind the proclamation.[1] Although Jackson stood by the edict, the following year he opted to issue a proclamation for "Human Rights Week" rather than "Gay Pride Day" to avoid additional criticism.

The contested relationship between Jackson and local gay and lesbian political constituencies mirrored similar coalitions during the last three decades of the twentieth century. In many cities, gay liberalism—with its focus on lobbying, litigation, and legibility as a political constituency—superseded gay liberation and homophile organizing as the dominant political framework for gay men and lesbians.[2] Building relationships with local, state, and federal elected officials (white as well as people of color) was crucial to securing key political objectives, including antidiscrimination ordinances, policing reform, and challenges to the ubiquitous homophobia that marked American life. This period saw critical alliances between gay and lesbian voters and Black mayors like Tom Bradley of Los Angeles, Harold Washington of Chicago, and Marion Barry of Washington, DC.[3] Maynard Jackson occupies a somewhat indeterminate place in the history of Black-gay political coalitions, given his seeming retreat from explicit support of gay rights after 1976. However, I argue that the controversy over gay pride in Atlanta not only illuminates the tensions that so often marked Black-gay political alliances; it also demonstrates how Black and gay political identities were imbricated in metropolitan politics.

As I have demonstrated over the past few chapters, Blackness and homosexuality were long mutually referential—whether it be in white supremacist fantasies about political decline or the ways that Black liberals navigated the homophobic Cold War state. Centering this moment brings into stark relief how associations between Blackness and sexual/gender nonconformity emerged within a new arena: local political contests over gay rights. Comparisons between discrimination on the basis of race and sexual orientation (and less often gender identity) were central to support for and antipathy toward Jackson's proclamation. Moreover, focusing on Atlanta illuminates how social conservatives' concerns over Black-gay political coalitions also reflected anxieties over the city's sexual geographies. As in other cities, counterculturalist hangouts, sex work, pornographic bookstores/theaters, and gay and lesbian social spaces proliferated during the 1960s and 1970s, challenging a host of social, gender, and sexual norms. For a cadre of political conservatives, concerns over these genders and sexualities were profoundly linked to the emergence of Atlanta as a majority-minority city. Rather than understanding the catalyst for urban politics as being primarily about race or—as Josh Sides notes—as a response to the increased visibility of particular forms of sexual and gender expression, an analysis of Atlanta demonstrates that both race and sexuality exerted great force over metropolitan politics in complex and ambivalent ways.[4]

Although the bulk of this chapter focuses on the controversy over mayoral recognition of gay pride in the 1970s, I conclude with a brief analysis of two moments in the 1980s that reveal the persistence and limits of Black-gay comparisons. The first is a moment of tension between the National Coalition of Black Gays and the National Gay Task Force as the latter initiated a public relations campaign to challenge homophobic reporting during the Atlanta child murders. The second is the ambivalent cultivation of gay and lesbian voters during the 1989 mayoral campaign between two Black candidates—Maynard Jackson, who was seeking a third term, and Michael Lomax, the longtime chairman of the Fulton County Commission. In centering these two moments, I am not asserting that they are the most consequential for understanding Black-gay political tensions or identities in Atlanta or nationally. Rather, they are suggestive of how the minoritarian status of sexual and gender minorities continued to be tethered to that of Black subjects.

Atlanta's Urban Regime and Gay Liberation

"Cops have been busting and harassing Gays for years," declared the cover of a 1971 issue of the *Great Speckled Bird*, Atlanta's leading countercultural newspaper. In blood-red ink across several comic book panels, "The Christopher Street Story" recounted the birth of gay liberation at the Stonewall uprising. On June 28, 1969, hundreds of sexual and gender dissidents violently challenged the police raid on the Stonewall Inn, a mob-owned bar in the Greenwich Village neighborhood of New York City frequented by queer patrons. Artist, author, and *Great Speckled Bird* "gay liberation" editor Steve Abbott's visual narrative departed from the conventional story in one critical way—the gruesome death of an arrested protester who ended his life rather than be exposed as a gay man.[5] It was this suicide, according to Abbott, that catalyzed protesters' anger into action, making the Stonewall uprising a rallying cry for gay political empowerment in New York City and beyond. The story then shifts to the local level, where Abbott identified key realms in which "gay sisters and brothers are oppressed in Atlanta, GA . . . by the churches, by the government, by almost everyone." The comic feature ends by calling for "gays" and "straight identified sisters and brothers" to march for an end to antigay thought and action. Beginning at Seventh and Peachtree Streets in Midtown and ending in a rally at nearby Piedmont Park, *Great Speckled Bird* readers were called on to "Smash Gay Oppression."[6]

The social and economic upheavals of World War II increased the visibility of sexual and gender dissidents in Atlanta. Queer migrants moved to the city for a host of reasons including employment, educational opportunities, and, perhaps, knowledge that the city offered opportunities for affirmation and intimacy. Class, gender, and race profoundly shaped spaces of queer sociality. For white middle-class men and women access to white segregated public and private spaces facilitated such connections. In the predominately white middle-class enclaves of north Atlanta, gay men gathered in spaces like the Wisteria Garden Cocktail Lounge tucked away in the back of the Camelia Garden restaurant, while lesbians frequented the Tick Tock Grill. In Midtown, piano bars and an Italian restaurant called Mama Mia's were popular places to socialize, and the Queen of Clubs featured male and female impersonator shows. The ability to meet in establishments with names like Mammy's Shanty, with its Pappy's Plantation Lounge bar located in the rear, highlights how white gay and lesbian Atlantans could access segregated spaces that trafficked in anti-Black stereotypes and antebellum nostalgia.[7]

Even though it appears there was a degree of interracial fraternization and some Black queer Atlantans were visible to their white counterparts (including a "bull dagger" named Big Peck who operated a well-known brothel in the early 20th century), the color line held firm.[8] Like their white counterparts, Black queer Atlantans largely socialized within intraracial spaces. For example, female impersonators performed at the all-Black Top Hat Club (which later became the Royal Peacock).[9] Similarly, Black men found space for intimacy in public and private places. For example, in 1955 two men were arrested "on suspicion of sodomy" after being spotted near one of their homes in Vine City, a neighborhood in the western part of Atlanta.[10]

As this last anecdote suggests, the visibility of queer subcultures did not go unnoticed by municipal stewards of sexual and gender normativity. City institutions embraced heteronormative sexual politics and antigay policies, placing Atlanta in line with most other metropolitan governments in the postwar era. During the late 1940s, local media narratives popularized fears over the sexual psychopath, a constructed figure understood to be psychologically abnormal and sexually depraved. Local law enforcement officials mobilized these and other statutes, like sodomy and morals charges, to disproportionately harass and prosecute gay men in the city. As John Howard analyzes, a well-publicized crackdown in 1953 revealed the importance of space in the municipal response to sexuality. In what was known as the Atlanta Public Library perversion case, several men were arrested and convicted of soliciting sex in public library restrooms. Moreover, Howard explicates the ways in which the desire to curtail public heterosexual intimacies in Piedmont Park exposed those same spaces as sites of same-sex intimacies, prompting increased policing. During the 1950s and 1960s, local citizens and social organizations regularly alerted authorities to what they perceived as salacious activities. In 1966, for example, the Parent-Teacher Association of Henry Grady High School called for "an all-out effort to rid [Piedmont] Park of 'sex perverts.'"[11]

That such repressive policing was common in Atlanta helped spark the emergence of gay liberation. Weeks after the Stonewall uprising in New York City, Atlanta police launched a raid on the Ansley Mall Mini-Cinema for showing Andy Warhol's homoerotic film *Lonesome Cowboy*. After halting the screening, officers interrogated, detained, and photographed customers and arrested the projector operator and cinema manager.[12] The event catalyzed the formation of the Atlanta Gay Liberation Front, which held the first gay pride march in 1971. The organization emerged out of the city's countercultural community, particularly *Great Speckled Bird* staff members. After the Gay Liberation Front folded in 1973 due to infighting, several other organizations emerged, including the Atlanta Lesbian Feminist Alliance (ALFA, 1972), the Georgia State University Gay Liberation Front (1973), and a local congregation of the Metropolitan Community Church (MCC, 1972), a gay-affirming Christian denomination. As we will see, such organizations would continue to be crucial to the city's growing prominence as a southeastern hub for queer life.[13]

In Atlanta, gay liberationists pursued good relationships with local officials, embodying how, in the words of Marc Stein, "white gay liberationists may have rejected conventional politics, [but] they sometimes worked through conventional political channels."[14] In July 1971, members of the Atlanta Gay Liberation Front met with Mayor Sam Massell and successfully advocated for representation on the Community Relations Commission, a representative body for various municipal constituencies that investigated allegations of discrimination and inequity.[15] The appointment of Charlie St. John, a gay activist and journalist, to the commission in 1972 was a significant step in the growth of "queer clout" in Atlanta. Gay liberationists in other cities undertook similar actions. Groups like the Committee for Homosexual Freedom in San Francisco and the Street Transvestite Action Revolutionaries (STAR) in New York City appealed to local governments for protections against discrimination on the basis of gender identity and/or sexual orientation. Gay liberationists also used the courts to issue challenges to gender and sexual oppression. Crucially, gender transgressors constituted a vanguard within gay liberationist movements nationwide. Transgender activists like Marsha P. Johnson and Sylvia Rivera (who founded STAR, a mutual aid organization) participated in the New York City Gay Liberation Front. Others began to articulate a trans liberationist perspective that advocated for an end to targeted policing, transphobia with gay and lesbian spaces, access to gender affirming medical care, and the end of medical pathologization of transgender persons.[16] As the 1970s continued, gay liberation gave way to a narrower political vision that centered visibility and legal reform as the a priori strategies for equality and self-determination. It was within this political context that Mayor Jackson acquiesced to the Gay Pride planning committee's request for a proclamation declaring June 26, 1976, "Gay Pride Day."

In requesting and receiving mayoral recognition, this cadre of gay rights activists sought to influence the city's urban regime of governance that had shaped the political and economic power structure since World War II. As Clarence Stone notes, an "urban regime" is not limited to the "machinery of government" but rather "the informal arrangements that surround and complement the formal workings of governmental authority."[17] By the late 1960s, three constituencies operated at the epicenter of these arrangements: the white corporate business community, elected officials, and African American elites. The first group, the white corporate business community, organized to shape municipal development by forming the non-profit Central Atlanta Improvement Association in 1941 to bolster Atlanta's place in the regional economy and shape the development of the central business district. During the postwar years, its leadership forged strong and—as we will see—at times contentious relationships with city hall and the mayor in particular. Elected officials, especially mayors, formed the second group. Prior to the early 1970s, the city's governing structure featured a weak mayoralty and a strong city council. However, Mayor William Hartsfield greatly enhanced the power of this office through informal mechanisms, including cultivating close ties to powerful business elites. Holding office almost continuously between 1937 and 1962, Hartsfield garnered the support of white and Black middle-class residents and successfully annexed key northern white Atlanta suburbs in 1952. His successor, Ivan Allen, who served as mayor until 1970, operated in a similar mode, overseeing downtown development, the construction of major highways and maintaining racial segregation in a city with an increasingly large African American population.[18]

The third group, African American elites, exercised increasing power within Atlanta's informal governance structure beginning in the 1940s. After emancipation, most Black Atlantans continued to labor in the broad service sector economy—working as domestics and laundresses, porters, and day laborers. Yet, at the same time, a growing cadre of elites emerged, anchored in the vibrant Black institutional life of the West End, Vine City, and

Auburn Avenue neighborhoods, with their educational institutions, organizations, prominent businesses, houses of worship, and entertainment venues. Politically empowered during the Great Depression through professional and political opportunities associated with the New Deal, Black political elites enacted a pragmatic vision of political advancement that often meant seeking piecemeal concessions from white elected officials and prioritizing the economic well-being of the Black middle class. Voter registration was a central strategy of this approach.[19] Prominent Black leaders formed the All-Citizens Registration Committee in 1946, the same year that the Supreme Court issued a stare decisis ("to stand by things decided") on the US Court of Appeals for the Fifth Circuit's decision in *Chapman v. King*, which stated that Georgia's whites-only primary was unconstitutional.[20] The drive registered 21,244 Black Fulton County residents and captured the attention of white elected officials (including Mayor Hartsfield), initiating a drive to attract African American votes in the 1949 election. This election ignited a biracial political coalition in which Black elites and white power brokers managed to avoid much of the racial rancor engulfing other major southern cities in the 1950s and 1960s, through a process of gradual desegregation and neighborhood transition. Hartsfield promoted this veneer of peaceful race relations, coining the pithy phrase "The City Too Busy to Hate" to lure and keep white residents and business interests in Atlanta.[21]

Demographic change and generational tensions within Black communities challenged this biracial coalition. By 1970, the African American population increased by 70,000 while the white population declined by 60,000, creating additional pressure for access to housing and more public spaces.[22] For supporters of racial segregation, the embrace of a rhetoric of "rights, freedom, and individualism" allowed for a successful shift from the language and action of strident demagoguery to the subtle invocation of rights and color blindness.[23] In Atlanta, this shift proved crucial to the growth of modern conservatism and acted as a bulwark against the advancements of civil rights mobilizations. As these demographic and political shifts unfolded, a younger generation of mostly Black activists clustered around the West End's Atlanta University Center became increasingly vexed by the gradual and compromising nature of the Black elite's political pragmatism. Rather than rely solely on litigation and the negotiations between Black and white elites that had marked the last two decades of racial advancement, they adopted more confrontational strategies—including boycotts, civil disobedience, and public appeals. Inspired by the Greensboro, North Carolina, sit-ins, activists from six historically Black colleges and universities launched their own series of sit-ins under the organization the Committee on Appeal for Human Rights and, later, joined with other regional activists to form the Student Nonviolent Coordinating Committee.[24] This challenge to the hegemony of Black political elites signaled the diversification of the Black electorate, creating an opening for a new generation of Black politicos in the late 1960s and 1970s.

The political ascendancy of Maynard Jackson profoundly reflected this shifting landscape. The grandson of prominent African American minister John Wesley Dobbs and a graduate of Morehouse College and North Carolina Central University School of Law, Jackson entered politics after a career as a lawyer for the poor. In 1968, he launched a failed campaign to win the US Senate seat held by Herman Talmadge, an ardent segregationist and former governor of Georgia. Undeterred, Jackson won the vice-mayoral position in 1969, serving under Sam Massell, the city's first Jewish mayor and the choice of the Black political establishment. Crucially, Jackson had failed to consult key Black political leaders prior to his first campaign for political office—a major indiscretion. And although this disregard contributed to his defeat in the senatorial race of 1968, his victory in the 1969 vice-mayoralty race indicated the Black elite's loosening grip on a diverse Black electorate.[25] In 1973, Jackson became Atlanta's first Black mayor, placing the city among a growing number of cities in which African Americans held key municipal positions and exercised greater control in urban politics.

The first three years of Mayor Jackson's tenure were a crucial time of municipal political transformation. The revised city charter gave increased power to the city council and the mayor (especially over financial matters), and the formerly at-large elections of city council members were replaced with majority district-specific elections, thus concentrating Black voting power. This increase in power combined with Jackson's bombastic personality as a challenger to the status quo framed a confrontation with long-standing business leaders. As Jackson criticized the lack of diversity in their ranks, he empowered new power brokers like neighborhood representatives, and advanced affirmative action policies in contract holding that expanded access to lucrative funds. Downtown business elites viewed his policies as a challenge to their largely undisturbed autonomy and control over municipal affairs. Many white Atlantans perceived Jackson as not only antagonistic to business interests but, indeed, anti-white. These tensions reached a critical point in the fall of 1974 when Harold Brockey, president of the Central Atlanta Progress (CAP, formerly known as the Central Area

Improvement Association), issued a letter decrying the mayor's actions, warning of the flight of white residents and capital. According to the *Atlanta Constitution*, Brockey's September 16 letter cited concerns over crime, a declining "downtown image," and challenges in recruiting workers given the "racial imbalance."[26]

Law enforcement was another key area of reform. Policing had long been a source of contention among Black residents. Police chief John Inman's tolerance of oppressive policing practices, opposition to Jackson's affirmative action policy to diversify the police force, and willingness to demote Black officers who challenged workplace discrimination placed him at odds with the new mayor. After a failed attempt to remove Inman, who had been appointed by Massell in 1972, Jackson created the director of public safety position to supplant him. Although his appointee, Reginald Eaves, was popular with many Black residents for his willingness to challenge abusive policing practices and implement affirmative action hiring policies, many white business elites viewed his appointment as an act of cronyism, given that both Eaves and Jackson attended Morehouse College.[27] It was within this broader moment of instability that Jackson issued the Gay Pride Day proclamation.

Gay Pride Day, Mayor Maynard Jackson, and Citizens for a Decent Atlanta

When Jackson issued his proclamation, he may have assumed it would be a marginal story, buried in the back pages of the local newspaper. It declared, "All citizens deserve basic legal rights regardless of race, sex, age, religious belief, economic status, national origin or sexual preference" and noted that the march sought "to emphasize two things: solidarity among the gay community and the need for legislative change to eliminate discrimination so that as myths and stereotypes are shattered change can come about."[28] However, negative responses quickly emerged from a cadre of semi-anonymous Atlantans, calling themselves Citizens for a Decent Atlanta (CDA). This group sought, and failed, to secure an injunction in the Fulton County Superior Court to reverse the proclamation.[29] Although CDA leadership remains a mystery, it appears they were members of the Christian business communities in Fulton and DeKalb Counties. The CDA largely spoke through their attorney, William Burke, who claimed his clients' anonymity reflected their "concerns about reprisals, not from the city, but from the gay community," largely in the form of vandalism of their businesses.[30] Such concerns reflected the continued linkages between homosexuality and criminality that many gay rights activists increasingly sought to distance themselves from.[31] Although the core leadership remained anonymous, Burke named several key supporters of the CDA, including attorney Ben T. Beasley Jr.; Dr. William Self, pastor of the Wieuca Road Baptist Church; Rev. Charles Stanley, pastor of First Baptist Church; Rev. John Sharp, pastor of West Hills Presbyterian Church; Harmon Moore, executive director of the Christian Council of Metropolitan Atlanta; and Jerry C. Nims, a scientist and entrepreneur who would later lead Jerry Falwell Sr.'s Moral Majority in the 1980s. Rather than ignore the CDA, Jackson held a press conference to clarify the proclamation's content and purpose. His accompanying press release said that "the city's proclamation does not condone homosexuality"; rather, it articulated support for a particular group of citizens' right "to seek public discussion and legislative action on the issue [of gay rights]."[32]

The challenge soon moved from the courthouse to the local press. On June 26, the CDA published advertisements in the *Atlanta Constitution* that according to Burke, cost "over $6,000" and were paid for by a handful of wealthy donors.[33] The CDA's name mirrored an older prominent anti-vice organization—Citizens for Decent Literature. Established in the mid-1950s, this Catholic organization formed a vanguard within New Right anti-obscenity campaigns.[34] While national in scope, there is evidence of its prominence in metropolitan Atlanta, with a chapter forming in Cobb County in the late 1960s.[35] It is possible that the CDA leadership intentionally referenced this older national organization as a way to attract those concerned about the proliferation of nonheteronormative behaviors and intimacies in the public landscape. The CDA's initial advertisement objected to the proclamation because it endorsed criminality, violated Judeo-Christian principles, and endangered Atlanta's national reputation. The first advertisement appeared on June 26, 1976, the same day formally recognized by the mayor as Gay Pride Day. Beneath the words "We Protest" in large, bold text at the top, the issuers stated they did "not wish to deny homosexuals freedom of expression that is guaranteed in the Constitution," but they did protest the role of local governments in legitimizing certain acts: "We do challenge the right of our Mayor unilaterally to affix our city's seal of approval to a sexual orientation which the majority of his fellow citizens believes to be against the moral law of Judeo-Christian tradition and the institution of the home family unit. Also, homosexual acts are considered a felony under Georgia Law."

This language echoes the rhetorical strategies of desegregation's opponents during the 1960s and early 1970s. The reference to the religious beliefs of "the majority of citizens" invokes the ways in which advocates of segregation sought to undermine the appeals of minority groups, and instead position the desires of the majority as worth defending. The phrase "the institution of the home family unit" mirrored concerns about the welfare of children and sexual morality during debates over school integration. And a reference to the felonious nature of "homosexual acts" aligned with the mobilization of racial statistics about crime that had long been used as justifications for the disproportionate policing, marginalization, and ultimately, segregation of Black subjects. The text also focused on the city's reputation, erroneously noting that Atlanta was the "only US city to have accorded official recognition to the homosexuals in this bi-centennial year." "We call upon Mayor Jackson to immediately rescind this embarrassing proclamation. If you agree," the CDA suggested, "why don't you contact City Hall?"

And many did. The advertisements successfully mobilized metropolitan residents, striking a particular chord with white Protestant ministers and congregants as well as some interracial interdenominational organizations. The ministerial leadership of the Moreland Avenue Church of Christ and Peachtree City Christian Church wrote the mayor independently, pleading with him to revoke the proclamation. Other clergy took to their physical and metaphorical pulpits to denounce gay pride and Mayor Jackson.[36] Although individual petitioners, congregations, and ministerial organizations were united in their opposition, they articulated their disagreement in different ways. The statements of the Christian Council of Metropolitan Atlanta (CCMA), an ecumenical organization, and the Atlanta Baptist Association (ABA) illustrate a range of responses. Founded in 1879, the CCMA sought to facilitate cooperation among Atlanta's various Christian congregations. By 1976, African American congregations had joined their ranks, including some churches affiliated with African Methodist Episcopal, National Baptist Convention, and Church of God in Christ denominations. The CCMA's letter to its membership about the proclamation struck a tone of polite disapproval, with the executive committee asserting that the "Mayor was in grievous error in this matter" and calling on member churches "after prayerful thought to make your feelings known by writing to the council your reactions in whatever manner you see fit," and they would in turn "apprise the Mayor." It continued, "We are sympathetic with those who are homosexual men and women, or otherwise classified as gay" and admitted that "the churches have often failed in their ministry to these persons."[37] That CCMA's executive director Harmon Moore publicly supported the CDA places into even starker relief the letter's tone of respectful disagreement rather than strident protest, potentially acknowledging the strong support for Mayor Jackson among Black Atlantans, some of whom filled the pews of churches affiliated with the CCMA.

In contrast, the ABA's public statement and the actions of some of its member congregations conveyed intense outrage. Several white Baptist ministers voiced their objections from their pulpits the day after the Gay Pride march. They were also the first constituency to actively call for Mayor Jackson to resign. For example, Rev. William Self, pastor of the large Wieuca Road Baptist Church in northern Atlanta, called for the mayor to "repent or resign" due to his perceived support of "devious behavior." He queried, "How can we talk up Atlanta if our leaders keep putting it down?"[38] Recognizing this groundswell of support, the ABA's director of missions, R. Edward Gilstrap, issued a memo encouraging pastors to organize a petition drive among their congregations calling for the repeal of the proclamation and Jackson's resignation. Gilstrap encouraged pastors to gather signatures during the Fourth of July holiday weekend as it was "the most advantageous time for gathering names." Whereas the ABA had long commented on sexual matters in the public sphere, by the middle of the 1970s white Protestant Christians no longer held the same sway in the press or with government officials.

Individual citizens also expressed their displeasure, sending letters to Mayor Jackson and the *Atlanta Constitution* whose tone ranged from the formal and polite to the derisive and insulting. "Sad Day! When a mayor of an international city will bow to the Gay Society and acknowledge their 'rights' in the pretense of being fair to them, shows your weakness and Ignorance [sic] and proves you are not qualified to sit in leadership of this great city," K. N. Meadows of Atlanta chastised.[39] Mary Grable, who resided in Buckhead, applauded Jackson's plans to close "massage parlors" but she was "strongly oppos[ed]" to Jackson's decision to recognize Gay Pride. "Atlanta is a beautiful city. We need to hold our standards up," she wrote to the mayor. The "message to homosexuals" should be "to tell them God loves them and that he can and wants to set them free," not to support public celebrations of gay pride. She concluded with an appeal to what she understood as the moral integrity of the city: "The Bible tells us 'Blessed is the nation (city!) whose God is the Lord.' I love Atlanta, the South and our nation deeply and believe that if we will honor God and walk in his ways he will bless us."[40] Finally, R. David Remaley's letter casts the mayor's controversial proclamation as one of many missteps. "From the firing [of] John Inman to 'gay pride day' this administration, at best, has been a sad disappointment to Atlantans with the kind of 'pride' which built this city," wrote Remaley. He went on to characterize these and other actions as "the liberal and often racist actions of this administration."[41] These letters traffic in narratives about Black mayoral leadership as not only inept but, indeed, a facilitator of crime, vice, and discrimination against white Atlantans.

Although the CDA's protest rallied disaffected segments of the white metropolitan community, it also drew support from some Black Atlantans. On July 11, one of the city's Black newspapers, the *Atlanta Daily World*, published a CDA advertisement radically different from its counterpart in the *Atlanta Constitution*. It was not an anonymously authored plea but, rather, featured the words and image of Rev. John D. Sharp, an African American minister who served as pastor of West Hills Presbyterian Church from 1971 to 1988.[42] Sharp's headline read, "We Need Your Help: Fathers, Mothers, Sisters, and Brothers," referencing both kinship ties and racial solidarity in the use of "brothers" and "sisters." By condemning the mayor's proclamation, Sharp articulated a moral argument that mirrored the CDA's advertisement—that homosexuality was sinful. Sharp characterized his plea to reverse Jackson's proclamation as "a basic stand by a God-fearing citizen . . . against the encouragement of a moral wrong as though it is a thing to celebrate and be proud of." He cited a number of biblical scriptures to bolster his assertion that homosexuality "is an abomination unto God and a dishonor to our own bodies."[43] He also articulated a political objection to comparisons between gay rights and Black civil rights. "Our Dream," Sharp wrote, "is being misused if we confuse Moral Wrongs with Civil Rights. . . The victories we achieved in our struggle for Civil Rights were not meant to promote or encourage moral wrongs." This reference to Dr. Martin Luther King Jr.'s "I Have a Dream" speech highlighted the minister's central premise: that the Black freedom struggle and the gay rights struggle were not only dissimilar but incompatible. Sharp concluded, "Let's help save the dream by asking our mayor to rescind the 'gay pride day' proclamation." The call to "help save the dream" added a layer of urgency to his missive, suggesting that Black political support for gay rights might endanger the advances of the civil rights movement.

Sharp's umbrage over the proclamation was, in part, a dismissal of the professed similarity between gay civil rights and Black civil rights, which had increasing purchase nationally. As this chapter's opening anecdote suggests, some gay liberals and even liberationists mobilized the rhetoric and tactics associated with the civil rights movement. And although people of color were a part of gay liberationist and gay liberal organizing during the 1970s, many national and local organizations remained largely white in their membership and cultural orientation.[44] As Christina Hanhardt argues, militant gay liberals sought to differentiate themselves from other urban dwellers associated with criminality, including people of color.[45] This distancing, combined with racism and cultural homogeneity in various organizations/institutions, further fused the association between whiteness and gay/lesbian identities. This seemed to hold true in Atlanta, where members of the Gay Pride planning committee and related organizations were overwhelmingly white. As Kevin Mumford asserts in his study of Philadelphia in the 1970s and early 1980s, Black political conservatives increasingly mobilized both moral and political objections to gay and lesbian organizers' assertions of a "just like race" formulation of rights.[46] Sharp, then, mirrored these efforts in his refutation of a rhetoric of similar estrangements. The radically different content and structure of the CDA's advertisement in the city's Black newspaper suggests that CDA leaders believed a different kind of appeal was necessary to mobilize support among Black subjects. Also, the assumed racial homogeneity of the CDA and its supporters may have been unappealing to some Black Atlantans who were perhaps wary of supporting a campaign launched by largely unknown white leaders. The editorial board of *Atlanta Daily World*, a Black newspaper, also expressed disapproval over the proclamation stating they "regret the mayor issued his proclamation because it may give undue recognition to the wrong side of this delicate question." The editorial continued, "We consider sexual abnormalities most unfortunate and degrading to society" and asserted they "are on the side of the great majority of black and white Americans" in their view of homosexuality as deviant. After recounting some basic contours of the controversy, the editorial concluded, "But we are glad the issue is now in the open and we welcome expressions on it."[47] The editorial's reluctance to pointedly condemn or support the proclamation may reflect a desire not to criticize the city's first Black mayor.[48]

However, there is another possible reason for some Black Atlantans' wariness in supporting the CDA—rumors that the leadership and their largely white Protestant Christian supporters were racist. In an interview with the *Great Speckled Bird*, Tyrone Brooks of the Southern Christian Leadership Conference (SCLC) asserted that the CDA consisted of "the same conservative racist businessmen . . . who are continuing to fight the Mayor and do everything they can to bring him and Reginald Eaves down." The reporters offered their own editorializing on this point: "Citizens for a Decent Atlanta are closet racists. They cannot get away with hollering 'nigger' because of the fight black people have waged to get their civil rights and the strength and unity they now possess. Instead, Citizens for a Decent Atlanta yells 'pervert' and 'queer,' using homosexuals as scapegoats for the real target—the new black city power structure."[49] The ABA statement also reflects unease about how some Atlantans might perceive the ecumenical group's disapproval of the mayor's proclamation. Gilstrap wrote, "It is not an issue of race, and many Black pastors stand alongside of you in their condemnation of the proclamation thusly made." That the ABA's own director of missions, who organized the petition drive among the city's Baptists, mentioned race suggests concerns that their antipathy toward the mayor was perceived as racially motivated.[50]

One illuminating perspective on the stakes of denying the affinity between gay and Black political mobilizations emerged from civil rights activist and state senator Hosea Williams. A Baptist minister and former member of Dr. King's inner circle, Williams was a visible presence in state and municipal politics. After two unsuccessful races, for governor of Georgia in 1966 and US Senate in 1972, Williams won a seat in the state senate, where he served until 1984. In an interview with local television news station WSB, he offered his strident support for the mayor and suspicions of the CDA: "Well, the thing that worries me about them is that they proclaim to be Christians, I've been told. And I think if you are a Christian, I think you ought to remember that part of the Bible where Jesus said to those that were stoning the prostitute 'Ye without sin cast the first stone.'" He then asked the reporter to consider the long-term implications of this opposition. "If we support the fact that Maynard Jackson is immoral or wrong for proclaiming Gay Day, there are those that will dispute the fact that he should have proclaimed SCLC Day or Civil Rights Day." In comparing the mayor's right to recognize certain underrepresented subjects, Williams astutely challenged viewers to focus less on their own reactions to homosexuality or gay rights and instead on two things: First, any criticism of the mayor's actions might have negative ramifications on issues that some viewers held dear, such as municipal recognition and support for civil rights organizations that only a decade before had been derided as immoral and criminal. Second, that those calling for the repeal of the proclamation and the removal of the mayor may be hostile to racial equality and Black political organizing.

In Williams's formulation, the ability of gay and lesbian Atlantans to organize for civil rights could be a barometer for the ability of African Americans to do the same.[51]

The overwhelming response of most Black Atlantans was support of the mayor or silence. When asked by *Great Speckled Bird* reporters about the response of Black Atlantans, SCLC official Brooks asserted that "the reaction in the black community will be very subtle." He continued, "These ministers just won't risk losing their congregations, which are often conservative and set in their ways," then stated that they would not oppose Jackson outright.[52] Like the editorial staff at the *Atlanta Daily World*, they adopted a subtle approach. However, some civil rights organizations vocally supported the mayor. Indeed, when Mayor Jackson held a press conference on June 25 to stand by the proclamation, he was accompanied by representatives from the Community Relations Commission, the National Association for the Advancement of Colored People (NAACP), the SCLC, and the American Civil Liberties Union (ACLU) of Georgia.[53] According to the *Great Speckled Bird*, the local chapter of the Urban League also supported the proclamation.[54]

Gay rights activists organized independently in response to the CDA and its allies. The Gay Pride Planning Committee expanded its membership to include the city's major gay and lesbian organizations, including ALFA, the Dykes of the Second American Revolution (known as DAR II), the Gay Center, MCC, Dignity (a Catholic affinity group), and Integrity (an Episcopalian affinity group). Now called the Gay Pride Alliance (GPA), the coalition largely focused on countering the CDA's homophobic campaign through protest and persuasion. The alliance identified representatives who could share information about gay rights and communities with members of the press, municipal officials, and civic groups.[55] In an open letter to the *Atlanta Constitution*, GPA representatives wrote, "We wish to thank the 'Concerned citizens for a decent Atlanta' for their generous gesture of contributing a three-quarter page ad as an advertisement for our Gay Pride Parade celebration June 26." Citing their standing as "hard-working honest citizens," the authors asserted that they were "willing to pay for equality and integrity" not with "dollars and cents . . . but rather with a Christian Faith . . . and a sense of freedom, justice and truth that will never die." The writers also linked the recognition of gay pride to that year's bicentennial celebration of the nation's founding, stating, "One of the original 13 colonies (Pennsylvania) has shown its originality again by its governor's declaring Gay Pride Week for the entire state." The letter's signatories—activists Robert Salo and Linda Regnier as well as "216 others"—indicated the growing numbers of "active members and friends of the Atlanta Gay community."[56] Activists also mounted a counterdemonstration in front of Wieuca Road Baptist Church and its vocal pastor, William Self, on July 11. Spearheaded by ALFA with support from the GPA, the demonstration was largely ignored by the city's media (with the *Great Speckled Bird* as a notable exception). While forty supporters demonstrated outside of the church, ten people wearing "Gay Pride" buttons attended a religious service inside "without incident." However, the demonstrators felt the ever-present threat of a violent response with the presence of "six plainclothes police officers and six off duty uniformed police officers," a stark reminder of the long-standing policing often faced by queer subjects.[57]

The National Gay Task Force (NGTF) sought to support local activists and Mayor Jackson as the controversy unfolded. NGTF cofounder and director Bruce Voeller wrote to the editor of the *Atlanta Constitution*, drawing on well-worn comparisons between race and sexual orientation. "Only a few years ago," he asserted, "one suspects the same 'Citizens for a Decent Atlanta' would have written similarly against blacks, claiming that intermarriage of the races is 'against the moral law of the Judeo-Christian tradition.'" Voeller subtly critiqued the Jackson administration and the limits of gestures recognition, noting that Atlanta lagged behind other cities that had antidiscrimination ordinances. He concluded with a call for "all civil libertarians and American gay taxpayers" to unmask the identities of the "CDA sponsors," exert financial pressure, and "show that civil rights are more than paper rights."[58] Voeller also reached out directly to Jackson, sharing a copy of Los Angeles mayor Tom Bradley's recently issued Gay Pride Week proclamation and writing "I hope these help."[59]

Like their detractors, supporters of the proclamation and gay rights generally wrote to the mayor and the local press. In a letter to Jackson, Ann Maury claimed, "There is substantial support [for the proclamation] and many are using the publicity caused by your position to speak about the issue and hopefully increase other people's awareness of the rights needed by homosexuals."[60] Harold R. Bodie sent a copy of the CDA advertisement to Mayor Jackson, inserting the letters "dis" into the phrase "If you [dis]agree." Citing his membership at First Baptist Church and residence in Ainsley Park, Bodie wrote, "What the chairman of the CDA or any member of the committee does in bed might be considered perverted by someone else."[61] Writing to the *Atlanta Constitution*, Jerry Higginbotham asserted that "being aware of the different sexual orientations of some of [Atlanta's] citizens, I support the mayor in his just and honest stand concerning this matter."[62] An anonymous Atlanta resident declared, "Come on, Atlanta, show that you're a progressive city, willing to stand up for human beings and not a bunch of narrow-minded bigots."[63] In addition to casting the opposition as bigots, some correspondents framed the CDA and their supporters as suburbanites and, therefore, illegitimate dissenters. Noting that many of the letters published on July 9 were written by people living outside the city limits, E. Russell wrote, "What right do these non-Atlanta residents have to complain about Jackson?" He continued, "These are the same people who when out of the state, will tell people who ask where they live that they are from Atlanta. But they are the same ones who violently oppose annexing their small townships to the city of Atlanta."[64] Ultimately, however, the mayor neither rescinded the proclamation nor resigned.

The Sexual Geographies of Atlanta

In postwar histories of Atlanta (and other US cities), scholars foreground race as a primary driver of municipal politics and spatial change. As they recount, Atlanta's moniker as "The City Too Busy to Hate" obscured how a partnership between capitalists and public officials instantiated racial inequality in housing policy, public space, hiring procedures, and law enforcement. Race, of course, is a multivalent category in which ideas about class, gender, and sexuality are always already present and informative. Shifting our attention to sexuality as well as race in the metropolitan Atlanta landscape, however, allows us to see a longer history of what Josh Sides calls a "moralist geography"—or how social conservatives asserted their particular vision of appropriate gendered and sexual behavior in public space and politics.[65] They did so in the postwar period (and the 1960s and 1970s in particular), as nonnormative sexualities and genders became increasingly visible in the actions of counterculturalists, sex workers, proprietors of pornographic theaters, bookstores and massage parlor owners, as well as queer residents. The opposition to Jackson's gay pride proclamation, then, is not only a story of race or a story of sexuality; rather, it is also a story about how the increasing demographic presence and political power of African Americans became associated with spaces for non-normative sexualities and genders.

The 1960s was a crucial time for the shifting racial and spatial demographics of Atlanta. Despite increasing Black political influence after the 1930s, by 1965 Black Atlanta residents were restricted to a small tract of city property, about 22 percent of the total area of the city despite being 43.5 percent of the city's population.[66] The displacement of Black residents through urban renewal and the placement of new public housing in predominantly Black areas compounded racial inequality. New challenges to the urban regime and racial segregation would shift the racial composition of the city, yet largely retain segregation. Despite this, Atlanta increasingly earned a reputation as a place of opportunity for African Americans and especially for professionals who relocated to the city in notable numbers during the 1970s. However, battles over residential segregation and access to schools and downtown businesses spurred the white flight that altered the city's demographics and politics.

Alongside these shifting racial demographics, three insurgent sexual geographies challenged the heteronormativity of the public sphere. First was the growing visibility of same-sex-desiring and gender-nonconforming Atlantans, who began to congregate around the Midtown area and Little Five Points. By the early 1970s, many queer Atlantans shifted from surreptitious intimacy to political organizing and visible public socializing. By the middle of the 1970s, Atlanta had emerged as a key hub of gay life in the southeast, perhaps due to comparatively less repressive policing practices and the anonymity one could assume in a large city. Others learned about the array of gay bars, clubs, bathhouses, and lounges from publications like *The Barb* and *Cruise*.[67] One venue, the After Dark bookstore, functioned not only as place to procure gay pornography but also as a space for socializing and sexual encounters.[68] Lesbians found community in spaces like the ALFA Omega's, a racially diverse softball team, and the Edge of Night House, a house for lesbians that eventually became the ALFA house.[69]

Second was the countercultural community that overlapped with these queer spaces. By 1966, there was a vibrant hippie subculture in the Midtown area, congregating around the Catacombs Café on Fourteenth Street Northwest, the Twelfth Gate on Tenth Street, and Piedmont Park. Counterculturalists' willingness to flout gender and sexual conventions drew the attention (and ire) of many Atlanta residents, city officials, and especially law enforcement, who forced the Catacombs to close in 1967.[70] Tensions between police, city officials, and counterculturalists reached a fever pitch in the fall of 1969, when police and hippies clashed violently in Piedmont Park. The incident became a flashpoint in the mayoral election that year when the four candidates traded barbs over previous statements and actions related to policing the Peachtree–Fourteenth Street area. Alderman Everett Millican, who regularly articulated a "law and order with justice" perspective, asserted he would clear the area of "hippies, homosexuals, sex deviates

FIGURE 5.1 Jerome McClendon, "Sex Worker Hiding Their Face as Police Serve the House of Erotica Court Papers," *Atlanta Journal-Constitution*, 1976. Jerome McClendon/*Atlanta Journal-Constitution* via Associated Press.

and drug pushers."[71] His opponent, Sam Massell, took a moderate position, citing his efforts as an alderman to work with the Community Relations Commission to broker better relations between counterculturalists and other residents.[72] The importance of hippie visibility to the 1969 election—fraught with questions about race and municipal demographics—indicated how profoundly sexuality, gender, and race shaped the political terrain in Atlanta.

Finally, the rise of various sex industries created consternation among a wide cross section of city residents and officials (see fig. 5.1). Sex work and pornography suppliers existed prior to the 1960s; however, the enervation of obscenity and prostitution laws at the federal, state, and local levels allowed these goods and services to circulate more freely. Moreover, Atlanta's emergence as a corporate center and convention town created a greater number of itinerant consumers for such illicit products. A range of businesses catered to the largely male conventioneers, including massage parlors, bathhouses, movie houses, sex toy vendors, and pornographic movie theaters/bookstores. Sex workers could also be found within and around these businesses, with the *Atlanta Constitution* estimating that "some 7,500 full or part-time prostitutes" could be found within the city limits. The press and police identified two prominent areas for such activity—the Triangle north of Baker Street and businesses between Ponce de Leon and Fourteenth Avenue, with particular concentration on the "Strip" segment of Peachtree Street between Eighth and Eleventh Streets.[73] Legal loopholes and ineffective policing (which often ignored the clientele) undermined efforts to close these establishments. For example, some massage parlors operated as venues for sex under the ruse of offering a legal service. And although Georgia State Legislators passed a law in 1975 criminalizing anyone who "erotically stimulates the genital organs of another . . . by manual or other bodily contact, exclusive of sexual intercourse," the parlors simply amended their offerings once again, making detection and prosecution difficult.

Prior to the late 1960s, much of the rhetoric assailing these forms of sexual and gender transgression was rooted in Christian moralizing (although such action continued, see fig. 5.2). Howard describes how Evangelical Christians exerted a powerful influence in postwar Atlanta governance, as they sought to assert their particular brand of morality.[74] Chief among these moralists were people and institutions associated with the Southern Baptist denomination. In 1954, for example, the ABA characterized Piedmont Park as "a hotbed" of sexual immorality, claiming that "fifteen hundred sex perverts can legally pursue their devilish designs in the park."[75] For some, Christian belief informed their watchfulness. Lt. J. L. Mosley of

FIGURE 5.2 Guy Hayes, "Religious Protestors Leading an Anti-pornographic Demonstration outside a Strip of Sex Industry Businesses," *Atlanta Journal-Constitution*, 1974. Guy Hayes/*Atlanta Journal-Constitution* via Associated Press.

the Atlanta vice squad told a reporter that "Atlanta folks are mostly church people and they are quick to report violations."[76] Baptist clergy and laity alike articulated a "moralist vision" in formal positions of governance.[77] For example, Pastor James P. Wesberry Sr. was the inaugural chairman and premier spokesperson for the Georgia Literature Commission. Created in 1953 by the state legislature, the committee was tasked with scrutinizing "literature which they have reason to suspect is detrimental to the morals of the citizens."[78] Similarly, Hinson McAuliffe, the solicitor general of Fulton County Superior Court who oversaw the 1969 raid of the Ainsley Mall Mini-Cinema for showing *Lonesome Cowboys* in 1969 and built a career as a smut fighter, was a devoted Baptist who taught Sunday school for decades.[79] Everett Millican, who articulated an anti-counterculturalist stance in his 1969 mayoral campaign, was an active member of Morningside Baptist Church and trustee for the Atlanta Baptist College.[80]

As the sexual geographies of Atlanta shifted, moralists diversified their rhetoric to include instrumentalist arguments. As Danielle Lindemann argues, instrumentalist arguments emphasize the negative consequences of the proliferation of sex and pornographic industries and, more specifically, how these particular businesses might violate existing statutes. As Lindemann notes, these arguments were not free of moralism, as they often relied on the same logics that undergirded those articulated by anti-vice reformers. However, these moralists—which included elected officials and business interests—did not foreground immorality as the chief rationale for regulation. Instead, their arguments pivoted around two points: First, that certain businesses (like bathhouses, massage parlors, and wrestling dens) were surreptitious sites for sex work, and therefore intentionally violated state laws. Second, that the proliferation of such businesses hurt the local economy by making the city, and downtown in particular, unattractive for conventions or new businesses. These arguments inverted the common logic that it was the city's vibrancy as a convention and corporate headquarters that made it a site for adult entertainment businesses. This strategy, which first appeared in the 1970s, would become more prominent in the 1980s and 1990s.[81]

While business elites and city officials used instrumental arguments for the regulation of sex industries, the proliferation of such activities became a point of contention between the Jackson administration and CAP. Speaking before the Atlanta City Council Public Safety Committee in January 1976, public safety director Eaves advocated for the legalization of sex work, asserting that "legalized prostitution would save us a lot of headaches" (see fig. 5.3). His statements raised concerns among some city council

FIGURE 5.3 Bill Mahan, "Mayor Maynard Jackson (right) Delivering the Oath to Reginald Eaves (left)," *Atlanta Journal-Constitution*, 1978. Bill Mahan/*Atlanta Journal-Constitution* via Associated Press.

members and attracted local media attention.[82] Eaves later clarified that he was interested in revisiting a number of so-called victimless crimes, including "prostitution, gambling, marijuana, pornography and homo-sexuality." Citing the difficulty in curtailing such activities, he noted that legalizing sex work would minimize the incursion of organized crime in the city, reduce "drug abuse" and venereal disease, as well as allow the police to focus their efforts on other criminal activity.[83] His comments elicited negative reactions from a number of city council members and downtown business elites, including Dan E. Sweat, the president of CAP. Sweat was in a key position to respond to Eaves's seeming policy shift around sex work. Taking the helm of CAP at the same time Jackson ascended to the mayor's office, Sweat possessed a wide-ranging background as a journalist and bureaucrat with the DeKalb County Commission, Atlanta's anti-poverty program, and Mayor Ivan Allen's administration. He assailed Eaves, saying that the official's running commentary on legalizing sex work encouraged "more prostitutes [to] come out from under the rock." In an August address to the Atlanta Rotary Club, Sweat identified a constellation of "problems" that law enforcement was unable (or perhaps unwilling) to deal with, including bathhouses, massage parlors, and sex work industries, growing Black unemployment, and organized crime.[84] An *Atlanta Constitution* editorial a month later expounded on his concerns about the city becoming "easy": "the fact that our top law enforcement official in the city suggests we can't control [sex work] through existing laws and should therefore legalize it encourages the pimps and prostitutes . . . to accelerate their operations." Race emerged as a crucial element in Sweat's commentary. Writing about the downtown area, he asserted, "The 'perception' problem is compounded by the fact that the pattern of prostitution downtown has become one in which most 'streetwalkers' are black and most call girls are white. As more and more of the prostitutes who solicit on the sidewalks are observed to be black, the assumption arises that Atlanta is 'easy' on black prostitutes, creating more serious overtones from the problem. This draws more so-called 'johns' into the downtown area and innocent women become targets for abuse and insults."

Sweat's statement linked Black political power with deviant Black sexualities and genders, suggesting that Jackson, Eaves, and others in the mayor's administration adopted racially discriminatory policing practices toward sex workers, policing elite (and seemingly white) "call girls" while leaving alone the everyday "streetwalker" (assumed to be Black). This allegation of differential policing echoed long-standing ideas that Black elected officials, at best, prioritized the needs of Black constituents to a fault and, at worst, were inept and corrupt (ideas that stretched back to the Reconstruction era when Southern redemptionists sought to undermine the political legitimacy of empowering the formerly enslaved). Finally, Sweat's commentary suggested that the proliferation of criminality and sexual debauchery would be particularly unattractive to local, regional, and national business interests—who would not want to relocate their business to Atlanta.

White business interests were not alone in their concern over the proliferation of sex work and other forms of behavior closely associated with public disorder. Black middle-class and elite Atlantans had long labored to dissolve perceptions of Black residential and commercial spaces as places of vice. As Danielle Wiggins argues, the increasing concern among Black business owners and elected officials over the proliferation of violent crime and "crimes against public order" in the late twentieth century has roots that extend to various racial uplift efforts in the early twentieth century. Citing

FIGURE 5.4 Mary Mangiafico, "Mayor Maynard Jackson with Lawyer Mary Welcome Shutting Down a Roman Bathhouse along a Strip of Adult Establishments," *Atlanta Journal-Constitution*, 1977. Dan Sweat, president of Central Atlanta Progress appears in the middle of the image. Nancy Mangiafico/*Atlanta Journal-Constitution* via Associated Press.

broad middle-class support for urban renewal and slum clearance as "sites for working class blacks to be rehabilitated," Wiggins demonstrates that Black officials, law enforcement, and business owners articulated a "broken windows" vision of policing in which quality-of-life laws were used to remove undesirables from the historic Auburn Avenue District in 1979 and the early 1980s.[85] Jackson's move to police sex work more broadly in 1976 and 1977 is a crucial precursor to this work.[86]

Jackson's decision to appoint Mary Welcome, the city's first Black city solicitor, to spearhead the crackdown may have been an intentional decision to decenter Eaves and his controversial commentary. A Baltimore native who previously served as the attorney general of the Virgin Islands, Welcome arrived in Atlanta in her early thirties a divorcée with a small son in tow. She vigorously took up the mayor's charge to assail the proliferation of sexual businesses in the city of Atlanta, with a focus on massage parlors and bathhouses. Notably, this initiative began in early July 1976 during the height of public outcry over the gay pride day proclamation. It is unclear whether the conservative outcry over the mayor's actions spurred this assault on other forms of nonheteronormativity or if the anti–sex businesses campaign was already planned. Regardless, the effect seems to be the same—to position the mayor as committed to policing certain vice industries while also supporting the rights of citizens to express themselves erotically.

The campaigns against bathhouses, massage parlors, and "streetwalker" sex workers yielded mixed results. Welcome and her staff sought to close establishments using statutes that prohibited the operation of businesses deemed to be "public nuisance[s]" and houses of prostitution. Vice and beat police officers increased their arrests of employees and customers of these Peachtree Street–area establishments during July and August. The campaigns did not have any substantive effects until that end of the year, however. After attempting to regulate the emerging adult industry businesses via zoning, the city council's Public Safety Commission passed two ordinances that allowed the city to exert greater control over the opening and operation of adult entertainment businesses. These expanded powers included background checks on owners and employees, a required certification of massage therapists, prohibiting hours of operation after 9:30 P.M. and broader investigative powers by the Bureau of Police Services.[87] By January 1977, four bathhouses—with names like Wild Mary's, Madame's Love Parlour, and Purple Passion Palace—had all closed their doors. In response, CAP launched an initiative known as the Peachtree Walk Project to revitalize the area by influencing businesses that would fill the empty storefronts.

Indeed, the headquarters for the new project occupied the former location of the once-infamous Roman Bathhouse, whose sign was ceremoniously removed in the spring of 1977 (see fig. 5.4). In the middle of 1977, a group known as the Midtown Business Association took over the initiative and the burden of funding it. The area began to attract new establishments, including a health food store, a gym, and a floral shop. City officials would continue to undertake campaigns to police sex businesses and sex work in that area during the rest of the 1970s.[88]

The political fallout over gay pride should not be seen as separate from skirmishes over the city's sexual and racial dynamics. That non-normative sexual geographies and Black municipal power became imbricated in Atlanta mirrors the larger processes recounted in this book: namely, how Blackness and queer sexual formations (and those associated with homosexuality in particular) continued to be linked—by those who supported the inclusion of those constituencies within the regime of urban governance and by those disturbed by the empowerment of one or both groups. As we shall see, Mayor Jackson's retreat from gay pride aligned with a reconciliation with business elites and the appeasement of social conservatives.

Civil Liberties Week 1977

The following year, gay rights activists once again requested that Mayor Jackson recognize Gay Pride Day with a mayoral proclamation. Writing to the mayor on May 5, 1977, GPA coordinators Linda Regnier and Vic Host implored the mayor to continue his enthusiastic support for the annual gay pride celebration. "We understand the terrific pressure this put you under last year, and we want you to know again that you are greatly respected throughout Atlanta—by people of all persuasions who are concerned with basic human rights and dignity." Their plea noted intensified conservative organizing nationwide. "Witness," the coordinators implored, "what is happening in Miami." They asserted that the "one way to prevent a gay witch-hunt here in Atlanta is to have a gay community that is open, viable, and visable [sic]."[89] The Miami-based Save Our Children campaign, which successfully overturned a county nondiscrimination ordinance and brought profound visibility to antigay mobilizations, added additional urgency to the GPA's request. Citing the passage of the June 7 referendum in Florida, the GPA "urg[ed] the lesbian and gay community to come out next Saturday for this important demonstration in defense of gay rights—and we especially urge Blacks, feminist [sic] and every supporter of basic human rights to join with us." To emphasize the coalitional nature of support for the rally, the press release named speakers from several organizations, including "the Atlanta National Organization for Women, Southern Christian Leadership Conference [and] the American Civil Liberties Union."[90] Opponents of the proclamation also began to mobilize, this time with support far beyond metropolitan Atlanta. During the spring of 1977, Governor George G. Busbee received petitions signed by hundreds of Georgians, urging him to prevent a second mayoral proclamation. The petitions shared the same banner: "We the undersigned citizens of Georgia join hands with the Women's Christian Temperance Union urge you [sic] to use your influence and the power vested in you as Governor of our State to ban 'Gay Pride Week' in our Capital City and throughout Georgia." Whereas some petitions emanated from the Atlanta metropolitan region (like Decatur), most were from small towns elsewhere in the state, like Covington, Alma, Americus, and Waycross and larger towns and cities like Douglas, Macon, Augusta and neighboring Martinez.[91]

Still haunted by the CDA protests of the previous summer and anticipating the upcoming mayoral election, Jackson and his advisers endeavored to appease Atlantans made uneasy by the proclamation and maintain good ties with the gay and lesbian community. Handwritten notes between close advisers and personnel in the Jackson administration indicate that finding this middle course was a priority. Adviser Tony Riddle asserted that "the [mayor's] statement must be clear and strong. Anything less will be seen as an indication of shame and wrong-doing." He continued, "Opponents of the Proclamation seem to fear it as a threat, they must be impressed that their rights of protest are not being called into question."[92] Another note from an unnamed staffer reveals a collective desire to manage the GPA's expectations. "The Gay Committee needs to *feel* a part of what [Jackson] is doing to prevent them from *asking* for separate clarification at their rally" (emphases in original).[93] As early as July 16, Jackson and his staff settled on the broad framing of "human rights" as a way to acknowledge residents' right to assemble and organize for gay equality without seeming to explicitly support gay rights. A draft of an unreleased press statement reflects this approach, asserting that any group requesting a mayoral proclamation had the right "to be permitted to live free from the burdens of discrimination based upon age, race, sex, religious or sexual preference and physical handicaps." It framed Jackson's commitments to civil liberties as a key outgrowth of his career as an attorney who "has fought long and hard for human rights and civil liberties," a supporter of the ACLU of Georgia, and a "responsible elected official." Therefore, the statement asserted, he was "absolutely obligated to protect the constitutionally provided rights of *all* Atlantans" (emphasis in original). Jackson declared the week of June 27–July 4, 1977, to be "Civil Liberties Week in Atlanta" and promised to hold a press conference with representatives from organizations like the NAACP, B'nai B'rith Anti-Defamation League, the National Organization for Women, the GPA, the ACLU, Community Relations Commission, SCLC, Georgians for the Equal Rights Amendment, Veterans of Foreign Wars, National Welfare Rights Organization, and environmental groups.[94]

The mayor's office surveyed Atlanta religious leaders in two different venues to ensure that a proclamation recognizing Civil Liberties Week would be uncontroversial. The first survey occurred during a monthly meeting between the mayor and "community religious leaders" in early June.[95] The second occurred through individual solicitations via telephone. Although many religious leaders were unavailable for comment, several offered their support for the Civil Liberties Week proclamation, including Rev. Robert E. Lee of Lutheran Church of the Redeemer, Bob Lupton of Youth for Christ, Father Michael A. Morris of Sacred Heart Catholic Church, and Imam Ibrahim Pasha of Muhammad's Mosque #15. Notably, Harmon Moore of the CCMA, who had supported the CDA one year prior, praised the mayor's effort, stating, "beautiful job." Moore's support was a key victory, signaling the extent to which Jackson had successfully avoided renewed controversy. However, the most surprising supporter was Rev. John D. Sharp of West Hills Presbyterian—the only Black minister publicly working with the CDA the previous summer. According to the notes of a June 23 conversation with a Jackson staff member, Sharp indicated he would "support [the] statement and applaud [it]" because it "covers everyone."[96]

The mayor's declaration of June 25–July 2 as "Civil Liberties Days" elicited support from more conservative segments of metropolitan Atlanta and dismay from gay rights activists. The *Atlanta Constitution* reported that members of Jackson's staff "had been meeting privately with representatives of the gay community to determine if a day recognizing the rights of all groups would be acceptable to the homosexuals."[97] Once the new proclamation was announced, gay and lesbian activists expressed profound disappointment with what they saw as a political retreat. In a front-page *Atlanta Constitution* article on June 22, Linda Regnier of the GPA asserted that although the mayor was "avoiding controversy," "there's no way he can put his foot half in and half out on the issue of civil rights." Vic Host characterized it as the mayor "copping out," stating that the broadly framed civil liberties proclamation "might backfire on him" and draw the disdain of those who supported gay pride and those who opposed it.[98] "The Proclamation," he declared, "was wishy-washy and meaningless." Notably, Vince Eagan, a candidate for mayor running on the Socialist Workers Party platform, also assailed Jackson for his retreat on gay rights. "Mayor Jackson has beat a cowardly retreat on gay rights at a time when gay people are under an attack nation-wide," Eagan argued, casting detractors of last year's proclamation as "the kind of right-wing pressure which supported Anita Bryant's anti-gay crusade in Miami."[99] The CDA and its supporters publicly praised what they saw as a victory rooted in their organizing the previous year. In a press release, the CDA praised Jackson, stating that he "has taken a statesman-like position in defending the rights of the vast majority of Atlanta citizens, in resisting the extreme pressure on him from a small group of militant moral anarchists." Jerry C. Nims, the CDA chairperson, asserted that GPA "harassed" the mayor and sought to malign the character of anti-gay organizers. "They're out to destroy Anita Bryant and her character," he charged.[100]

Eaves also notably shifted his public statements about gay rights and the policing of homosexuality. Even as he indicated support for the decriminalization of sex work, he also suggested that laws targeting "homosexuality, adultery and fornication" needed to be "updated . . . Some should probably be retained and some deleted." Eaves also commented on the hiring of gay men and lesbians for the police force: "My personal preference would be to hire males and females who can do the job and that's it. If being a homosexual would be a handicap it should be considered and if it wouldn't, it shouldn't."[101] These statements mirrored his comments at a panel hosted by the State Bar of Georgia in December the previous year. Appearing on a panel with MCC pastor Jim N. Snow, Eaves discussed then historic tensions between the police department and Atlanta's gay community. Notably, Snow "chided" Eaves about the persistent harassment of gay men at Piedmont Park, stating that "a gay person has the right to go to [the park], meet a person and then go home to their own privacy." Eaves seemed to agree, stating, "I personally believe a person's sexual activity is private and if it does not infringe on another person it should be legalized."[102] The notion of privacy, as Clayton Howard argues, was mobilized by a wide cross section of political and everyday actors to support their particular visions of sexuality and family. This included both political conservatives who sought to blunt the rhetoric of sexual liberalization and some gay men and lesbians who sought to cast same-sex intimacy as a private and personal matter. As Howard notes, such rhetoric not only worked to reinscribe the heteronormativity of the state but also sharpened distinctions between those gay and lesbian Atlantans who might be understood as embodying some normative ways of being and those who could not or would not.[103] Notably, Eaves retreated from his stance on the hiring of gay men and lesbians to the police force the following summer—a mere three weeks after the mayor declined to issue a second Gay Pride Day proclamation. He also asserted that he would reinstate a question about homosexuality that had been removed from the lie detector test administered to police applicants. When asked for his rationale, Eaves cited, "a feeling of 'antagonism' between present officers and homosexuals hired for the force." He stated, "I don't think I need that additional problem. I'm still fighting the feeling against hiring women [and] African Americans."[104] These conservative shifts in policy during the twelve months after the Gay Pride Day proclamation controversy suggests how profoundly the CDA's attacks affected the Jackson administration and municipal governance. Moreover, the looming 1977 mayoral election prompted Jackson and his supporters to curry favor from broad segments of the Atlanta electorate, a move that marginalized gay and lesbian activists at the same time that antigay organizing was intensifying nationwide. The relationship between Black politicians, Black communities, and local gay political organizations continued to be marked by moments of coalition and fracture well into the 1980s.

The "Gaying of Atlanta" in the 1980s

The *Atlanta Constitution* acknowledged the city's growing queer community in a December 12, 1982 subheading that read "from a small group of marchers in 1971, the city's homosexual community has grown to become more visible, diversified, and politically influential." However, such "diversity" did not appear to include race. The prevalence of whiteness in the article—from the identification of queer-friendly neighborhood spaces outside of traditional Black neighborhoods to the seeming whiteness of those pictured in the feature—is striking. Writer Barbara Gervais Street referenced queer people of color just twice: First, in a reference to Black and White Men Together, an organization that supported gay interracial couples and challenged racism and homophobia, and, second, in a quote from Bill

Martin, identified as the Black co-owner of gay periodical the *Metropolitan Gazette*. Martin asserted that "the Blacks who are openly gay live in Midtown. But the majority of Black gays are closet cases. They tend to stay isolated." Martin's reference to "closet cases" implied that Black gay Atlantans hid their sexual orientation in response to homophobia within their communities and, potentially, a lack of self-acceptance.[105] As articulated earlier in this chapter, the implicit racialization of queer space as white and Black spaces as homophobic (and straight) unfolded locally and nationally. In Atlanta, these dynamics were somewhat different, given the scale and vibrancy of Black/multiracial queer community and political organizing. This chapter concludes not with a full accounting of these dynamics but with a brief interrogation of two moments that suggest the ambivalent relationship between conceptualizations of Black, gay/lesbian, and Black gay and lesbian political subjectivities.

The late 1970s and 1980s were a time of active gay and lesbian political organizing in Atlanta. In 1977, the Gay Democratic Club (later known as the First Tuesday Democratic Association) formed to bolster a visible gay and lesbian voting constituency that might exert influence in the municipal governing structure. The organization surveyed candidates about gay rights issues, built relationships with preexisting and new gay and lesbian organizations, and held voter registration drives among other activities. Although the Lesbian and Gay Rights Chapter of the ACLU was first formed in 1981, it built upon more than fifteen years of advocacy by the ACLU of Georgia against the punitive policing of queer Atlantans. The Atlanta Gay Center (AGC) was founded, partially, in response to Anita Bryant's highly publicized attendance at the Southern Baptist Convention, held in Atlanta in June 1978. Originally called the Atlanta Coalition on Human Rights, the center was established in recognition of the need for a "community service center for people who are gay."[106] The AGC acted as a central social service agency, providing "mental and physical health" services, legal services, and other forms of support. In 1980, the Atlanta Business and Professional Guild formed to represent the interests of lesbian and gay businesses and white-collar workers, as well as offer opportunities to network.[107]

In 1979, the Gay Atlanta Minority Association (GAMA) emerged as "a third world socio political organization dedicated to the understanding of gay issues among minorities in Atlanta."[108] GAMA worked closely with a number of other groups, including the First Tuesday Democratic Association and the AGC (where their office was housed). An events calendar for GAMA's second anniversary offers insight into its programming: holding educational workshops at the AGC, attending a concert by R & B songstress Millie Jackson at the Fox Theater, dancing the night away at a night club called the Answer and celebrating Mr. and Miss GAMA at the Celebrity Room.[109] GAMA was one of many Black, Latinx, Native American, and Asian American gay and lesbian organizations that emerged nationwide in the 1970s and 1980s and worked to challenge homophobia within their own communities while also challenging racism and privilege within white gay/lesbian social spaces and organizations.[110] In Los Angeles, the Association of Black Gays challenged the discriminatory entry policies at local gay clubs through boycotts and campaigned on behalf of incarcerated Black gay men.[111] It was local organizing of Black gay and lesbian activists in Washington DC and Baltimore that resulted in the creation of the National Coalition of Black Gays (NCBG, and later the National Coalition of Black Lesbians and Gays). The first national Black gay rights organization, the NCBG centered the concerns of Black queer communities through advocacy, challenging racism in mainstream LGBTQ+ organizations and the publication of *Black/Out*.[112]

Racism within gay and lesbian social as well as political institutions made organizations like GAMA and NCBG especially important. An undated community survey by the Friends for Lesbian and Gay Outreach indicates the pervasiveness of anti-Blackness within some of Atlanta's queer spaces. The questionnaire sought to assess the prevalence of discriminatory practices at gay bars or clubs and the lack of participation of people of color in Atlanta's annual pride march celebrations. The fifty- self-identified Black and white respondents reveal a consistent pattern of discrimination at the city's bars and clubs, including requiring multiple forms of identification from Black patrons, being denied entry, told the establishment was a "private club," and experiencing other forms of hostility. One Black respondent who had recently moved from Washington, DC, noted the prevalence of racism: "In some cases it seems like the 'old south' I've heard so much about. And this is supposed to be 'the New Atlanta.' Sometimes it makes me wonder??!!"[113]

At this time, the Atlanta child murders became a flashpoint for conversations about racism, urban inequality, and sexuality. From July 1979 to May 1981, the disappearance of thirty Black children, teenagers, and young adults—later found to have been murdered—created a municipal crisis that exposed the limited gains for working-class Black communities under the Jackson administration. While law enforcement officials began to understand the disappearances and murders as potentially linked in August 1980, the delay in identifying suspects and the disappearance of an additional sixteen youths deepened mistrust among many Black Atlantans. Despite widespread rumors that the Ku Klux Klan was largely responsible for the murders, narratives about the possibility of sexual violence soon emerged in the media.[114] Given the long-standing equivalencies between homosexuality and pedophilia, it is unsurprising that local and national gay and lesbian organizations felt compelled to respond to media coverage of the unfolding tragedy. From Anita Bryant and the Save Our Children campaign a few years earlier to the growing influence of Jerry Falwell Sr.'s Moral Majority—which characterized gay rights as a threat to the American family—gay rights activists nationwide were especially sensitive to equations between pedophilia and homosexuality. In Atlanta, some gay rights activists issued press releases affirming support for the victims' families and sought to distance the unknown perpetrator(s) from the gay and lesbian community. In an April 8 statement, Frank Scheuren, a member of the Community Relations Commission and president of the local chapter of the Catholic gay affinity group Dignity Inc., challenged the use of "homosexual" to reference the alleged sexual motivations for the murders, asserting that "we are not talking straight or gay sex but demented sex." Scheuren also amplified the efforts of local gay organizations in supporting the families of those slain and missing, including GAMA members who had participated in the "Saturday searches" and the Atlanta Business and Professional Guild's call for its members to wear green ribbons in support.[115]

Beginning on March 16, 1981, the NGTF prepared to respond to the growing speculation that the perpetrator might be gay. Discussions between Scheuren and Charles Hosley of GAMA surfaced the possibility of a fundraising campaign among gay and lesbian communities, presumably to support the families of missing or slain youths and to aid search efforts. Too, the NGTF called for a coordinated press conference in four cities to address the unfolding crisis. NGTF co-executive director Charles F. Brydon secured the participation of several organizations, including the Parents of Gays (which would become PFLAG), three religious organizations (Dignity, Metropolitan Community Church and Integrity, an Episcopalian gay affinity group), as well as the NCBG. In a memo titled "Joint Action on Atlanta Child Murders," Brydon framed the press conference as designed "not to respond to this speculation"—that the perpetrator was gay—but instead to "express the concerns of lesbians, gay men and the parents of gay people to this seemingly unending tragedy." This support continued to be framed as outside of the organization's narrow focus on lesbian and gay issues, as evidenced by the NGTF declining to create a fundraising campaign to support the families of missing and slain children. The memo noted that "fundraising within the gay community for a purpose outside the community is unprecedented" and that there were concerns that many members of the gay and lesbian community would not be supportive.[116] In another undated memo, the NGTF asserted that "all gay people, not just gay parents, have a responsibility in the healthy development of not only their own children but of all children." Stating that everyone had a responsibility to combat the "social and economic conditions" that supposedly rendered working-class Black children vulnerable to violence, the statement asserted, "We must search out ways to take children out of these urban 'pockets of poverty' and provide them with means to develop into healthy, productive adults."

This characterization of Black children as social deviants given their impoverished urban upbringing mirrored popular and academic discourse about urban Black families that extended back to the early twentieth century. In particular, these linkages between poverty, urban ghettoes, and deviancy reflect the continued influence of the 1965 federal report *The Negro Family: The Case for National Action*. Written by Daniel Patrick Moynihan, then an assistant secretary of the Department of Labor, the report called for federal policies to shore up nuclear two-parent households and thereby limit the necessity of public support. In particular, the report articulated concerns about what Moynihan characterized as a "black matriarchy:" namely, that Black women's historical roles as wage earners undermined Black men's role as patriarchs. As Kevin Mumford asserts, the report—and its subsequent reverberations through federal policy circles and Black political discourse—also evinced a concern that Black boys might grow up without ideal male role models and, thus, embrace sexual deviancy, which often included extramarital sex, abandonment of family, and (less often) effeminacy and/or homosexuality.[117] It is notable, then, that the NGTF echoed this rhetoric of pathological Black family formations that might, indeed, reify the connections between urban poverty and queerness. Such characterizations marked local coverage of the abductions and murders. For example, an *Atlanta Constitution* article about slain youth Anthony Hill used sensational language to describe his life: "For Hill, life consisted of a jumbled melange [*sic*] of many interrelated elements: hunger, poverty, neglect, criminal behavior and homosexuality." Asserting that Hill spent one of his last nights alive at a home "where an admitted homosexual lived," the reporting noted that police were considering "the possibility of homosexual activity" as a related factor in his killing.[118] Vague references to "hustling" in some of the press coverage also reinscribed notions of criminality as generational and pathological.[119]

A week later, the NCBG issued a scathing response to the proposed press conference. In their response, Executive Director Billy Jones and board cochairs Gilberto Gerald and Sandra Small recounted conversations within the national organization and with chapter representatives "especially in Atlanta" and "other third world leaders." They noted that "just as fundraising within the lesbian/gay community for a purpose outside the community is unprecedented so is strong support for the struggles of blacks without precedence by mainstream organizations such as NGTF. Coming from a framework of being a one issue movement, we question the motive (and necessity) of seeking publicity for what is indeed a worthy cause—but perhaps for the wrong reason." The reason, the response implied, was not to identify the perpetrators of these murders or support the grieving families and grieving communities. Rather, their response asserted, the NGTF's rationale was primarily about distancing (white) gay and lesbian communities from associations with pedophilia and criminality more broadly. Referencing concerns over antigay backlash stemming from press coverage, the NCBG asserted, "It will be the Black lesbian and gay community that will receive the heaviest backlash." This claim reflected both the continued spatial segregation of Black and white communities (gay and straight) and how homophobic anger over the Atlanta child murders would inevitably target those most closely associated with Black communities—Black queer subjects. However, their response implicitly rejected the increasingly prominent rhetoric that cast communities of color—and especially Black communities—as hyper-homophobic and more likely to assault white gay men and lesbians.

The NCBG leadership also challenged the NGTF and other national gay rights groups to embrace coalitional politics. The missive writers urged "mainstream organizations" to expand their political vision to "actively support all oppressed groups such as women, low income, people of color, youth, physically challenged, etc., " and said that "coalitions and networks must be established not only during periods of crisis, but also during periods of relative peace." This call for coalition building reflected a feminist of color tradition in which recognition of oppressions as interlocking and mutually reinforcing formed a crucial bridge to understanding and shared action. Civil rights activist and Black feminist artist Bernice Johnson Reagon crucially theorized of coalition as challenging: "You don't get a lot of food in coalition. You don't get fed a lot in a coalition you have to give and it is different from your home."[120] This kind of coalitional work was not limited to Black feminists and feminists of color—gay liberationists and lesbian feminists also engaged in coalitional politics during the 1960s and 1970s. However, the separatist and single-issue focus of gay liberalism was on full display, largely fomenting the ability to grapple with the structural oppressions that affected Black and queer communities.

It appears that the NGTF, while sensitive to the NCBG's criticism, doubled down on its commitment to intervene in media coverage of the murders. In a memo to representatives of gay religious affinity groups, Brydon affirmed the NGTF's concern over the murders as "socially concerned citizens," dismissing the NCBG's challenge and stating, "speculation by a few people that we are acting out of some other motive is simply that— speculation."[121] On May 7, the remaining organizations issued a joint statement that not only (a) supported a fundraising and green ribbon campaign to support the families of slain and missing Black youth but also (b) mobilized a comparative framework that linked anti-Black racism with homophobia.[122] In a May 12 press release, the NGTF noted: "As targets of prejudice and discrimination ourselves, gay people recognize the pestilence of bigotry in whatever guise it may present itself. We understand the interrelationship of all human and civil rights issues."[123]

As issues of race emerged within the local and national gay rights landscape, the interrelationship between Black elected officials in Atlanta and local gay and lesbian constituencies persisted, albeit in complicated ways. Mayor Andrew Young, Jackson's successor who served as mayor from 1982 to 1990, adopted a largely distant and conservative approach toward organized gay and lesbian communities. Young, a former civil rights activist and the ambassador to the United Nations under President Jimmy Carter, vacillated between quiet relationship building with gay voters and appeals to more conservative elements of the city's political structure by differentiating gay rights from other civic concerns. During his first two years in office, he publicly negotiated with local gay rights activists over the mayor's role in supporting gay rights. After refusing to sign a petition titled "Lesbian/Gay/Transpersons Pride Day," Young cast himself as a "defender" of the civil rights of all Atlantans rather than an advocate. He noted: "I make a distinction between gay rights and gay pride. I'm a strong advocate of people's human rights, regardless of their racial, religious, ethnic, or sexual orientation. But I tried to explain to them, I was never an advocate of black pride. I mean, I understand it, but I think that's not something that can come from the political situation."[124] Human rights, in Young's formulation, transcend categories of identification. Here, Young identifies "pride" as a shorthand for self-esteem and valuation that, although having potential political impacts, is unrelated to the machinery of governance. This comparison suggests how Blackness continued to be a reference point for gay identification and political orientations. And although Young seemed to assert that he understood himself as a "defender of gays" rather than an "advocate of gays," his framing overlooks how city officials (in Atlanta and elsewhere) had long cultivated a reputation as advocates and representatives for any number of constituencies.[125] Like Jackson before him, Mayor Young experienced pushback to his refusal to recognize gay pride. MCC minister Jimmy Brock noted the mayor's intransigence with disappointment, asserting the importance to "any minority" of official recognition: "We feel that Mayor Young should understand this, given his background in civil rights."[126] Notably, other Atlanta officials formed closer ties with gay and lesbian activists. Perhaps most notable in this regard was John Lewis, who had been a student activist with the Student Nonviolent Coordinating Committee and served as an at-large member of the Atlanta City Council from 1981 to 1986—a period of expansive growth of gay political clout. Rather than keep gay and lesbian voters at arm's length, Lewis built strong relationships, actively campaigning in gay bars around the city. In 1988 the Human Rights Campaign honored Lewis, by then a new congressperson in the US House of Representatives, as a gay rights supporter during its first fundraiser in the southeast. Lewis is quoted as saying that he had "'fought too long and hard against bigotry and racism' to ignore the struggle for gay rights."[127]

The 1989 mayoral election was a crucial moment in which the relationship between the mayor's office and local gay political interests seemed to strengthen and converge. That year, former Mayor Jackson and Fulton County Commissioner Michael Lomax competed to succeed Young. A former college educator and president of Dillard University, Lomax, who was a decade younger than his storied opponent, had previously served as the chair of the Fulton County Commission, which functioned as a de facto legislative body for the county. Both men became the earliest mayoral candidates not only to attend a gay pride celebration (a sign that the event had lost its political toxicity) but also to appoint special political liaisons to conduct targeted outreach to gay voters. However, their campaigns differed in the perceived centrality of gay constituencies within their political coalitions. It became clear that summer that Lomax's outreach to gay political communities was a central aspect of his campaign. He created a multipoint platform that addressed issues like hate crimes legislation; more funding for HIV/AIDS-related services, including housing; and efforts to mitigate antigay discrimination in local governmental agencies. Lomax formed a committee for "Gay and Lesbian Issues" that included individuals from organizations including the Gay March Committee and ACT-UP Atlanta. Crucially, Lomax's campaign seemed to especially recognize the importance of Black gay and lesbian leaders and organizations as key partners. To that end, the campaign planned a fundraiser in March 1989 with "a primary invitation list include [sic] people from the African American lesbian and gay community."[128]

Notably, the late 1980s would mark the emergence of new Black gay and lesbian organizations in the city of Atlanta, including the African American Lesbian and Gay Alliance (AALGA). Founded in 1989 in gay rights organizer Duncan Teague's living room, AALGA became a central space of organizing for gay men and lesbians of African descent.[129] After the passing of cofounder Marquis Walker from an AIDS-related illness, AALGA established an award in his honor to highlight the contribution of Black gay and lesbian community members, like Carolyn Mobley, the first female cochair, a founding member and deacon of First Metropolitan Community Church, and a former board member of the AGC, and allies like Mercedes King, wife of civil rights leader Lonnie King, who lost two sons to AIDS and donated her Bedford Pine neighborhood home as a potential site for the AGC.[130] Notably, Lomax gave the keynote address at this same awards dinner in 1988.[131]

Compared to Lomax, Jackson was slower to recognize and actively court gay and lesbian voters. In an internal memo for the Jackson campaign, two staffers "strongly advised" the former mayor to raise his visibility among this growing cohort of voters. The perception that Jackson was an inconsistent ally was based on his overreliance on his record as mayor (almost eight years prior) and (according to the memo) opponents' efforts to cast Jackson as apathetic to gay voters' concerns. Citing the dramatic growth of gay and lesbian organizations in Atlanta and other mayors' success in building coalitions with gay voters, the memo concluded, "It is important that Maynard be consistent with the community in terms of who he is, how he views the community struggles for parity and how he is going to support the community." Although the report is undated, it seems that Jackson and his campaign representatives subsequently pursued many of the recommendations, including actively addressing key issues, engaging in outreach to local gay and lesbian communities, and attending events (like Gay Pride).[132]

Both campaigns, however, relied on Blackness and the Black freedom struggle as a rhetorical touchstone for understanding the concerns and history of Atlanta's gay and lesbian communities. Jackson's campaign workers used such comparisons in internal memos to remind the candidate of the importance of gay pride, noting "This is the 20th anniversary of Stonewall—the Montgomery Boycott of Gay and Lesbian Rights." In a report titled "Questions Maynard Is Likely to Be Asked," the authors cited allegations that police officers had called representatives of Metropolitan Atlanta Council of Gay and Lesbian Organizations "faggot" and "dyke" as they walked in the annual Martin Luther King Jr. Day parade earlier that year.[133] "What would happen if a white officer openly referred to a black citizen as 'nigger'?" the authors asked. Both references mobilized key aspects of Black political and social life—disparaging violent language and a key moment within the Black freedom struggle—as frames through which to understand the experiences and political histories of gay and lesbian subjects. Advisers in the Lomax campaign used similar rhetorical frames. For example, staffers prepared some notes about a May 25 meeting between the candidate and Legislate Equality for Gays and Lesbians (LEGAL), an affinity group for Democratic voters in Atlanta. The memo read, "Ms. Cathy Woolard [a member of the Atlanta March Committee] has suggested if a question in the Gay and Lesbian community 'bothers' you, please substitute the term 'Black' for Gay and Lesbian and then answer the question accordingly." It concluded that "she would rather hear you say 'I Don't Know,' than 'shoot from the lip' like Maynard Jackson."[134] The suggestion not only indexes a sense that Jackson only said what constituents wanted to hear—and perhaps, at times, seemed inauthentic—but also illustrates a default framing of gay political issues through the lens of Black political concerns.

Perhaps no other issue exemplifies this practice more than Lomax's controversial proposal to extend municipal affirmative action policies to gay- and lesbian-owned businesses. The Minority Business Enterprise Program was a key innovation during Jackson's first mayoral term in which the city would reserve 20 percent of contracts to build the Hartsfield Airport and, later, other municipal projects.[135] This policy offered a crucial platform for Black businesses to initiate successful bids for city contracts and help them overcome structural challenges such as a lack of experience with similar projects, low-quality plans, and limited access to the informal networks of shared knowledge for successful applications. Jackson's tenacity on this issue, according to Stone, "was integral to the reordering of relationships in Atlanta" by increasing opportunities for Black-owned firms to compete and creating incentives for previously white-owned firms to cultivate Black partners so as to be eligible for the program.[136] The initiative also fostered the sort of biracial cooperation that had marked the relationship between city hall and downtown business elites before Jackson's first term.[137] Lomax proposed a daring amendment to this program: granting gay- and lesbian-owned businesses eligibility for the 20 percent of funds set aside for minority-owned firms. The responses were swift and varied. Some segments of local gay and lesbian communities supported the proposal, including Jeffrey Laymon, chairperson of the Metropolitan Atlanta Council of Gay and Lesbian Organizations, who used a minoritarian framework to argue for the proposed amendment. Referencing "women" and "racial minorities," Laymon asserted that gay and lesbian Atlantans were "sort of a different minority because we are not an obvious minority. . . . We can often be an invisible minority." But the proposal drew criticism from some county commissioners and city council members who believed extending minority status to gay and lesbian Atlantans might be "impractical" and may not survive a legal challenge. The head of the Atlanta Business League, a consortium of Black business owners, expressed concerns about adding another category of people to the Minority Business Enterprise Program.[138] Notably, the day after Lomax was publicly quoted as supporting the proposal, he "backpedaled" and stated that he was misquoted about unequivocally extending eligibility to gay and lesbian business owners—instead, he believed that the city should study the prevalence of gay discrimination in city contracting as a part of an ongoing review of discrimination at the municipal level.

Crucially, Lomax's subsequent withdrawal from the mayoral race foreclosed a unique mayoral debate cosponsored by SCLC and LEGAL. Slated for September, the proposed debate was set to feature three panelists asking questions. In his letter to the Lomax campaign, LEGAL member Richard Jones observed that each organization created a list of question categories and "surprisingly they were identical!" These were "Public Safety, Housing and Homelessness, Drugs, Economic Development, and Affirmative Action/Civil Rights."[139] The proposed partnership between the two entities signaled the growing prominence of gay rights organizations and voters within Atlanta politics and the coalitions forming between (at least) some African American and gay rights organizations, creating spaces for dialogue.[140] As we shall see in the next chapter, however, these coalitions did not easily translate into affirmation of Black queer subjects within their ranks or in the communities they served.

However, deepening relationships between gay constituencies and Black mayors created some possibilities for Black gay and lesbian Atlantans to move more fully into public life. Joan Garner, a native of Washington, DC, who relocated to Atlanta, began to work for the Lomax campaign after a friend recruited her. She remembered the challenges of political organizing, including a lack of acceptance in the broader Black community and the political apathy among Black gay men and lesbians. "We would try to organize political LGBT stuff for the Black community. And we get twenty-five people. But then you'd have a party over here at Texas and you'd get five hundred black lesbians out there . . . [and] we weren't out." Yet she remembered how her isolation in largely white gay and lesbian organizations shifted after joining the AALGA. "I felt like I've come home," she remembered. After Lomax's withdrawal from the campaign, Garner went on to work in Jackson's campaign as a liaison to the gay and lesbian community and, ultimately, serve in several governmental posts including to the License Review Board, the cochair of the Public Safety Commission, and as a member of the Fulton County Commission.[141]

The Ambivalence of Black Liberals

With the election of Ronald Reagan in 1980 and the continued ascendancy of social conservatism, supporters of gay and Black civil rights faced emboldened and often overlapping adversaries. Black-gay political coalitions became more visible and potent during the 1980s and 1990s in cities like Chicago and Washington, DC. In Atlanta, as elsewhere, these relationships were marked by affinity and conflict. The revolt against Mayor Jackson's recognition of Gay Pride Day in 1976 is notable not only because it indexes the increasing power of a mobilized religious right but also because it powerfully demonstrates how the emergence of gay rights was connected to fears of criminality and sexual deviance long associated with Black governance. As the 1970s gave way to the 1980s, a framework in which Black racial identity as a political reference point for gay and lesbian voters became more profoundly entrenched in the political landscape. However, the deepening distance between "Black" and "gay" as lived, embodied identities would limit the actions of mainstream Black civil rights organizations, like the SCLC, from being most able to intervene in a deepening health crisis disproportionately affecting Black communities: HIV/AIDS.

6 Saving the RACE

The SCLC/WOMEN and Ambivalent Approaches to HIV/AIDS, 1986–1993

. . . .

On August 13, 1987, the Women's Organizational Movement for Equality Now, the female auxiliary of the Southern Christian Leadership Conference (known as SCLC/WOMEN), convened a luncheon at their annual conference in New Orleans, Louisiana. In many respects, the printed program seem conventional. Printed on a bi-folded piece of salmon-colored paper, the schedule features an opening prayer, welcome message, keynote address, theatrical skit, and closing remarks. However, a photograph in the program indicates that a surprising degree of gravity marked this annual gathering. The image features members of the Everyday Theater Youth Ensemble of Washington, DC, a young adult troupe that performed educational skits for "at-risk youth." A four-piece band appears in the left-hand corner of the photograph, and several individuals lie prostrate in the foreground. However, it is the presence of three figures, arms outstretched, dressed in dark hooded robes, that give the image its most patently menacing quality, invoking a history of lynching and racial terror. Titled "Until Death Do Us Part," the play illustrates how drug abuse and the acquired immunodeficiency syndrome (AIDS) threaten the lives of Black youth. This message dovetailed with the luncheon's theme: "Liberation from the New Lynch Mobs: AIDS, Drugs and Teenage Pregnancy."[1] The SCLC/WOMEN's framing of these three non-normative states—living with AIDS, drug use, and teenage pregnancy—as fundamental threats to the well-being of African Americans reflects an inherent tension within the organization's messaging about AIDS (and the human immunodeficiency virus or HIV). On the one hand, this list can be understood as deviant behaviors that threatened individual and communal wellness. On the other hand, the association of these ailments with racial terror suggests that members of SCLC/WOMEN understood anti-Blackness to be a key factor in their proliferation, with consequences that were corporeal, psychological, and political.

Between 1986 and 1993, SCLC/WOMEN devoted much of their collective energies to challenging the ubiquitous belief that HIV/AIDS was exogenous to Black communities and their concerns. In conferences large and small and through two federally funded educational programs as well as public relations campaigns, the SCLC/WOMEN disseminated basic information about these illnesses and forms of prevention, including safe-sex methods, harm-reduction practices for intravenous (IV) drug users, as well as drug and sexual abstinence. In her foundational work on Black communal responses to HIV/AIDS, Cathy Cohen frames the SCLC/WOMEN as belatedly engaging with AIDS work and articulating a relative conservatism about sexuality and IV drug use that placed them at the rearguard of African American AIDS service providers during the 1980s and early 1990s.[2] She asserts that the SCLC "actively work[ed] to increase awareness and provide services . . . yet cautiously refrain[ed] from redefining AIDS as a political issue that demands the attention and action of those in and outside of African-American communities."[3] According to Cohen, the SCLC embodied typical Black mainstream institutional and political responses to the growing HIV/AIDS crisis; they were "mixed, limited, and often reluctant."[4]

This chapter uses the ascription of the "mixed" nature of the SCLC/WOMEN's AIDS work as a point of departure to argue that a profound ambivalence marked their efforts to educate Black communities about this illness. The SCLC/WOMEN's educational programs, I argue, struggled to shift from a *rhetoric of risk* to a *rhetoric of vulnerability*. A *rhetoric of risk* emphasized individual behaviors (and thus individuals) as the cause of increasing rates of HIV/AIDS in Black communities, largely ignoring structural factors that facilitated disproportionate rates of transmission. Moreover, SCLC/WOMEN's initial focus on women and children living with HIV/AIDS did little to combat the stigmatization of particular behaviors associated with the illness (including IV drug use, same-sex intimacy, and sex work). By contrast, another initiative known as the RACE program endeavored to articulate a *rhetoric of vulnerability* that acknowledged structural factors that enhance vulnerability to HIV/AIDS. Crucially, this program began to directly address the behavioral stigma associated with the disease. Yet the importance of African American churches as key partners impeded the RACE program's ability to address the homophobia at the core of much HIV/AIDS stigma.

In returning to the SCLC/WOMEN's HIV/AIDS programming, I frame this ambivalence as, in part, an outgrowth of five decades of engagement between notions of Blackness and homosexuality in American politics at the core of this book, particularly as this engagement was experienced by Black mainstream liberal political organizations like the SCLC. In recent years, studies of cultural, political, and medical responses to HIV/AIDS in Black communities illuminate a diverse cross-section of responses and mobilizations against this devastating illness.[5] Indeed, varied aspects of the SCLC/WOMEN's activism mirror those Dan Royles identifies in other Black HIV/AIDS organizations: a desire for "culturally competent" programming, collaboration with groups and institutions that were important to Black communities, and a focus on the social determinants of health.[6] I am also interested in considering the SCLC/WOMEN's work within the context of their umbrella organization's support of gay rights, indicating the limits of a civil rights coalitional framework. Thus, this chapter begins with an overview of the SCLC, SCLC/WOMEN, and their entry into HIV/AIDS work. I then shift to analyze their early AIDS work (largely undertaken through conferences and the "Spreading the Word about AIDS" campaign). The chapter concludes with an analysis of the RACE program and its ambivalent articulation.[7]

Contextualizing the SCLC/WOMEN's Entry into AIDS Work

The SCLC's revitalization and expanded political activity created the context for their entry into AIDS work in the mid-1980s. Although largely remembered as the organizational home of Dr. Martin Luther King Jr., a cadre of ministers (including Ralph Abernathy of Montgomery, Alabama, Fred Shuttlesworth of Birmingham, Alabama) and veteran progressive organizers (Ella Baker, Bayard Rustin, and Stanley Levinson) created the SCLC as a coalitional organization that would act as a conduit between Black clerical leadership and grassroots political communities throughout the South. Between its founding in 1957 and the late 1960s, the SCLC participated in prominent mobilizations of the modern civil rights movement, including nonviolent civil disobedience and voter registration drives in Georgia, Alabama, and Florida. Its standing diminished in the late 1960s due to a series of events, including the assassination of Dr. King in 1968 and the perceived failure of the Poor People's Campaign to advocate for antipoverty measures that same year.[8] Moreover, the SCLC experienced heightened internal strife marked by discord, disorganization, and the perception of declining relevance in an increasingly militant Black political landscape.

In the late 1970s, the SCLC reemerged as a respected and active organization—coinciding with a moment of intensified white supremacist organizing and racial retrenchment—and buoyed by the election of Rev. Joseph Lowery as its new president in 1977. The son of a pool hall owner and entrepreneur in Huntsville, Alabama, Lowery developed a righteous indignation over racial injustice after being assaulted by a white police officer. During his inaugural placement as the young pastor of Warren Street Methodist Church in Mobile, Alabama, he joined an interracial coalition to desegregate the city's busing system in 1956—an action that led him to join other ministers and organizers to found the SCLC. He remained active in the organization during the 1960s, eventually relocating to Atlanta in 1968 to assume a leadership position and continue in ministry at Central United Methodist Church (and later Cascade United Methodist Church).[9] His election as SCLC president after Abernathy's departure initiated a series of dramatic organizational changes, including the creation of municipal-based chapters with dues-paying memberships, increased administrative centralization, and aggressive fundraising initiatives.[10] The organization's political scope also broadened, centering a vision of racial justice that championed electoral political empowerment, expanded economic opportunities, freedom from racial terror, and the role of Black American communities as a moral voice in international affairs.[11]

The founding of Women's Organizational Movement for Equality Now (SCLC/WOMEN) in 1979 institutionalized a long history of Black women's activism and leadership within the organization and in the civil rights movement broadly. Women's contributions to the movement's ideologies and organizations had often been marginalized, with female organizers typically functioning as bridge leaders. Belinda Robnett defines bridge leaders as being "able to cross the boundaries between the public life of a movement organization and the private spheres of adherents and potential constituents." Bridge leaders' multifaceted contributions included forming relationships with individual communities, conveying local needs to national leaders (and vice versa), and effectively executing campaigns despite being largely excluded from formal and executive leadership positions. The SCLC's orientation as a Christian entity rooted in Black churches encouraged what historian Barbara Ransby calls "a patriarchal ethos," creating a "man's domain" in which participating Black ministers often articulated traditional and limiting notions about appropriate roles for women—as wives, mothers, and potential sexual partners.[12] Despite these challenges, Black women were essential to the success of the SCLC, in both formal and informal capacities. Longtime radical organizer Ella Baker served as acting executive director after the SCLC's founding. Educator Septima Poinsette Clark brought her transformative citizenship workshops to the organization, serving as its director of education and facilitating the Citizenship Education Program. Carole F. Hoover oversaw SCLC fundraising

efforts but, mirroring the patriarchal logics of the organization, was initially excluded from executive committee membership.[13] Coretta Scott
King kept the organization viable and politically salient during its most
troubled period following her husband's assassination. Black women's
leadership was also crucial at the local level, despite the continued domi-
nance of formal leadership positions by male ministers.[14] More numerous
are the women whose names fail to appear in histories of the organization,
who participated in the citizenship schools, mass mobilizations, and fundraising efforts while Black charismatic ministerial leadership dominated
the headlines.

That the SCLC/WOMEN was created in Evelyn Gibson Lowery's Atlanta
home indicates her central role in the vision and viability of the auxiliary
(see fig. 6.1).[15] Born in 1927 to well-educated middle-class parents in Memphis, Tennessee, Lowery engaged in civil rights activism alongside and
separate from her husband, whom she married in 1948, despite being largely
remembered as a supportive spouse and first lady. However, it was a near-
death experience—when a Klansman's bullet nearly struck her during a
demonstration in Decatur, Alabama—that moved her to form a women's
auxiliary.[16] In an interview about the founding of SCLC/WOMEN in 1979,
Lowery referenced the unrecognized presence of women in the SCLC, asserting, "It was time for the women to come out front."[17] The group prioritized
issues related to Black families, women, and children but also undertook
work in other realms, including "health and wellness, education and international affairs."[18] In the late 1980s and early 1990s the auxiliary members
devoted much of their energy and programming to HIV/AIDS education.

According to Cathy Cohen, two factors delayed the entry of mainstream
Black institutions like the SCLC/WOMEN into AIDS work.[19] First was the
disease's disproportionate association with (white) gay men, which had been
forged in the earliest years of the epidemic. In 1981, a quick succession of
published medical papers suggested the emergence of a new communica-
ble disease among gay men, in which patients suffered from rare conditions
including pneumocystis carinii pneumonia (PCP) and Kaposi's sarcoma
(KS). The increasing number of deaths among gay men from this mysterious illness prompted public health officials to adopt the term "gay-related
immune deficiency," cementing the illnesses' association with homosexuality. By August 1982, the US Centers for Disease Control (CDC) had
shifted the disease's designation to the acquired immunodeficiency syndrome (AIDS) in recognition of the growing number of cases among other
groups: Haitians, IV drug users, and hemophiliacs.[20] Public officials identified

FIGURE 6.1 William Anderson Bridges, "Demonstrations during the Save Our Children March Walk for the Missing and Murdered Children of Atlanta, 1980," *Atlanta Journal-Constitution*, 1980. W. A. Bridges Jr./*Atlanta Journal-Constitution* via Associated Press. Evelyn Lowery is featured third from the left and Rev. Joseph Lowery appears third from the right.

a causative virus—HIV—in 1984, clarifying the possibility of transmission across various demographics.[21] Nevertheless, HIV/AIDS continued to be understood through what Cindy Patton characterizes as a "queer paradigm."[22] This queer paradigm—in which HIV/AIDS continued to be linked with non-normative sexualities and homosexuality in particular—persisted, forming a crucial barrier to widespread political and collective mobilizations to support the growing numbers of individuals living with the virus and syndrome.

While the public face of the epidemic was largely white gay men, the proliferation of HIV/AIDS among communities of color, in part, through intravenous drug use and the sexualized drug economy was a crucial catalyst for action by Black political organizations. The economic blight that characterized many Black and brown urban communities made participation in the drug trade a viable way to be economically self-sufficient and for others to cope with past traumas and present-day adversity. The proliferation of abandoned spaces created opportunities for IV drug users to gather and share needles and other drug paraphernalia. Moreover, with the rise of crack cocaine use, a sexualized drug trade emerged in which sexual acts could be exchanged for money and/or drugs. As Celeste Watkins Hayes notes in her study of women living with HIV/AIDS, injuries of inequality—"big and small wounds to personal, familial and communal well-being"—create compounding vulnerabilities to various kinds of harm.[23] Viewed through this lens, it is less surprising that the epidemic disproportionately impacted those who were most marginal in Black communities: Black queer men, women, and children.

A second factor that delayed the entry of mainstream Black organizations into AIDS work is what Manning Marable characterized as the increasingly hostile political terrain marked by "[Ronald] Reagan, racism and capitalist economic reaction [which] provide the terrain for black struggle."[24] The Reagan administration's policies represented a broader assault on race-conscious policies (like affirmative action) as well as social programs that benefited working-class people of color generally. These policies compounded the effects of structural economic shifts, which profoundly impacted African Americans, including continued deindustrialization, capital flight from industrial centers, and rising unemployment.[25] Pathologizing images of Black communities circulated with increased vigor—the violent Black criminal, the greedy welfare queen—fueling antipathy toward race-conscious policies. Drug use (heroin and later crack cocaine) increased in Black communities, devastating those in the grips of addiction, their families, and communities. The national war on drugs compounded this devastation, with its militarization of local and federal law enforcement agencies, a widening net of social control and surveillance, and growing forms of mass incarceration.[26] However, the growing numbers of Black people "haunted by the risks" of living with and dying from AIDS increasingly alarmed Black elected officials, health-care providers, and mainstream organizations like the SCLC, prompting action.

The SCLC/WOMEN and a Rhetoric of Risk

The specific catalyst for the SCLC/WOMEN's entry into AIDS work in 1986 is unclear. However, there are several likely factors. By 1986, African Americans represented 24 percent of the cumulative reported AIDS cases (6,990 cases).[27] By 1989, African American women (ages fifteen to forty-four) accounted for 57.6 percent of all AIDS cases, while 54.5 percent of all pediatric AIDS cases were among Black children.[28] These numbers may have attracted the attention of SCLC/WOMEN members, given their commitment to promoting wellness for Black women, children, and families. The presence of a large community of Black medical professionals and the CDC's headquarters in Atlanta may have heightened the SCLC/WOMEN's awareness of HIV/AIDS's impact on minority communities.[29] Moreover, the year 1986 witnessed a greater number of Black elected officials, political organizations, and churches expressing concern about the disease.[30] SCLC/WOMEN appear to have been a part of that shift.

SCLC/WOMEN's entry into HIV/AIDS work should be viewed alongside and within a broader matrix of African American HIV/AIDS activism and networks of care. In the late 1980s and 1990s, a cadre of organizations emerged to combat the disease, with varied approaches.[31] Organizations like Blacks Educating Blacks about Sexual Health Issues in Philadelphia and Balm in Gilead in New York City labored within Black neighborhoods and churches to spread knowledge about AIDS and challenge the stigma around homosexuality. Others, like Gay Men of African Descent and the National Task Force on AIDS Prevention, specifically targeted Black gay and bisexual men. To be sure, Black gay men and lesbians formed a vanguard against the epidemic. The conviction that Black communities knew best how to reach those most at risk was commonly held among African American led organizations engaged in AIDS work. "No one," wrote AIDS activist and Detroit gay rights activist Floyd Dunn, "knows our needs better than we do. In a world of self-interests, we cannot rely on others to fight for us without us. Every time we do, we get swept under the rug."[32] For those living with HIV/AIDS, the urgency of the work was corporeal and personal. Rodney McCoy Jr., an HIV health educator, articulated with poetic vibrancy the fear that stalked his work. "Every cough/ every bruise/ has me fingering my neck/ haunted by the risks/ wondering if I will be next."[33]

The SCLC/WOMEN initially prioritized knowledge sharing and awareness in their AIDS work. The group sponsored five regional conferences across the state of Georgia, two national conferences (Atlanta in 1986 and Washington, DC in 1987), and three smaller events on World AIDS Day (held on December 1) over a two-year period. These gatherings brought together medical practitioners, professionals, and SCLC members to learn basic facts about HIV/AIDS (including epidemiology and prevention strategies) and its impact on Black communities. This programming relied heavily on public health officials—like Donald Hopkins, deputy director of the CDC, and Dr. Wayne Greaves, chief of infectious disease at Howard University

Hospital—and gay rights and AIDS activists—like Gil Gerald, director of the National Coalition of Black Lesbians and Gays, and Gil Robison, a gay rights activist and lobbyist for the Atlanta lesbian and gay political organization First Tuesday Democratic Association—to educate conference participants.[34] These conferences established the SCLC as one of the most visible mainstream national Black political organizations to take up HIV/AIDS as a central concern.

The success of these conferences and the availability of federal funding encouraged the SCLC/WOMEN to create the National AIDS Minority Information Education and Training Program (NAMIETP), also called the National AIDS Awareness Program. NAMIETP expanded the auxiliary's HIV/AIDS educational work and established offices in six metropolitan communities with substantive Black populations: the deindustrializing midwestern cities of Detroit, Michigan, Kansas City, Missouri, and Dayton, Ohio; the southern sunbelt cities of Atlanta, Georgia, and Charlotte, North Carolina; and the much smaller Deep South community of Tuscaloosa, Alabama. NAMIETP administrators chose communities with vibrant SCLC and SCLC/WOMEN chapters, which presumably could support the programming.[35] With funding from the CDC, the first campaign—"Spreading the Word about AIDS"—adopted a "community diffusion model" in which administrators identified community needs and "community leaders" who would act as program partners. The NAMIETP defined "community leaders" as "representatives of local businessmen and women, churches, civic and community grassroots organizations along with federal state and local health care agencies," all of which suggests that the organization subscribed to classist conceptualizations of leadership. In each city, NAMIETP administrators engaged in wide-ranging activities, including hosting safe-sex educational parties at public housing facilities and private residences, training "professionals and nonprofessionals" about HIV/AIDS, initiating outreach to IV drug users through the formation of "street teams," and creating "various art forms to education youth about HIV infection and AIDS."[36]

The CDC was the primary funder of the NAMIETP and thus influenced its HIV/AIDS programming. As the CDC increasingly devoted resources to HIV/AIDS prevention, gay and lesbian organizations and institutions were often the first to receive funding and support. However, the growing number of people of color living with HIV/AIDS prompted the CDC to devote increasing resources to Indigenous, Hispanic, Black, and Asian American/Pacific Islander communities, largely funneled through state and local health-care agencies, as well as the United States Conference of Mayors.[37]

As the need to partner with organizations for people of color intensified, the CDC increasingly extended funding to non-health-care organizations like the SCLC/WOMEN. A second phase of funding (1989–1993), which allowed a select number of existing grantees to expand their programming, facilitated the creation of the Reducing AIDS through Community Education (RACE) program.[38]

Whereas outside funding created the NAMIETP, Black women's labor and skill proved essential to its formulation, execution, and maintenance. Although Evelyn Lowery acted as the principal investigator on the CDC grant and had ultimate authority over the program, the SCLC/WOMEN hired Black professional women with experience in social work, public health, and the private sector to oversee daily operations. Brenda Taylor-Hines served as the first national director of the program, which was based in Atlanta. Until her departure in 1989, Taylor supervised staff, oversaw the program's finances, acted as a liaison between the CDC and SCLC leadership, publicized the program, and built relationships with public health officials, educational institutions, public housing communities, and Black civic institutions.[39] Six local site coordinators managed campaigns in their own communities, held HIV/AIDS informational sessions, identified community partners and cultivated relationships with them, oversaw an office with volunteer staff, submitted progress reports to the national leadership, and maintained budgets. Forming community partnerships was the most important part of the site coordinators' responsibilities, as these groups facilitated the NAMIETP's engagements with local communities. Community partners included churches, educational institutions, civic groups, HIV/AIDS organizations, gay and lesbian groups, and public officials.[40] The site coordinators were as diverse as the cities they called home. Recruited by the local SCLC, Tuscaloosa leader Eva Harris Owens worked in the private sector prior to her leadership in the NAMIETP. Margie Shannon brought a decade's worth of drug abuse treatment and social service work in Los Angeles, California, and Montgomery, Alabama, to her position as the site coordinator of the Atlanta program—the most prolific and productive of all of the sites.[41] In Dayton, Ohio, Mississippi native and former civil rights activist Flonzie Brown Wright dedicated her life to AIDS education and other social justice causes. Cheryl Thompson Marsh, a Detroit native, had experience in marketing and merchandising before joining the NAMIETP as the site coordinator in the Motor City.[42] The only exception to the prevalence of Black female leadership was in Charlotte, where both site coordinators were men (Keith Sherrill and Reverend Norman Kerry).

That Black women's labor and skill proved essential to the program's execution not only reflected the NAMIETP's location within the women's auxiliary of the SCLC and a longer history of Black women's leadership with the organization; it also mirrored the development of a growing cohort of Black women committed to AIDS work during the 1980s and early 1990s. This cohort was sustained in part by the increased number of social service agencies dedicated to providing support to people living with HIV/AIDS within Black institutions and in municipalities with large minority populations. A growing number of professional AIDS service providers coexisted with the leaders of independent organizations that sought to support people living with HIV/AIDS. For example, in 1989 Black women's health activist Dázon Dixon Diallo founded Sister Love to support HIV-positive women in Atlanta. New York City resident Pernessa Seele established Harlem Prayer Week as a day of national awareness of HIV/AIDS in Black communities and would later found Balm in Gilead, one of the most prominent Black HIV/AIDS organizations.[43] The entrance of Black women into AIDS work is one manifestation of a Black women's health activism rooted in experiences of enslavement and emerging as a realm of activism in the late nineteenth century. Black women were critical participants, regularly occupying grassroots positions within health organizing, building relationships with patients, and acting as intermediaries between physicians and those seeking care.[44] SCLC/WOMEN site coordinators built on this tradition, connecting public health officials, physicians, and local communities.

The SCLC/WOMEN's initial programming—the "AIDS in the Black Community" conferences and the "Spreading the Word about AIDS" campaign—articulated a *rhetoric of risk*. Here, I use "risk" to refer to "someone or something that creates or suggests a hazard."[45] For the SCLC/WOMEN, the "hazard" was HIV transmission, the "something" was non-normative behaviors understood as heightening individual exposure to the virus, and the "someone" were individuals who engaged in those behaviors. If the source of risk was individualized, the experience of risk, as articulated by the SCLC/WOMEN campaigns, was individual and collective. The organization repeatedly emphasized how HIV/AIDS would impair the health and futures of individuals, while also framing the illness as endangering Black communities and Black political futures as a whole. Two distinct ideologies informed the rhetoric of risk: that of biomedical individualism on the one hand and racial uplift on the other hand. Conceptualized by Elizabeth Fee and Nancy Krieger, biomedical individualism identifies a health paradigm in which people are "'free' to 'choose' health behaviors," placing the primary responsibility of health on individuals and leaving "little place for understanding how behaviors are related to social conditions and constraints or how communities shape individuals' lives."[46] This health framework usually prioritizes the viewpoints of scientists, medical practitioners, and public health experts over the knowledge of patients and their communities, reinforcing a medical perspective that isolates individual health from interpersonal, institutional, and structural factors that inform "health behaviors."[47]

The NAMIETP rooted prevention strategies in a biomedical individualist frame, largely aligning itself with contemporary mainstream public health approaches to HIV prevention. For example, a common list of actions "for Blacks to prevent AIDS" appeared within public-facing materials, including national conference programs and NAMIETP publicity materials. These prevention strategies included appeals to eschew IV drug use, avoid sharing needles or other drug paraphernalia, refrain from having sexual intercourse with IV drug users or individuals "suspected of having AIDS," and engage in monogamous sexual relationships.[48] This biomedical individualist approach supported a key aspect of the "queer paradigm" that continued to inform perceptions of people living with HIV/AIDS—namely, that they were solely responsible for their own health.[49]

The potency of racial uplift narratives also informed the SCLC/WOMEN's rhetoric of risk. A response to the degradations of slavery and white supremacy, racial uplift has dueling connotations. One understanding of uplift encapsulates "personal or collective spiritual transcendence of worldly oppression and misery" and thus "liberationist theology."[50] Another variation, which became increasingly prominent in the late nineteenth century, prioritized self-help, social mobility, and the adoption of elite standards of comportment.[51] While racial uplift as a strategy largely operated in a context of formal barriers to racial equality (like de jure segregation), a related manifestation of its most pernicious facets continued during the post–civil rights era. Cohen's theory of secondary marginalization denotes how minoritarian elites continued to police and discipline community members whose behaviors failed to align with dominant norms. These elites did so within a milieu marked by "a symbolic opening of dominant society" in which some racial minorities are able to achieve economic, political, and social empowerment while the vast majority continue to experience profound marginalization.[52] Such policing, as Cohen notes, harms the collective political strategies long employed by Black communities and enact further harm on its most marginal members. The SCLC's political vision largely embraced the sexual, gender, and economic status quo, seeking inclusion for African Americans rather than radical transformation of existing institutions and social structures.

The concept of "liberation lifestyles" most concretely captures the SCLC/WOMEN's use of the rhetoric of risk during their auxiliary's early AIDS work. Rev. Joseph Lowery created this expression in 1985 to encapsulate the SCLC's conviction that various social behaviors (monogamous sex, refraining from drug use, financial independence, etc.) formed a crucial aspect of African American empowerment. This phrase had a prominent place within the SCLC/WOMEN's AIDS conferences—it appeared in the presidential greeting for the 1987 conference program, where Reverend Lowery identified "liberation lifestyles" as "THE most effective weapon against AIDS" (emphasis original). Calling on African Americans to "put into motion the[ir] historical, unique and creative gifts," the SCLC president warned conference participants to "not fall victim to any assault from without by default (and *our fault*) from within!" (emphasis added). "Liberation lifestyles," he asserted, promised to render Black communities "'free at last' from substance abuse, perverted priorities, sexual promiscuity and other self-destruct[ive] lifestyles." The antidote included "the strengthening of family values . . . and *one-on-one* relationships with commitment" (emphasis added).[53] Rev. Lowery's invocation of "free at last"—a lyric from a spiritual and a prominent quote from Dr. King's "I Have a Dream" speech—aligns non-normative behaviors (including certain sexual intimacies and drug/alcohol use) with interpersonal, institutional, and structural racism that circumscribed Black political, economic, and social life. Less explicit are potential references to same-sex intimacy in the phrases "perverted priorities" and "sexual promiscuity." In the context of the phrase "family values"—a term mobilized by social conservatives to cast heterosexual married couples and biological families as an ideal social formation—Rev. Lowery implicitly positions same-sex intimacies as fundamental threats to Black communal integrity, marginalizing Black queer communities.

If the SCLC/WOMEN's rhetoric of risk clearly vilified a particular set of individual behaviors, marking them as dangerous, their programming adopted a varied approach regarding which constituencies were at risk. In general, the organization centered women, adolescents, and children in its early programming. Evelyn Lowery clearly demarcated which segments of Black communities deserved their attention, writing, "AIDS strikes at the very core of our community—our women and children."[54] The visibility of women and adolescents in the SCLC/WOMEN's programming reflected the auxiliary's commitment to "emphasize women's issues [and] children's needs" as well as the greater visibility of these constituencies within African American mainstream responses to HIV/AIDS in the late 1980s.[55] Crucially, the emphasis on women and children living with AIDS further marginalized Black queer men and gender variant people in communal HIV/AIDS responses, offering an implicit message about which people living with HIV/AIDS deserved care.

If Black women and adolescents emerged *as being at risk*, SCLC/WOMEN rhetoric also positioned these same groups *as being risks*, to themselves and others, mirroring the racial uplift rhetoric that historically identified Black women and girls as particularly vulnerable to certain kinds of moral corruption and, thus, deserving of heightened intraracial surveillance and policing. During the late nineteenth and early twentieth centuries, African Americans in political and social institutions believed Black women played a crucial role in the empowerment of the race, a view that was largely rooted in assumptions about sexuality, reproduction, and child-rearing. Notions of racial futurity often centered children and adolescents as well, prompting greater concern over their behavior and well-being during the late nineteenth and early twentieth centuries.[56] These legacies are evident in the bifurcated manner in which the SCLC/WOMEN's programming framed how these groups experienced risk.

A NAMIETP flyer dramatically illustrates the rhetoric of risk. On the black-and-white flyer, a photograph with an ebullient infant wearing a diaper and smiling into the camera contrasts with the prominently displayed header: "He Has His Daddy's Smile and His Mother's AIDS." Smaller text warns about the possible transmission of HIV from mothers to their infants, although it does not specify breastfeeding or childbirth as the source of infection. Subsequent text identifies IV drug use as the central vector of risk and issues a series of stern commands: "Don't use DRUGS! If you are an intravenous drug user don't share needles! Don't have sex with an IV drug user and if you do for goodness sakes, try to protect yourself by using a CONDOM! . . . Don't share a bed with someone who shares a needle!"[57] It concludes by informing the viewer that "54% of the women and children in the U.S.A. who have AIDS are BLACK!!!"[58] This terse communication reflects the proscriptive mentality at the heart of the rhetoric of risk. Within its biomedical individualist frame of health behavior, the flyer does little to address the structural factors that might contribute to intravenous drug use and/or unprotected sex. It assumes relatively easy access to condoms and ignores barriers to condom use (e.g., a lack of knowledge about appropriate application or resistance from partners). Even without depicting Black mothers, the flyer positions them as primarily responsible for preventing HIV/AIDS transmission to their children. Finally, the centering of heterosexual intimacies that result in reproduction erases other constituencies living with and dying from HIV/AIDS.

The rhetoric of risk also appeared in the SCLC/WOMEN's chief outreach strategy to adolescents: a theatrical production titled *Choices: The AIDS Play*. Written for SCLC/WOMEN by Margo Williams-Moorer and Ralph Williams, the play mirrored the 1987 convention/luncheon performance in its messaging (of AIDS as a fatal condition) and its Black teenage protagonists. *Atlanta Journal-Constitution* staff writer Henrietta Spearman recounts the inaugural staging of *Choices: The AIDS Play* as performed by local Atlanta high school students in the winter of 1989. The protagonist is a high school basketball star, Carl Robertson, who dies from an AIDS-related illness (and who acquired HIV after a one-time experimentation with drugs).[59] The plot recounts the journey of his resurrected spirit from the grave to his high school, where he witnesses the consequences of his passing: the grief and shock of classmates at a memorial service, the misconceptions about AIDS, the revelation that he has exposed his girlfriend to the virus. The central message is that a momentary decision could lead to HIV/AIDS, and multiple dire consequences: illness and death, communal mourning, and the possibility of transmitting the virus to others. Performed gratis for one year across metropolitan Atlanta, the play rearticulated the SCLC/WOMEN's emphasis on individualized risk and the need for both community care and policing. By rooting Carl's illness in a one-off use of IV drugs and positioning him implicitly as heterosexual, the play fundamentally erases other groups as vulnerable (including populations who engage in habitual drug use /or same-sex intimacy).[60]

Notably, the play's program moves beyond the plot to demonstrate the potential material costs of an HIV/AIDS diagnosis through the biographical profiles of the adolescent actors. Each actor's biography narrates their accomplishments to date, their career aspirations, and their thoughts about the dangers of HIV/AIDS. Dan, who portrayed Carl and hoped to become an engineer, asserted, "One day AIDS as well as other obstacles attempting to destroy our advancement will be conquered." Kamaria, whose dreams of being an actress spurred her decision to tour Europe that summer with an acting troupe, said, "AIDS will crumble all of your dreams to dust." Aspiring cardiologist or biochemist Bianca warned that the "threat of AIDS has increased dramatically and will inevitably destroy the teenage population if we do not make a choice to avoid its 'harmful grasp.'"[61] By highlighting the individual utterances of these young Black Atlantans, the program reinforced the consequences of HIV/AIDS to individual actors' futures and those of Black communities more broadly. Although the individualist rhetoric around HIV/AIDS prevention never fully dissipated, in 1990 the NAMIETP's expanded programming marked a shift in the organization's rhetoric of HIV/AIDS, rooted in a collective and inclusive understanding of community.

Maurice O'Brian Franklin, the RACE Program, and a Rhetoric of Vulnerability

Launched in 1990, the RACE program reflected continuity and change from earlier educational programming. Although it maintained the same municipal sites, funding source (the CDC), organizational structure, mission, and operating features as its predecessor there were some key differences. Notably, the RACE program relied more heavily on feedback from public health experts during its conceptualization. The NAMIETP hired Dr. Stephen A. Thomas, an assistant professor of public health at the University of Maryland–College Park, as a consultant for the new program, seeking his expertise in AIDS education and drug/alcohol abuse.[62] Another crucial shift was the prioritization of Black religious institutions as community partners. The turn to faith communities (and churches in particular) as primary community partners is unsurprising given their long-standing centrality within Black communities and the SCLC's orientation as a Black ministerial organization. NAMIETP sought partnerships with religious communities such as the Nation of Islam, the American Muslim Mission, the Church of God in Christ, and the Union of Black Episcopalians.[63] Despite the diverse orientation of the targeted denominations, Baptist and Church of God in Christ congregations most often participated in the RACE program— perhaps reflecting the importance of preexisting relationships between the SCLC and SCLC/WOMEN chapters and these congregations.

Another programmatic shift endeavored to democratize the dissemination of HIV/AIDS information. A newly adopted "training of trainers model" certified workshop participants to hold informational sessions independent of the SCLC or SCLC/WOMEN. Workshop components included an overview of basic HIV/AIDS information, a video presentation from Reverend Lowery titled "AIDS in the Black Community," a glossary of HIV/AIDS terminology, a list of local HIV/AIDS service organizations, and a module titled "Homosexuality and the Church."[64] Site coordinators also administered a Knowledge, Attitudes, Beliefs, and Behavior (KABB) survey, that "assess[ed] knowledge, attitudes, and behaviors as they relate to HIV infection" and quantified the program's impact on an individual basis. Targeting two broad groups defined as "professionals" and "nonprofessionals," the survey featured a pre- and postworkshop assessment that allowed the NAMIETP to measure how much information attendees retained after each session. Administrators gauged the workshop's impact by the number of participants and the KABB survey responses, in part to comply with the need to provide quarterly reports to the CDC.[65]

Arguably the most consequential change was the hiring of Maurice O'Brian Franklin as the RACE program's national coordinator. Raised in a close and affirming family in Paul's Valley, Oklahoma, Franklin told me during an oral history interview that he identified that he was "different" at a young age. When he was a college student at the University of Oklahoma in the early 1980s, his exposure to vibrant gay social circles, emerging political organizing on campus, and a growing awareness of the AIDS crisis shaped his self-identification. "I was still dealing with the whole stigma of being black and homosexual," Franklin remembered. "I wanted to affirm both, but how do you do that at that time period?" He did so through a practice of care, saying "I had to love me first and I was not going to allow anybody to deny who I am."[66] After graduating from college, he enlisted in the U.S. Navy, serving as a medical service officer at the Naval Hospital at Portsmouth, Virginia. Despite the intensified policing of gay men, lesbians, and transgender service members under the Reagan-era military, queer community was readily available. "All of the nurses, male and female, . . . were gay or lesbian," he remembered. "It just seemed that being gay in the military at the time just wasn't a big deal." During his time off, Franklin socialized in various gay clubs in Norfolk—"an act of liberation or defiance," he remembered, given the vigilance of civilian and military police. These affirming spaces coexisted with the daily suffering of hospitalized service members—many of them Black and Latinx men—dying from AIDS-related illnesses. "I met many Black gay and Latino men during that experience," he remembered, "that I befriended because I wanted to do at that time what I could to save their lives." Franklin's care took the form of caring for those who were largely shut away in a ward, left to "deteriorate," left to die. He also culled together "whatever information was coming out of San Francisco" to spread awareness about AIDS to various communities: gay service members, his colleagues at the Naval Hospital, and parishioners in Norfolk's African American churches. His commitment to HIV/AIDS work persisted, leading to work with the American Red Cross and the National Education Association during the next two years. He then successfully applied for the position leading the SCLC/WOMEN's AIDS program.[67]

Under Franklin's guidance, the RACE program inaugurated a shift in the SCLC/WOMEN's rhetoric from individualized risk centered on particular constituencies (women, children, adolescents) to a framework of vulnerability that was collective and conscious of structural causes (or a *rhetoric of vulnerability*). The RACE program increasingly highlighted socioeconomic factors as a key driver of the disproportionate rates of HIV/AIDS in Black communities, including barriers to education, lower income, and "limited community health resources among disadvantaged Black populations." In a CDC grant application, SCLC/WOMEN declared, "only interventions that recognize these socioeconomic barriers have any chance of success in these communities."[68] This identification of structural forces shaping the spread of HIV/AIDS reflects a partial shift in understanding prevention from individual choices to what critical Adam Geary calls "state intimacies." "State intimacies" refers to a set of conditions (often perpetuated/maintained by the state) that enhance a particular demographic's structural vulnerability to HIV/AIDS—including poverty that heightens weakened immune systems and poor health, social/dating networks structured by residential segregation, mass incarceration, and so forth.[69] Many Black Americans found themselves not at the margins of the crisis but rather in an enmeshed web of conditions that structured their and their loved ones' enhanced vulnerability. Thus, while continuing to offer mainstream behavioral forms of prevention, the RACE program increasingly recognized and referenced structurally induced vulnerability in its public rhetoric.

This framing of racialized vulnerability undergirds the explicit turn to Black nationalist rhetoric and imagery in the RACE program. Indeed, even the acronym positions the program as one that explicitly sought to politically empower Black communities. Explicit invocations of racial solidarity are most evident in the organization's ephemera and publicity, which characterize HIV/AIDS as a racial political concern. One prominent brochure cover depicts a phalanx of figures in Black nationalist colors, the SCLC seal that includes Dr. Martin Luther King Jr.'s visage, and a drawing of Rev. Lowery's face, frozen in mid-exhortation. The text articulates the collective effects of HIV/AIDS on Black communities, stating, "The African American Community is currently being beat up by AIDS. . . . We need your help to stop [it]." Large print grabs the attention of the reader and, again, centers HIV/AIDS as a communal concern: "Sad but true our community is being ruined by disease and despair," "Black People Get AIDS Too," "AIDS Does Not Discriminate," and "Save the Race!" Inside, the trifold pamphlet is littered with facts and resources: the percentage of Black Americans living with AIDS, information about the RACE program, and the telephone number of an AIDS information hotline.[70]

The striking use of brightly colored human figures in the programming materials illustrates the turn toward this rhetoric of vulnerability and an ethic of care. There are large and small red, black, and green silhouettes, suggesting a range of gender expressions, adults, and minors. Their forward motion in a column seems to reference histories of mobility and collective struggle—an escape from bondage, a journey of migration, the advance of demonstrators in civil disobedience. This collectivity is countered by an isolated red figure—perhaps read as masculine—who is doubled over, as if weighed down by some burden: the stigma of illness, the debilitating nature of a compromised immune system? A cluster of figures in black and green seem to depict what might be interpreted as a nuclear heterosexual Black family unit—with a mother, father, and two children. A Black mother and child-like figure appear to disintegrate as they follow the father and the other child, depicted in green. Even the SCLC/WOMEN's placement of figures communicates important information about their understanding of collectivity. The position of what might be a nuclear family at the forefront signals the imagined importance of the heterosexual nuclear family in the forward political movement of Black communities while also suggesting their vulnerability. The next two figures (the falling red masculine figure and a green feminine figure with outstretched arms) convey the centrality of gendered care for those suffering with HIV/AIDS, while perhaps also acknowledging how Black men experienced disproportionate rates of HIV/AIDS.[71]

Although the RACE program initially sought to counteract persistent communal apathy about HIV/AIDS, it did not extend that intervention to the homophobia at the core of HIV/AIDS stigmatization until it partnered primarily with Black churches. Many church leaders and laity alike embraced a vision of "liberation" akin to that espoused by Reverend Lowery— one that sought freedom from racial oppression while failing to interrogate intracommunal sexual and gender oppression. This resistance was rooted (in part) in the prevalence of Christian scriptural interpretation that cast homosexuality as—to quote the site coordinators—"not acceptable."[72] The existence of homophobia within some Black religious institutions has been well documented. In addition to prohibitive statements issued from pulpits, queer congregants have (to varying degrees) been actively policed or tolerated in exchange for their silence. Not all Black churches and religious institutions articulated homophobic views. Indeed, congregations and ministerial leadership alike have had contradictory and complex relationships to sex, sexuality, and gender. However, many ministers participating in the RACE program objected to any educational programs that might be perceived as condoning extramarital sex (of any kind, but same-sex sex in particular). In a 1990 survey, ministers expressed alarm that the "church's primary message of abstinence and monogamy" might get lost within the RACE training session.[73] More broadly, congregants believed that some forms of transmission (like infection through blood transfusion) were more tolerable than others (certain sexual behavior and drug use). Some went even further in their judgmental assessments, claiming that queer men diagnosed with HIV/AIDS were "getting what they deserve." Not surprisingly, this type of hostility and fear prevented some churches from joining RACE networks. In Tuscaloosa, for example, inaugural site coordinator Nikki Oakes-Freeman lamented the apathy and hostility of some local ministers to HIV/AIDS during the spring of 1990. She put it bluntly: "Black Ministers don't give a durn about AIDS." Oakes-Freeman elaborated that many ministers she encountered were afraid of being labeled "the AIDS preacher" and were "wary of being associated with the disease because it can be transmitted sexually and has been associated with homosexuals."[74]

RACE program staff and collaborators increasingly identified the need to challenge sexual stigma and homophobia to achieve their aims. In a 1990 survey, local administrators "suggested the church has a responsibility to deal with the phobia around sexuality and homosexuality specifically, and that the church must not be judgmental towards homosexuals."[75] It was Franklin, however, who most directly and powerfully articulated a vision of HIV/AIDS activism that was intersectional and transgressive. He drew on his years of AIDS educational work and his deep involvement in emerging national and regional Black gay organizations, including Black and White Men Together, the African American Lesbian and Gay Alliance (AALGA), and Gay Men of African Descent.[76] He actively sought partnerships with gay-affirming HIV/AIDS organizations like the National Association of Black and White Men Together's National Task Force on AIDS Prevention. As Brett Stockdill notes in his study of AIDS activism, Franklin mirrored other AIDS activists of color in his commitment to working within organizations of color to challenge both homophobia and the general silence around HIV/AIDS.[77]

Franklin's contribution to policy development and his public rhetoric was transformative but short-lived. He crafted a module within the RACE program that explicitly addressed homosexuality and homophobia. Collaborating with Reverend Mariah McFadden of Mariah Walker AME Church in Kansas City, Missouri, Franklin adopted her workshop titled "Homosexuality and the Church." Although there is evidence this module was implemented in Kansas City and Dayton, it is unclear if it became a required part of all trainings.[78] The module's content reflected the public-facing message of Christian compassion toward all people and drew upon scripture for inspiration to overcome fear. The impact of this module seems mixed. Some participants claimed it was the most important component of the RACE program workshop. Another participant asserted that they were "convinced that AIDS is no longer a homosexual disease" but that "the [site coordinator] speaker made the inference that AIDS is a punishment."[79] This final comment suggests how local implementation could dramatically shape and potentially undermine the transformative potential of these programmatic interventions.

Franklin's public rhetoric consistently linked racism and homophobia, framing both as antithetical to the NAMIETP. A 1991 address in New Orleans best exemplifies Franklin's ideological commitment to intersectional activism. In this speech, he challenged the assertions that same-sex intimacies constituted a departure from "normal" and "natural" behavior and represented the influence of white values and the emasculation of Black men. "The truth about the entire sexual spectrum is [that it is] as much a Black thing as it is anybody else's thing," He declared. "There is no honor in fighting racism while embracing sexism. There is no honor in fighting sexism while embracing homophobia. . . . . Justice can no longer mean just us for far too much of our potential as a group has been left behind."[80] Here, Franklin uses the notion of linked fate, not to homogenize or flatten difference but rather to facilitate recognition, respect, and coalition across differences within Black communities.

NAMIETP collaborators included other prominent individuals who publicly assailed homophobia in Black churches and communities. For example, the three keynote speakers at the SCLC/WOMEN AIDS conference in 1991 represented the vanguard of Black ministerial leadership on affirming gay congregants and challenging sexual stigma within Black communities. Willie T. Barrow, pastor of the Vernon Park Church of God in Chicago, Illinois, Cecil Williams, pastor of the Glide Memorial Church in San Francisco, and Bishop Leotine Kelly, the first Black women to be elected as a bishop in the United Methodist Church, all assailed the homophobia apparent in some Black ministers' sermons along with their apathy toward AIDS.

Kelly asserted, "There's a theology developing that AIDS is God's curse on a certain group of people. I don't think AIDS is the will of God. The answer to AIDS is the will of God."[81] That the conference featured these three individuals suggests the degree to which—at least at the national level—there was a concerted effort to partner with ministers interested in challenging homophobia as well as the proliferation of HIV/AIDS. In addition, the content and tenor of the 1991 conference suggests how far the SCLC/WOMEN had strayed from emphasizing women and children in their rhetoric. The efforts of Franklin and his collaborators reflected a vibrant national movement of straight and queer activists, artists, and clerics who challenged homophobia and the marginalization of queer voices and bodies within Black religious institutions during the 1980s and 1990s. For example, Detroit lesbian activist and minister Renee McCoy asserted that many Black queer folk felt "exiled to the wilderness" because "the church thinks we have the wrong lifestyles." She called on Black churches to "heed the call of a God of pure love and reach out and heal and liberate all people."[82] Ministers like James Tinney of Washington, DC and Carl Bean of Los Angeles created congregations and organizations that were explicitly queer affirming and attentive to the cultural importance of Black religious liturgies and practices. These and other spiritual leaders sought to create oases of affirmation and support in the midst of anti-queer sentiments in some houses of worship.

The SCLC articulated its own ambivalent sentiments on gay rights. Publicly and privately, leadership within the SCLC and WOMEN identified with and supported the political struggles of lesbian and gay communities and yet limited such intervention in the very heart of Black communities. As we have seen in chapter 5, the SCLC supported Mayor Maynard Jackson's recognition of Gay Pride Day in 1976. Such efforts continued into the 1980s and 1990s. In the spring of 1991, the *SCLC National Magazine* featured an article about the rise of homophobic violence and vitriol from far-right groups. Reported by the Center for Democratic Renewal (a coalition of civil rights organizations devoted to exposing white supremacists groups), the article drew crucial connections between antigay and anti-Black sentiment among far right organizations.[83] More substantively, in 1992, the SCLC joined with other civil rights groups at a press conference in front of Dr. King's tomb in Atlanta to contest President Bill Clinton's proposed "Don't Ask, Don't Tell, Don't Pursue" policy that sought to reduce the regular purges of gay and lesbian military service members that had been commonplace since World War II. Touted as a reform, this policy allowed gay and lesbian Americans to serve in the armed forces as long as they did not disclose their sexual orientation. Linking the SCLC's support for the equal treatment for gays and lesbians to the Black freedom struggle, Rev. Lowery asserted that "it would be ridiculously and drastically inconsistent for us to support the denial of lesbians and gays to equal opportunity and equal access to serve their country in the military."[84] Local SCLC chapters also seemed to support Black gay organizers. The SCLC chapter of Greater Los Angeles honored Carl Bean, the founder and bishop of Unity Fellowship Church. Spokesperson Kevin C. Spears viewed the recognition of Bean and his work as sending a message to Black churches: "For the SCLC—which is one of the traditional black civil rights organizations—to recognize the work of the Unity Fellowship Church is saying the . . . African American church needs to recognize there are persons in our community that represent alternative lifestyles. We have to move forward."[85] There is evidence that Evelyn and Joseph Lowery believed that homophobia had no place in progressive political organizing. As Franklin asserted in a private letter, "Dr. Lowery and Mrs. Lowery have been very outspoken about the acceptance and the unveiling of homosexuality within the community of conscience."[86] Given the Lowerys' importance to the vision of both the SCLC and WOMEN, their views may have facilitated the increasing number of collaborations between gay-affirming HIV/AIDS groups and SCLC AIDS programing.

Ultimately, Franklin found the SCLC to be hostile to the concerns of Black queer communities. Despite his formal leadership role and successes, he felt increasingly isolated and unsatisfied within the SCLC/WOMEN. "I felt isolated because I felt like the part of the work I was doing wasn't doing [anything] for the community that was impacted the most," he remembered.[87] This combined with "rumblings . . . around the issue of sexual orientation" set the stage for a confrontation. In 1991, Duncan Teague, a founding member of the AALGA, asked Franklin for help writing a grant to support their HIV/AIDS work among men who have sex with men. Teague's proposed Chiwara Project sought to "empower the community leaders to facilitate prevention education presentations that assist men who have sex with men."[88] Such outreach efforts proved profoundly important given the dearth of resources in Black gay and lesbian communities. "I was in a lot of different places trying to do as much [as] I can to impact our entire community," Franklin remarked. "We needed a strong black gay community" to slow the spread of HIV/AIDS in particular. Creating a program that provided "systematic and culturally appropriate HIV/AIDS awareness" emanating from an "openly visible African American lesbian or gay organization" would have far-reaching implications on the ability to transmit safe-sex messages to Black men who have sex with men. Organizationally, the Chiwara Project adopted a workshop model with ten participants each. Word of mouth and publicity through Black gay bars was a key component of the program's plan for success. Moreover, the grant articulated the importance of partnering with Black lesbian organizations, which "interrelate with the target population and have profound influence on their lives."[89]

When Franklin asked if the SCLC/WOMEN might cowrite the grant with the AALGA, Evelyn Lowery issued a firm no. "We don't do that kind of work," Franklin remembered her saying. He was enraged by her callousness. "I wrote that grant because to me that was the community that was hit the hardest, and if I couldn't do this for my own community, then what the fuck am I doing?"[90] Upon discovering Franklin's disobedience, Lowery chastised the national director. In response, Franklin wrote a scathing letter in which he characterized Lowery as unavailable, self-serving, and fundamentally homophobic. "As an African American gay male who is living in the age of HIV infection, I am stunned at your insensitivity toward the needs of individuals like myself who have no benefit in this city of any HIV/AIDS prevention drives being direct[ed] at our community," he wrote.[91] His letter reflected two key characteristics of late-twentieth century gay political organizing: the deliberate linking of present day mobilizations to a longer freedoms struggle (invoking the beloved community of King and Reverend Lowery), and looking back to the Harlem Renaissance for antecedents and ancestors. Quoting Harlem Renaissance poet Langston Hughes's "I Too Sing America" created a profound genealogy of anti-racist and anti-heterosexist articulation. His stinging conclusion, "justice can no longer mean just us within SCLC/ WOMEN," was a profound indictment of how homophobia and certainly heterosexism circulated with the organization.[92] NAMIETP and the churches it partnered with embraced a limiting and exclusionary vision of who should be included in conversations about health and communal wellness.

Yet the very implementation of the RACE program through churches may have created opportunities to subvert and challenge sexual stigma as well as promote AIDS awareness to Black queer communities. Queer bodies, gender expressions, and sexualities have always been a (in)visible part of Black religious institutions. Churches have been sites of liberation and policing, affirmation and aspersions, tolerance and derision. The experiences of Black queer folk in these spaces is, of course, not a uniform story. The nature of ecstatic worship and singing in many churches make them sites of contradiction and complexity with regard to sexuality and eroticism. C. Riley Snorton identifies this ambiguity noting, "feminine and queer aesthetics . . . serve as a predominant mode of articulation and expression of black determination" within these spaces, even as they are disavowed.[93] More pointedly, E. Patrick Johnson asserts, "the black church has always been a site of contradictions where sexuality is concerned. In fact, one might argue that the body is one organizing site of multiple and competing signifiers within the black church service."[94] In addition to the potential eroticism of Black churches, surreptitious knowledge about taboo sexual behaviors might actually be transmitted through public and private conversations in this space. The cultural uses of the church by queer Black folk have been legion; Johnson, for instance, has documented how Black queer men transfer church music and forms of bodily movement to gay clubs to collapse neat distinctions between the secular and the sacred.[95] Identifying this legacy of Black religious spaces as places of subversion and transgression, then, is crucial when considering the degree to which the vital information shared by the SCLC/WOMEN's programming circulated among diverse constituencies that experienced vulnerability to HIV/AIDS.

The Consequences of Black Liberal Ambivalence

Although it is possible that Black queer persons received important health information from the NAMIETP and SCLC/WOMEN, their inconsistency in addressing the (homo)sexual stigma of HIV/AIDS undermined their efforts. By the mid-1990s, the SCLC/WOMEN and SCLC largely abandoned HIV/AIDS work, turning their attention to other forms of programming. Franklin ultimately left the organization to work in the growing national organizations that sought to center Black gay and lesbian concerns. However, the SCLC/WOMEN's foray into AIDS education reveals the level of contradiction and complexity with which Black liberal political organizations encountered politicized ideas about homosexuality. As we have seen, Black liberals have adopted varied and ambivalent strategies that included continued investments in heteropatriarchal ideals about sex, gender, sexuality, and kinship rooted in decades-long understandings of demonstrating fitness for citizenship and challenging some of those same ideals (at times through coalitions with gay and lesbian political communities). The SCLC/WOMEN's ambivalent responses to the AIDS crisis exposes the limited efficacy of heteronormativity within Black communities as a political strategy as well as its continued stronghold as a path for empowerment. It also reveals the possibility of contradiction within Black liberal organizations—that they might espouse support for LGBTQ+ rights while abandoning the very efforts that might advance such equity within their organizations and broader communities.

Epilogue

• •

This book ends not with a rumination on the past but rather, a brief engagement with two events that index the moment of this book's completion, the present. The first is a 2022 Pew Research Center study titled "Race Is Central to Identity for Black Americans and Affects How They Connect with Each Other," and the second is the domestic politics surrounding the detention of US Olympian and professional athlete Brittney Griner in 2022. I begin with two moments of violence—epistemological and material, collective and individual—because they gesture toward one of the central implications this book endeavors to trace: that the long-standing ambivalent relationship between Black and gay political categories/identities conspires to compound the structural vulnerabilities to harm that affect Black queer subjects.

The Pew Research Center survey measured the degree to which Black Americans articulate the importance of their racial identity to their sense of self and the degree of "connectedness" to other people of African descent.[1] Conducted in the fall of 2021 as an online survey of "3,912 Black US adults," the study's major finding was that 76 percent of respondents believed that their race "is extremely or very important to how they think about themselves." Moreover, 52 percent of respondents stated that "everything or most things that happen to Black people in the United States affect what happens in their own lives."[2] However, the study revealed key fault lines of division and forms of disconnection among Black Americans based on regional location, class, educational level, ethnicity, and sexual/gender identity. It is in this last realm that a sense of disconnectedness emerges. An overwhelming majority of respondents (60 percent) believe that "they have few things or nothing in common with LGBTQ Black people." Only 14 percent of those surveyed believed they had "everything or most things in common with Black people who identify as lesbian, gay, bisexual, transgender or queer." While the number of respondents vary across generations, the proportional distributions remain fairly consistent. Among respondents over the age of sixty-five, 10 percent said they had some or most things in common. Those aged fifty to sixty-four had fairly similar numbers.[3] The distribution among younger generations is striking. The next age group (thirty to forty-nine years of age) echoes the lack of connection with 54 percent stating they had "few things/nothing" in common with Black LGBTQ+ Americans, 27 percent had "some things" in common, and 14 percent had "everything/most things" in common. The numbers for those aged 18–29 are similar: 54 percent stated they had "few things/nothing in common," 24 percent had "some things" in common, and 21 percent had "everything/most things." Polls and numbers can obscure as much as they reveal, flattening complicated realities and quotidian experience. The data does not interrogate the varied experiences of Black LGBTQ+ folks who labor, worship, and live within the same institutions, neighborhoods, and collectivities as other people of African descent. The data does not interrogate bonds and kinship ties that elide simple designations like "affirmation," "tolerance," "denigration," and "marginalization." And yet the poll is suggestive of how non-normative genders and sexualities continue to function as a marker of differentiation within politicized concepts of Black racial identity. What are we to make of these numbers at a time in which Black LGBTQ+ visibility in the media, politics, and popular culture is at an all-time high? What are we to make of these numbers in the aftermath of the movement for marriage equality, which gained support from the vast majority of mainstream Black political figures and organizations? What are we to make of these numbers when the organizers of the Movement for Black Lives—many of whom articulate a Black queer feminist lens and also identify as queer, non-binary, and/or trans—are forming a powerful vanguard against state and interpersonal violence?

The second moment is the detention and ultimate release of Brittney Griner, an Olympian, professional basketball player, and Black gender-nonconforming lesbian. On February 17, 2022, Russian authorities detained Griner at Moscow's Sheremetyevo Airport for allegedly carrying a vaporizer with hashish oil, an illegal substance. She was subsequently charged and convicted of cannabis possession and sentenced to a nine-year prison term.[4] Griner was not unknown in Russia. In fact, she visited the country several times since the mid-2010s with other Women's National Basketball Association (WNBA) players to play in the Russian Women's Basketball Premier League. She and others did so to supplement their low salaries. As of 2019, the base WNBA salary was $120,600 compared to the $5.4 million for male players in the National Basketball Association (NBA), laying bare the stark pay inequities between the sibling leagues.[5] Although Griner's salary is higher—$227,000 per year—it is still dramatically smaller than her marquee counterparts in the NBA.[6] A week after her detainment, Griner's plight became widely known as Russia invaded Ukraine. While this international crisis enhanced the precarity of her incarceration, the deeply antigay and anti-Black sentiments among the Russian government enhanced her vulnerability to violence. For the first few months of Griner's detainment, her wife, Cherelle Griner, family, and teammates said little publicly about her case, fearing it might have a negative impact on her timely release.[7] The State Department's decision in early May to classify her detainment as unlawful prompted a shift in strategy in which her teammates, WNBA and NBA executives, and finally, government officials began to speak out. On June 23, 2022, a coalition of progressive organizations banded together to demand greater action from the diplomatic corps and the White House. Organizations that signed onto this effort included the NUL, the NAACP, the Human Rights Campaign, the National Action Network, the National Organization for Women, and GLAAD (formerly known as the Gay and Lesbian Alliance Against Defamation). A day later, the House of Representatives passed a bipartisan resolution calling for her release and return to the United States.[8] Cherelle Griner was a crucial force in this campaign, publicizing the lack of concern among the diplomatic corps and President Biden's administration. For months, no major Black civil rights organizations or mainstream LGBTQ+ rights groups mobilized to raise awareness about her case. That Griner's plight gained greater traction in June—the month of Gay Pride and the recently federally recognized holiday Juneteenth—is suggestive of the neoliberal logics of centering marginalized subjects during moments of heightened visibility. However, organizations like Black Feminist Futures labored to keep Griner's plight visible while also highlighting the intersectional forces that compounded her vulnerability to neglect and state violence.[9] Whereas many hailed Griner's release in December 2022 and praised the Biden administration for their labors, some—especially far-right political conservatives—decried her release in lieu of other detained Americans. Some juxtaposed Griner's detainment with that of Paul Whelan, a white former marine and employee of a US auto parts supplier who was convicted and sentenced to a fourteen-year prison sentence for espionage. Current and former elected officials as well as conservative political commentators mischaracterized Griner, calling her "anti-American," a drug-using criminal, and a celebrity (rather than an Olympian and skilled athlete). Former president Donald Trump, for example, claimed that Griner "openly hated our country," in part because she walked off the basketball court during a 2020 game in protest of the unarmed killings of African Americans.[10] Other commentators cited Griner's intersectional identity as a Black lesbian as the rationale for the Biden administration's advocacy on her behalf. Michael Savage, a conservative radio host, asserted "the choice of Griner over Whelan may reflect the preference of Biden's political base. The WNBA star and celebrity is also a black lesbian, who protested the US national anthem. Whelan is a middle-aged white man and a US Marine." Owen Shroyer, a host on the far-right website *Infowars*, stated that Griner "is a Black gay woman, [a] liberal, and now they know she's going to come back and be a good Democrat spokesperson." Matt Walsh of the *Daily Wire* referenced the right-wing outrage over the alleged teaching of critical race theory in public schools in his commentary on the prisoner exchange. He tweeted, "The rules of intersectionality dictate that the black woman gets freed first. That's one of the primary factors driving this, whether we want to admit it out loud or not."[11] In their commentary, then, Griner was an avatar for the intersecting constituencies of the Democratic Party as well as the party's support for LGBTQ+ rights and Black civil rights.

The complex relationship between Black and gay political identities illustrated in the Griner case and Pew survey emerged, in part, out of the post–World War II Black freedom struggle and challenges to it. *Ambivalent Affinities* has traced critical moments in which ideas about homosexuality crossed paths with contests over Black political empowerment. In the 1940s and 1950s, civil rights organizations intentionally chose to engage with state formations in ways that were not only anti-Black and hostile to radicalism but that also, increasingly, saw gender variance and same-sex intimacy as threats to be punished. These engagements extended to the local level in the 1970s and 1980s, as Black elected officials worked to build relationships with multiracial (but in many places largely white) gay and lesbian electoral con-stituencies in the face of, at times, united antigay and anti-Black sentiment. The long history of Blackness as being defined by non-normative genders and sexualities informed the strategies that individuals and organizations pursued to achieve autonomy and empowerment to be sure. However, I argue that scholars (and, indeed, the public) must also attend to the power of the heteronormative state as an influential force that shaped the strate-gies of mainstream civil rights organizations.

But the state did not act alone. Rather, I offer a reading of backlash to the modern civil rights movement as fundamentally about sexual and gen-der disorder. It was not so much that the anti-communism at the core of postwar antigay discourse and anti–civil rights discourse acted as a bridge to connect queerness and Blackness. Rather, it is that the grammars of devi-ance that had long marked anti-Black thought and action were easily elided to include what emerged in the mid-twentieth century as the "queerest" of sexual and gender formations: homosexuality. These grammars acted as a cudgel that undermined efforts for racial, sexual, and gender liberation—but also extended a hand in allyship to African Americans antagonistic to sexual and gender dissidence. These are not the only moments in which such crossings occurred nor, do I assert, are they the most important. But they are suggestive of how contests over white supremacy created conditions in which notions of Black racial equality and concretizing boundaries of homosexuality were imbricated. A book can only do and be so many things. However, it is my hope that others will take up these insights, stories, and questions that have historical, historiographical, political, and material impacts.

I have aimed to offer a historical amendment to the importance of race in the concretization of homosexuality and heterosexuality as well as queerness more broadly. A small but powerful body of scholarship demonstrates how racial hierarchies, a Black-white binary, and spaces of interracial sociality became crucial sites for medical, legal, and popular understandings of homosexuality and heterosexuality during the late nineteenth century and first half of the twentieth century.[12] Scholars have begun to analyze how, after World War II, Blackness continued to be a reference point for homosexuality, as well as how Black communities themselves sought to understand sexual and gender variance.[13] It was not simply limited to the realm of homophile / gay rights organizing, growing queer enclaves, or even federal and state homophobic policies and practices. Scholars should consider the postwar Black freedom struggle—and challenges to it—as key arenas in which ideas about homosexuality and heterosexuality were being constituted during this period. The postwar civil rights movement in particular became an organic place in which this binary was contested and racialized, in large measure because of how Blackness continued to be a reference point for non-normative genders and sexualities. This articulation—of Blackness as always already queer and as a crucial reference point for sexual and gender binaries—amplifies how sexuality and gender have historically been constitutive of racial categories and Black racial formations in particular.

This book is indebted to and in conversation with historically minded scholarship that centers Blackness and queerness. In the twenty or so years since Michele Mitchell and Matt Richardson outlined both the historical "silence" around Black LGBTQ+ communities and "compulsory heterosexuality," within African American history, a number of studies have sought to fill the void.[14] Indeed, in the more than ten years since I began this project, more and more historically minded work has amplified the intellectual, artistic, and political labor of Black queer subjects.[15] Also, as I have written elsewhere, Black women's and gender history in particular has been an especially crucial field for intersectional interrogations of variant genders and sexualities.[16] However, it continues to be the case that most work about Black queer subjects emerges from outside the discipline of history and that compulsory heterosexuality continues to mark African American historiography broadly. I raise this not to suggest that the discipline of history is the only nor the ideal place for Black queer histories to "reside" but to amplify the need for additional historically minded work within and outside of the discipline on such topics. Furthermore, *Ambivalent Affinities* most clearly stands as an invitation to consider the possibilities when we think about Blackness and queerness (with an attentiveness to ways of being and identification that fall under a historically specific classification of homosexuality) not only as the lived experience of intersectional subjects but also as mutually imbricated political, social, economic, and epistemological formations. Building on the critical work of Black queer studies and queer of color critique, this work encourages greater attentiveness to these formations as a way to illuminate both the lived experiences of Black queer and transgender communities and the normalizing forces that deepen certain kinds of exclusion.

Politically, *Ambivalent Affinities* offers one historical narrative about the challenges of articulating an intersectional political praxis attentive to formations of power and forging Black-gay political coalitions (especially those rooted in liberal or left-of-center politics). This text implicitly follows the call of organizer and political scientist Cathy Cohen to access the "radical potential of queer politics." In her influential essay "Punks, Bulldaggers, and Welfare Queens: The Radical Potential of Queer Politics?," Cohen notes that one of the "great failings" of queer political formations in the 1980s and 1990s was "their inability to incorporate into analysis of the world and strategies for political mobilization the roles that race, class, and gender play in defining people's differing relations to dominant and normalizing power." She calls for political formations that are "organized . . . around a more intersectional analysis of who and what the enemy is and where our potential allies can be found."[17] I hope that this history offers critical insights into not only the growing number of histories that consider how Black subjects have historically been excluded from heteronormativity but how the very production of homosexuality as a political category is simultaneously tethered to the non-normativity of Blackness as a way to stigmatize both while disassociating them in an attempt to forestall organizing coalitions. *Ambivalent Affinities* endeavors to honor Cohen's warning to not have "movement building be rooted in our shared history or identity but in our shared marginal relationship to dominant power which normalizes, legitimizes, and privileges" by amplifying the latter processes.[18] Having a clearer understanding not only of the siloed ways that Black and LGBTQ+ subjects (who may be Black) have experienced, and continue to experience, structural inequities and marginalization but of how these two political categories have functioned ambivalently offers historical context for how freedom fighters have labored in the past and will continue to do so in the present and future.

Ultimately, these histories have material impacts for Black queer and transgender subjects. There is a long history of Black queer subjects looking backward, seeking ancestral traces—of those whose experiences mirror our own. Of those who constructed knowledges and ways of being that challenged the normalizing impulses of their communities and the nation-state. In addition, we also need histories that attend to the normalizing forces that continue to impinge on the varied lived experience of these communities. In his autobiographical essay "Sissies at the Picnic: The Subjugated Knowledges of a Rural Black Queer," Roderick Ferguson offers a visible connection between the forces of normalization and concretization that attend to "progress" and the material impacts on sexual and gender dissidents. Recounting the crucial place of Black sissies in the small rural Black community of Manchester, Georgia, Ferguson declares, "To remember the past, we must act against the storm of progress. We who look to history critically and queerly do so by reckoning with the mighty winds of progress in whatever forms they may come—civil rights, the Christian Right, modern homosexuality. Others may see these movements as entirely separate, but all of them throw piles of debris at our feet, heaping that wreckage in the varied name of progress. It is important to recognize that this wreckage is actually made up of the bones of people like Edward Larue," a Black queer elder from Ferguson's childhood who experienced the social violence of homophobia and the corporeal violence of AIDS.[19]

Ambivalent Affinities is deeply invested in excavating those forces of normalization that create these forms of wreckage in an attempt to lay bare the varied forces that impact Black queer subjects, politics, and the worlds they sought and continue to seek to make. It is my hope that this study creates greater space for other inquiries that center both the epistemologies and experiences of Black sexual and gender dissidents as well as the structural forces that shape their lives.

Acknowledgments

Every book has an origin story. This book has two. One story begins when, as an undergraduate at the University of Michigan, I watched the film *Paris Is Burning*. After my encounter with this documentary, I assumed there would be a significant amount of historical work about Black Lesbian, Gay, Bisexual, Transgender, and Queer communities—but I was wrong. My concern over this absence animates this project, alongside other intellectual interests presented herein. The other story is about self-possession and knowledge. I felt queer long before I knew its implications for sexual desire and/or gender expansiveness. The queerness of being a Black girl in predominately white educational and residential spaces; the queerness of well-known Black intimacies and kinship structures that offered transgressive alternatives alongside the well-worn narratives of Black middle-class respectability that marked my childhood. This book, then, is the amalgamation of my scholarly and personal knowledges.

Over the years, various funding sources have supported this work. They include the Department of History and the Program in American Studies at Princeton University; Frances S. Summersell Center for the Study of the South; College Academy for Research, Scholarship, and Creative Activity Grant from the Department of Gender and Race Studies at the University of Alabama; Stuart A. Rose Manuscript, Archives, and Rare Book Library, Emory University; and Phil Zwickler Memorial Research Grants from the Division of Rare and Manuscript Collections, Cornell University. I want to thank the archivists at the repositories I consulted for this project including those at the Kenan Research Center, Atlanta History Center; Archives Research Center, Robert W. Woodruff Library at Atlanta University Center; Stuart A. Rose Manuscript Archives and Rare Book Library, Emory University; National Archives at College Park, College Park, Maryland; Alabama Department of Archives and History, Montgomery, Alabama; Archives and Special Collections, Auburn University–Montgomery, Montgomery, Alabama; Georgia State Archives; Department of Archives and Special Collections, University of Mississippi; Library of Virginia, Richmond, Virginia; Special Collections, Washington University in Saint Louis, Saint Louis, Missouri; W. S. Hoole Library Special Collections Library, University of Alabama, Tuscaloosa, Alabama; Manuscript Division, Library of Congress; and Moorland Spingarn Research Center, Howard University. A special thank-you to Kerrie Cotton Williams at the Archives Division, Auburn Avenue Research Library, and Brenda Marsden at the Human Sexuality Collection at the Division of Rare and Manuscript Collections, Cornell University Library. Finally, I want to thank Maurice O'Brian Franklin for his generosity and patience in sharing his story for this project.

When I approached Rhonda Y. Williams at a conference in 2015, I could not imagine how that meeting would lead to the book finding a home with the Justice, Power, and Politics series at the University of North Carolina Press. I deeply appreciate Rhonda's and Heather Ann Thompson's support for this project. Working with Brandon Proia has been a delight. I have so appreciated his sage advice, encouragement, and superhuman patience as I labored to let the book go. Dawn Durante oversaw the final stages of the production process. I am grateful for her generous and critical feedback on some pivotal parts of the manuscript. I extend my sincere gratitude to entire editorial staff at the University of North Carolina Press. I want to also thank the development and copy editors at Ideas on Fire for their feedback and support of this manuscript.

I have been fortunate to be supported and shaped by several teachers and mentors during my time as a student. As an undergraduate at the University of Michigan, I had the great fortune to build a relationship with Julius Scott III. His deep knowledge of histories of the Black Atlantic and love of teaching inspired me to be a historian. Although I never took a course with Martha S. Jones, she agreed to supervise my undergraduate honors thesis. Her generous support cemented my desire to attend graduate school. During the summer of 2005, I had the opportunity to work with Keith A. Mayes under the Summer Research Opportunity Program at the University of Minnesota–Twin Cities. Keith's mentorship and later friendship has been invaluable, despite years between conversations. Attending graduate school at Princeton University proved to be one of the most challenging and rewarding experiences of my life. Several faculty members in the History Department became supportive and substantive intellectual interlocutors including Daniel Rodgers, Kevin Kruse, and Hendrik Hartog. Vera Candiani offered a model of fierce scholarly independence and rigor. Joshua Guild's support, kindness, and deep knowledge of the postwar Black freedom struggle made me a better scholar. I arrived at Princeton the same year Margot Canaday joined the faculty, a fortuitous development that proved essential to my deepening interests in the history of sexuality and LGBTQ+ history in particular. Her kindness and support for my work has made all the difference for my career. Tera W. Hunter's model of intellectual curiosity, scholarly rigor and professionalism have been profoundly influential. Her various pieces of advice remain a touchstone as I continue to interrogate the possibilities of this profession.

My three years as an Assistant Professor at the University of Alabama–Tuscaloosa was an unforeseen gift. The sprawling campus on the Black Warrior River provided a critical homeplace to nurture my Black feminist praxis—a praxis that has enhanced my life and scholarship in more ways than I can measure. As a faculty member, I received critical support from the College of Arts and Sciences and the Departments of American Studies and Gender and Race Studies. Associate Dean for Humanities and Fine Arts Tricia McElroy offered steadfast support. I benefited from regular engagement with a cohort of faculty across a number of units including Hilary Green, Hali Felt, Stefanie Fishel, Latrise Johnson, Jennifer Kenney, and Jennifer Purvis. Long conversations with Utz McKnight about scholarship, pedagogy, and academia were affirming and illuminating. I am appreciative for his mentorship and friendship then and now. My friendship with Elizabeth McKnight blossomed over terrible Panera coffee and long walks. Our bond is rooted in a feminist ethic of care that I value deeply.

Academia is, indeed, a serendipitous profession. This serendipity led me back to my undergraduate alma mater, the University of Michigan. My first two years as an LSA Collegiate Fellow introduced me to a critical cohort of scholars of color who (in ways large and small) sustained me, including Savi Namboodiripad, Luiz Zaman, Beza Merid, Margo Mahan, Raevin Jimenez, Jessica Walker, and Cristina Perez. Anne Curzan has been deeply supportive during her time in the dean's office. I have found profoundly supportive colleagues in my units, history and women's and gender studies. I especially want to thank those colleagues who gathered on Zoom eight months into the pandemic to offer feedback on my manuscript. A sincere thank-you to Stephen Berrey, Andrea Bolivar, James Cook, Nadine Hubbs, Charlotte Karem Albrecht, Matthew Lassiter, Sara McClelland, Peggy McCracken, Victor Mendoza, Anthony Mora, Ava Purkiss, Gayle Rubin, Alexandra Stern, Abigail Stewart, Ruby Tapia, and Heather Ann Thompson. Valerie Traub offered line edits and comments on the entire manuscript in the months before the workshop, an act of generosity I will always cherish. Matthew Countryman and LaKisha Simmons offered close readings of the book and have been steadfast mentors during my time at the University of Michigan. Earl Lewis and Mary C. Kelley engaged the manuscript during my third-year review and offered critical feedback and professional advice. An array of other colleagues have provided invaluable professional advice and support (beyond those already mentioned): Paulina Alberto, Allison Alexy, Kathryn Babayan, Josh Cole, Henry Cowles, Anna Bonnell Freidin, Deborah Dash Moore, Diedre De La Cruz, Christian de Pee, Angela Dillard, Jesse Hoffnung-Garskof, Sue Juster, Anna Kirkland, Earl Lewis, Diana Louis, Ellen Meuhlberger, Kenneth Mills, Helmut Puff, Mrinalini Sinha, Matthew Spooner, Ruby C. Tapia, Ruth Tsoffar, Jeffrey Veidlinger, Stephen Ward, Liz Wingrove, Yi-Li Wu, and Jason Young. I am especially grateful for the friendship, humor, and critical perspectives from a group of current and former faculty of color. Brandi Hughes's wisdom, candor, and eloquence has deepened my understandings of the possibilities of scholarly life within and outside the ivory tower. Raevin Jimenez's comradery, institutional insight, and wit have been invaluable. Conversations with Kira Thurman about life and academia (along with lots of great memes) have made me laugh out loud and see the silver linings of the profession. Ava Purkiss's humor, kindness, and professional savvy have been an anchor and balm in moments of professional and personal challenge.

Beyond my academic institutions, I have had the great fortune of engaging with and being supported by a wide array of scholars and academic venues. Audiences at the University of Kentucky, Yale University, Princeton University, and Oberlin College have greatly improved this work. The following scholars have touched me and my work in various ways—I owe them a great deal of thanks: Cathy Cohen, Darius Bost, Brett Gadsden, David Green, Cheryl Hicks, Pippa Holloway, Kwame Holmes, John Howard, Jared Leighton, Jeffrey McCune, Joanne Meyerowitz, LaShonda Mims, Melynda J. Price, Tim Retzloff, Renee Romano, Crystal Sanders, Timothy Stewart Winter, Leah Wright Rigueur, and Cookie Woolner. I owe a special note of thanks to two people: Sarah Haley, who has been a constant supporter since we first met at Princeton University (Sarah as a postdoctoral fellow and I as a shy graduate student), and Christina Hanhardt, whose advocacy and advice have been crucial during the last few years of working on the manuscript. Their professional and intellectual generosity continue to amaze me.

I am deeply grateful for the communities of Black women and women of color I have had the pleasure to count as friends and community across various institutional and geographic home spaces: Valeria Lopez Fadul's brilliance, style, and love of heavy metal; Justene Hill Edwards's positivity, mirth, and love of all things cashmere; and Tikia Hamilton's generosity, humor, and wisdom all inspire. I have been especially fortunate to find supportive and loving Black queer community near and far, including Brittney Edmonds, K. B. Dennis Meade, Deanna Smith, and Regine Cashay West. Priyanka Pathak's unwavering inner compass and conviction has inspired me for almost twenty years. Thank you for always being there.

I am the daughter, granddaughter, and great-granddaughter of Black folks living in and with ties to Albion, Michigan. Hearing stories about Black communities in this small industrial city on the Kalamazoo River made me want to be a historian and has been an enduring source of my deep reverence for stories too often excluded from official chronicles, popular publications, and public memory. I want to thank the extended Powell family in particular for their love and support. My cousin Tish Surae Powell has been a constant presence in my life, regularly fulfilling a big sister role. My grandparents—Rosie Bell Powell, Dianne (Bennett) Jones, and Charles W. Jones—all nurtured my love of knowledge. Although they did not live to hold this book in their hands, I honor them with its completion. Damien Parker entered our family with good humor and patience (fielding too many questions about medical complaints to count). I thank him for his support. My parents' support has been steadfast and ardent (although I am glad they no longer have to ask when this book will be done!). Charles Allen Jones's kindness, determination, and fundamental optimism continue to inspire me. Judy Sharlene (Powell) Jones's faith, curiosity, and gregariousness have been a balm more times than I can count. My twin sister Jessica Danielle Jones is more than a sibling. She is a confidant, an intellectual interlocutor, and a source of laughter, comfort, and truth-telling. My gratitude for her presence in my life cannot be measured. Finally, yet foremost, I thank and praise God.

Notes

Abbreviations

AARL   Archives Division, Auburn Avenue Research Library on African American Culture and History, Atlanta, GA

ADAH   Alabama Department of Archives and History, Montgomery, AL

AHC   Kenan Research Center, Atlanta History Center, GA

ARC   Archives Research Center, Robert W. Woodruff Library at Atlanta University Center, GA

ASCUM   Department of Archives and Special Collections, University of Mississippi, Oxford, MS

AUM   Archives and Special Collections, Auburn University–Montgomery, AL

DRMC   Human Sexuality Collection, Division of Rare and Manuscript Collections, Cornell University Library, Ithaca, NY

GA   Georgia Archives, Jonesboro, GA

LC   Library of Congress, Washington, DC

LOV   Library of Virginia, Richmond, VA

MARBL   Manuscript Archives and Rare Book Library, Emory University, Atlanta, GA

MSRC   Moorland Spingarn Research Center, Howard University, Washington, DC

NACP   National Archives at College Park, MD

RWC   Right Wing Collection, Special Collections and Archives, University of Iowa, Iowa City

RWF   Robert Woodruff Library, Emory University, Atlanta, GA

WBMA   Walter J. Brown Media Archives and Peabody Awards Collection, University of Georgia Libraries, Athens

WSHL   W. S. Hoole Library Special Collections Library, University of Alabama, Tuscaloosa

WUSL   Special Collections, Washington University in Saint Louis, MO

A Note on Language

1. Profound shifts in the conceptualization of and terminology for gender nonconformity and same-sex intimacy (commonly placed under the banner of homosexuality) occurred during this period. My thinking about this is informed by: Stein, *Rethinking the Gay and Lesbian Movement*, and Hanhardt, *Safe Space*.

2. Stryker, *Transgender History*, 1.

3. Cohen, "Punks, Bulldaggers, and Welfare Queens," and Rubin, "Thinking Sex."

Introduction

1. For more about the 1993 mobilization, see Ghaziani, *The Dividends of Dissent*, and Stein, *Rethinking the Gay and Lesbian Movement*.

2. Beemyn notes that "despite the efforts of trans activists and some cis LGB allies" "transgender" was not included in the name of the 1993 mobilization: "The 1993 march organizers were persuaded by trans activists to add trans people to the events platform, which, among other demands, called for a LGBT civil rights law and legislation banning discrimination against LGBT people." For more on this, see Beemyn, "LGBTQ Movement, Trans Inclusion In/exclusion," 4.

3. The poem is called "Let America Be America Again." Hughes's sexuality has been the subject of much scholarly debate and contention. For more on this conversation, see Rampersad, *The Life of Langston Hughes*, and Vogel, "Closing Time."

4. For discussions about the Black gay cultural renaissance generally, and the long Black gay 1980s, see Allen, *There's a Disco Ball between Us*; Bost, *Evidence of Being*; Royles, *To Make the Wounded Whole*, 79–84.

5. Alec Larson, "Activists Plan Protest of NAACP," *Philadelphia Tribune*, July 6, 1993, 2D.

6. For video footage of Wilson's speech, see "Gay and Lesbian March on Washington," C-SPAN, April 15, 1993, https://www.c-span.org/video/?40062-1/gay-lesbian-march-washington; Linda Wheeler, "NAACP Adds Support to Gay Rights March," *Washington Post*, March 4, 1993, D3.

7. "Activists Plan Protest of NAACP," *Philadelphia Tribune*, July 6, 1993, 2D.

8. "Homosexuality in America," C-SPAN April 21, 1993, https://www.c-span.org/video/?39906-1/homosexuality-america.

9. Foucault, "Nietzsche, Genealogy, History," 146.

10. The phrase "provocative disruption" references the work of literary critic Omise'eke Natasha Tinsley. Tinsley forwards a call for an expansive Black queer analytic, writing that "relationships between shipmates [during the transatlantic slave trade] read as queer relationships. Queer not in the sense of a 'gay' or same-sex loving identity waiting to be excavated from the ocean floor but as a praxis of resistance. Queer in the sense of marking disruption to the violence of the normative order and powerfully so. . . . It disrupts provocatively." See Tinsley, "Black Atlantic, Queer Atlantic," 199.

11. Shah, "Queer of Color Estrangement and Belonging," 262–263.

12. Shah frames survival and belonging as queer of color responses to forms of estrangement. See Shah, "Queer of Color Estrangement and Belonging," 265–272.

13. The literature on slavery indexing forms of Black estrangement is too numerous to list here. For a small cross-section, see White, *Ar'n't I a Woman?*; Jones, *Labor of Love*; Morgan, *Laboring Women*; Camp, *Closer to Freedom*; Glymph, *Out of the House of Bondage*; Mustakeem, *Slavery at Sea*; Brown, *Good Wives, Nasty Wenches, and Anxious Patriarchs*; Stevenson, *Life in Black and White*.

14. See, for example, Hunter, *Bound in Wedlock*; Penningroth, *The Claims of Kinfolk*; Williams, *Help Me to Find My People*.

15. See, for example, Rosén, *Terror in the Heart of Freedom*; Haley, *No Mercy Here*; Gross, *Colored Amazons*; Hicks, *Talk with You like a Woman*; LeFlouria, *Chained in Silence*.

16. Kandaswamy, *Domestic Contradictions*; Roberts, *Killing the Black Body*; Scott, *Contempt and Pity*; Williams, *The Politics of Public Housing*.

17. For more on how urban leisure and same-sex subcultures developed within interracial spaces like cabarets, dance halls, and vice districts, see Mumford, *Interzones*; Vogel, *The Scene of Harlem Cabaret*; Chauncey, *Gay New York*; Somerville, *Queering the Color Line*; Heap, *Slumming*.

18. The rise of sexual psychopathy laws in the 1930s (which targeted individuals alleged to engage in same-sex sex and gender nonconformity) mirrored a growing awareness at the federal level of homosexuality as a discreet set of practices and something to be punished. Federal laws and policies deepened this form of exclusion through its deliberate exclusion of identified homosexuals from key benefits of citizenship including naturalized citizenship immigration, social welfare benefits, and military service. The Lavender Scare witnessed the discursive coupling of political subversion with "sexual perversion," in the loss of employment for individuals in the public and private sectors to a profound degree. For more on this, see Bérubé, *Coming Out under Fire*; Johnson, *The Lavender Scare*; Canaday, *The Straight State*; Freedman, "'Uncontrolled Desires'"; Robertson, "Separating the Men from the Boys"; Chauncey, "The Postwar Sex Crime Panic"; Howard, *The Closet and the Cul-de-Sac*.

19. For select works on post-World War II gay, lesbian, and transgender political activism see D'Emilio, *Sexual Politics, Sexual Communities*; Boyd, *Wide-Open Town*; Stewart-Winter, *Queer Clout*; Stein, *City of Sisterly and Brotherly Loves*; Stein, *Rethinking the Gay and Lesbian Rights Movement*; Batza, *Before AIDS*; Sides, *Erotic City*; Hanhardt, *Safe Space*; Hobson, *Lavender and Red*.

20. For works on histories of race and conservatism, see Dillard, *Guess Who's Coming to Dinner Now?*; Kruse, *White Flight*; Lassiter, *The Silent Majority*; Crespino, *In Search of Another Country*; Wright Rigueur, *The Loneliness of the Black Republican*.

21. Dillard, *Guess Who's Coming to Dinner Now?*; Frank, "The Civil Rights of Parents"; Strub, *Perversion for Profit*.

22. Here, I am indebted to and building upon the work of John Howard in *Men Like That* which documents similar associations in Mississippi.

23. See Scott, *Contempt and Pity*.

24. For an overview of these developments, see Thompson, "The Racial History of Criminal Justice." For some representative works, see Muhammad, *The Condemnation of Blackness*; Fortner, *Black Silent Majority*; Thompson, *Blood in the Water*; Hinton, *From the War on Poverty to the War on Crime*; Murakawa, *The First Civil Right*; Alexander, *The New Jim Crow*.

25. For an overview of these developments, see Ritchie and Whitlock, "Criminalization and Legalization"; Stein, "Law and Politics." See also Canaday, *The Straight State*; Chauncey, *Gay New York*; Eskridge, *Dishonorable Passions*; Freedman,

"Uncontrolled Desires"; Hanhardt, *Safe Space*; Stewart-Winter, "Queer Law and Order"; Sears, *Arresting Dress*; Johnson, *The Lavender Scare*.

26. Hanhardt, *Safe Space*.

27. Dawson, *Black Visions*, 15.

28. A rich interdisciplinary literature documents how liberal actors (as elected officials, bureaucrats, and policy experts) contributed to the maintenance and deepening of racial inequality. See Sugrue, *The Origins of Urban Crisis*; Murakawa, *The First Civil Right*; Melamed, *Represent and Destroy*; Katznelson, *When Affirmative Action Was White*.

29. The literature on the multifaceted nature of African American political activism after World War II is voluminous. On African American activism during the early Cold War years and the influence of geopolitics, see Anderson, *Eyes off the Prize*; Biondi, *To Stand and Fight*. On the influence of Cold War geopolitics and decolonization movements, see Borstelmann, *The Cold War and the Color Line*; Dudziak, *Cold War Civil Rights*; Merriweather, *Proudly We Can Be Africans*; Slate, *Colored Cosmopolitanism*. For classic histories of the civil rights movement and relevant organizations in the South, see Morris, *The Origins of the Civil Rights Movement*; Chafe, *Civilities and Civil Rights*; Carson, *In Struggle*; Branch, *Parting the Waters*. For histories of Black freedom struggles in the North and West, see Countryman, *Up South*; Gadsden, *Between North and South*; Sugrue, *The Origins of Urban Crisis*; Sugrue, *Sweet Land of Liberty*; Thompson, *Whose Detroit?*; Dillard, *Faith in the City*; Self, *American Babylon*. For additional scholarship about Black Nationalism and the Black Radical Tradition, see Tyson, *Free Radio Dixie*; Woodard, *A Nation within a Nation*; Joseph, *Waiting until the Midnight Hour*; Ransby, *Ella Baker and the Black Freedom Movement*; Spencer, *The Revolution Has Come*; Farmer, *Remaking Black Power*; Jeffries, *Bloody Lowndes*. For legal histories of the modern civil rights movement, see Kluger, *Simple Justice*; Brown-Nagin, *Courage to Dissent*.

30. For organizational histories of these entities, see Reed, *Not Alms but Opportunity*; Sullivan, *Lift Every Voice*; Fairclough, *To Redeem the Soul of America*; Peake, *Keeping the Dream Alive*.

31. In making this formulation, I in no way seek to flatten the ideological (or tactical) diversity of constituencies that sought to counter the gender and sexual status quo. The literature on gay and lesbian activism is incredibly broad. For a cross section of this work, see D'Emilio, *Sexual Politics, Sexual Communities*; Boyd, *Wide-Open Town*; Stewart-Winter, *Queer Clout*; Stein, *City of Sisterly and Brotherly Loves*; Stein, *Rethinking the Gay and Lesbian Movement*; Batza, *Before AIDS*; Sides, *Erotic City*; Hanhardt, *Safe Space*; Hobson, *Lavender and Red*; Mims, Drastic Dykes.

32. Hanhardt, *Safe Space*.

33. As Chandan Reddy asserts, "To think of race, sexuality, and US globalism through and with 'amendments' rather than with the metaphor of 'intersections' is to suggest the importance of historical, political, and epistemological structures that organize these formations are linked or intersected, and what kinds of logic fasten their coincidence" (*Freedom with Violence*, 16). While this book continues to think

about "intersections" and "crossings," I acknowledge that there are other ways of conceptualizing the relationship between Blackness and queerness. For more on how sexuality amends race, see Reddy, *Freedom with Violence.*

34. Writing about intersectionality and its application by (inter)disciplinary academics is voluminous. My use of intersectional is rooted in canonical works by Black feminist scholars and by Black feminist historians. See Combahee River Collective, "A Black Feminist Statement"; Crenshaw, "Mapping the Margins"; Collins, *Black Feminist Thought*; Higginbotham, "African American History and the Metalanguage of Race."

35. Higginbotham, "African American History and the Metalanguage of Race," 267.

36. Hanhardt, "The Radical Potential of Queer Political History?", 145–149.

37. For example, see Jenkins, *Private Lives, Proper Relations*; Hartman, *Scenes of Subjection*; Sharpe, *Monstrous Intimacies*; Abdur-Rahman, *Against the Closet.*

38. My perspective is informed by Roderick Ferguson, who writes that the "intersection of blackness and homosexuality requires that we both illustrate the regulatory function of heteronormative conformity and identify those sites that prompt alternative and oppositional readings of African American non-heteronormativity" ("Nightmares of the Heteronormative," 420). Also see Ferguson, *Aberrations in Black.*

Chapter 1

1. This letter is one of several pieces of correspondence between Lemuel Brown and Charles Hamilton Houston about the serviceman's court-martial. A copy of this letter may be found in the papers of Truman K. Gibson, who replaced William Hastie as the civilian aide to the Secretary of War in 1943 after Hastie's resignation. See Lemuel Brown to Charles H. Houston, May 14, 1944, California, Court-Martials, Records of the Civilian Aide Subject Files "Hastie Files," Records of the Office of the Secretary of War, Record Group 107, NACP. The original letter and related correspondence may be found in the Charles Hamilton Houston Papers. See Lemuel Brown to Charles H. Houston, May 14, 1944, Charles Hamilton Houston Papers, box 163–7, folder 27, Manuscript Division, MSRC. Correspondence between Houston and Brown indicates that Brown's parents were familiars of Houston and resided in Washington, DC.

2. For more on Charles Hamilton Houston's activism and life, see McNeil, *Groundwork.* There is a rich and growing scholarship on the enhanced militancy of African American political, social, and economic activism from the Great Depression through World War II, and into the late 1940s. For a small cross-section of this literature, see Kelley, *Hammer and Hoe*; Honey, *Southern Labor and Black Civil Rights*; Bates, *Pullman Porters*; Dudziak, *Cold War Civil Rights*; Anderson, *Eyes off the Prize*; Korstad, *Civil Rights Unionism*; Biondi, *To Stand and Fight*; Brown-Nagin, *Courage to Dissent.*

3. Charles H. Houston to Lemuel Brown, June 8, 1944, Charles Hamilton Houston Papers, box 163–7, folder 27, Manuscript Division, MSRC.

4. Like his predecessor William H. Hastie, Gibson possessed marginal authority to address complaints of racism by Black service members. For more on Gibson in the context of efforts to alleviate discrimination, see McGuire, *Taps for a Jim Crow Army*, 2–5, 34, 99. For a firsthand account of his efforts, see Gibson, *Knocking Down Barriers*.

5. See Lemuel Brown to Charles H. Houston, December 15, 1946, Charles Hamilton Houston Papers, box 163–7, folder 27, Manuscript Division, MSRC.

6. Lemuel Brown to Charles H. Houston, December 15, 1946, Charles Hamilton Houston Papers, box 163–7, folder 27, Manuscript Division, MSRC.

7. Katznelson, *When Affirmative Action Was White*, 113.

8. At the conclusion of his letter, Brown asked Houston about the viability of filing a lawsuit "for each year of my life that has been messed up as a result of the action taken against me by the US Army and the War Dept. [*sic*] and the U.S. Govt. [*sic*]." Houston replied over two months later, having "thought about [his letter] a great deal." However, Houston doubted the viability of his case and suggested, "I think we will have to go about the matter in a different way." See Lemuel Brown to Charles H. Houston, December 15, 1946, and Houston to Brown, February 1947, Charles Hamilton Houston Papers, box 163–7, folder 27, MSRC.

9. Throughout the chapter, I use a number of terms to refer to individuals serving within the army and navy including GIs and service members.

10. Both Margot Canaday and Allan Bérubé have examined the overlapping experiences of gay men, lesbians, and African Americans within the World War II–era military and their treatment by the state. Bérubé notes, "The war experiences of Black and gay veterans ran parallel in more ways than suggested by the rhetorical comparisons in postwar literature." Canaday also examines the overlapping experiences between the two groups and the intense stigmatization of Black same-sex-desiring veterans in the postwar era. See Bérubé, *Coming Out Under Fire*, 252; Canaday, *The Straight State*, 148, 150.

11. For more on the NAACP's involvement in protests to create greater opportunities for African American laborers in war-related industries, including the 1941 March on Washington movement, see Bracey and Meier, "Allies or Adversaries?"; Sullivan, *Lift Every Voice*, 243, 253–255, 266, 274–278.

12. Whereas Russell uses the word "heteronormativity" to describe African Americans' increasing denigration of certain forms of sexual and gender dissidence, I believe it is more accurate to place the NAACP's actions within the framework of the politics of respectability. As outlined by Evelyn Brooks Higginbotham in her study of the National Baptist Convention's female auxiliary around the turn of the twentieth century, the politics of respectability entailed the adoption of Victorian morality and an emphasis on communal uplift to counter racist stereotypes. Although a number of scholars have contributed to the development of this important framework, Victoria Wolcott's work on Black women's activism in interwar Detroit, Michigan, illuminates the waning influence of bourgeois respectability in lieu of more masculine rhetoric "of respectability that placed self-determination and community survival above public presentations of bourgeois life" (Wolcott, *Remaking Respectability,* 9). However, a concern with individual comportment as

well as adherence to sexual and gender norms continued to exert a powerful influence within Black politics and collective strategies for communal uplift. LaShawn Harris argues that working-class Black women in interwar New York "complicated normative versions of respectability" in their informal work (Harris, *Sex Workers,* 3). For more on the development of the politics of respectability in Black communities, see Higginbotham, *Righteous Discontent*; Gaines, *Uplifting the Race*; Wolcott, *Remaking Respectability*; Mitchell, *Righteous Propagation*; Harris, *Sex Workers*. For more on deepening homophobia in Black communities during the postwar period, see Hamilton, "Sexual Politics and African American Music"; Retzloff, "Seer or Queer?"; Russell, "The Color of Discipline"; Leonard, "Containing 'Perversion.'"

13. "Should I Sacrifice to Live 'Half-American,'" *Pittsburgh Courier,* January 31, 1942, 3.

14. Although there were some expanded opportunities for officer training, the military continued to be characterized by racial inequality. To quote Ira Katznelson, "the United States, in effect, had two armies—one white, one Black. Not entirely separate, they were utterly unequal" (*When Affirmative Action Was White,* 82). For more on discrimination, see Katznelson, *When Affirmative Action Was White,* 80–113; Mershon and Schlossman, *Foxholes and Color Lines,* 13–24.

15. See Katznelson, *When Affirmative Action Was White,* 80–113; Mershon and Schlossman, *Foxholes and Color Lines,* 13–24.

16. Wynn, *African American Experience during World War II,* 86.

17. For more on the specific behaviors targeted by the undesirable discharge, see Bérubé, *Coming Out under Fire,* 139. A Soldier to the Afro American, "Suffering Northern Indignities," May 10, 1943, in McGuire, *Taps for a Jim Crow Army,* 170.

18. Wynn, *African American Experience during World War II,* 53.

19. I did not encounter evidence that the military disproportionately targeted African Americans in their anti-homosexual campaigns.

20. The one most often leveled at Black servicemen was the Section VIII discharge (especially 615–360, and 615–368/369). The navy did not have specific regulations but issued directives that urged for the discharge of "habitual homosexuals." For more on this, see Bérubé, *Coming Out Under Fire,* 138–139. For more on abusive treatment of Black service members, see Sullivan, *Lift Every Voice,* 272.

21. See Edward F. Witsell to Jesse O. Dedmon January 8, 1946, folder General Correspondence January–March 1946, II: G10, National Association for the Advancement of Colored People Records, Manuscript Division, LC.

22. McGuire, *Taps for a Jim Crow Army,* 161.

23. Bérubé, *Coming Out Under Fire,* 128–148.

24. Bérubé, *Coming Out Under Fire,* 139–144.

25. For more on the experiences of gay men and lesbians in psychiatric wards, military hospitals, and "queer stockades," see Bérubé, *Coming Out Under Fire,* 210–227.

26. Report of the Proceedings of the Board of Officers, January 22, 1948, William E. White, folder 8 Discharge Review White, William E., II: G9, National Association for the Advancement of Colored People Records, Manuscript Division, LC.

27. Bérubé does not specify the exact document that enumerated these figures. Using figures enumerated in the January 8, 1946, memorandum of Major General Edward Witsell of the War Department, 18 percent of the blue discharges issued during the war appear to have been given for homosexuality. See Bérubé, *Coming Out Under Fire*, 147, and note xxiv.

28. Bérubé, *Coming Out Under Fire*, 262.

29. For more on the GI Bill, see Katznelson, *When Affirmative Action Was White*, 115–121.

30. Katznelson, *When Affirmative Action Was White*, 121–129. For more about the experiences of Black veterans and the VA, see Onkst, "'First a Negro . . . Incidentally a Veteran.'"

31. Bérubé, *Coming Out Under Fire*, 230.

32. McGuire, *Taps for a Jim Crow Army*, 22.

33. Canaday, *The Straight State*, 150.

34. John H. Young III, "Blue Discharges under Fire: GIs Denied Benefits," *Pittsburgh Courier*, October 20, 1945, 1.

35. For more on the shifting contours of the Veteran Administration's policies toward service members removed for homosexuality, as well as congressional attempts to intervene in such policies, see Bérubé, *Coming Out Under Fire*, 230–235, 229; Canaday, *The Straight State*, 158–163.

36. Thurston Lane to Truman K. Gibson, April 20, 1947, box 183, Records of the Civilian Aide Subject Files "Hastie Files," Records of the Office of Secretary of War, Record Group 107, NACP. Thousands of veterans mobilized to amend their blue discharges or access benefits. For more about the strategies these men employed, see Bérubé, *Coming Out Under Fire*, 235–243; Canaday, *The Straight State*, 152–158.

37. In 1910, a group of Black and white reformers, social scientists, and philanthropists created the NAACP to combat the deepening disfranchisement and racial terrorism that gripped the South as well as the de facto segregation and widespread prejudice that characterized Black life in the North. Sullivan, *Lift Every Voice*, 15.

38. Biondi, *To Stand and Fight*, 16.

39. For more on the growth of NAACP membership and Ella Baker's efforts in this regard, see Sullivan, *Lift Every Voice*, 285–286, 293.

40. For the scope of NAACP's wartime and immediate postwar activism, see Sullivan, *Lift Every Voice*, 237–333, Guglielmo, "A Martial Freedom Movement."

41. For more about the Veterans' Affairs Bureau and its work challenging residential segregation, see Woods, "Almost 'No Negro Veteran.'"

42. Minutes of the Meeting of the Board of Directors, October 9, 1944, folder Board of Directors: Inauguration of Veterans' Affairs, I: A-148, National Association for the Advancement of Colored People Papers, Manuscript Division, LC.

43. Jesse O. Dedmon to Madison S. Jones, March 24, 1947, folder General Correspondence cont. January–June 1947, II: BG-10, National Association for the Advancement of Colored People Papers, Manuscript Division, LC.

44. For examples, see "Capt. Dedmon Named NAACP Vet's Secretary," *New York Amsterdam News*, December 30, 1944, 5A; "Veterans Secretary Named by NAACP," *New Journal and Guide*, January 6, 1945, 3; "Named Vets' Secretary," *Chicago*

Defender, January 6, 1945, 9; "NAACP Veterans' Secretary Named," *Baltimore Afro-American,* January 6, 1945, 3.

45. See Bérubé, *Coming Out Under Fire,* 238, 241.

46. "Secretary of War's Discharge Review Board," September 6, 1946, and Navy Department, "Administrative Regulations and Procedures Governing the Panel and Boards Established to Review Discharges and Dismissals Pursuant to Section 301 of Servicemen's Readjustment Act of 1944," n.d. Both may be found in the folder Discharge Reviews Miscellaneous Letter 1946–1950, II: G8, National Association for the Advancement of Colored People Records, Manuscript Division, LC.

47. Leonard J. Johnson to Jesse O. Dedmon (March 1950, date uncertain), folder Discharge Review "I–J" 1943–1950, II: G7, National Association for the Advancement of Colored People Records, Manuscript Division, LC.

48. Elon Bruce to Jesse Dedmon, June 27, 1947, folder Discharge Reviews "B" 1945–1950, II: G6, National Association for the Advancement of Colored People Records, Manuscript Division, LC.

49. Attar T. Gibson to Judge Advocate General's Office, May 7, 1947, folder Discharge Reviews "G" 1945–1950, II: G7, National Association for the Advancement of Colored People Records, Manuscript Division, LC.

50. Case of Alfred Harrison, folder Discharge Reviews "H" 1945–1950, II: G7; and Case of James Perkins, folder Discharge Review Perkins, James 1947, II: G8, National Association for the Advancement of Colored People Records, Manuscript Division, LC.

51. Canaday, *The Straight State,* 156–158; Bérubé, *Coming Out Under Fire,* 265–266.

52. Herbold, "Never a Level Playing Field," 106.

53. T. O. Kraabel to Henry Nord, January 20, 1948, folder Discharge Reviews "N" 1945–1950, II: G8, National Association for the Advancement of Colored People Records, Manuscript Division, LC.

54. Bérubé, *Coming Out Under Fire,* 278.

55. Sullivan, *Lift Every Voice,* 288.

56. Henry Nord to Paul Dedmon (*sic*), February 17, 1948, folder Discharge Reviews "N" 1945–1950, II: G8, National Association for the Advancement of Colored People Records, Manuscript Division, LC.

57. Bérubé, *Coming Out Under Fire,* 235.

58. Daniel E. Byrd to Franklin H. Williams, March 21, 1946; and Daniel E. Byrd to Jesse O. Dedmon, April 10, 1946, folder Discharge Reviews "B" 1945–1950, II: G6, National Association for the Advancement of Colored People Records, Manuscript Division, LC.

59. Sullivan, *Lift Every Voice,* 288.

60. Elon Bruce to Jesse Dedmon, June 27, 1947, folder Discharge Reviews "B" 1945–1950, II: G6, National Association for the Advancement of Colored People Records, Manuscript Division, LC.

61. Willis Austin to Unknown, undated, folder 7 Soldier Trouble "A" 1942–1950, II: B152, National Association for the Advancement of Colored People Records, Manuscript Division, LC.

62. Chauncey, "The Postwar Sex Crime Panic"; Kunzel, *Criminal Intimacy.*

63. See D'Emilio, *Sexual Politics, Sexual Communities*; Chauncey, *Gay New York*; Kunzel, *Criminal Intimacy*.

64. See Chauncey, *Gay New York*; Chauncey, "The Postwar Sex Crime Panic"; Kunzel, *Criminal Intimacy*.

65. Bérubé, *Coming Out under Fire*; Canaday, *The Straight State*; D'Emilio, *Sexual Politics, Sexual Communities*. Also see Foucault, *The History of Sexuality Vol. 1*.

66. For more on the development of post–World War II gay community and political life, see D'Emilio, *Sexual Politics, Sexual Communities*; Faderman, *Odd Girls and Twilight Lovers*; Johnson, *The Lavender Scare*; Meeker, *Contacts Desired*.

67. Report of the Proceedings of the Board of Officers, January 22, 1948, William E. White, folder 8 Discharge Review White, William E., II: G9, National Association for the Advancement of Colored People Records, Manuscript Division, LC.

68. See Kunzel's *Criminal Intimacy* for more on this argument.

69. Bérubé, *Coming Out under Fire*, 86–87, 212–213, 224.

70. It is also possible that such depictions may have been fabricated to denigrate White and his friends.

71. Report of the Proceedings of the Board of Officers, January 22, 1948, William E. White, folder 8 Discharge Review White, William E., II: G9, National Association for the Advancement of Colored People Records, Manuscript Division, LC.

72. Bérubé, *Coming Out Under Fire*, 105.

73. Bérubé, *Coming Out Under Fire*, 106–113.

74. Bérubé, *Coming Out Under Fire*, 392.

75. This is in notable contrast to several other NAACP-affiliated attorneys, including Charles Hamilton Houston, Franklin Williams, and Thurgood Marshall.

76. The NAACP did not pursue a homosexuality-related discharge review for Henry Nord because he had already appeared before the Army Discharge Review Board in Saint Louis, Missouri.

77. For more on the role of rumor during the 1943 Detroit riots, see Johnson, "Gender, Race, and Rumours."

78. For more on the NAACP's engagement with interracial couples and miscegenation as well as general histories of interracial marriage and miscegenation law, see Romano, *Race Mixing*; Pascoe, *What Comes Naturally*; Stein, *Sexual Injustice*. Pascoe's text has the most complete discussion of the NAACP's engagement with miscegenation law.

79. Pascoe, *What Comes Naturally*, 191–204.

80. Chen, *The Fifth Freedom*, 41–42. For more on the postwar struggle to resuscitate and preserve the FEPC and its importance for Black freedom struggle historiography, see Chen, *The Fifth Freedom*, 32–87.

81. "NAACP to Senate: Vote FEPC Funds," *Chicago Defender*, June 17, 1944, 3.

82. Memorandum to Thurgood Marshall from Leslie Perry, May 21, 1945, folder General Correspondence May–August 1945, II: G9, National Association for the Advancement of Colored People Records, Manuscript Division, LC.

83. Jesse O. Dedmon, "When G.I. Joe Comes Home," May 19, 1945, folder Discharge Reviews "N" 1945–1950, II: G8, National Association for the Advancement of Colored People Records, Manuscript Division, LC. Dedmon reiterated the im-

perative nature of such appeals during a veterans conference at Howard University in November 1945, stating "All Negroes who have received other than honorable discharges are urged to file [an] application for a review of the same." "Report of the NAACP Veterans Conference," November 1945, folder General Correspondence November–December 1945, II: G10, National Association for the Advancement of Colored People Records, Manuscript Division, LC.

84. "Veterans Conference," folder General Correspondence November–December 1945, II: G10, National Association for the Advancement of Colored People Records, Manuscript Division, LC.

85. "NAACP Manual for Veterans' Committee," folder Branch Veterans Committees by States "A–G" 1945–1948, II: G1, National Association for the Advancement of Colored People Records, Manuscript Division, LC.

86. "The Army Blue Discharge Certificate," *Atlanta Daily World*, November 24, 1945, 6.

87. Walter White to Jesse O. Dedmon, August 10, 1948; Jesse O. Dedmon to Walter White, September 10, 1948, folder General Correspondence cont. July–December 1948, II: G11, National Association for the Advancement of Colored People Records, Manuscript Division,LC.

88. See Mershon and Schlossman, *Foxholes and Color Lines*, 183–185.

89. Jesse O. Dedmon to Walter White, September 10, 1948, folder General Correspondence cont. July–December 1948, II: G11, National Association for the Advancement of Colored People Papers, Manuscript Division, LC.

90. For more on this, see Anderson, *Eyes off the Prize*.

91. The literature on Black radicalism during the 1930s, 1940s, and 1950s is robust. For some key works on this period, see Gore, *Radicalism at the Crossroads*; Harris, "Marvel Cooke"; Kelley, *Hammer and Hoe*; Kelley, *Freedom Dreams*; McDuffie, *Sojourning for Freedom*; McDuffie, "Black and Red"; Ransby, *Ella Baker and the Black Freedom Movement*.

92. For more on the Lavender Scare, see Dean, *Imperial Brotherhood*; Johnson, *The Lavender Scare*.

93. "War Veteran Wins Army Battle, Will Get Benefits," *Los Angeles Sentinel*, July 11, 1963, A1.

94. See, for example, "Bishop, Organist Face Court Trial," *Baltimore Afro-American*, April 13, 1940, 1; for examples of the visibility of same-sex desire in Black churches, see Retzloff, "Seer or Queer?"; Best, *Passionately Human*.

Chapter 2

1. John W. Hamilton to Anonymous Supporters, October 25, 1956, *White American News Service*, Reel 51, RWC. Also in folder 3: White Sentinel, 1954–1971, box 1, J. D. Rowlett Collection, GA.

2. Johnson, *The Broken Heart of America*.

3. Rothstein, *The Color of Law*, 85.

4. For more about radical right organizing in Saint Louis, Missouri see Johnson, *The Broken Heart of America*, 291–336.

5. "Study in Animosity," *Saint Louis Post-Dispatch*, April 13, 1952. Copied in the following: "(National) Citizens' Protective Association, John W. Hamilton," Dossier, October 1954, folder NUL Administration Department General Department File Subversion of the UL John Hamilton, I: A50, National Urban League Records, Manuscript Division, LC.

6. "(National) Citizens' Protective Association, John W. Hamilton," Dossier, October 1954, folder NUL Administration Department General Department File Subversion of the UL John Hamilton, I: A50, National Urban League Records, Manuscript Division, LC.

7. His relationship with the local Republican leadership is unknown, but they may have frowned upon his activism. He was subsequently removed in the wake of his arrest and trial. For notice of his removal, see "St. Louis Election Officials Resign," *Jefferson City Post-Tribune*, November 29, 1956, 19; "John Hamilton Out as Election Official Here," *Saint Louis Argus*, November 30, 1956, 1.

8. See *Reed, Alms Not Opportunity*.

9. "Red Feather Tours," folder 18 Community Chest, 1949–1955 box 4, Urban League of Saint Louis, WUSL.

10. Parris and Brooks, *Blacks in the City*, 165–169, 369.

11. For more on Black women's political struggles in St. Louis, see Ervin, *Gateway to Equality*.

12. Flyer, "Where Does Your Money Go: 58 Chests-Funds Support Anti-White Urban League," undated, included in United Community Funds and Councils of American memorandum dated February 19, 1958, folder United Community and Councils 1956–1959, I: B14, National Urban League Records, Manuscript Division, LC.

13. "Sales of Philip Morris Cigarettes Drop 48%," *White Sentinel*, March 1958, folder Hate Groups, 1957–1958, I: B3, National Urban League Records, Manuscript Division, LC.

14. M. Leo Bohanon to William Charles, October 22, 1953, folder 36, box 4, Urban League of Saint Louis, WUSL.

15. *White Sentinel*, March 1958, folder Hate Groups, 1957–1958, I: B3, National Urban League Records, Manuscript Division, LC.

16. Brochure, "Where Does Your Money Go: 58 Chests-Funds Support Anti-White Urban League," undated, included in United Community Funds and Councils of American memorandum dated February 19, 1958, folder United Community and Councils 1956–1959, I: B14, National Urban League Records, Manuscript Division, LC.

17. Flyer, "Where Does Your Money Go: 58 Chests-Funds Support Anti-White Urban League," undated, included in United Community Funds and Councils of American memorandum dated February 19, 1958, folder United Community and Councils 1956–1959, I: B14, National Urban League Records, Manuscript Division, LC. See image above article beginning "Oakridge Tenn.," *White Sentinel*, October 1955, 1 and "A Result of Integration in Kirkwood, Mo. Schools," *White Sentinel*, November 1955, 1, 5. Both copies are located in folder 7, box 4, Race Relations Collection, ASCUM.

18. Flyer, "Where Does Your Money Go: 58 Chests-Funds Support Anti-White Urban League," undated, included in United Community Funds and Councils of American memorandum dated February 19, 1958, folder United Community and Councils 1956–1959, I: B14, National Urban League Records, Manuscript Division, LC.

19. For scholarship that explores the linkages between interracial space and homosexuality, see Mumford, "Homosex Changes."

20. England, letter to the editor, *Little Rock Arkansas Democrat*, October 7, 1956, folder NUL Newspaper Clippings Attacks against Urban League 1956, I: N75, National Urban League Records, Manuscript Division, LC.

21. G. F. J., letter to the editor, *Little Rock Arkansas Democrat*, September 17, 1956, folder NUL Newspaper Clippings Attacks against Urban League 1956, I: N75, National Urban League Records, Manuscript Division, LC.

22. "Negro-Aid Group Will Lose Funds," *New York Times*, September 15, 1956, 6; "States Rights Group Would Bar League Aid," *Norfolk Journal and Guide*, October 27, 1956, box 4, Urban League of Saint Louis, WUSL.

23. "Urban League Cut Off Chest Fund Case," *Jacksonville Florida Star*, September 15, 1956.

24. "As Drive Draws Urban League Withdraws from Community Chest," *Norfolk Ledger Star*, October 9, 1956.

25. Jo Hyde, "Urban League Requests Omission from Chest," *Richmond Times-Dispatch*, October 6, 1956; "As Drive Draws Urban League Withdraws from Community Chest," *Norfolk Ledger Star*, October 9, 1956.

26. Charles X. Sampson, memorandum, "Urban League–Chest and United Fund Relationship," undated, folder Subversion and the UL Miscellaneous, I: A50, National Urban League Records, Manuscript Division, LC.

27. Theodore Kheel to James A. Linen, July 31, 1957, folder United Community Funds and Councils 1956–1959, I: B14, National Urban League Records, Manuscript Division, LC.

28. "South Cuts Funds of Urban League," *New York Times*, November 18, 1957, fol. NUL Newspaper Clippings Attacks against Urban League 1956, I: N75, National Urban League Records, Manuscript Division, LC.

29. Nelson C. Jackson, memorandum, "Conference with Lyman Ford and Ralph Blanchard," to R. Maurice Moss, May 10, 1956, folder Subversion and the UL Memoranda General, I: A49, National Urban League Records, Manuscript Division, LC.

30. James A. Linen to Theodore Kheel, September 9, 1957, folder United Community and Councils 1956–1959, I: B14, National Urban League Records, Manuscript Division, LC.

31. See "Questions the Chest on League Support," September 24, 1956, *Richmond VA News-Leader*, folder NUL Newspaper Clippings Attacks against Urban League 1956, I: N75, National Urban League Records, Manuscript Division, LC.

32. I ascertained this by examining numerous examples of press coverage and from NUL correspondence. NUL officials and their affiliates never identified individuals within the local or national Community Chests as a problem. Additionally, NUL reached out to UCFCA officials; both organizations shared information

regarding these attacks. See Nelson C. Jackson, memorandum, "Conference with Lyman Ford and Ralph Blanchard," to R. Maurice Moss, May 10, 1956, folder Subversion and the UL Memoranda General, I: A49, National Urban League Records, Manuscript Division, LC; James A. Linen to Theodore Kheel, September 9, 1957, folder United Community and Councils 1956–1959, I: B14, National Urban League Records, Manuscript Division, LC. Charles X. Sampson, UCFCA director of field services, seemed especially supportive of the Urban League and kept the NUL updated on the nature of attacks. For examples of correspondence with Urban League officials, see Charles X. Sampson, memorandum, "Urban League–Chests and United Funds Relationships," The Urban League Files, folder Subversion and the UL Miscellaneous, I: A50, National Urban League Records, Manuscript Division, LC; Sampson to Nelson Jackson, November 16, 1956, folder United Community Funds and Councils, 1956–1959, I: B14, National Urban League Records, Manuscript Division, LC; Jackson to Sampson, September 9, 1957, folder United Community Funds and Councils, 1956–1959, I: B14, National Urban League Records, Manuscript Division, LC.

33. For specific references to NUL strategies for organizing with social work groups and organized labor, see Nelson C. Jackson, memorandum, "Southern Trip February 28–March 21, 1956," to Urban League Executives, April 16, 1956, folder United Community Funds and Councils 1956–1959, I: B14, National Urban League Records, Manuscript Division, LC; Nelson C. Jackson, memorandum, "Attacks against the Urban League for Use at St. Louis Meeting," to Lester B. Granger, May 16, 1956, folder Subversion and the UL Memoranda General 1956, I: A49, National Urban League Records Manuscript Division, LC; Marian D. Simmons to Thomas A. Webster, May 8, 1956, folder Subversion and the Urban League Local Affiliates 1956, I: A49, National Urban League Records, Manuscript Division, LC.

34. Nelson C. Jackson, memorandum, "Southern Trip February 28–March 21, 1956," to Urban League Executives, April 16, 1956, folder United Community Funds and Councils 1956–1959, I: B14, National Urban League Records, Manuscript Division, LC; Nelson C. Jackson, memorandum, "Attacks against the Urban League for Use at St. Louis Meeting," to Lester B. Granger, May 16, 1956, folder Subversion and the UL Memoranda General 1956, I: A49, National Urban League Records, Manuscript Collection, LC.

35. Lester B. Granger, memorandum, to Nelson C. Jackson, May 16, 1956, folder Subversion and the UL Memoranda General, 1956, I: A49, National Urban League Records, Manuscript Division, LC.

36. Writing to Granger in May, Nelson Jackson suggested the "use of public relations media to positively tell the story of the local urban league in an effort to offset lies and false propaganda by hate groups." Lester B. Granger, memorandum, to Nelson C. Jackson, May 16, 1956, folder Subversion and the UL Memoranda General, 1956, I: A49, National Urban League Records, Manuscript Division, LC.

37. R. Maurice Moss, memorandum to NUL Executive Committee and Staff, June 8, 1956, folder Subversion and the UL Memoranda General 1956, I: A49, National Urban League Records, Manuscript Division, LC.

38. It appears that the NUL shared copies of the dossier with Community Chests throughout the South. For example, see Nelson C. Jackson, memorandum,

"Telephone Call from Tom Wintersteen Executive Director Welfare Council of Dade County . . ." to Lester B. Granger, June 5, 1956, folder Subversion and the UL Memoranda General 1956, I: A49, National Urban League Records, Manuscript Division, LC.

39. The dossier does not contain any salacious information on Hamilton or other members of the NCPA. It quite simply recounts the basic chronology of the organization, published statements, and Hamilton speeches. See Summary Data, "John W. Hamilton, National Citizens' Protective Association," folder NUL Administration Department General Department File Subversion of the UL John Hamilton, I: A50, National Urban League Records, Manuscript Division, LC.

40. Harry Alston to Jack (surname unknown), October 8, 1956, folder Community Services Department Special File White Citizens Council Correspondence (General) 1956–1963, I: B22, National Urban League Records, Manuscript Division, LC.

41. The following account of the alleged molestation is contained in a copy of the police report obtained by the NUL. Police Report of John Hamilton, October 13, 1956, folder Subversion and the UL Miscellaneous, I: A50, National Urban League Records, Manuscript Division, LC. In Atlanta Urban League Papers: box 24 Administrative Files, 1943–1961, series 6 Grace Hamilton, 1942–1961 (1967), Subgroup II Presidents' Files, 1922–1990, Atlanta Urban League Papers, ARC.

42. *State of Missouri v. John Wilson Hamilton*, 310 S.W. 2d 906 (1958).

43. M. Leo Bohanon to Nelson C. Jackson, October 16, 1956, folder Community Services Department Special File White Citizens Council St. Louis, MO, I: B23, National Urban League Records, Manuscript Division, LC. It appears that Bohanon may have informed other Urban League chapters of the moral charges against Hamilton based on a letter he wrote to a member of the Fort Worth Urban League, in which he enclosed a copy of the *Saint Louis Globe-Democrat* article. M. Leo Bohanon to Velma McEwen, October 16, 1956, folder Community Services Department Special File White Citizens Council St. Louis, MO, I: B23, National Urban League Records, Manuscript Division, LC.

44. "John W. Hamilton Arrested on Morals Charges," *Saint Louis Globe-Democrat*, October 16, 1956, n.p.

45. This memorandum is simply addressed to "city editors" making it impossible to definitively determine the intended recipients. I assume that he sent it to African American and mainstream newspapers. See Guichard Parris, memorandum, "A Suggested Subject for Editorial Treatment," box 24, Administrative Files, 1943–1961, series 6 Grace Hamilton, 1942–1961 (1967), Subgroup II Presidents' Files, 1922–1990, Atlanta Urban League Papers, ARC. Also located in folder News Releases 1956, I: E37, National Urban League Records, Manuscript Division, LC.

46. Minutes of Meeting of Board of Directors October 18, 1956, box 2, Urban League of Saint Louis, WUSL.

47. Nelson C. Jackson, memorandum, to Executive Secretaries, October 18, 1956, folder Community Services Department Special File White Citizens Council Correspondence General 1956–1963, I: B22, National Urban League Records, Manuscript Division, LC.

48. Charles Sampson to Nelson Jackson, November 1, 1956, folder Community Services Department special file White Citizens Council Correspondence (General) 1956–1963, I: B22, National Urban League Records, Manuscript Division, LC.

49. Unfortunately, there was no accompanying documentation specifying when the report was received or who forwarded it to the national office or the Atlanta branch. However, copies of this document can be found in the NUL Papers as well as the papers of the Atlanta Urban League. Police report of John Hamilton, October 13, 1956, folder Subversion and the UL Miscellaneous, I: A50, National Urban League Records, Manuscript Division, LC, in Atlanta Urban League Papers, box 24 Administrative Files, 1943–1961, series 6 Grace Hamilton, 1942–1961 (1967), Subgroup II Presidents' Files, 1922–1990, Atlanta Urban League Papers, ARC.

50. Lester Granger, "Manhattan and Beyond," *New York Amsterdam News*, November 24, 1956, 8.

51. Nelson C. Jackson to M. Leo Bohanon, October 19, 1956, folder 8, National Urban League Nelson C. Jackson Director of Community Services 1956, box 18, I: A50, National Urban League Records, Manuscript Division, LC.

52. M. Leo Bohanon to Olive Samuel, October 22, 1956, folder 8, National Urban League Nelson C. Jackson Director of Community Services 1956 box 18, I: A50, National Urban League Records, Manuscript Division, LC.

53. For a very small sample of this literature, see Dailey, "Sex, Segregation, and the Sacred"; Feimster, *Southern Horrors*; Hodes, *White Women, Black Men*; McGuire, *At the Dark End of the Street*; Rosén, *Terror in the Heart of Freedom*; Smith, *How Race Is Made*.

54. Notably, Thaddeus Russell does draw some connections between intensifying homophobia in the Black press and the work of civil rights organizations. See Russell, "The Color of Discipline."

55. Dean, *Imperial Brotherhood*, 63–168.

56. Dean, *Imperial Brotherhood*, 63–168.

57. For more on the emergence of the NUL, see Reed, *Not Alms but Opportunity*.

58. Granger, "Manhattan and Beyond," *New York Amsterdam News*, November 24, 1956, 8.

59. The *Pittsburgh Courier*, the *Norfolk New Journal and Guide*, the *Rockford Crusader*, the *Saint Louis Argus*, and the *Baltimore Afro-American* all featured articles about Hamilton's arrest and trial. "Editor of Race-Baiting Paper Faces Morals Trial," *Norfolk New Journal and Guide*, October 27, 1956, 11; "Hate Sheet Editor, Sex Deviate," *Rockford Crusader*, November 2, 1956, 8; "White Sentinel Editor Guilty of Perversion," *Pittsburgh Courier*, March 2, 1957, 23.

60. Roberts and Klibanoff, *The Race Beat*, 76.

61. Jenkins, *Moral Panic*, 61–64.

62. For more on the history of the sexual psychopath, see Chauncey, "The Postwar Sex Crime Panic"; Freedman, "'Uncontrollable Desires'"; Jenkins, *Moral Panic*.

63. A key word search of major Black newspapers digitized on Proquest Historical Newspapers reveal ninety-one references to "sex maniac" during the 1950s alone.

64. "8 Year Old Boy Attacked Near Home by Sex Maniac," *Norfolk New Journal and Guide*, July 22, 1950, D2; "Girls Feared Sex Victims," *Los Angles Sentinel*, September 25, 1952, A1.

65. Roger Maddox, "Menace in Our Midst—Sex Crimes: No Child Is Safe from This Evil!" *Baltimore Afro-American*, April 7, 1956, 20E.

66. Gallon, *Pleasure in the News*, 4.

67. Gallon, *Pleasure in the News*. Simon D. Elin Fisher argues that the Black press as a crucial space for knowledge sharing about gender (and sexual) nonconformity. See Fisher, "Challenging Dissemblance."

68. See Leonard, "'Containing Perversion'"; Russell, "The Color of Discipline."

69. For more on Prophet Jones and his queer sex scandal, see Retzloff, "Seer or Queer?"; Conerly, "Queering the Black Church."

70. Chauncey, "The Postwar Sex Crime Panic."

71. For examples of this, see "White Sentinel Editor Guilty of Perversion," *Pittsburgh Courier*, March 2, 1957, 23; "Leader of Race Hate Group Guilty on Morals Charge," *Norfolk New Journal and Guide*, March 2, 1957, C1; "White Citizens Council Editor Guilty," *Baltimore Afro-American*, March 2, 1957, 1; "Editor of Race-Baiting Paper Faces Morals Trial," *Norfolk New Journal and Guide*, October 27, 1956, 11.

72. Romesburg, "'Wouldn't a Boy Do?'"

73. See *State of Missouri v. John Wilson Hamilton*, 310 S.W. 2d 906 (1958).

74. See Carroll, *Race News*.

75. On October 3, 1956, two white men in a vehicle approached the youth and asked where they could "find some girls." When the shoeshine boy noted they could visit a nearby hotel, they asked him to accompany them to provide directions. Once in the vehicle, they asked the boy to "do something nasty" (alternately described as an "unnatural sex act"). An African American cabdriver saw the vehicle going the wrong way on a one-way street and was alarmed further when "one of the men force[d] the boy's head down" after seeing the cabdriver. The cabdriver followed them, blowing his horn, and forced them to pull over. Police, who were alerted by the cabdriver's actions, then arrested them. Initially, it was reported that charges were not brought against the men, but less than a month later, a trial date had been set. Although they were charged with child molestation and delinquency charges, the court failed to serve them because they could not be located. See "Prosecutor Fails to Press Charges Involving Youth," *Saint Louis Argus*, October 5, 1956, 1; "Charge 2 Who Took Shoe Shine Boy," *Saint Louis Argus*, October 26, 1956, 1; "Fail to Serve 2 in Abduction Case of Youth," *Saint Louis Argus*, November 30, 1956, 1.

76. See "John Hamilton Is Guilty," *Saint Louis Argus*, February 22, 1957, 1; "Police Told Hamilton Kept Other Male Dates," *Saint Louis Argus*, October 19, 1956, 1.

77. Howard Woods, "Portrait of a White Supremacist," *Pittsburgh Courier*, November 24, 1956, 8. There was also a second part to this article: Howard B. Woods, "Portrait of a White Supremacist," *Pittsburgh Courier*, December 1, 1956, C6.

78. See two images near "Police Report on John Wilson Hamilton," *Saint Louis Argus*, November 19, 1956, 15; "John Hamilton Out as Election Official Here," *Saint Louis Argus*, November 30, 1956, 1.

79. "Room 311," *Saint Louis Argus*, October 19, 1956, 14. The editorial's title is the number of the Saint Nicholas hotel room the youth and Hamilton shared that night.

80. This is an amalgamation of the city's two leading newspaper titles—the *Saint Louis Globe-Democrat* and the *Saint Louis Post-Dispatch*.

81. "Confusin' Ain't It," *Saint Louis Argus*, October 19, 1956, 14.

82. Richard Howell, Letter to the Editor, *Baltimore Afro-American*, March 9, 1957, 4.

83. Dorothy Lemmons, Letter to the Editor, "Shocked," *Saint Louis Argus*, October 26, 1956.

84. For more about the importance of sexuality in the Black public sphere from 1925 to 1940, see Gallon, *Pleasure in the News*.

85. Joyce Caldwell, Editorial, *Saint Louis Argus*, November 2, 1956, 14.

86. Beulah Parks, Letter to the Editor, *Baltimore Afro-American*, March 9, 1957, 4.

87. "Editor of the White Sentinel Held on Morals Charge," *Saint Louis Post-Dispatch*, October 16, 1956, C3; "Molesting Charge against John W. Hamilton Dropped," *Saint Louis Post-Dispatch*, October 20, 1956, 3A; "Johns W. Hamilton Convicted by Jury," *Saint Louis Post-Dispatch*, February 21, 1957, 14D.

88. In addition to the general southern newspapers reviewed, I also consulted the *Jackson Clarion Ledger*, the *Atlanta Constitution*, and the *New Orleans Times Picayune*.

89. "White Sentinel Editor Accused of Sodomy," *Washington Post and Times Herald*, October 17, 1956, B3.

90. Walter Winchell, "Broadway and Elsewhere," *Logansport* (IN) *Pharos-Tribune*, March 4, 1957, 4.

91. Roberts and Klibanoff, *The Race Beat*.

92. Editor's Corner, *American Nationalist*, May 25, 1953, 2; Press Report, *American Nationalist*, January 1956, 2.

93. Press Report, *American Nationalist*, March 1957, 4.

Chapter 3

1. Garrow, *Protest at Selma*, 2.

2. Joseph Doherty to George C. Wallace, March 22, 1965, folder 5, box SG030822, Governors George C. and Lurleen B. Wallace Collection, ADAH.

3. The Florida Legislative Investigation Committee was also colloquially known as the Johns Committee after its chairman, Charley Johns, a state senator who served as governor from 1953 to 1955.

4. An exception is historian Stacy Braukman, who asserts that the committee's homophobia was one aspect of southerners articulations of anti-communism. For more, see Braukman, *Communists and Perverts*.

5. Howard, *Men Like That*, 147.

6. Throughout the chapter, I use phrases "Alabama voting rights demonstrations" or "voting rights demonstrations" to refer to a series of demonstrations that took place in February and March 1965. Most of the key nationally visible clashes took place in March, as did the rumors of alleged impropriety.

7. Leighton, "Freedom Indivisible," 263–289.

8. For a brief overviews of the sexual politics associated with the Alabama voting rights demonstrations, see Dailey, "Sex, Segregation, and the Sacred," 138–142; McGuire, *At the Dark End of the Street*, 174–189; Eagles, *Outside Agitator*; Friedland, *Lift Up Your Voice*; Garrow, *Protest at Selma*; May, *The Informant*; Stanton, *From Selma to Sorrow*.

9. William L. Dickinson speaking on "March on Montgomery—the Untold Story," on March 30, 1965, Congressional Record 6333–6335.

10. Garrow, *Protest at Selma*, 31–39.

11. For more on this, see Garrow, *Protest at Selma*, 221–224.

12. Roberts and Klibanoff, *The Race Beat*, 376.

13. Violence as a part of white supremacist action was not uniformly embraced. While most white racial militants, the Ku Klux Klan, and other more radical groups believed that violence was a useful and necessary tool in the protection of white supremacy. More moderate segregationist groups, like the Citizens' Councils, most state entities, and the business community wanted to avoid violence. For more on this point, see Webb, *Rabble Rousers*; McMillen, *The Citizens' Council*; Bartley, *The Rise of Massive Resistance*.

14. Garrow, *Protest at Selma*, 35.

15. It is worth noting that the national press largely ignored Jackson's death. This suggests more broadly how the loss of African American lives was not deemed as noteworthy and, therefore, not as valuable as their white counterparts. Roberts and Klibanoff, *The Race Beat*, 384.

16. Roberts and Klibanoff, *The Race Beat*, 375–394.

17. For a broad overview of the demonstrations, see Garrow, *Protest at Selma*, 131–132.

18. Roberts and Klibanoff, *The Race Beat*, 360–361.

19. Bodroghkozy, *Equal Time*, 377.

20. Roberts and Klibanoff, *The Race Beat*, 407.

21. Roberts and Klibanoff, *The Race Beat*, 360–361.

22. Carter, *The Politics of Rage*, 232–233; Wallace, "The Way We See It," 51, 60–61.

23. For a detailed discussion of Workman and Waring, see Bedingfield, *Newspaper Wars*, 149–169.

24. There were a handful of moderate southern newspaper editors who consistently advocated for moderation with federal officials, national unity, and deplored the violence that characterized some of the resistance to desegregation. Notable figures include Ralph McGill of the *Atlanta Constitution*, Buford Boone of the *Tuscaloosa News*, and Hodding Carter Jr. of the *Greenville Delta Democrat Times*. For more on these figures, see Roberts and Klibanoff, *The Race Beat*, 24–43.

25. These suits were eventually thrown out because, under Alabama law, all related action had to take place within the state. For more on this, see Roberts and Klibanoff, *The Race Beat*, 126–142.

26. Roberts and Klibanoff, *The Race Beat*, 126–142.

27. Woods, *Black Struggle, Red Scare*.

28. Ted Pearson, "Pink-Hued Smoke Hangs over Integration Drive," *Birmingham News*, March 27, 1965, 6.

29. "Making the Best of the Bad," *Montgomery Advertiser*, March 26, 1965, 4.

30. Despite chief editor Virginus Dabney's relatively moderate views, editorials about civil rights demonstrations became increasingly conservative during the 1950s and 1960s. Roberts and Klibanoff, *The Race Beat*, 114.

31. "Why They Lose Their Heads," *Richmond Times Dispatch*, March 18, 1965, 16.

32. J. J. Mallory, "New Low," *Montgomery Advertiser*, March 21, 1965, 4A.

33. Woods, *Black Struggle, Red Scare*, 71, 152.

34. For more on general use of civil war memory during the mid-twentieth century contests over racial equality, see Blight, *American Oracle*.

35. As Michael Bronski notes, "The beat movement and homosexual culture were inextricably intertwined." For more on the beats' connection to LGBTQ+ history, see Bronski, *A Queer History of the United States*, 200.

36. Howard, *Men Like That*, 147.

37. John Howard's analysis of these trends is a crucial intervention into southern race relations and queer sexualities. For more on this, see Howard, *Men Like That*, 142–166. This section also includes his analysis of Aaron Henry and Bill Higgs, civil rights activists whose same-sex attractions were mobilized to undermine their legitimacy in the public sphere.

38. Tom Lankford, "Hep-Talking Beatniks Dig Demonstrations in Alabama," *Birmingham News*, March 21, 1965, A-4.

39. "Untitled," *Montgomery Advertiser*, March 12, 1965, 10.

40. Insularity from laity disapproval often determined an individual minister's ability to engage in activism. For further information, see Friedland, *Lift Up Your Voice*, 10–15.

41. For more on clerical participation in the modern civil rights movement, see Friedland, *Lift Up Your Voice*.

42. For more on anticlericalism in southern resistance to desegregation, see Chappell, *A Stone of Hope*, 125–135.

43. M. H. Smith, "Costume Boom," *Montgomery Advertiser*, March 21, 1963, 4A.

44. "Impersonation of Clergy—Alabama," *Race Relations Law Reporter* 10 (1965–1966): 1364–1365.

45. Dailey, "Sex, Segregation, and the Sacred," 121–122.

46. Roberts and Klibanoff, *The Race Beat*, 230.

47. "Making the Best of Bad," *Montgomery Advertiser*, March 26, 1965, 4.

48. "Making the Best of Bad," *Montgomery Advertiser*, March 26, 1965, 4.

49. Dailey, "Sex, Segregation and the Sacred," 138–142.

50. Leslie Carpenter, "Harassing Bobby K.," *Abilene Reporter-News*, March 21, 1965, 8-B.

51. "Lovemaking in Open Definitely Occurred in Selma Prayer Vigil," *Birmingham News*, March 28, 1965, A10.

52. In a survey of the correspondence to Senators John Sparkman and Lister Hill of Alabama in March and April 1965, this article was sent to them in at least one hundred individual letters.

53. "Demonstrations Religious Leaders Alabama Resolution," *Race Relations Law Reporter* 10 (1965–1966): 1364–1365.

54. United Press International, "Promiscuous Behavior Charges Leveled," *Nashville Banner*, March 24, 1965, 1; Associated Press, "Alabama Legislature Raps Rights Marchers Conduct," *Charleston News Courier*, March 25, 1965, 8D.

55. "Selma Orgies Charged by Alabama Lawmaker," *Los Angeles Times*, March 31, 1965, 8; "House Told Drunkenness, Sex Orgies Marked Part of Selma Rights March," *Washington Post*, March 31, 1965, A9; "Selma March Said Marked by Sex Orgies," *Birmingham News*, March 31, 1965, 8.

56. "House Told Drunkenness, Sex Orgies Marked Part of Selma Rights March," *Washington Post*, March 31, 1965, A9.

57. Associated Press, "Selma Orgies Charged by Alabama Lawmaker," *Los Angeles Times*, March 21, 1965, 8. The secondary headline is "Communists behind March, he asserted on House Floor, Statements hit as garbage."

58. Buchwald was a syndicated columnist. This particular story appeared in the *Boston Globe* and the *Los Angeles Times*. See Art Buchwald, "Those Civil Rights 'Orgies'—They Shall Be Overcome," *Los Angeles Times*, April 6, 1965, D1; Art Buchwald, "Where the Boys Are Going," *Boston Globe*, April 7, 1965, 5.

59. Excerpt reprinted in "News Printed, Not Rumors of Every Kind from Selma," *Birmingham News*, March 27, 1965, 6.

60. "Saw No Orgies During March Editor Reports," *Los Angeles Times*, April 27, 1965, 5; "Newsman Doesn't Find Immorality on March," folder 158 Civil Rights Correspondence, c. 1965, box 89-06, William L. Dickinson Congressional Papers, AUM.; see also "The News—Briefly," *Christian Science Monitor*, April 29, 1965, 2.

61. "Selma Orgies Charged by Alabama Lawmaker," *Los Angeles Times*, March 31, 1965, 8.

62. "Negro Hits Mongrelization," *El Paso Herald Post*, March 31, 1965, C2; "Bevel Lashes Out at Charges of Immorality," *Birmingham News*, March 31, 1965, 4.

63. McGuire, *At the Dark End of the Street*, 191–220.

64. Anonymous to William L. Dickinson, undated, folder 189 Anti-Dickinson, box 89-04, William L. Dickinson Congressional Papers, AUM.

65. C. R. Rowan to William L. Dickinson, undated, folder 189 Anti-Dickinson, box 89-04, William L. Dickinson Congressional Papers, AUM.

66. Sara C. Mayberry to William L. Dickinson, April 27, 1965, folder 189 Anti-Dickinson, box 89-04, William L. Dickinson Congressional Papers, AUM.

67. Welsey Crowe to William L. Dickinson, April 25, 1965, folder 189 Anti-Dickinson, box 89-04, William L. Dickinson Congressional Papers, AUM.

68. These transcripts include statements from members of the National Guard, State Troopers, State Highway Patrol and the Montgomery County and City Police. These transcripts are located in folder 141 Civil Rights Affidavits, box 3, William L. Dickinson Congressional Papers, AUM.

69. These documents were provided by George L. Singelmann, secretary of the Citizens' Council of Greater New Orleans (letter undated). It is unclear if this material was requested by Dickinson or simply sent to him. The following items are

located in this folder: Statement of Wayne Martin Long to the Pasadena Police Department, January 21, 1953; Pasadena Police Record Bayard Rustin 1953; Felony Report Bayard Rustin Pasadena Police Department. A flyer titled "Girls, Girls, Girls" is also located in this folder. See folder 142 Civil Rights Evidence, box 3, William L. Dickinson Congressional Papers, AUM.

70. Untitled and undated memorandum, folder 141 Civil Rights Affidavits, box 3, William L. Dickinson Congressional Papers, AUM.

71. William L. Dickinson to J. Edgar Hoover, April 16, 1965, folder 165 Civil Rights Correspondence H, box 89-03, William L. Dickinson Congressional Papers, AUM.

72. J. Edgar Hoover to William L. Dickinson April 20, 1965, folder 165 Civil Rights Correspondence H, box 89-03, William L. Dickinson Congressional Papers, AUM.

73. See Leighton, "Freedom Indivisible," 215–260.

74. William L. Dickinson speaking on "March on Montgomery—the Untold Story," on April 27, 1965, Congressional Record 8592–8598.

75. See debate on "March on Montgomery—the Untold Story," on April 27, 1965, Congressional Record 8598–8600.

76. "Clerical Rights Workers Deny March Immorality," *Los Angeles Times*, April 29, 1965, 7; "Clergy, Nun Deny Charges against Selma-Montgomery Marchers," *Boston Globe*, April 29, 1965, 13.

77. For more on Joseph McCarthy's experience with lavender baiting, see Dean, *Imperial Brotherhood*, 147–168.

78. Edward Strickland to William L. Dickinson, April 28, 1965, folder 177 Civil Rights Correspondence S 1965, box 89-04, William L. Dickinson Congressional Papers, AUM.

79. William L. Dickinson to Edward Strickland, April 29, 1965, folder 177 Civil Rights Correspondence S 1965, box 89-04, William L. Dickinson Congressional Papers, AUM.

80. Although a number of cases loosened the grip of obscenity law, the 1957 U.S. Supreme Court case *Roth v. United States* was consequential. It narrowed the definition of obscenity to "whether to the average person, applying contemporary standards, the dominant theme of the material taken as a whole appeals to prurient interest." See Strub, *Perversion for Profit*, 62–63.

81. For an in-depth analysis of the history of obscenity law, including *Roth v. United States* see Strub, *Obscenity Rules*.

82. Although gay men and lesbians were better able to create a collective public sphere through publications during the 1960s, they also benefited (directly and indirectly) from the production of expositions of homosexuality directed toward a general audience. See Meeker, *Contacts Desired*, 51–98, 109–112.

83. Meeker, *Contacts Desired*, 112.

84. Simmons, "Public Stereotypes of Deviants."

85. Henry and Curry, *Fire Ever Burning*, 124. For press coverage of this see "Hold Henry Guilty, Libel," *Laurel Leader Call*, December 2, 1963, 2. For coverage see "Court Reverses Libel Ruling Against Henry," *Greenville Delta Democrat Times*, March 29, 1965, 1; "Mississippi Libel Verdict is Overturned," *Abilene Reporter News*, March 29, 1965, 2A.

86. See Stewart-Winter, "The Fall of Walter Jenkins"; Dean, *Imperial Brotherhood*, 221–226.

87. "Four Indicted, Accused of Plot to Libel Kuchel," *Los Angeles Times*, February 18, 1965, 1; Lawrence E. Davies, "Kuchel, Target of Rumors, Fights Back and Takes His Accusers to Court," *New York Times*, February 28, 1965, 69; Ronald Einstoss, "Effort to Link Kuchel, Jenkins Let to Affidavit," *Los Angeles Times*, March 5, 1965, 2; Jack Jones, "3 Admit Errors in Kuchel Libel Case," *Los Angeles Times*, June 29, 1965, 3.

88. McGuire, *At the Dark End of the Street*, 212–224; Persons, *The True Selma Story*.

89. Persons, *The True Selma Story*, 2.

90. Persons, *The True Selma Story*, 7.

91. For more, see Chauncey, *Gay New York*.

92. Dailey, "Sex, Segregation, and the Sacred," 138–142.

93. Mikell, *Selma*.

94. The anxiety over queer sexual behavior is somewhat unsurprising given the figures who facilitated his ability to write this exposé. Mikell thanked several key Alabama officials for their cooperation, including Governor Wallace, Representative Dickinson, and Sheriff James G. Clark. See Mikell, *Selma*.

95. Mikell, *Selma*.

96. Bob Marsh, "Sorrow of Selma," folder 261 B April 1965, box 498, Lister Hill Papers, WSHL.

97. Charles Bishop, "A True Picture of the Alabama Story," Bainbridge, Georgia (undated). Located in folder 156 Civil Rights Correspondence B 1965, box 89–03, William L. Dickinson Congressional Papers, AUM.

98. For more on Myron C. Fagan and the Educational Guild, see Persons, *The True Selma Story*; Slide, *Actors on Red Alert*, 4–6.

99. Cinema Educational Guild Inc., *Martin Luther King and His "Civil Rights Urinators,"* Calvin Fred Craig Papers, MARBL.

100. For more on the broad nature of civil rights backlash, see Nickerson, *Mothers of Conservatism*; McGirr, *Suburban Warriors*; Sugrue, *Sweet Land of Liberty*.

101. Although women's voices may have been marginalized in segregationist groups, this was not the case among anti-communists circles, where women occupied an important and vocal place. For more on this, see Nickerson, *Mothers of Conservatism*.

102. See Stock Letter, folder 370 Civil Rights Correspondence 1966, box 89-06, William L. Dickinson Congressional Papers, AUM.

103. George Burruss Jr. to William L. Dickinson, undated, folder 370 Civil Rights Correspondence 1966, box 8906, William L. Dickinson Congressional Papers, AUM.

104. Kirby Walker to William L. Dickinson, April 13, 1965, folder 182 Civil Rights Correspondence W, box 89-04, William L. Dickinson Congressional Papers, AUM.

105. Paul J. Wilson to William L. Dickinson, undated, folder 182 Civil Rights Correspondence W, box 89-04, William L. Dickinson Congressional Papers, AUM.

106. Harold J. Olson to William L. Dickinson, April 7, 1965, folder 173 Civil Rights Correspondence O, box 89-04, William L. Dickinson Congressional Papers, AUM.

107. R. J. Robinson to William L. Dickinson, n.d., folder 175 Civil Rights Correspondence R 1965, box 89-04, William L. Dickinson Congressional Papers, AUM.

108. G. R. Swift to William L Dickinson, April 30, 1965, folder 177 Civil Rights Correspondence O, box 89-04, William L. Dickinson Congressional Papers, AUM.

109. See Somerville, *Queering the Color Line.*

110. Heap, *Slumming*; Mumford, *Interzones.*

111. Helen Coolidge to William L Dickinson, March 30, 1965, folder 158 Civil Rights Correspondence C, box 89-06, William L. Dickinson Congressional Papers, AUM.

112. Mrs. Edwin Pierce to John Sparkman, April 4, 1964, box 26 (no files), Accession Number 66A89, John Sparkman Papers, WSHL.

113. Major Olenius Olson Jr. to William L. Dickinson April 14, 1965, folder 173 Civil Rights Correspondence O, box 89-04, William L. Dickinson Congressional Papers, AUM.

114. C. T. Clarke to William Dickinson, March 31, 1965, folder 159 Civil Rights Correspondence C, box 89-06, William L. Dickinson Congressional Papers, AUM.

115. Arthur J. Hansel to Governor George Wallace, March 12, 1965, folder 153 Incoming Correspondence C–H et al. 1965, box 8, James A. Hare Papers, WSHL.

116. This reference appeared in the American Nazi Party publication *The Stormtrooper.*

117. William L. Gowan to William L. Dickinson, April 6, 1965, folder 163 Civil Rights Correspondence G 1965, box 89-03, William L. Dickinson Congressional Papers, AUM.

118. W. Pearl W. Phinney to Edward Willis, April 4, 1965, folder 173 Civil Rights Correspondence P 1965, box 89-06, William L. Dickinson Congressional Papers, AUM.

119. Mrs. Arden Porter to William L. Dickinson, April 29, 1965, folder 173 Civil Rights Correspondence P 1965, box 89-06, William L. Dickinson Congressional Papers, AUM.

120. Bill Eaton to William L. Dickinson, May 6, 1965, folder 161 Civil Rights Correspondence E 1965, box 89-06, William L. Dickinson Congressional Papers, AUM.

121. George Warren to George Wallace, folder 15 Governor (1963–1968) George Wallace Out of State Correspondence 1963–1966 ca. Mississippi, box SG030721, Governors George C. and Lurleen B. Wallace Papers, ADAH.

122. John A. Darden to President L. B. Johnson April 10, 1965, folder 265 D 1965, box 498, Lister Hill Papers, WSHL.

123. Boyd, *Wide-Open Town*, 231–236.

124. Broadside, folder 170 Civil Rights Correspondence M 1965, box 89-03, William L. Dickinson Congressional Papers, AUM.

Chapter 4

1. "Fruits of Mixing," *The Citizen* October 1956, 4, microfilm 4275, reel v. 1–12 1955–1968, RWF.

2. "'Gay' Minister Marries Black and White Wacs," *The Citizen*, December 1973, 23.

3. It is possible that this minister was Ray Broshears, a multifaceted gay activist who embodied what Christina Hanhardt calls militant gay liberalism, or "a non-apologetic, visibility-oriented approach to gay-centered left-liberal political reforms." For more on Broshears, see Hanhardt, *Safe Space*, 90–99.

4. "Germany Must Perish," *Rockwell Report*, October 15, 1961, 5.

5. Webb, *Massive Resistance*.

6. Two biographies on George Lincoln Rockwell and subsequent studies of the ANP contain rich biographical information. See Simonelli, *American Fuehrer*; Schmaltz, *Hate*.

7. In *Rabble Rousers*, Clive Webb diversifies the organizations that participated in the southern response to the modern civil rights movement. Certain groups, which he characterizes as "white racial militants," embraced a far-right ideology that advocated violence, espoused anti-Semitism, and embraced some aspects of fascism. See Webb, *Rabble Rousers*, 6–10.

8. Schmaltz, *Hate*, 207; Simonelli, *American Fuehrer*, 34.

9. See Phillips-Fein, "Conservatism." For more thoughts on the nomenclature of political conservatives, see Hendershot, *What's Fair on the Air*, 8–9.

10. For more on the historiography interrogating the imbrication of homo-eroticism, homosexuality, and Nazism in Germany, see Heineman, "Sexuality and Nazisms."

11. According to Simonelli, "nothing . . . matched Rockwell's visceral abhorrence of homosexuals" and "homosexual[s] with the ranks of the ANP was a constant concern to Rockwell and a source of speculation among his enemies." Further, persistent rumors about various high-ranking ANP members like Matt Koehl and Leonard Holstein also dogged the organization. See Simonelli, *American Fuehrer*, 77–79.

12. "Playboy Interview: George Lincoln Rockwell, a Candid Conversation with the Fanatical Fuhrer of the American Nazi Party," *Playboy*, April 1966, 82, 154, box 132 Radical Right General 1966, Southern Regional Council Collection, AARL.

13. This contrasted with the Daughters of Bilitis's publication *The Ladder*, which initially circulated among a limited number of subscribers and many more who received the publications secondhand. Meeker, *Contacts Desired*, 51–96, 109–112.

14. Johnson, *The Lavender Scare*, 182–195. ANP concern over homophile political organizing predated the hearings by over a year, however.

15. Meeker, *Contacts Desired*, 32.

16. Alison Hunter, "Editorial," *One Magazine*, March 1962, 4.

17. Based on a survey of *One Magazine*, it appears these images were taken from other publications and attributed to the homophile magazine. "Only a Nazi Reformation Can Destroy This Filthy Cancer," *Rockwell Report*, June 15, 1962, 2–3, reel 6, RWC.

18. "Fairies Handbook," *Rockwell Report*, May 1965, 11.

19. See McGirr, *Suburban Warriors*; Nickerson, *Mothers of Conservatism*.

20. "U.S.A. Decaying from Within: Talmudists and Communists Subverting Nation thru Immorality," *Common Sense*, February 1, 1965, 1. According to *Common Sense*, this article was reprinted from the *Liberty League, U.S.A.* newspaper.

21. Chandler appears as a kind of antecedent to Anita Bryant, spokeswoman of the 1977 Save Our Children campaign in Dade County, Florida, which repealed an ordinance that banned discrimination on the basis of sexual orientation.

22. See Folder 183, White Conservative Newspapers 1964–1965, box 9, James A. Hare Papers, WSHL.

23. "How the Jews Have Made 'Spoiled Brats out of Independent Americans,'" *Rockwell Report*, March 1, 1962, 4, reel 6, RWC.

24. "Jews Use White Morality," *Rockwell Report*, December 1, 1962, 3, reel 6, RWC.

25. "Portrait of the Enemy," *Rockwell Report*, April 1966, reel 6, RWC.

26. "How Jews Have Made 'Spoiled Brats' out of Independent Americans," *Rockwell Report*, March 1, 1962, 1, reel 6, RWC.

27. Dean, *Imperial Brotherhood*; Johnson, *The Lavender Scare*.

28. Savage, *JFK, LBJ, and the Democratic Party*, 240.

29. "Poem to a Wild Pansy," *Rockwell Report*, November 1964, 9, reel 6, RWC.

30. Chauncey, *Gay New York*, 155.

31. "What Makes an Anti-Nazi," *Rockwell Report*, March 1966, 12–14, reel 6, RWC.

32. This is not to suggest that most segregationists did not hold similar views. Anti-Semitism was rampant in many organizations. Further, civil rights activists, Black and white, were widely assumed to be operating under the control of the Communist Party and the Soviet Union. For more on the prevalence of anti-communism in massive resistance and segregationist political mobilizations, see Woods, *Black Struggle, Red Scare*.

33. "Only a Nazi Reformation Can Destroy This Filthy Cancer," *Rockwell Report*, June 15, 1962, 2–3, reel 6, RWC.

34. "'Dignified' Niggers," *Rockwell Report*, April 1964, 4.

35. "Disgrace for the White Race, Bold Victory for Nazis," *Rockwell Report*, September 1963, 2; "Reds Use Negro Fronts," *Rockwell Report*, October 1963, 3–4, reel 6, RWC.

36. "Disgrace for the White Race: Bold Victory for the Nazis," *Rockwell Report*, September 1963, 2.

37. "The Fairies' Handbook," *Rockwell Report*, May 1965, 11.

38. "What Makes an Anti-Nazi," *Rockwell Report*, March 1966, 13.

39. Notably, this rumor was referenced by a correspondent to Representative William L. Dickinson less than two years later. See Capt. Seth D. Ryan, "Nazi Hatelets," *The Stormtrooper*, September–October 1963, 7, reel 6, RWC.

40. Wade, *The Fiery Cross*.

41. "Playboy Interview: Robert Shelton, a Candid Interview with the Klan's Notorious Imperial Wizard," *Playboy*, April 1966, 47.

42. This is not to suggest that anti-communism was not a crucial part of their ideology—it was.

43. Jane Dailey, conversely, exposes the crucial linkages between religiosity and notions of racial difference. She argues, "It was through sex that racial segregation in the South moved from being a local social practice to a part of the divine plan for the

world." Clive Webb, in his study of white racial militants, argues that religious sentiment was an important part of mobilizations against racial desegregation. He demonstrates how militant segregationist Bryant J. Bowles, president of the National Association for the Advancement of White People, relied heavily on the support and clout of fundamentalist and evangelical churches in his campaign to reverse the integration of Lakeview Avenue High School in Milford, Delaware in the fall of 1954. See Dailey, "Sex, Segregation, and the Sacred after *Brown*"; Webb, *Rabble Rousers*, 25–27. For more on Bryant J. Bowles, see the fuller chapter in Webb, *Rabble Rousers*, 15–38.

44. Dailey, "Sex, Segregation, and the Sacred after *Brown*."

45. The entire curse is as follows: "Cursed be Canaan! The Lowest of slaves will he be to his brothers. He also Said Blessed be the Lord, the God of Shem! May Canaan be the slave of Shem. May God Extend the territory of Japheth may Japheth live in the tents of Shem and many Canaan be his slave." See Genesis 9:25–27. For entire story, see Genesis 9:20–29.

46. Whereas most interpretations in the early modern period focused on Ham's viewing of his father's nakedness, other writers incorporated different sexual crimes like castration and having sex on the Ark (an act expressly forbidden). A number of competing interpretations of the curse of Ham existed during the medieval and early modern eras, linking it to sexual deviance. One version asserts that Ham castrated Noah, while another asserts that Ham engaged in forbidden copulation on the Ark during the flood. Finally, another interpretation asserts that before the flood, the giants (to which Noah and his family belonged) engaged in various lecherous and sexual acts including sex with other men. For more see Chappell, *A Stone of Hope*, 125–135; Whitford, *The Curse of Ham*, 24–25, 51, 53–55.

47. See Dailey, "Sex, Segregation, and the Sacred after *Brown*," 123n7.

48. United Klans of America, *God Is the Author of Segregation* (Tuscaloosa, AL: Imperial Press, 1967), 11–14, box 1, folder 15, Calvin Fred Craig Papers, MARBL.

49. United Klans of America, *God Is the Author of Segregation*, 13–14.

50. "Genesis Nine," *Fiery Cross*, November 1969, 29.

51. Others were unwilling to interpret biblical scripture to sanction racial segregation. Chappell argues that historians have devoted an inordinate amount of attention to segregationist biblical arguments like the Hamitic story of the curse, stating that religious appeals were overwhelmingly ineffective. Chappell, *A Stone of Hope*, 125–135.

52. For more on anticlericalism among advocates of segregation, see Chappell, *A Stone of Hope*, 125–135.

53. Although the subject matter was enough to attract the UKA's attention, the fact that the conference organizer, Canon Walter D. Dennis, was African American certainly created an additional imperative to cover the story. See Edward B. Fiske, "Episcopal Clergy Here Call Homosexuality Morally Neutral," *New York Times*, November 29, 1967, 1, 39.

54. Instead, the clerics were moving toward viewing same-gender relationships as "morally neutral and in some instances a good thing." Although this tolerance is notable for the time period, it is not synonymous with viewing same-sex intimacy as a moral and positive form of relationality.

55. Circuit Rider Pamphlet, folder 22: Circuit Riders, Inc., box 1: Correspondence 1952–1964 Segregationist and Other Right-Wing Literature, Dr. H. Norton Mason Collection, LOV.

56. Although the Circuit Rider cover letter is undated, the article appeared in the *San Francisco Sunday Chronicle* on January 3, 1965. See "Angry Ministers Rip Police," *San Francisco Sunday Chronicle*, January 3, 1965, 1A.

57. See, for example, Robert Shelton, "Editorial," *Fiery Cross*, July 1970, inside front cover, unpaginated; "Along the Black Front," *Fiery Cross*, November 1970, 17; Calvin Fred Craig Papers, MARBL; "Imperial Wizard Speaks to St. Petersburg College," *Fiery Cross*, April 1970, 5–10; "Along the Black Front," *Fiery Cross*, November 1970, 17; Calvin Fred Craig Papers, MARBL.

58. "Fiery Flashes," *The Fiery Cross*, October 1971, 17, reel 51, RWC.

59. For a history of the experiences of sexual and gender dissidents within leftist political organizing, and the Community Party in particular, see Lecklider, *Love's Next Meeting*.

60. Meeker, *Contacts Desired*. For more on strains of gay and lesbian political organizing, see Stein, *Rethinking the Gay and Lesbian Movement*.

61. For more on this within the larger history of battles over pornography in the post–World War II United States, see Strub, *Perversion for Profit*.

62. Here, I refer to the most notable cases, *Brown v. Board of Education* in 1954 and 1955 and *Loving v. Virginia* case in 1967, which invalidated miscegenation law.

63. Strub, *Perversion for Profit*, 125–129.

64. Melvin Sexton, "Editorial," *Fiery Cross*, April 1969, inside front cover, unpaginated.

65. Carl F. Lyons, "The New 'Morality,'" *Fiery Cross*, 1972, 22.

66. Strub, *Perversion for Profit*, 125–129.

67. Johnson, *The Lavender Scare*.

68. "LBJ's Homo Haven," *Fiery Cross*, February 1968, 26–28, reel 51, RWC.

69. Robert Shelton, "Editorial," *Fiery Cross*, May 1968, 2, reel 51, RWC.

70. "Comics Section," *Fiery Cross*, August 1967, box 6, Southern Regional Council Collection, AARL.

71. "Comics Section," *Fiery Cross*, August 1967, 7, box 133 Resistance Groups KKK 1966, Southern Regional Council Collection, AARL.

72. See, for example, McGuire, *At the Dark End of the Street*.

73. For more on this, see Cuordileone, "'Politics in an Age of Anxiety'", and Estes, *I Am a Man*.

74. The Janus-faced nature of white southern preoccupations with Black sexuality is evident in the alleged production of a play called *This Is Integration*. Civil rights advocate and writer Lillian Smith described the production as one in which teenagers, some of whom were in blackface, engaged in "highly erotic love-making between white and negro high school students." Staged and funded by "white citizens councils" in various parts of the South in 1961, Smith claimed "the audiences giggle hysterically during the play. . . . They are both aroused and shocked." "Lillian Smith Raps 'Racial Gangsters,'" *Washington Post*, March 8, 1961, C16.

75. "Along the Black Front," *Fiery Cross*, September 1968, 17, reel 51, RWC.

76. "Along the Black Front," *Fiery Cross*, November 1970, 17; Calvin Fred Craig Papers, MARBL.

77. Meyerowitz, *How Sex Changed*.

78. "Along the Black Front," *Fiery Cross*, January 1970, 28, reel 51, RWC.

79. "Along the Black Front," *Fiery Cross*, June 1968, 29, reel 51, RWC. In invoking this disease, the article referenced the increasing visibility of sickle cell anemia as a politicized metaphor for the historic pain of African Americans. Although this was true nationally, some segregationists manipulated information about the disease to legitimize legal challenges to federal mandates for the desegregation of public schools, claiming to protect the "pure blood" of white southerners. For more on the general politicized history of sickle cell anemia, see Wailoo, *Dying in the City of the Blues*. For the efforts of Mississippi segregationists to mobilize misinformation about sickle cell anemia and race, see Forbes and Smithers, "Combatting the 'Communistic Mulatto Inspired Movement.'"

80. Skidmore, "Constructing the 'Good Transsexual.'" For analysis of how Black gender-variant subjects are figured within the African American press and used to mediate questions about race, community, and citizenship, see Snorton, *Black on Both Sides*, 139–175.

81. One of the images features Dame Margaret Rutherford, a British actress who unofficially adopted Hall. "Along the Black Front," *Fiery Cross*, March 1969, 29, reel 51, RWC.

82. From 1968 to 1971, four articles about marriage between two members of the same sex were featured—always with an image.

83. "New York Pastor Joins Two Black Women in 'Holy Union,'" *Fiery Cross*, June 1971, 18, reel 51, RWC.

84. "Along the Black Front," *Fiery Cross*, August 1971, reel 51, RWC.

85. Considering *Fiery Cross*'s tendency to identify the race of African Americans, it is unlikely that McConnell's partner was Black if not identified as such. "Along the Black Front," *Fiery Cross*, November 1970, 17, Calvin Fred Craig Papers, MARBL.

86. Pascoe, "Sex, Gender, and Same-Sex Marriage."

87. Several studies have interrogated the manner in which ideas about race influenced developing notions of homosexuality. See Mumford, *Interzones*; Somerville, *Queering the Color Line*; Somerville, *"Queer Loving;"* Duggan, *Sapphic Slashers*; Meyerowitz, ""How Common Culture Shapes the Separate Lives."

88. Mumford, "The Trouble with Gay Rights."

89. "In the past, the Negro played the role of a second-class citizen. Now that he is gradually achieving his rightful place as a first-class citizen, there are those who are trying to replace the Negro with the homosexual. We do not intend to play a second-class role either." Frank Kameny to Robert Bissel, May 30, 1969, folder 7 B Miscellaneous 1962–1983, Bi-Bri, box 2, Frank Kameny Papers, LC.

90. The CCA was created in 1956 at a meeting of segregation advocates from eleven states in New Orleans. See Dailey, "Sex, Segregation, and the Sacred after *Brown*," 142.

91. Dailey, "Sex, Segregation, and the Sacred after *Brown*," 152.

92. McMillen, *The Citizens' Council*, 124.

93. McMillen, *The Citizens' Council*, 116–155.

94. McMillen, *The Citizens' Council*, 29–30.

95. McMillen, *The Citizens' Council*, 153, 414.

96. CCA leaders attempted to distance themselves from anti-Semitism, but it persisted among grassroots members and several prominent individuals like Georgian power broker Roy V. Harris. For more, see McMillen, *The Citizens' Council*, 160–161, 413.

97. For more on the Sex Information and Education Council of the United States and national battles over sex education, see McMillen, *The Citizens' Council*, 1017–1056; Irvine, *Talk about Sex*.

98. For more on Orange County activism on this issue, see McGirr, *Suburban Warriors*.

99. Homosexuality was one of the sexual behaviors invoked. Citing an alleged government-sponsored organization, Evans asserts they stated it "can be neither for nor against illegitimacy, homosexuality, premarital sex—nor any other manifestation of human sexual phenomena." See Medford Evans, "Tree of Knowledge? Sex Education in Integrated Schools," *The Citizen*, June 1969, 18, box 2, Citizens' Council Collection, ASC-UM.

100. See end of chapter 3 for information about this entity.

101. "Methodist Sex Films," *The Citizen*, September 1972, 23, reel 26, RWC.

102. McGirr, *Suburban Warriors*, 227–231.

103. This violence could take on racial overtones laws associated with the war on drugs combined with long-standing inequities in policing, convictions, and sentencing.

104. Kunzel, *Criminal Intimacy*, 149–190.

105. "Suit Alleges Black Inmates Raping Whites," *The Citizen*, May 1973, 23, reel 26, RWC.

106. "Four White Convicts Tell of Abuse by Blacks," *The Citizen*, September 1974, 23, 26, reel 26, RWC.

107. Although the origins of this group are less clear, it may be the progenitor organization of the current Council of Conservative Citizens. This Citizens' Council–like group whose current publication shares the same name, emerged from the ashes of the Saint Louis Citizens' Councils. Neither McMillen nor Bartley addressed massive resistance or Citizens' Councils in Missouri, where the *Citizens' Tri-State Informer* was published. Yet it does appear that this group mirrored many other local/state Citizens' Councils in that it experienced some initial political strength and then dwindled over the course of the 1960s and 1970s. The Council of Conservative Citizens was founded in 1985 and continues to exert a presence among white supremacist groups today. For more, see Somerville, *Queering the Color Line*; "U.S. Forces Race-Mixing at Missouri Penitentiary," *Citizens' Tri-State Informer*, January 1974, 1, 9; "White Inmates Protest Black Terror," *Citizens' Tri-State Informer*, June 1974, 1, reel 26, RWC.

108. "Prison Furloughs," Illinois Scene, *Citizens' Tri-State Informer*, July 1974, 6, reel 26, RWC.

109. Peterson, "Furlough."

110. Articles in these publications linked same-sex desire with popular culture, political liberalism, and moral decay. An anonymously authored manifesto titled "I Am a Sick American" claimed disgust with the presence of homosexuality in films. And in "A Strange Set of Values," the anonymous author asserted, "Tel Aviv not only tolerates homosexuality but in some instances encourages the practice." "I Am a Sick American," *Citizens' Tri-State Informer*, January 1974, 8, reel 26, RWC; "A Strange Set of Values," *The Councilor*, September 14, 1970, 2, reel 26, RWC.

111. Terry McGinnity, "Survival: The Natural Way," *The Citizens' Report*, November 1970, 2, reel 26, RWC.

112. "Skinny Dippers," *The Councilor*, August 30, 1970, 2, reel 26, RWC.

113. "Madison (C&F)," *The Councilor*, September 14, 1970, 2, reel 26, RWC.

114. *Citizens' Tri-State Informer*, January 1974, 1, reel 26, RWC.

115. "Negro and Jewish Politicians Honor Queer Perverts," *The Attack*, November 1976, 5.

116. For more on alliances between LGBTQ+ and African American communities, see Stewart-Winter, *Queer Clout*.

Chapter 5

1. This speculative reconstruction of events is based on coverage of the *Atlanta Constitution* and WSB-TV, a news station headquartered in Atlanta. See Neil Swan, "Gay Pride Day without Inc.," *Atlanta Constitution*, June 27, 1976, 7B. File Master #41 6/24/76 through 6/30/76, FM00041. WSB-TV Videotape Collection, WBMA.

2. This is not to suggest that transgender subjects did not also participate in gay liberation, gay liberalism or articulate other political visions. However, much of gay liberalism was cisgender in its orientation. For examples of transgender activists within the liberal Gay Activist Alliance, see Stein, *Rethinking the Gay and Lesbian Movement*, 101.

3. See Stewart-Winter, *Queer Clout*.

4. See Sides, *Erotic City*, 10.

5. For more on Steve Abbott, see the review of his novel *Beautiful Aliens*: David Grundy, "Steven Abbott, *Beautiful Aliens*," last modified July 9, 2020, https://www.chicagoreview.org/steve-abbott-beautiful-aliens/.

6. Cover, *Great Speckled Bird*, June 28, 1971.

7. Chenault, "An Unspoken Past," 105–107.

8. Kuhn, Joye, and West, *Living Atlanta*, 189.

9. See "Top Hat," *Atlanta Daily World*, November 2, 1945, 5.

10. "Police Arrest Two for Morals Charge," *Atlanta Daily World*, May 8, 1955, 1. It does not appear that local authorities disproportionately targeted Black men for such infractions. This observation is based on a perusal of local sodomy convictions from the 1930s through the 1960s.

11. For more on the long history of child protection, see Frank, "Save Our Children."

12. Marini, "'Looking for a City,'" 63–64.

13. Around 250 people attended. See Fleischmann and Hardman, "Hitting below the Bible Belt."

14. Stein, *Rethinking the Gay and Lesbian Movement*, 86.

15. See Alex Coffin, "No City Hiring Bias Homosexuals Advised," *Atlanta Constitution*, July 9, 1971, 1A; Stone, *Regime Politics*, 7; Martin, *Atlanta and Its Environs*, 500.

16. See Stryker, *Transgender History*.

17. Stone, *Regime Politics*, 3.

18. See Stone, *Regime Politics*; Lassiter, *The Silent Majority*; Kruse, *White Flight*.

19. See Ferguson, *Black Politics in New Deal Atlanta*; Brown-Nagin, *Courage to Dissent*.

20. This decision was bolstered by *Smith v. Allwright* two years earlier.

21. See Stone, *Regime Politics*; Lassiter, *The Silent Majority*; Kruse, *White Flight*; Brown-Nagin, *Courage to Dissent*.

22. Stone, *Regime Politics*, 77.

23. See Lassiter, *The Silent Majority*; Kruse, *White Flight*.

24. See Kruse, *White Flight*; Brown-Nagin, *Courage to Dissent*. For more on the Student Nonviolent Coordinating Committee's activities, see Tuck, *Beyond Atlanta*; Holsaert et al., *Hands on the Freedom Plow*; Carson, *In Struggle*.

25. Hobson, *The Legend of the Black Mecca*, 50–59.

26. John Huey Jackson, "Brockey Sending Corrections," *Atlanta Constitution*, November 15, 1974, 9A. Later that fall, Jackson and Brockey sought to blunt the damage of this disagreement between city hall and business elites. They issued a joint rebuttal of the framing in the press—not just in Atlanta but in national outlets like the *New York Times* and *Business Week* as well. They characterized it as a productive exchange of views rather than a sign of contentious relations.

27. Noted in Hank Ezell, "Jackson Keeps Busy: Flower in Flap," *Atlanta Constitution*, January 13, 1974, 4A.

28. For an account of the 1976 controversy over Gay Pride Day in Atlanta see Mims, *Drastic Dykes*. Margo George, "Citizens for a Decent Atlanta vs Gay Pride," *Great Speckled Bird* 9, no. 7 (August 1976): 8.

29. Neil Swan, "Gay Pride Rally without Incident," *Atlanta Constitution*, June 27, 1976, 7B.

30. George mentions the CDA leaders were affiliated with the Christian Businessmen's Committee. See Margo George, "Citizens for a Decent Atlanta vs Gay Pride," *Great Speckled Bird* 9 no. 7 (August 1976): 10.

31. See Hanhardt, *Safe Space*.

32. Jackson administration, "News Release," June 25, 1970, series 1st and 2nd Terms, box 56, folder 10, Maynard Jackson Mayoral Administrative Records, ARC.

33. Jim Burkett founded Christian Financial Concepts, Inc. in 1976. This organization later provided financial advice to Protestant Evangelical churches and individuals. For more on Burkett, see Kay Powell, "Larry Burkett Taught Lessons of God, Money," *Atlanta Constitution*, July 8, 2003, B6.

34. For more on the history and importance of the Citizens for Decent Literature, see Strub, *Perversion for Profit*, 80–115.

35. See Mrs. W. F. Elliott, "Rotten Apples," *Atlanta Constitution*, May 19, 1968, SM5.

36. See, for example, Woodland Hills Baptist Church, *The Messenger*, July 11, 1976, series 1st and 2nd Term, box 56, folder 11, Maynard Jackson Mayoral Administrative Records, ARC; Theo Carter, "An Open Letter to the Honourable [*sic*] Maynard Jackson," *Riverside Review*, July 4, 1976, series 1st and 2nd Term, box 56, folder 11, Maynard Jackson Mayoral Administrative Records, ARC.

37. Executive Committee to Churches of Metropolitan Atlanta, Memo: The Mayor of Atlanta's Gay Pride Day Proclamation, July 7, 1976, box 56, folder 14, series 1st and 2nd Term, Maynard Jackson Mayoral Administrative Records, ARC.

38. Alice Murray, "Baptist Leaders Call for Mayor to Quit," *Atlanta Constitution*, June 30, 1976, 3-A.

39. K.N. Meadows to Maynard Jackson, July 4, 1976, box 56, folder15, Maynard Jackson Mayoral Administrative Records, ARC.

40. Mary Grable to Maynard Jackson, received July 20,1976, series 1st and 2nd Term, box 56, folder 10, Maynard Jackson Mayoral Administrative Records, ARC; for another example from a resident outside of the city (Conley, Georgia), see Patti Pitts to Maynard Jackson, July 16, 1976, series 1st and 2nd Term, box 56, folder 10, Maynard Jackson Mayoral Administrative Records, ARC.

41. Letter to the Editor, *Atlanta Constitution*, July 9, 1976, 4A.

42. Sharp later cofounded the organization Concerned Black Clergy in response to the Atlanta child murders, a tragic two-year period in which thirty Black youths were abducted and murdered. The group's relief programs also supported the city's indigent and homeless population. See J. E. Geshwiler, "John Sharp, Minister to the Poor, Homeless," *Atlanta Journal-Constitution*, July 10, 2004, E4.

43. Advertisement, "We Need Your Help," *Atlanta Daily World*, July 11, 1976, 10.

44. For an extended meditation on whiteness in gay and lesbian spaces, see Bérubé, "How Gay Stays White."

45. Hanhardt, *Safe Space*.

46. Mumford, "The Trouble with Gay Rights."

47. Editorial, "A Timely Issue," *Atlanta Daily World*, July 1, 1976, 6.

48. A brief survey of editorials suggests that the *Atlanta Daily World* coverage of the mayor was generally favorable.

49. Margo George and David Massey, "The Controversy," *Great Speckled Bird* 9, no. 7 (August 1976): 12.

50. Margo George and David Massey, "The Controversy," *Great Speckled Bird* 9, no. 7 (August 1976): 12.

51. File Master #41 6/24/76 through 6/30/76, FM00041, WSB-TV Videotape Collection, WBMA.

52. Margo George and David Massey, "The Controversy," *Great Speckled Bird* 9, no. 7 (August 1976): 11.

53. Jim Gray, "Jackson Will Not Withdraw His Gay Pride Proclamation," *Atlanta Daily World*, June 26, 1976, 1A.

54. Margo George and David Massey, "The Controversy," *Great Speckled Bird* 9, no. 7 (August 1976): 11.

55. Margo George and David Massey, "The Controversy," *Great Speckled Bird* 9, no. 7 (August 1976): 11.

56. Gay Pride Week Planning Committee, "Letter to the Editor," *Atlanta Constitution*, July 9, 1976, 4A.

57. Margo George and David Massey, "Gay Pride vs Citizens for a Decent Atlanta," *Great Speckled Bird* 9, no. 7 (August 1976): 11–12.

58. Bruce Voeller, "Letter to the Editor," *Atlanta Constitution*, July 26, 1976, 4A.

59. Bruce Voeller to Maynard Jackson, July 20, 197, box 56, folder 14, series 1st and 2nd Term, Maynard Jackson Mayoral Administrative Records, ARC.

60. Ann Maury to Maynard Jackson, July 6, 1976, box 56, folder 15, series 1st and 2nd Term, Maynard Jackson Mayoral Administrative Records, ARC. For a similar letter, see William Power to Maynard Jackson, June 30, 1976, box 56, folder 11, series 1st and 2nd Term, Maynard Jackson Mayoral Administrative Records, ARC.

61. Harold L. Bodie to Maynard Jackson, received July 8, 1976, box 56, fol. 15, series 1st and 2nd Term, Maynard Jackson Mayoral Administrative Records, ARC. For another example of support for the proclamation written on a CDA advertisement, see Paul E. Abstein to Maynard Jackson, n.d., box 56, folder 15, series 1st and 2nd Term, Maynard Jackson Mayoral Administrative Records, ARC.

62. Jerry Higginbotham, letter to the editor, *Atlanta Constitution*, July 9, 1976, 4A.

63. Anonymous, letter to the editor, *Atlanta Constitution*, July 9, 1976, 4A.

64. E. Russell, letter to the editor, *Atlanta Constitution*, June 26, 1976, 4A.

65. Sides, *Erotic City*.

66. Baylor, *Race and the Shaping of Twentieth Century Atlanta*, 83.

67. Ron Taylor, "Gay Life: Basheron Prowl Break Up 'Cruising,'" *Atlanta Constitution*, May 11, 1975, 10 A.

68. Joe Brown, "The Gay Life," *Atlanta Constitution*, April 24, 1976, 8B.

69. For more about Atlanta Lesbian communities, see Mims, *Drastic Dykes*.

70. Ann Carter, "Hangouts of Hippies Closed as Hazard," *Atlanta Constitution*, July 23, 1967, 18B.

71. Alex Coffin, "Run Hippies Out: Millican," *Atlanta Constitution*, September 22, 1969, 2B.

72. Alex Coffin, "Cook, Massell Swap Heated Accusations," *Atlanta Constitution*, September 24, 1969, 1A.

73. Joe Brown and Frederick Allen, "Sex for Sale—and City's Paying Price," *Atlanta Constitution*, June 27, 1976, 1A, 6A.

74. See Howard, "The Library, the Park and the Pervert," 122–125.

75. "Baptists Study Report of Park Delinquency," *Atlanta Constitution*, October 20, 1954, 1.

76. Lloyd Bryant, "Vice Squad Here Small, Keep Busy," *Atlanta Constitution*, September 5, 1955, 33.

77. For more on moralists and sex radicals, see Sides, *Erotic City*.

78. Lisby, "'Trying to Define What May Be Indefinable,'" 76.

79. James Dodson, "Exit the Smut Fighter," *Atlanta Weekly*, August 15, 1982, 11.

80. See biographical advertisement that appeared in the *Atlanta Constitution*. Advertisement, "Who Is Millican?" *Atlanta Constitution*, October 1, 1969, 10A.

81. Lindemann, "From Fire and Brimstone to Property Values."

82. Jim Gray, "Need to Control It: Eaves Says Prostitution Should Be Made Legal," *Atlanta Constitution*, January 14, 1976, 2A.

83. Sharon Bailey, "Eaves: Revise 'Victimless Crime' Laws," *Atlanta Constitution*, January 15, 1976, 1A.

84. Sam Hopkins, "Eaves Blasted on Prostitution," *Atlanta Constitution*, August 3, 1976, 1A.

85. Wiggins, "'Order as well as Decency,'" 2, 5.

86. It's notable that news reporting suggests Jackson moved to crack down on sex businesses after being solicited by two sex workers while driving through downtown Atlanta in the summer of 1976. Joe Brown and Frederick Allen, "Sex for Sale—and City's Paying Price," *Atlanta Constitution*, June 27, 1976, 1A, 6A.

87. "Anti-Bathhouse Bills Approved," *Atlanta Constitution*, December 12, 1976, 9A.

88. Tina McElroy, "Revitalizing 'The Strip': New Businesses Are Moving into Once-Blighted Area," *Atlanta Constitution*, May 2, 1978, 1B. For more on original partnership, see Jay Lawrence, "Strip Revitalization Effort Begins Today," *Atlanta Constitution*, March 4, 1977, 1A, 8A.

89. Linda Regnier and Vic Host to Maynard Jackson, May 5, 1977, box 56, folder 16, series 1st and 2nd Term, Maynard Jackson Mayoral Administrative Records, ARC.

90. Gay Rights Alliance (spokesperson Linda Regnier), "Press Release," n.d., box 56, folder 16, series 1st and 2nd Term, Maynard Jackson Mayoral Administrative Records, ARC.

91. For these petitions, see "1977–1978 Gay Pride Week," Correspondence and Subject Files, 1975 through 1979-C37650, RCB 1975–1983 Gov. George D. Busbee, GA.

92. Note, Tony Riddle 6/22, box 56, folder 10, series 1st and 2nd Term, Maynard Jackson Mayoral Administrative Records, ARC.

93. Anonymous, note, June 17, 1977, box 56, folder 16, series 1st and 2nd Term, Maynard Jackson Mayoral Administrative Records, ARC.

94. "A Statement by Mayor Maynard Jackson," box 56, folder 16, series 1st and 2nd Term, Maynard Jackson Mayoral Administrative Records, ARC.

95. See this key passage in news article: "Rev. John Sharp, minister of the Westhills Presbyterian Church, reported that a group of about 20 community religious leaders who meet monthly with Jackson warned the mayor last week about the consequences of a Gay Pride Day." Lynn Martin and Ken Willis, "There'll Be No 'Gay Pride Day,'" *Atlanta Constitution*, June 24, 1977, 1A, 22A.

96. Assortment of documents related to campaign, box 56, folder 16, series 1st and 2nd Term, Maynard Jackson Mayoral Administrative Records, ARC.

97. "Jackson Pressured for Gay Pride Day," *Atlanta Constitution*, June 21, 1977, 6B.

98. Lynn Martin, "Mayor Afraid, Gay Leaders Say," *Atlanta Constitution*, June 22, 1977, 1A.

99. Lynn Martin and Ken Willis, "There'll Be No 'Gay Pride Day,'" *Atlanta Constitution*, June 24, 1977, 1A, 22A.

100. Lynn Martin, "Group Praises Mayor on 'Liberties Days,'" *Atlanta Constitution*, June 25, 1977, 6A.

101. Sharon Bailey, "Eaves: Revise 'Victimless Crime' Law," *Atlanta Constitution*, January 15, 1976, 1A, 22A.

102. Sam Hopkins, "Sexual Privacy Gains Approval," *Atlanta Constitution*, December 5, 1975, 6B.

103. Howard, *The Closet and the Cul-de-Sac*.

104. Ken Willis, "Eaves Rules Out Homosexuals as City Policemen," *Atlanta Constitution*, July 15, 1977, 1A, 20A.

105. Barbara Gervais Street, "The Gaying of Atlanta," *Atlanta Constitution*, December 12, 1982, 11–13, 32.

106. "Statement of Purpose," folder 2 Atlanta Gay Center Organizational Setup, box 4, MSS 773, Atlanta Lesbian and Gay History Thing Publications, AHC.

107. Fleischmann and Hardman, "Hitting Below the Bible Belt," 418.

108. "What Is GAMA?" *Atlanta Gay Central*, November December 1979, folder 6 Atlanta Gay Center AGC Newsletters, 1979–1982, box 47, MSS 773, Atlanta Lesbian and Gay History Thing Publications, AHC.

109. Beginning in 1980, GAMA held a Miss GAMA Pageant at the Sweet Gum Head, a prominent gay bar on Cheshire Bridge Road. "GAMA's Second Birthday—a Week of Celebration—a Rainbow," folder 5 Gay Atlanta Minority Association, 1981, undated box 46, MSS 773, Atlanta Lesbian and Gay History Thing Publications, AHC. "1981 Miss GAMA Pageant," pamphlet folder 5 Gay Atlanta Minority Association, 1981, undated box 46, MSS 773, Atlanta Lesbian and Gay History Thing Publications, AHC.

110. For overview, see Stein, *Rethinking the Gay and Lesbian Movement*, 123–124.

111. Quin, "To Stamp Out the Oppression."

112. Pritchard, "As Proud of our Gayness."

113. "Community Survey," folder 9 Friends for Lesbian/Gay Outreach Community Survey, box 50, MSS 773, Atlanta Gay and Lesbian History Thing, AHC.

114. See Hobson, *The Legend of the Black Mecca*, 94–130.

115. Miscellaneous documents in folder 22 Media: Atlanta Child Murders, box 150, National Gay and Lesbian Task Force records, #7301, DRMC.

116. "Joint Action on Atlanta Child Murders," National Gay Task Force, April 21, 1981, folder 22 Media: Atlanta Child Murders, box 150, National Gay and Lesbian Task Force records, #7301, DRMC.

117. Mumford, "Untangling Pathology."

118. Gail Epstein, "Victim Lived in a Nightmare, Died in One," *Atlanta Constitution*, May 1, 1981, 1A, 14 A.

119. For example, in one article from March 23, 1981, staff writer Linda Field quoted sociologist Bernard Headley as he spoke to the National Association of Blacks in Criminal Justice. Headley framed the murders as reflective of the profound distance between public representations of Black political progress in public and the status of most Black Atlantans. Using the framework of the "underclass," Headley referenced a culture of "hustling" that exposed working-class children to additional corporeal precarity. He is quoted as saying, "not only is it true that most of the boys were hustlers, but they descended from generations in which hustling and being able to turn a fast buck were the primary means of survival." See Linda Field,

"Sociologist Says Child Murders Reflect Blacks' Powerless," *Atlanta Constitution*, March 23, 1981, 14A.

120. See Reagon, "Coalition Politics," 346.

121. "Joint Action on Atlanta Child Murders," Charles F. Brydon to Dignity International (F. Scheuren), Integrity (J. Lawrence and Donn Mitchell) and UFMCC (T. Perry and N. Wilson), undated, folder 22 Media: Atlanta Child Murders, box 150, National Gay and Lesbian Task Force records, #7301, DRMC.

122. "Joint Statement on Atlanta Child Murders," May 7, 1981, folder 22 Media: Atlanta Child Murders, box 150, National Gay and Lesbian Task Force records, #7301, DRMC.

123. "National Gay Leaders Issue Joint Statement on Atlanta Child Murders," May 12, 1981, folder 22 Media: Atlanta Child Murders, box 150, National Gay and Lesbian Task Force records, #7301, DRMC.

124. Robin Toner, "Young Won't Put City Stamp on Gay Pride," *Atlanta Constitution*, April 27, 1983, 8A.

125. Robin Toner, "Gays Becoming Key Factor in City Politics," *Atlanta Constitution*, June 26, 1983, 1D, 9D.

126. Robin Toner, "Young Won't Put Stamp on Gay Pride," *Atlanta Constitution*, April 27, 1983, 8A.

127. "Gays Honor Cong. Lewis," *Atlanta Daily World*, May 26, 1988, 1.

128. Joan P. Garner and Henry McTerry to Beth Schapiro, "Proposal for Financial Assistance," January 13, 1989, folder 33 Lomax Campaigns: Campaign Issues, Gay and Lesbian Rights, 1989, box 25, Michael Lomax Papers, MARBL.

129. "Duncan Teague Honored by Georgia House of Representatives for His Tireless Advocacy," Georgiaequality.org, February 24, 2017, https://georgiaequality.org /2017/02/duncan-teague-honored-georgia-house-representatives-tireless-advocacy /, https://lgbtqreligiousarchives.org/profiles/duncan-teague.

130. For examples of these awards, see "Marquis Walker to Be Honored at AALGA Awards Dinner," *Southern Voice*, September 29, 1988, 13; Davanna Jones and Wendy Morse, "AALGA Honors Mobley at Dinner," *Southern Voice*, October 27, 1988.

131. The Women of Color Caucus of this group eventually formed a separate organization, ZAMI, that centered the social, political, health, and wellness concerns of Black lesbians. For more, see Finding Aid, ZAMI Records, AARL.

132. Peter C. White III and Christopher Hawkins, "Maynard Jackson for 1989: Campaign Information the Gay and Lesbian Community," folder 1, box 50 Campaign Series, Campaign 1977, Maynard Jackson Mayoral Administrative Records, ARC.

133. See Matt Moline, "MACGLO MLK Marchers Receive Mixed Crowd Response," *Southern Voice*, February 29, 1989, 3.

134. "Notes for Legal Meeting," May 15, 1989, folder 33 Lomax Campaigns: Campaign Issues, Gay and Lesbian Rights, 1989, box 25, Michael Lomax Papers, MARBL.

135. However, the roots of the program extended to a push to expand minority contract holders for the building of the Metropolitan Atlanta Rapid Transit Authority train.

136. Stone, *Regime Politics*, 145.

137. For more on the history of the Minority Business Enterprise Program and its place within the urban regime of governance, see Stone, *Regime Politics*, 136, 144–146, 165–166.

138. David Corvette, "Lomax: Include Gays in Affirmative Action," *Atlanta Constitution*, July 20, 1989, A1, A10; Larry Copeland and Deborah Scoggins, "Lomax Backpedaling on Gay Business Plan," *Atlanta Constitution*, July 21, 1989, D1, D6.

139. Richard Jones to Kevin Ross, March 20, 1989, folder 6, box 50: Campaign Series Campaign 1977, Maynard Jackson Mayoral Administrative Records, ARC.

140. Darryl G. Gray and Richard E. Jones to Kevin Ross and Beth Shapiro, March 16, 1989, folder 33 Lomax Campaigns: Campaign Issues, Gay and Lesbian Rights, 1989, box 25, Michael Lomax Papers, MARBL.

141. Johnson, *Honey Pot*, 140–147. Also see Arielle Kass, "Joan Garner, 65—Fulton County commissioner dedicated to her community—LGBT, AIDS, public health advocate lost battle with cancer," *Atlanta Journal-Constitution*, April 19, 2017, B5.

Chapter 6

1. Created in 1984 by an urban theatre program that sought to speak directly to the lives of district residents, this troupe of young adults offered "prevention" messages for "at-risk youth" about violence, alcohol, and drug abuse, and the acquired immunodeficiency syndrome. Faulk, "Prevention Messages"; SCLC/ WOMEN Convention Luncheon, "Liberation from the New Lynch Mobs: AIDS, Drugs and Teenage Pregnancy," folder 48/3 Annual Convention Luncheon Programs 1984–1994, box 48, SCLC/ WOMEN, Inc. Records, MARBL.

2. Historian Jennifer Brier defines "AIDS work" as collapsing the distinction between activist and service organizations. The SCLC/WOMEN's HIV/AIDS programming encompasses both components, making AIDS work an appropriate designation. See Brier, *Infectious Ideas*, 4.

3. Cohen, *Boundaries of Blackness*, 276.

4. Cohen, *Boundaries of Blackness*, 256.

5. For more see Cohen, *Boundaries of Blackness*; Woubshet, *Calendar of Loss*; Bost, *Evidence of Being*; Royles, *To Make the Wounded Whole*.

6. See Royles, *To Make the Wounded Whole*, 5.

7. SCLC/WOMEN administrator—to understand the internal logics of the organization. Unfortunately, I was unable to secure permissions to reproduce some of the SCLC/WOMEN imagery and promotional materials.

8. For more on the origins and organizing of the SCLC during the modern civil rights movement, see Garrow, *Bearing the Cross*; Fairclough, *To Redeem the Soul of America*.

9. Peake, *Keeping the Dream Alive*. See also Kissah Thompson, "Civil Rights Leader Worked with King," *Washington Post*, March 29, 2020, C9; Douglas Martin, "Rev. Joseph E. Lowery, Civil Rights Leader and King Aide, Dies at 98," *New York Times*, March 28, 2020, 24N.

10. Peake, *Keeping the Dream Alive*, 330–332.

11. Peake, *Keeping the Dream Alive*, 330–332.

12. Peake, *Keeping the Dream Alive*, 330–332.

13. Robnett, *How Long? How Long?*, 95.

14. Robnett, *How Long? How Long?*

15. Kitty J. Pope notes, "Mrs. Lowery has been her husband's constant and supportive companion since the early days of the Civil Rights demonstrations and marches. Amid attempted bomb threats in Mobile and Birmingham, Alabama, she courageously participated in demonstrations for freedom and equality alongside her husband. She marched in the Selma-Montgomery March in 1965 and the anniversary marches thereafter." There is evidence of Mrs. Lowery's activism beyond the SCLC—one account claims she fearlessly walked her daughter Cheryl into a segregated Birmingham school in the early 1960s, quoting scripture the entire way. See Pope, *Beside Every Great Man*, 150. For reference to her desegregation foray, see Cobb, *On the Road to Freedom*.

16. Members of Decatur, Alabama's Black community alerted the SCLC to the plight of Tommy Hines, a developmentally disabled Black man facing charges of assaulting a white woman. Rev. Lowery and the SCLC immediately launched a series of protests that drew 1,500 supporters, fifty Ku Klux Klan members, and dozens of National Guard troops. Klan members showered the demonstrators with bullets, two of which narrowly missed Mrs. Lowery as she drove a car at the rear of the march. "Afterwards," she noted many years later, "I felt like my life must have been spared for something." See Pope, *Beside Every Great Man*, 150.

17. See Pope, *Beside Every Great Man*, 150.

18. Summary, folder 27/8 Program for Children with Parents Infected by AIDS, 1991, SCLC/ WOMEN, Inc. Records, MARBL.

19. Cohen, *Boundaries of Blackness*, 78–119.

20. The Center for Disease Control was renamed the Centers for Disease Control and Prevention in 1992. Notably, the CDC removed Haitians from the risk-group category in 1985. For accounts of these early years of HIV/AIDS, see Shilts, *And the Band Played On*; Whiteside, *HIV/AIDS*; Engel, *The Epidemic*; Epstein, *Impure Science*; Brier, *Infectious Ideas*.

21. Curran, Jaffe, and the CDC, "AIDS: The Early Years."

22. Patton, "AIDS: Lessons from the Gay Community."

23. Watkins-Hayes, *Remaking a Life*, 13.

24. Marable, "Reagan, Race, and Reaction," 2.

25. For a general picture of Black political fortunes during the 1980s, see Marable, *Black American Politics*. Budget cuts shrunk the welfare rolls and undermined school lunch programs. Nonmilitary federal jobs also decreased, narrowing a key pathway of upward Black economic mobility.

26. Marable, *Black American Politics*.

27. Centers for Disease Control and Prevention, *AIDS Weekly Surveillance Report—United States AIDS Program*, December 29, 1986.

28. Public health officials argued that the disproportionate rates of transmission reflected higher rates of IV drug use, sexual intercourse with an IV drug user, and

mother-to-child transmission via childbirth and/or breastfeeding were largely responsible for the disproportionate rates of transmission. See Gayle, Selik, and Chu, "Surveillance for AIDS and HIV."

29. Cohen, *Boundaries of Blackness*, 101–111.

30. There is no evidence of one particular event as the catalyst for the organization's interest in HIV/AIDS. In general, the SCLC and SCLC/WOMEN's entry into AIDS work mirrors a growing concern among Black institutions and media outlets over the disease.

31. Cohen, *Boundaries of Blackness*; Royles, *To Make the Wounded Whole*.

32. Dunn, "When to Fight, When to Care," *Sojourner*, 65.

33. McCoy, *Sojourner*, 65. For more on Black gay men's organizing during the HIV/AIDS crisis, with a particular focus on performance and the arts, see Woubshet, *Calendar of Loss*; Bost, *Evidence of Being*.

34. National Conference on AIDS Saturday May 31, 1986, folder 42/5 Centers for Disease Control National AIDS Minority Information and Education Project Grants, 1988, box 5, SCLC/ WOMEN, Inc. Records, MARBL.

35. SCLC/WOMEN National AIDS Minority Information Education and Training Program Summary, folder 40/24 Program Summaries, box 40, SCLC/WOMEN, Inc. Records, MARBL.

36. SCLC/WOMEN National AIDS Minority Information Education and Training Program Summary, folder 40/24 Program Summaries, box 40, SCLC/WOMEN, Inc. Records, MARBL.

37. Bailey, "Community-Based Organizations and CDC."

38. Holman et al., "Increasing the Involvement of National and Regional Racial and Ethnic Minority Organizations."

39. Organizing Black Communities to Combat AIDS, folder 41/13 Centers for Disease Control, National AIDS Minority Information and Educational Project Grants, 1988, box 41, SCLC/WOMEN, Inc. Records, MARBL.

40. Organizing Black Communities to Combat AIDS, folder 41/13 Centers for Disease Control, National AIDS Minority Information and Educational Project Grants, 1988, box 41, SCLC/WOMEN, Inc. Records, MARBL.

41. Shannon worked for the Lighthouse Counseling Center in Montgomery, Alabama and the Suicide Prevention Center in Los Angeles, California. See Margie A Shannon, Resume, folder 38/19 Atlanta, Georgia program site, 1988–1990, box 38, SCLC/WOMEN, Inc. Records, MARBL.

42. Cheryl Thompson Marsh, Resume, folder 39/11 Detroit Michigan Program site 1988–1989, box 39, SCLC/WOMEN, Inc. Records, MARBL.

43. Shannon and Dixon joined female AIDS workers at two consecutive Women in AIDS Prevention conferences—first in Washington, DC, and then in Atlanta. Issues raised during these gatherings included access to health care and treatment, the CDC's exclusion of women from their HIV/AIDS definitions, and an intersectional analysis of how classism, racism, sexism, and homophobia inhibited the ability to fight the illness. For more, see Dazon Dixon (on behalf of Women AIDS Prevention Project), Letter, c. 1989, folder 38/4 Sister to Sister: Women of Color AIDS Network, box 38, SCLC/WOMEN, Inc. Records, MARBL.

44. Responding to racial disparities in health care, many Black practitioners and health activists adopted a relationist Black health paradigm—one that emphasized segregation, economic marginalization, and racial discrimination as key determinants for African Americans' comparatively worse health (rather than cultural norms or biological inferiority). For more, see McBride, *From TB to AIDS*.

45. *Merriam-Webster*, s.v. "risk (n.)," accessed May 15, 2020, https://www.merriam -webster.com/dictionary/risk.

46. Fee and Krieger, "Understanding AIDS," 1481.

47. Fee and Krieger, "Understanding AIDS."

48. For more on typical prevention strategies during the early SCLC/WOMEN campaigns, see contents of folder 41/15 Centers for Disease Control, National AIDS Minority Information and Education Project Grants, February 1989, box 41, SCLC/ WOMEN, Inc. Records, MARBL.

49. Patton, "AIDS."

50. Gaines, *Uplifting the Race*, 1.

51. Gaines, *Uplifting the Race*, 1.

52. See Cohen, *Boundaries of Blackness*, 63–70.

53. Joseph Lowery, "Foreword," AIDS in the Black Community Program, folder 48/1 AIDS and the Black Community 1987, box 48, SCLC/WOMEN, Inc. Records, MARBL.

54. Draft of AIDS in the Black Community, folder 25/2 AIDS Education Handbook (draft), undated, box 25, SCLC/WOMEN, Inc. Records, MARBL.

55. Program for Children with Parents Infected by AIDS 1991, fol. 27/8 Program for Children with Parents Infected by AIDS, 1991, box 27, SCLC/WOMEN, Inc. Records, MARBL.

56. Mitchell, *Righteous Propagation*; Carby, "Policing the Black Woman's Body."

57. Flyer, folder 39/11 Detroit, Michigan Program Site 1988–1989, box 29, SCLC/ WOMEN, Inc. Records, MARBL.

58. Flyer, folder 39/11 Detroit, Michigan Program Site 1988–1989, box 29, SCLC/ WOMEN, Inc. Records, MARBL.

59. Henrietta Spearman, "Youths in AIDS Play Want to Get Message to Their Peers," February 9, 1989, and "Talented Teens Inform Peers of Their 'Choices,'" February 9, 1989, *Atlanta Journal- Constitution*, located in folder 32/5 Press, circa 1988–1989, box 32, SCLC/WOMEN, Inc. Records, MARBL.

60. Although the script is not available, SCLC/WOMEN documents and press accounts allow for a preliminary analysis of the production.

61. Program, fol. 39/2 Choices, the AIDS Play circa 1989, box 39, SCLC/WOMEN, Inc. Records, MARBL.

62. Evelyn Lowery to Stephen Thomas, September 20, 1989, folder 42/2 Centers for Disease Control, National AIDS Minority Information and Education Project, grants June–December 1989, box 42, SCLC/WOMEN, Inc. Records, MARBL.

63. This folder contains stock letters to the following faith leaders/organizations: Iman Warith Dean Muhammad (American Muslim Mission), Bishop J. P. Patterson (Church of God in Christ), Honorable Louis Farrakhan (Nation of Islam), Rev. Albert Cleage Jr. (the Pan-African Orthodox Christian Church), Rev. Edrick Bain (Union of Black Episcopalians), Edward B. Smith (Gospel Music Workshop

of America), Dr. E. V. Jones (National Baptist Convention Center of America), and Dr. Theodore Jemison (National Baptist Convention). All letters dated June 4, 1990. See folder 32/7 Program Mailings, 1990, box 32, SCLC/WOMEN, Inc. Records, MARBL.

64. M. Franklin to Site Coordinators, April 24, 1990 "Goals and Objectives of Race," folder 36/19 Goals and Objectives, 1989–1990, box 36 and "What We Have Learned," folder 43/6 Centers for Disease Control, National AIDS Minority Information and Education Project Grants, 1993, box 43, SCLC/WOMEN, Inc. Records, MARBL.

65. See Evaluation Plan undated, folder 41/15 Centers for Disease Control, National AIDS Minority Information and Education Project grants, February 1989, box 41, SCLC/WOMEN, Inc. Records, MARBL.

66. Maurice O'Brian Franklin, interview by author, July 30, 2018.

67. Maurice O'Brian Franklin, interview by author, July 30, 2018.

68. See Maurice O'Brian Franklin and Evelyn G. Lowery, "R.A.C.E. A National Minority Organization: A Continuation Grant Application submitted to the Centers for Disease Control," folder 42/4 Centers for Disease Control, National AIDS Minority Information and Education Project grants, January–July 1990, box 41, SCLC/WOMEN, Inc. Records, MARBL.

69. Geary, *Anti-Black Racism and the AIDS Epidemic*.

70. See RACE Program Pamphlet, folder 32/1 National STD/HIV Prevention Conference, Session Packets, box 32, SCLC/WOMEN, Inc. Records, MARBL.

71. See RACE Program Pamphlet, folder 32/1 National STD/HIV Prevention Conference, Session Packets, box 32, SCLC/WOMEN, Inc. Records, MARBL.

72. Charles Taylor, "Black Ministers Don't Give a Durn [*sic*] about AIDS," *Richmond News Leader*, August 7, 1990, folder 34/10 Tuscaloosa, Alabama program site, 1989–1991, box 34, SCLC/WOMEN, Inc. Records, MARBL.

73. RACE AIDS Prevention Survey, folder 32/11 RACE, AIDS Prevention, 1991, box 32, SCLC/WOMEN, Inc. Records, MARBL.

74. Charles Taylor, "Black Ministers Don't Give a Durn [*sic*] about AIDS," *Richmond News Leader*, August 7, 1990, folder 34/10 Tuscaloosa, Alabama program site, 1989–1991, box 34, SCLC/WOMEN, Inc. Records, MARBL.

75. RACE AIDS Prevention Survey, folder 32/11 RACE, AIDS Prevention, 1991, box 32, SCLC/WOMEN, Inc. Records, MARBL.

76. Various documents indicate Franklin's involvement with a number of community organizations, including Letter to Maurice from National Task Force on AIDS Prevention of the National Association of White and Black Men Together, folder 29/11 Correspondence 1990–1994, box 29; press clipping featuring Franklin's involvement in the Coalition of African Descent, see Robert J. Vickers, "Anti-gay Remarks at Morehouse Provoke Activists," *Atlanta Journal-Constitution*, B1, B4, undated, folder 50/4 Newspaper Clippings about SCLC/WOMEN undated, box 50; Correspondence with African American Lesbian and Gay Alliance, folder 44/3 Georgia Department of Human Resources, People of Color Initiatives grant application, 1993; box 44, SCLC/WOMEN, Inc. Records, MARBL.

77. Stockdill, *Activism against AIDS*.

78. "Homosexuality and the Church," folder 33/10 RACE Training Manuals undated, box 33, SCLC/WOMEN, Inc. Records, MARBL.

79. NAP Training Evaluation, 37/20 RACE Undated, box 37, SCLC/WOMEN, Inc. Records, MARBL.

80. "Speech by Maurice O'Brian Franklin to No/AIDS Task Force," *SCLC National Magazine* 20, no. 5 (November/December 1991): 78.

81. Teresa L. Grigsby, "SCLCWOMEN's AIDS Conference," *SCLC National Magazine* 21, no. 1 (January/February 1992): 22–28.

82. Renee McCoy, "We Are Exiles from Our Own Communities," folder 30/13 Homosexuality, circa 1990–1991, box 30, SCLC/WOMEN, Inc. Records, MARBL.

83. "New Report Highlights Homophobic Violence," *SCLC National Magazine* 19, no. 1 (March/April 1990): 119–120.

84. "SCLC Joins Civil Rights Coalition—Reiterates Its Call for Fair Treatment of Gays and Lesbians in Military," *SCLC National Magazine* 22, no. 4 (August/September/October 1993): 38–39.

85. Larry B. Stammer, "SCLC to Honor of Church for Minority Gays," *Los Angeles Times*, January 16, 1993, B10.

86. Maurice O'Brian Franklin to Michael D. Blackwell, folder 26 Correspondence 1991–1992, box 26, SCLC/WOMEN, Inc. Records, MARBL.

87. Maurice O'Brian Franklin, interview by author, July 30, 2018.

88. SCLC/WOMEN and African American Lesbian Gay Alliance, "The Chiwara Project: Healthy Loving Awareness," folder 44/ 3 Georgia Department of Human Resources, People of Color Initiatives grant application, 1993, box 44, SCLC/WOMEN, Inc. Records, MARBL.

89. SCLC/WOMEN and African American Lesbian Gay Alliance, "The Chiwara Project: Healthy Loving Awareness," folder 44/ 3 Georgia Department of Human Resources, People of Color Initiatives grant application, 1993, box 44, SCLC/WOMEN, Inc. Records, MARBL.

90. Maurice O'Brian Franklin, interview by author, July 30, 2018.

91. Maurice O'Brian Franklin to Evelyn Lowery, September 9, 1992, folder 44/3 Georgia Department of Human Resources, People of Color Initiatives grant application, 1993, box 44, SCLC/WOMEN, Inc. Records, MARBL.

92. Maurice O'Brian Franklin to Evelyn Lowery, September 9, 1992, folder 44/3 Georgia Department of Human Resources, People of Color Initiatives grant application, 1993, box 44, SCLC/WOMEN, Inc. Records, MARBL.

93. For more on this, see Snorton, *Nobody Is Supposed to Know;* 94–120.

94. Johnson, "Feeling the Spirit in the Dark," 399–416.

95. Johnson, "Feeling the Spirit in the Dark," 399–416.

Epilogue

1. Cox, Edwards, and Arditi, *Race Is Central*.

2. Cox, Edwards, and Arditi, *Race Is Central*, 8.

3. Twelve percent said they had "everything/most things in common," 24 percent said they had "some things in common," and 63 percent said they had "few things/nothing in common." See Cox, Edwards, and Arditi, *Race Is Central*, 32.

4. For early coverage of Brittney Griner's detention, see Michael Crowley and Jonathan Abrams, "Brittney Griner, Star W.N.B.A. Center Is Detained in Russia," *New York Times*, March 5, 2022.

5. Laurel Wamsley, "What Brittney Griner's Detention in Russia Tells Us about Basketball Gender Pay Gap," *National Public Radio*, April 14, 2022.

6. Jude Ephson and Nikki Main, "Griner's Cash: What Is Brittney Griner's Salary?" *U.S. Sun,* May 13, 2022.

7. Jonathan Abrams and Tania Ganguli, "Brittney Griner's Circle Turns to a Common Strategy: Silence," *New York Times*, March 11, 2022.

8. Amanda Musa and CNN Sport Staff, "Dozens of Organizations Sign Letter Calling on President Biden to Strike Deal for Brittney Griner's Release," CNN.com, June 23, 2022, 10:23 A.M., https://www.cnn.com/2022/06/23/sport/brittney-griner-wife-president-biden-spt-intl/index.html. For the House of Representatives resolution for Griner's release, see "Calling for the Immediate Release of Brittney Griner, a Citizen of the United States, Who Was Wrongfully Detained by the Government of the Russian Federation in February 2022," HR1132, 117th Congress (2022).

9. For more on the campaign by Black Feminist Futures, see, "Together We Were Able to #BringBrittneyHome," *Black Feminist Futures*, Accessed January 5, 2023, https://blackfeministfuture.org/bringbrittneyhome/

10. Jonathan Weisman and Ken Bensinger, "Blowback over Griner's Release Exposes Depth of America's Divisions," *New York Times*, December 9, 2022.

11. For a collection of right-wing commentators' attacks on Brittney Griner, see Ethan Collier and Charis Hoard, "Following Brittney Griner's Release from Russian Detainment, Right-Wing Media Figures Blast Her with Racist Attacks," Media Matters, December 9, 2022, https://www.mediamatters.org/fox-news/following-brittney-griners-release-russian-detainment-right-wing-media-figures-blast-her.

12. For works about the imbrication of racial and sexual classifications in emerging conversations about homosexuality, see Terry, *An American Obsession*; Somerville, *Queering the Color Line*. For more on leisure and urban same-sex subcultures developed within interracial spaces like cabarets, dance halls, and vice districts facilitating the exchange of Black cultural forms with white queer men, see Vogel, *The Scene of Harlem Cabaret*; Chauncey, *Gay New York*; Heap, *Slumming*.

13. For works that consider racialization in gay/lesbian politics as well as the intersections of African American politics and gay/lesbian politics, see Peacock, "Race, the Homosexual"; Stewart-Winter, *Queer Clout*; Hanhardt, *Safe Space*; Mumford, "The Trouble with Gay Rights."

14. Mitchell, "Silences Broken"; Richardson, "No More Secrets."

15. This is a rapidly growing body of literature that considers Black same-sex intimacy and gender nonconformity from a historical perspective. Book monographs include Allen, *There's a Disco Ball Between Us*; Bailey, *Butch Queen Up in Pumps*; Best, *Passionately Human*; Bost, *Evidence of Being*; Chauncey, *Gay New York*; Enke, *Finding the Movement*; Gallon, *Pleasure in the News*; Haley, *No Mercy Here*; Hartman, *Wayward Lives*; Heap, *Slumming*; Johnson, *Sweet Tea*; Johnson, *Black. Queer. Southern. Women*; Johnson, *Honey Pot.* Kennedy and Davis, *Boots of Leather*; Mumford, *Interzones*; Mumford, *Not Straight, Not White*; Ross, *Sissy In-*

surgencies; Royles, *To Make the Wounded Whole*; Schwarz, *Gay Voices of the Harlem Renaissance*; Snorton, *Black on Both Sides*; Somerville, *Queering the Color*; Woubshet, *Calendar of Loss*; Vogel, *The Scene of Harlem Cabaret*. Cookie Woolner's forthcoming book *The Famous Lady Lovers: Black Women and Queer Desire before Stonewall* is an important addition to this list. Dissertations includes Bailey, "'As Proud of Our Gayness'"; Cabello, "Queer Bronzeville"; Chenault, "An Unspoken Past"; Gonzaba, "Because the Night"; Leighton, "Freedom Indivisible." More numerous are articles that examine this phenomenon. For example, see Conerly, "Queering the Black Church"; Fisher, "Challenging Dissemblance"; Garber, "A Spectacle in Color"; Grantmyre, "'They Lived their Life'"; Hamilton, "Sexual Politics and African-American Music"; Retzloff, "Seer or Queer?"; Russell, "The Color of Discipline."

16. See Jones, "Finding Home."

17. Cohen, "Punks Bulldaggers, and Welfare Queens," 457.

18. Cohen, "Punks, Bulldaggers, and Welfare Queens," 458.

19. Ferguson, "Sissies at the Picnic," 194.

Bibliography

Manuscript Collections

Atlanta, Georgia
  Archives Division, Auburn Avenue Research Library
    Southern Regional Council Collection
  Archives Research Center, Robert W. Woodruff Library at
      Atlanta University Center
    Atlanta Urban League Papers
  Kenan Research Center, Atlanta History Center
    Atlanta Lesbian and Gay History Thing Publications
  Stuart A. Rose, Manuscript Archives and Rare Book Library, Emory University
    Calvin Fred Craig Papers
    Southern Christian Leadership Conference Papers
    Women's Organizational Movement for Equality Now Inc./SCLC Papers
    Michael A. Lomax Papers
College Park, Maryland
  National Archives at College Park
    Records of the Civilian Aide Subject Files "Hastie Files," Records of the
      Office of the Secretary of War

Digital Collections

Athens, Georgia
  Walter J. Brown Media Archives and Peabody Awards Collection,
      University of Georgia Libraries
    WSB-TV Newsfilm Collection

Microfilm Collections

Iowa City, Iowa
  Special Collections and Archives, University of Iowa
    Right Wing Collection of the University of Iowa Libraries, 1918–1977
Ithaca, New York
  Division of Rare and Manuscript Collections, Cornell University Library
    National Gay Task Force Records

Montgomery, Alabama
    Alabama Department of Archives and History
        Governors George C. and Lurleen B. Wallace Collection
    Archives and Special Collections, Auburn University–Montgomery
        William L. Dickinson Congressional Papers
Morrow, Georgia
    Georgia State Archives
        J. D. Rowlett Collection
        Governor-Executive Department—Governors Subject Files (aka Incoming
            Correspondence)
Oxford, Mississippi
    Department of Archives and Special Collections, University of Mississippi
        Race Relations Collection
Richmond, Virginia
    Library of Virginia
        Dr. H. Norton Mason Collection
Saint Louis, Missouri
    Special Collections, Washington University in Saint Louis
        Urban League of Saint Louis Papers
Tuscaloosa, Alabama
    W. S. Hoole Library Special Collections Library, University of Alabama
        Lister Hill Papers
        John Sparkman Papers
        James A. Hare Papers
Washington, DC
    Manuscript Division, Library of Congress
        National Association for the Advancement of Colored People Records
        National Urban League Records
        Frank Kameny Papers
    Moorland Spingarn Research Center, Howard University
        Charles Hamilton Houston Papers

Newspapers and Periodicals

Abilene Reporter-News
American Nationalist
Baltimore Afro-American
Birmingham News
Boston Globe
Charleston News Courier
Chicago Defender
Christian Science Monitor
The Citizen
Citizens (Tri-State) Informer
Common Sense

El Paso Herald Post
Fiery Cross
Jacksonville Florida Star
Jefferson City Post-Tribune
Logansport (IN) Pharos-Tribune
Los Angeles Sentinel
Los Angeles Times
Montgomery Advertiser
Nashville Banner
New York Amsterdam News
Norfolk Ledger Star

Norfolk New Journal and Guide
One Magazine
Pittsburgh Courier
Richmond Times-Dispatch
Rockford Crusader

Rockwell Report
Saint Louis Argus
Saint Louis Globe-Democrat
Saint Louis Times-Dispatch
Washington Post and Times Herald

Cases

State of Missouri v. John Wilson Hamilton, 310 S.W. 2d 906 (1958)

Dissertations

Bailey, Johnny. "'As Proud of Our Gayness, as We Are of Our Blackness': The Political and Social Development of the African American LGBTQ Community in Baltimore and Washington, D.C., 1975–1991." PhD diss., Morgan State University, 2017.

Cabello, Tristan. "Queer Bronzeville: Race, Sexuality and Culture in Black Chicago, 1920–1985." PhD diss., Northwestern University, 2011.

Chenault, Wesley. "An Unspoken Past: Atlanta Lesbian and Gay History, 1940–1970." PhD diss., University of New Mexico, 2008.

Frank, Gillian. "Save Our Children: The Sexual Politics of Child Protection in the United States, 1965–1990." PhD diss., Brown University, 2009.

Gonzaba, Eric. "Because the Night: Nightlife and Remaking the Gay Male World, 1970–2000." PhD diss., George Mason University, 2019.

Leighton, Jared E. "Freedom Indivisible: Gays and Lesbians in the African American Civil Rights Movement." PhD diss., University of Nebraska, 2013.

Marini, Angelica. "'Looking for a City': Community, Politics, and Gay and Lesbian Rights in Atlanta, 1965–1993." PhD diss., Auburn University, 2018.

Wallace, David James. "The Way We See It: Massive Resistance, Southern Myth and Media Suppression." PhD diss., University of Colorado–Boulder, 2011.

Books and Articles

Abdur-Rahman, Aliyyah. Against the Closet: Black Political Longing and the Erotics of Race. Durham, NC: Duke University Press, 2012.

Alexander, Michelle. The New Jim Crow: Mass Incarceration in the Age of Colorblindness. New York: New Press, 2010.

Allen, Jafari. There's a Disco Ball between Us: A Theory of Black Gay Life. Durham, NC: Duke University Press, 2022.

Anderson, Carol. Eyes off the Prize: The United Nations and the African American Struggle for Human Rights, 1944–1955. Cambridge: Cambridge University Press, 2003.

Bailey, Marlon M, Butch Queen Up in Pumps: Gender, Performance, and Ballroom Culture in Detroit. Ann Arbor: University of Michigan Press, 2013.

Bailey, Marvin E. "Community-Based Organizations and CDC as Partners in HIV Education and Prevention." In "CDC's HIV Public Information and Education Programs," special issue, *Public Health Reports* 106, no. 6 (November–December 1991): 702–708.

Bartley, Numan V. *The Rise of Massive Resistance: Race and Politics in the South during the 1950's.* Baton Rouge: Louisiana State University Press, 1969.

Bates, Beth Tompkins. *Pullman Porters and the Rise of Protest Politics in Black America, 1925–1945.* Chapel Hill: University of North Carolina Press, 2001.

Batza, Katie. *Before AIDS: Gay Health Politics in the 1970s.* Philadelphia: University of Pennsylvania Press, 2018.

Baylor, Ronald H. *Race and the Shaping of Twentieth-Century Atlanta.* Chapel Hill: University of North Carolina Press, 2000.

Bedingfield, Sid. *Newspaper Wars: Civil Rights and White Resistance in South Carolina, 1935–1965.* Urbana-Champaign: University of Illinois Press, 2017.

Beemyn, Genny. "LGBTQ Movement, Trans Inclusion In/exclusion From." In *The Sage Encyclopedia of Trans Studies,* edited by Abbie E. Goldberg and Genny Beemyn, 492–496. Thousand Oaks, CA: Sage, 2021.

Bérubé, Allan. *Coming Out under Fire: The History of Gay Men and Women in World War II.* 20th anniversary ed. Foreword by John D'Emilio and Estelle B. Freedman. Chapel Hill: University of North Carolina Press, 2010.

———. "How Gay Stays White and What Kind of White It Stays." In *My Desire for Gay History: Essays in Gay, Community and Labor History,* 202–230. Chapel Hill: University of North Carolina Press, 2011.

Best, Wallace D. *Passionately Human, No Less Divine: Religion and Culture in Black Chicago, 1915–1952.* Princeton, NJ: Princeton University Press, 2005.

Biondi, Martha. *To Stand and Fight: The Struggle for Civil Rights in Postwar New York City.* Cambridge, MA: Harvard University Press, 2006.

Blight, David W. *American Oracle: The Civil War in the Civil Rights Era.* Cambridge, MA: Harvard University Press, 2011.

Bodroghkozy, Aniko. *Equal Time: Television and the Civil Rights Movement.* Urbana: University of Illinois Press, 2012.

Borstelmann, Thomas. *The Cold War and the Color Line: American Race Relations in the Global Arena.* Cambridge, MA: Harvard University Press, 2001.

Bost, Darius. *Evidence of Being: The Black Gay Cultural Renaissance and the Politics of Violence.* Chicago: University of Chicago Press, 2019.

Boyd, Nan Alamilla. *Wide-Open Town: A History of Queer San Francisco to 1965.* Berkeley: University of California Press, 2003.

Bracey, John H., Jr., and August Meier. "Allies or Adversaries? The NAACP, A. Phillip Randolph and the 1941 March on Washington." *Georgia Historical Quarterly* 75, no. 1 (Spring 1991): 1–17.

Branch, Taylor. *Parting the Waters: America in the King Years* 1954–63. New York: Simon & Schuster, 1988.

Braukman, Stacy. *Communists and Perverts under the Palms: The Johns Committee in Florida, 1956–1965.* Gainesville: University of Florida Press, 2012.

Brier, Jennifer. *Infectious Ideas: U.S. Political Responses to the AIDS Crisis.* Chapel Hill: University of North Carolina Press, 2009.

Bronski, Michael. *A Queer History of the United States.* Boston: Beacon, 2011.

Brown, Kathleen M. *Good Wives, Nasty Wenches, and Anxious Patriarchs: Gender, Race and Power in Colonial Virginia.* Chapel Hill: University of North Carolina Press, 1996.

Brown-Nagin, Tomiko. *Courage to Dissent: Atlanta and the Long History of the Civil Rights Movement.* Oxford: Oxford University Press, 2011.

Camp, Stephanie. *Closer to Freedom: Enslaved Women and Everyday Resistance in the Plantation South.* Chapel Hill: University of North Carolina Press, 2004.

Canaday, Margot. *The Straight State: Sexuality and Citizenship in Twentieth Century America.* Princeton, NJ: Princeton University Press, 2009.

Carby, Hazel. "Policing the Black Woman's Body in an Urban Context." *Critical Inquiry* 18, no. 4 (Summer 1992): 738–755.

Carroll, Fred. *Race News: Black Journalists and the Fight for Racial Justice in the Twentieth Century.* Urbana-Champaign: University of Illinois Press, 2017.

Carson, Clayborne. *In Struggle: SNCC and the Black Awakening of the 1960s.* Cambridge, MA: Harvard University Press, 1981.

Carter, Dan T. *The Politics of Rage: George Wallace, the Origins of the New Conservatism, and the Transformation of American Politics.* Baton Rouge: Louisiana State University Press, 2000.

Chafe, William H. *Civilities and Civil Rights: Greensboro, North Carolina, and the Black Struggle for Freedom.* Oxford: Oxford University Press, 1980.

Chappell, David L. *A Stone of Hope: Prophetic Religion and the Death of Jim Crow.* Chapel Hill: University of North Carolina Press, 2004.

Chauncey, George. *Gay New York: Gender, Urban Culture, and the Making of the Gay Male World, 1890–1940.* New York: Basic Books, 1994.

———. "The Postwar Sex Crime Panic." In *True Stories from the American Past,* edited by William Graebner, 160–179. New York: McGraw Hill, 1993.

Chen, Anthony S. *The Fifth Freedom: Jobs, Politics and Civil Rights in the United States, 1941–1972.* Princeton, NJ: Princeton University Press, 2009.

Cobb, Charles E., Jr. *On the Road to Freedom: A Guided Tour of the Civil Rights Trail.* Chapel Hill: Algonquin Books of Chapel Hill, 2008.

Cohen, Cathy J. *The Boundaries of Blackness: AIDS and the Breakdown of Black Politics.* Chicago: University of Chicago Press, 1999.

———. "Punks, Bulldaggers, and Welfare Queens: The Radical Potential of Queer Politics?" *GLQ* 3, no. 4 (1997): 437–465.

Collins, Patricia Hill. *Black Feminist Thought: Knowledge, Consciousness, and the Politics of Empowerment.* Boston: Unwin Hyman, 1990.

Combahee River Collective. "A Black Feminist Statement." In *Words of Fire: An Anthology of African-American Feminist Thought,* edited by Beverly Guy Sheftall, 231–240. New York: New Press, 1995.

Conerly, Gregory. "Queering the Black Church: Notes from the Black Press, 1945–1960." *Journal of African American History* 104, no. 2 (Spring 2019): 201–226.

Countryman, Matthew. *Up South: Civil Rights and Black Power in Philadelphia.* Philadelphia: University of Pennsylvania Press, 2006.

Cox, Kiana, Khadijah Edwards, and Tanya Arditi. *Race Is Central to Identity for Black Americans and Affects How They Connect with Each Other.* Washington, DC: Pew Research Center, April 2022.

Crenshaw, Kimberlé. "Mapping the Margins: Intersectionality, Identity Politics, and Violence against Women of Color." *Stanford Law Review* 43, no. 6 (July 1991): 1241–1299.

Crespino, Joseph. *In Search of Another Country: Mississippi and the Conservative Counterrevolution.* Princeton, NJ: Princeton University Press, 2007.

Cuordileone, K. A. "'Politics in an Age of Anxiety': Cold War Political Culture and the Crisis in American Masculinity, 1949–1960." *Journal of American History* 87, no. 2 (September 2000): 515–545.

Curran, James W., Harold W. Jaffe, and the Centers for Disease Control and Prevention. "AIDS: The Early Years at CDC's Response." *Morbidity and Mortality Weekly Report* 60, no. 4 (October 7, 2011): 64–69.

Dailey, Jane. "Sex, Segregation, and the Sacred after *Brown*." *Journal of American History* 91, no. 1 (2004): 119–144.

Dawson, Michael. *Black Visions: The Roots of Contemporary African-American Political Ideologies.* Chicago: University of Chicago Press, 2001.

Dean, Robert D. *Imperial Brotherhood: Gender and the Making of Cold War Foreign Policy.* Amherst: University of Massachusetts Press, 2001.

D'Emilio, John. *Sexual Politics, Sexual Communities: The Making of a Homosexual Minority in the United States, 1940–1970.* 2nd ed. Chicago: University of Chicago Press, 1998.

Dillard, Angela D. *Faith in the City: Preaching Radical Social Change in Detroit.* Ann Arbor, MI: University of Michigan Press, 2007.

———. *Guess Who's Coming to Dinner Now? Multicultural Conservatism in America.* New York: New York University Press, 2001.

Dudziak, Mary L. *Cold War Civil Rights: Race and the Image of American Democracy.* Princeton, NJ: Princeton University Press, 2000.

Duggan, Lisa. *Sapphic Slashers: Sex, Violence, and American Modernity.* Durham, NC: Duke University Press, 2001.

Eagles, Charles W. *Outside Agitator: Jon Daniels and the Civil Rights Movement in Alabama.* Chapel Hill: University of North Carolina Press, 1993.

Engel, Jonathan. *The Epidemic: A Global History of AIDS.* New York: Harper Collins, 2006.

Enke, Finn. *Finding the Movement: Sexuality, Contested Space, and Feminist Activism.* Durham, NC: Duke University Press, 2007.

Epstein, Steven. *Impure Science: AIDS, Activism, and the Politics of Knowledge.* Berkeley: University of California Press, 1998.

Ervin, Keona. *Gateway to Equality: Black Women and the Struggle for Economic Justice in St. Louis.* Lexington: University of Kentucky Press, 2017.

Eskridge, William N., Jr. *Dishonorable Passions: Sodomy Laws in America, 1861–2003.* New York: Penguin Press, 2008.

Estes, Steve. *I Am a Man!: Race, Manhood, and the Civil Rights Movement.* Chapel Hill: University of North Carolina Press, 2005.

Faderman, Lillian. *Odd Girls and Twilight Lovers: A History of Lesbian Life in Twentieth-Century America.* New York: Columbia University Press, 1991.

Fairclough, Adam. *To Redeem the Soul of America: The Southern Christian Leadership Conference and Martin Luther King, Jr.* Athens: University of Georgia Press, 1987.

Farmer, Ashley D. *Remaking Black Power: How Black Women Transformed an Era.* Chapel Hill: University of North Carolina Press, 2017.

Faulk, Ralph. "Prevention Messages through the Performing Arts." *Prevention Pipeline* 8, no. 1 (January/February 1995): 49–50.

Fee, Elizabeth, and Nancy Krieger. "Understanding AIDS: Historical Interpretations and the Limits of Biomedical Individualism." *American Journal of Public Health* 83, no. 10 (October 1993): 1477–1486.

Feimster, Crystal N. *Southern Horrors: Women and the Politics of Rape and Lynching.* Cambridge, MA: Harvard University Press, 2009.

Ferguson, Karen. *Black Politics in New Deal Atlanta.* Chapel Hill: University of North Carolina Press, 2002.

Ferguson, Roderick. *Aberrations in Black: Toward a Queer of Color Critique.* Minneapolis: University of Minnesota Press, 2004.

——. "Nightmares of the Heteronormative." *Journal of Cultural Research* 4, no. 4 (2000): 419–444.

——. "Sissies at the Picnic: The Subjugated Knowledges of a Black Rural Queer." In *Feminist Waves, Feminist Formations: Life Stories from the Academy,* edited by Hokulani Aikau, Karla Erickson, and Jennifer L. Pierce, 188–196. Minneapolis: University of Minnesota Press, 2007.

Fisher, Simon D. Elin. "Challenging Dissemblance in Pauli Murray Historiography, Sketching History of the Trans New Negro." *Journal of African American History* 104, no. 2 (Spring 2019): 201–226.

Fleischmann, Arnold, and Jason Hardman. "Hitting below the Bible Belt: The Development of the Gay Rights Movement in Atlanta." *Journal of Urban Affairs* 26, no 4 (2004): 407–426.

Forbes, Amy Wise, and Amanda Smithers. "Combatting the 'Communistic Mulatto Inspired Movement to Fuse the Two Ethnic Groups.'" *Social History of Medicine* 31, no. 2 (May 2018): 392–413.

Fortner, Michael Javen. *Black Silent Majority: The Rockefeller Drug Laws and the Politics of Punishment.* Cambridge, MA: Harvard University Press, 2015.

Foucault, Michel. *The History of Sexuality Vol. 1 An Introduction.* Translated by Robert Hurley. New York: Random House, 1978.

——. "Nietzsche, Genealogy, History." In *Language, Counter-Memory Practice: Selected Essays and Interviews,* edited by D. F. Bouchard, 78–100. Ithaca, NY: Cornell University Press, 1977.

Frank, Gillian. "'The Civil Rights of Parents': Race and Conservative Politics in Anita Bryant Campaign in Anita Bryant's Campaign against Gay Rights in 1970s Florida." *Journal of the History of Sexuality* 22, no. 1 (January 2013): 126–160.

Freedman, Estelle. "'Uncontrollable Desires': The Response to the Sexual Psychopath, 1920–1960." *Journal of American History* 74 no. 1 (June 1987): 83–106.

Friedland, Michael B. *Lift Up Your Voice like a Trumpet: White Clergy and the Civil Rights and Antiwar Movements, 1954–1973*. Chapel Hill: University of North Carolina Press, 1998.

Gadsden, Brett. *Between North and South: Delaware, Desegregation, and the Myth of American Sectionalism*. Philadelphia: University of Pennsylvania Press, 2013.

Gaines, Kevin K. *Uplifting the Race: Black Leadership, Politics, and Culture in the Twentieth Century*. Chapel Hill: University of North Carolina Press, 1996.

Gallon, Kim. *Pleasure in the News: African American Readership and Sexuality in the Black Press*. Urbana-Champaign: University of Illinois Press, 2020.

Garber, Eric. "A Spectacle in Color: The Lesbian and Gay Subculture of Jazz Age Harlem." In *Hidden from History: Reclaiming the Gay and Lesbian Past*, edited by Martin B. Duberman, Martha Vicinus, and George Chauncey, 318–331. New York: Penguin, 1991.

Garrow, David J. *Bearing the Cross: Martin Luther King, Jr., and the Southern Christian Leadership Conference*. New York: Perennial Classics, 1999.

——. *Protest at Selma: Martin Luther King, Jr., and the Voting Rights Act of 1965*. New Haven, CT: Yale University Press, 1978.

Gayle, Jacob A., Richard M. Selik, and Susan Y. Chu. "Surveillance for AIDS and HIV Infection among Black and Hispanic Children and Women of Childbearing Age, 1981–1989." *Morbidity and Mortality Weekly Report* 39, no. SS-3 (July 1990): 23–30.

Geary, Adam. *Anti-Black Racism and the AIDS Epidemic: State Intimacies*. New York: Palgrave Macmillan, 2014.

Ghaziani, Amin. *The Dividends of Dissent: How Conflict and Culture Work in Lesbian and Gay Marches on Washington*. Chicago: University of Chicago Press, 2008.

Gibson, Truman K., Jr., with Steve Huntley. *Knocking Down Barriers: My Fight for Black America—a Memoir*. Evanston, IL: Northwestern University Press, 2005.

Glymph, Thavolia. *Out of the House of Bondage: The Transformation of the Plantation Household*. Cambridge: Cambridge University Press, 2008.

Gore, Dayo. *Radicalism at the Crossroads: African American Women Activists in the Cold War*. New York: New York University Press, 2011.

Grantmyre, Laura. "'They Lived Their Life and They Didn't Bother Anybody': African American Female Impersonators and Pittsburgh's Hill District, 1920–1960." *American Quarterly* 6, no. 4 (December 2011): 983–1011.

Gross, Kali N. *Colored Amazons: Crime, Violence, and Black Women in the City of Brotherly Love, 1880–1910*. Durham, NC: Duke University Press, 2006.

Grundy, David. "Steven Abbott, *Beautiful Aliens*." *Chicago Review*, July 9, 2020, https://www.chicagoreview.org/steve-abbott-beautiful-aliens/.

Guglielmo, Thomas A. "A Martial Freedom Movement: Black G.I.'s Political Struggles during World War II." *Journal of American History* 104, no. 4 (March 2018): 879–903.

Haley, Sarah. *No Mercy Here: Gender, Punishment, and the Making of Jim Crow Modernity.* Chapel Hill: University of North Carolina Press, 2016.

Hamilton, Marybeth. "Sexual Politics and African-American Music; or, Placing Little Richard in History." *History Workshop Journal* 46 (Autumn 1998): 160–176.

Hanhardt, Christina. "The Radical Potential of Queer History?" *GLQ* 25, no. 1 (2019): 145–149.

———. *Safe Space: Gay Neighborhood History and the Politics of Violence.* Durham, NC: Duke University Press, 2013.

Harris, LaShawn. "Marvel Cooke: Investigative Journalist, Communist and Black Radical Subject." *Journal for the Study of Radicalism* 6, no. 2 (Fall 2012): 91–126.

———. *Sex Workers, Psychics and Numbers Runners: Black Women in New York City's Underground Economy.* Urbana-Champaign: University of Illinois Press, 2016.

Hartman, Saidiya. *Scenes of Subjection: Terror, Slavery, and Self-making in Nineteenth Century America.* Oxford: Oxford University Press, 1997.

———. *Wayward Lives, Beautiful Experiments: Intimate Histories of Riotous Black Girls, Troublesome Women, and Queer Radicals.* New York: Norton, 2020.

Heap, Chad. *Slumming: Sexual and Racial Encounters in American Nightlife, 1885–1940.* Chicago: University of Chicago Press, 2009.

Heineman, Elizabeth D. "Sexuality and Nazisms: The Doubly Unspeakable?" *Journal of the History of Sexuality* 11, nos. 1–2 (January–April 2002): 22–66.

Hendershot, Heather. *What's Fair on the Air? Cold War Right-Wing Broadcasting and the Public Interest.* Chicago: University of Chicago Press, 2011.

Henry, Aaron, and Constance Curry. *Aaron Henry: The Fire Ever Burning.* Jackson, MS: University of Mississippi Press, 2000.

Herbold, Hilary. "Never a Level Playing Field: Blacks and the GI Bill." *Journal of Blacks in Higher Education* 6 (Winter 1994–1995): 104–108.

Hicks, Cheryl D. *Talk with You like a Woman: African American Women, Justice, and Reform in New York, 1890–1935.* Chapel Hill: University of North Carolina Press, 2010.

Higginbotham, Evelyn Brooks. "African American History and the Metalanguage of Race." *Signs* 17, no. 2 (Winter 1992): 251–274.

———. *Righteous Discontent: The Women's Movement in the Black Baptist Church, 1880–1920.* Cambridge, MA: Harvard University Press, 1993.

Hinton, Elizabeth. *From the War on Poverty to the War on Crime: The Making of Mass Incarceration in America.* Cambridge, MA: Harvard University Press, 2016.

Hobson, Emily K. *Lavender and Red: Liberation and Solidarity in the Gay and Lesbian Left.* Oakland: University of California Press, 2016.

Hobson, Maurice J. *The Legend of the Black Mecca: Politics and Class in the Making of Modern Atlanta.* Chapel Hill: University of North Carolina Press, 2017.

Hodes, Martha. *White Women, Black Men: Illicit Sex in the Nineteenth-Century South.* New Haven, CT: Yale University Press, 1999.

Holman, Priscilla B., William C. Jenkins, Jacob A. Gayle, Carlton Duncan, and Bryan K. Linsey. "Increasing the Involvement of National and Regional Racial and Ethnic Minority Organizations in HIV Information and Education." In "CDC's HIV Public Information and Education Programs," special issue, *Public Health Reports* 106, no. 6 (November–December 1991): 687–694.

Holmes, Kwame. "What's the T: Gossip and the Production of Black Gay Social History." *Radical History Review* 122 (2015): 55–69

———. "Beyond the Flames: Queering the History of the 1968 D.C. Riot." in *No Tea, No Shade: New Writings in Black Queer Studies*, Vol. 2, edited by E. Patrick Johnson, 304–322. Durham, NC: Duke University Press, 2016.

Holsaert, Faith S., Martha Prescod Norman Noonan, Judy Richardson, Betty Garman Robinson, Jean Smith Young, and Dorothy M. Zellner. *Hands on the Freedom Plow: Personal Accounts by Women in the SNCC*. Urbana-Champaign: University of Illinois Press, 2012.

Honey, Michael. *Southern Labor and Black Civil Rights: Organizing Memphis Workers*. Urbana: University of Illinois Press, 1993.

Howard, Clayton. *The Closet and the Cul-de-Sac: The Politics of Sexual Privacy in Northern California*. Philadelphia: University of Pennsylvania Press, 2019.

Howard, John. "The Library, the Park and the Pervert: Public Space and Homosexual Encounter in Post-War World II Atlanta." In *Carryin' On in the Lesbian and Gay South*, edited by John Howard, 107–113. New York: New York University Press, 1997.

———. *Men Like That: A Southern Queer History*. Chicago: University of Chicago, 1999.

Hunter, Eric, ed. *Sojourner: Black Gay Voices in the Age of AIDS*. New York: Other Countries Press, 1993.

Hunter, Tera W. *Bound in Wedlock: Slave and Free Black Marriage in the Nineteenth Century*. Cambridge, MA: Harvard University Press, 2019.

Irvine, Janice M. *Talk about Sex: The Battles over Sex Education in the United States*. Berkeley: University of California Press, 2002.

Jeffries, Hassan Kwame. *Bloody Lowndes: Civil Rights and Black Power in Alabama's Black Belt*. New York: New York University Press, 2010.

Jenkins, Candice. *Private Lives, Proper Relations: Regulating Black Intimacy*. Minneapolis: University of Minnesota Press, 2008.

Jenkins, Philip. *Moral Panic: Changing Concepts of the Child Molester in Modern America*. New Haven, CT: Yale University Press, 1998.

Johnson, David K. *The Lavender Scare: The Cold War Persecution of Gays and Lesbians in the Federal Government*. Chicago: University of Chicago Press, 2004.

Johnson, E. Patrick. *Black. Queer. Southern. Women: An Oral History*. Chapel Hill: University of North Carolina Press, 2018.

———. "Feeling the Spirit in the Dark: Expanding Notions of the Sacred in the African-American Gay Community." *Callaloo* 21, no. 2 (Spring 1988): 399–416.

———. *HoneyPot: Black Southern Women Who Love Women*. Durham, NC: Duke University Press, 2019.

——. *Sweet Tea: Black Gay Men of the South*. Chapel Hill: University of North Carolina Press, 2008.

——. *No Tea, No Shade: New Writings in Black Queer Studies*. Durham, NC: Duke University Press, 2016.

Johnson, Marilynn S. "Gender, Race, and Rumours: Re-examining the 1943 Race Riots." *Gender & History* 10, no.2 (July 1998): 252–277.

Johnson, Walter. *The Broken Heart of America: St. Louis and the Violent History of the United States*. New York: Basic Books, 2020.

Jones, Jacqueline. *Labor of Love: Black Women, Work, and the Family, from Slavery to the Present*. New York: Basic Books, 2010.

Joseph, Peniel. *Waiting 'Til the Midnight Hour: A Narrative History of Black Power in America*. New York: Holt Paperbacks, 2006.

Kandaswamy, Priya. *Domestic Contradictions: Race and Gendered Citizenship from Reconstruction to Welfare Reform*. Durham, NC: Duke University Press, 2021.

Katznelson, Ira. *When Affirmative Action Was White: An Untold History of Racial Inequality in Twentieth-Century America*. New York: Norton, 2005.

Kelley, Robin D. G. *Freedom Dreams: The Black Radical Imagination*. Boston: Beacon, 2003.

——. *Hammer and Hoe: Alabama Communists during the Great Depression*. Chapel Hill: University of North Carolina Press, 1990.

Kennedy, Elizabeth Lapovsky, and Madeline D. Davis. *Boots of Leather, Slippers of Gold: The History of a Lesbian Community*. New York: Routledge, 1993.

Kluger, Richard. *Simple Justice: The History of* Brown v. Board of Education *and Black America's Struggle for Equality*. New York: Vintage, 2004.

Korstad, Robert. *Civil Rights Unionism: Tobacco Workers and the Struggle for Democracy in the Mid-twentieth Century South*. Chapel Hill: University of North Carolina Press, 2003.

Kruse, Kevin M. *White Flight: Atlanta and the Making of Modern Conservatism*. Princeton, NJ: Princeton University, 2005.

Kuhn, Cliff, Harlon E. Joye, and E. Bernard West. *Living Atlanta: An Oral History of the City, 1914–1948*. Athens: University of Georgia Press, 2005.

Kunzel, Regina G. *Criminal Intimacy: Prison and the Uneven History of Modern American Sexuality*. Chicago: University of Chicago Press, 2008.

Lassiter, Matthew. *The Silent Majority: Suburban Politics in the Sunbelt South*. Princeton, NJ: Princeton University Press, 2006.

Lecklider, Aaron. *Love's Next Meeting: The Forgotten History of Homosexuality and the Left in American Culture*. Berkeley: University of California Press, 2021.

LeFlouria, Talitha. *Chained in Silence: Black Women and Convict Labor in the New South*. Chapel Hill: University of North Carolina Press, 2015.

Leonard, Kevin Allen. "'Containing Perversion': African Americans and Same-Sex Desire in Cold War Los Angeles." *Journal of the History of Sexuality* 20, no. 3 (September 2011): 545–567.

Lindemann, Danielle. "From Fire and Brimstone to Property Values: The Changing Style of Arguments against Pornographic Industries, Atlanta, 1969–1997." *Sociological Perspectives* 52, no. 1 (Spring 2009): 81–101.

Lisby, Gregory C. "'Trying to Define What May Be Indefinable': The Georgia Literature Commission, 1953–1975." *Georgia Historical Quarterly* 84, no. 1 (Spring 2000): 72–97.

Marable, Manning. *Black American Politics: From the Washington Marches to Jesse Jackson.* London: Verso, 1985.

———. "Reagan, Race and Reaction: Black Political Realignment in the 1980s." *Black Scholar* 13, no. 6 (Fall 1982): 2–15.

Martin, Harold H. *Atlanta and Environs: A Chronicle of Its People and Events, 1940s–1970s, Vol. III.* Athens: University of Georgia Press, 1987.

May, Gary. *The Informant: The FBI, the Ku Klux Klan, and the Murder of Viola Liuzzo.* New Haven, CT: Yale University Press, 2005.

McBride, David. *From TB to AIDS: Epidemics among Urban Blacks since 1900.* Albany: State University of New York Press, 1991.

McDuffie, Erick S. "Black Liberation, the Cold War and the Horne Thesis." *Journal of African American History* 96, no. 2 (Spring 2011): 236–247.

———. "Black and Red: Black Liberation, The Cold War, and the Horne Thesis." *Journal of African American History* 96, no. 2 (Spring 2011): 236–247.

———. *Sojourning for Freedom: Black Women, American Communism, and the Making of Black Left Feminism.* Durham, NC: Duke University Press, 2011.

McGirr, Lisa. *Suburban Warriors: The Origins of the New American Right.* Princeton, NJ: Princeton University Press, 2001.

McGuire, Danielle. *At the Dark End of the Street: Black Women, Rape, and Resistance—a New History of the Civil Rights Movement from Rosa Parks to the Rise of Black Power.* New York: Knopf, 2010.

McGuire, Phillip, ed. *Taps for a Jim Crow Army: Letters from Black Soldiers in World War II.* Lexington: University Press of Kentucky, 1993.

McMillen, Neil R. *The Citizens' Council: Organized Resistance to the Second Reconstruction, 1954–1964.* Urbana: University of Illinois Press, 1994.

McNeil, Genna Rae. *Groundwork: Charles Hamilton Houston and the Struggle for Civil Rights.* Philadelphia: University of Pennsylvania Press, 1983.

Meeker, Martin. *Contacts Desired: Gay and Lesbian Communications and Community, 1940s–1970s.* Chicago: University of Chicago Press, 2006.

Melamed, Jodi. *Represent and Destroy: Rationalizing Violence in the New Racial Capitalism.* Minneapolis: University of Minnesota Press, 2011.

Merriweather, James H. *Proudly We Can Be Africans: Black Americans and Africa, 1935–1961.* Chapel Hill: University of North Carolina Press, 2002.

Mershon, Sherie, and Steven Schlossman. *Foxholes and Color Lines: Desegregating the U.S. Armed Forces.* Baltimore: Johns Hopkins University Press, 2003.

Meyerowitz, Joanne J. "How Common Culture Shapes the Separate Lives: Sexuality, Race, and Mid-twentieth-Century Social Constructionist Thought." *Journal of American History* 96, no. 4 (March 2010): 1057–1084.

———. *How Sex Changed: A History of Transsexuality in the United States.* Cambridge, MA: Harvard University Press, 2002.

Mikell, Robert Mosley. *Selma.* Charlotte, NC: Citadel Press, 1966.

Mims, La Shonda. *Drastic Dykes and Accidental Activists: Queer Women in the Urban South*. Chapel Hill: University of North Carolina Press, 2022.

Mitchell, Michele. *Righteous Propagation: African Americans and the Politics of Racial Destiny after Reconstruction*. Chapel Hill: University of North Carolina Press, 2004.

———. "Silences Broken, Silences Kept: Gender and Sexuality in African American History." *Gender & History* 11, no. 3 (November 1999): 433–444.

Morgan, Jennifer. *Laboring Women: Reproduction and Gender in New World Slavery*. Philadelphia: University of Pennsylvania Press, 2004.

Morris, Aldon. *The Origins of the Civil Rights Movement: Black Communities Organizing for Change*. New York: Free Press, 1984.

Muhammad, Khalil Gibran. *The Condemnation of Blackness: Race, Crime, and the Making of Modern Urban America*. Cambridge, MA: Harvard University Press, 2010.

Mumford, Kevin J. "Homosex Changes: Race, Cultural Geography and the Emergence of the Gay." *American Quarterly* 48, no. 3 (September 1996): 395–414.

———. *Interzones: Black/White Sex Districts in Chicago and New York in the Early Twentieth Century*. New York: Columbia University Press, 1997.

———. *Not Straight, Not White: Black Gay Men from the March on Washington to the AIDS Crisis*. Chapel Hill: University of North Carolina Press, 2016.

———. "The Trouble with Gay Rights: Race and the Politics of Sexual Orientation in Philadelphia, 1969–1982." *Journal of American History* 98, no. 1 (2011): 49–72.

———. "Untangling Pathology: The Moynihan Report and Homosexual Damage, 1965–1975." *Journal of Policy History* 24, no. 1 (2012): 53–73.

Murakawa, Naomi. *The First Civil Right: How Liberals Built Prison America*. Oxford: Oxford University Press, 2014.

Mustakeem, Sowande. *Slavery at Sea: Terror, Sex, and Sickness in the Middle Passage*. Urbana-Champaign: University of Illinois Press, 2016.

Nickerson, Michelle M. *Mothers of Conservatism: Women and the Postwar Right*. Princeton, NJ: Princeton University Press, 2012.

Onkst, David H. "'First a Negro . . . Incidentally a Veteran': Black World War Two Veterans and the G.I. Bill of Rights in the Deep South, 1944–1948." *Journal of Social History* 31 no. 3 (Spring 1998): 517–543.

Parris, Guichard, and Lester Brooks. *Blacks in the City: A History of the National Urban League*. Boston: Little and Brown, 1971.

Pascoe, Peggy. "Sex, Gender, and Same-Sex Marriage." In *Is Academic Feminism Dead: Theory in Practice*, edited by the Social Justice Group at the Center for Advanced Feminist Studies, University of Minnesota, 86–129. New York: New York University Press, 2000.

———. *What Comes Naturally: Miscegenation Law and the Making of Race in America*. Oxford: Oxford University Press, 2009.

Patton, Cindy. "AIDS: Lessons from the Gay Community." *Feminist Review* 30 (Autumn 1988): 105–111.

Peacock, Kent W. "Race, the Homosexual, and the Mattachine Society of Washington, 1961–1970." *Journal of the History of Sexuality* 25, no. 2 (May 2016): 267–296.

Peake, Thomas R. *Keeping the Dream Alive: A History of the Southern Christian Leadership Conference from King to the Nineteen-Eighties.* New York: Peter Lang, 1987.

Penningroth, Dylan. *The Claims of Kinfolk: African American Property and Community in the Nineteenth Century South.* Chapel Hill: University of North Carolina Press, 2004.

Persons, Albert C. *The True Selma Story: Sex and Civil Rights.* Birmingham, AL: Esco Publishers, 1965.

Peterson, Bryce E. "Furlough." In *The Encyclopedia of Criminology and Criminal Justice,* edited by Jay S. Albanese, 1–5. Hoboken, NJ: Wiley, 2014.

Phillips-Fein, Kim. "Conservatism: A State of the Field." *Journal of American History* 98, no. 3 (December 2011): 723–743.

Pope, Kitty J. *Beside Every Great Man . . . Is a Great Woman: African American Women of Courage, Intelligence, Strength, Beauty and Perseverance.* Edited by Jarmell H. Boyd-Sims. Phoenix: Amber Books, 2005.

Pritchard, Eric Darnell. "As Proud of Our Gayness As We Are of Our Blackness: Race-ing Sexual Rhetorics in the National Coalition of Black Lesbians and Gay." *Sexual Rhetorics: Methods, Identities, Publics.* Edited by Jonathan Alexander and Jacqueline Rhodes, 159–171. New York: Routledge Press, 2016.

Quin, Kevin C. "'To Stamp Out the Oppression of All Black People': Ron Grayson and the Association of Black Gays, 1975–1979." *Journal of African American History* 104, no. 2 (Spring 2019): 227–249.

Rampersad, Arnold. *The Life of Langston Hughes Volume 1: 1902–1941, I Too Sing America.* Oxford: Oxford University Press, 1986.

Ransby, Barbara. *Ella Baker and the Black Freedom Movement: A Radical Democratic Vision.* Chapel Hill: University of North Carolina Press, 2003.

Reagon, Bernice Johnson. "Coalition Politics: Turning the Century." In *Home Girls: A Black Feminist Anthology,* 343–356. New Brunswick, NJ: Rutgers University Press, 1983.

Reddy, Chandan. *Freedom with Violence: Race, Sexuality, and the US State.* Durham, NC: Duke University Press, 2011.

Reed, Touré F. *Not Alms but Opportunity: The Urban League and the Politics of Racial Uplift, 1910–1950.* Chapel Hill: University of North Carolina Press, 2008.

Retzloff, Timothy. "Seer or Queer? Postwar Fascination with Detroit's Prophet Jones." *GLQ* 8, no. 3 (2002): 271–296.

Richardson, Matt. "No More Secrets No More Lies: African American History and Compulsory Heterosexuality." *Journal of Women's History* 15, no. 3 (Autumn 2003): 63–76.

Ritchie, Andrea J., and Kay Whitlock. "Criminalization and Legalization." In *The Routledge History of Queer America,* edited by Don Romesburg, 300–314. New York: Routledge, 2018.

Roberts, Dorothy. *Killing the Black Body: Race, Reproduction, and the Meaning of Liberty.* New York: Vintage, 1997.

Roberts, Gene, and Hank Klibanoff. *The Race Beat: The Press, the Civil Rights Struggle, and the Awakening of a Nation*. New York: Knopf, 2006.

Robertson, Stephen. "Separating the Men from the Boys: Masculinity, Psychosexual Development, and Sex Crime in the United States, 1930s–1960s." *Journal of the History of Medicine and Allied Sciences* 56, no. 1 (January 2001): 3–35.

Robnett, Belinda. *How Long? How Long? African-American Women in the Struggle for Civil Rights*. Oxford: Oxford University Press, 1997.

Romano, Renee C. *Race Mixing: Black-White Marriage in Post-war America*. Cambridge: Cambridge University Press, 2003.

Romesburg, Don. "'Wouldn't a Boy Do?' Placing Early-Twentieth Century Male Youth Sex Work into Histories of Sexuality." *Journal of the History of Sexuality* 18, no. 3 (September 2009): 367–392.

Rosén, Hannah. *Terror in the Heart of Freedom: Citizenship, Sexual Violence, and the Meaning of Race in the Postemancipation South*. Chapel Hill: University of North Carolina Press, 2009.

Ross, Marlon B. *Sissy Insurgencies: A Racial Anatomy of Unfit Manliness*. Durham, NC: Duke University Press 2022.

Royles, Dan. *To Make the Wounded Whole: The African American Struggle against HIV/AIDS*. Chapel Hill: University of North Carolina Press, 2020.

Rubin, Gayle. "Thinking Sex: Notes for a Radical Theory of the Politics of Sexuality." In *Deviations: A Gayle Rubin Reader*, 137–181. Durham, NC: Duke University Press, 2011.

Russell, Thaddeus. "The Color of Discipline: Civil Rights and Black Sexuality." *American Quarterly* 60, no. 1 (March 2008): 101–128.

Savage, Sean J. *JFK, LBJ, and the Democratic Party*. Albany: State University of New York Press, 2004.

Schmaltz, William H. *Hate: George Lincoln Rockwell and the American Nazi Party*. Washington, DC: Brassey's, 1999.

Schwarz, A. B. Christa. *Gay Voices of the Harlem Renaissance*. Bloomington: Indiana University Press, 2003.

Scott, Darryl. *Contempt and Pity: Social Policy and the Image of the Damaged Black Psyche, 1880–1996*. Chapel Hill: University of North Carolina Press, 1997.

Sears, Clare. *Arresting Dress: Cross Dressing, Law and Fascination in Nineteenth-Century San Francisco*. Durham, NC: Duke University Press, 2014.

Self, Robert O. *American Babylon: Race and Struggle for Postwar Oakland*. Princeton, NJ: Princeton University Press, 2005.

Shah, Nayan. "Queer of Color Estrangement and Belonging." In *The Routledge History of Queer America*, edited by Don Romesburg, 262–275. New York: Routledge, 2018.

Sharpe. Christina. *Monstrous Intimacies: Making Post-slavery Subjects*. Durham, NC: Duke University Press, 2010.

Shilts, Randy. *And the Band Played On: Politics, People, and the AIDS Epidemic*. New York: St. Martin's, 1987.

Sides, Josh. *Erotic City: Sexual Revolutions and the Making of Modern San Francisco*. Oxford: Oxford University Press, 2011.

Simmons, J. L. "Public Stereotypes of Deviants." *Social Problems* 13, no. 2 (Autumn 1965): 223–232.

Simonelli, Frederick J. *American Fuehrer: George Lincoln Rockwell and the American Nazi Party*. Urbana: University of Illinois Press, 1999.

Skidmore, Emily. "Constructing the 'Good Transsexual': Christine Jorgensen, Whiteness and Heteronormativity in the Mid-twentieth Century Press." *Feminist Studies* 37, no. 2 (Summer 2011): 270–300.

Slate, Nico. *Colored Cosmopolitanism: The Shared Struggle for Freedom in the United States and India*. Cambridge, MA: Harvard University Press, 2017.

Slide, Anthony. *Actors on Red Alert: Career Interviews with Five Actors and Actresses Affected by the Blacklist*. Lanham, MD: Scarecrow, 1999.

Smith, Mark M. *How Race Is Made: Slavery, Segregation, and the Senses*. Chapel Hill: University of North Carolina Press, 2006.

Snorton, C. Riley. *Black on Both Sides: A Racial History of Trans Identity*. Minneapolis: University of Minnesota Press, 2017.

——. *Nobody Is Supposed to Know: Black Sexuality on the Down Low*. Minneapolis: University of Minnesota Press, 2014.

Somerville, Siobhan. *Queering the Color Line: Race and the Invention of Homosexuality in American Culture*. Durham, NC: Duke University Press, 2000.

——. "Queer Loving." *GLQ* 11, no. 3 (2005): 335-370.

Spencer, Robyn. *The Revolution Has Come: Black Power, Gender, and the Black Panther Party in Oakland*. Durham, NC: Duke University Press, 2016.

Stanton, Mary. *From Selma to Sorrow: The Life and Death of Viola Liuzzo*. Athens, GA: University of Georgia, 2000.

Stein, Marc. *City of Sisterly and Brotherly Loves: Lesbian and Gay Philadelphia, 1945-1972*. Philadelphia: Temple University Press, 2004.

——. "Law and Politics: 'Crooked and Perverse' Narratives of LGBT Progress." In *The Routledge History of Queer America*, edited by Don Romesburg, 315–330. New York: Routledge, 2018.

——. *Rethinking the Gay and Lesbian Movement*. New York: Routledge, 2012.

——. *Sexual Injustice: Supreme Court Decisions from Griswold to Roe*. Chapel Hill: University of North Carolina Press, 2010.

Stevenson, Brenda. *Life in Black and White: Family and Community in the Slave South*. Oxford: Oxford University Press, 1997.

Stewart-Winter, Timothy. "The Fall of Walter Jenkins and the Hidden History of the Lavender Scare." In *Intimate States: Gender, Sexuality, and Governance in Modern US History*, edited by Margot Canaday, Nancy F. Cott, and Robert O. Self, 211–234. Chicago: University of Chicago Press, 2021.

——. *Queer Clout: Chicago and the Rise of Gay Politics*. Philadelphia: University of Pennsylvania Press, 2017.

——. "Queer Law and Order: Sex, Criminality, and Policing in the Late-twentieth Century United States." *Journal of American History* 102, no. 1 (June 2015): 61–72.

Stockdill, Brett C. *Activism against AIDS: At the Intersections of Sexuality, Race, Gender, and Class.* Boulder, CO: Lynne Rienner, 2003.

Stone, Clarence N. *Regime Politics: Governing Atlanta, 1946–1988.* Lawrence: University Press of Kansas, 1989.

Strub, Whitney. *Obscenity Rules: Roth v. United States and the Long Struggle over Sexual Expression.* Lawrence: University Press of Kansas, 2013.

———. *Perversion for Profit: The Politics of Pornography and the Rise of the New Right.* New York; Columbia University Press, 2010.

Stryker, Susan. *Transgender History.* Berkeley, CA: Seal, 2008.

Sugrue, Thomas. *The Origins of Urban Crisis: Race and Inequality in Postwar Detroit.* Princeton, NJ: Princeton University Press, 1996.

———. *Sweet Land of Liberty: The Forgotten Struggle for Civil Rights in the North.* New York: Random House, 2009.

Sullivan, Patricia. *Lift Every Voice: The NAACP and the Making of the Civil Rights Movement.* New York: New Press, 2010.

Terry, Jennifer. *An American Obsession: Science, Medicine, and Homosexuality in Modern Society.* Chicago: University of Chicago Press, 1999.

Thompson, Heather Ann. *Blood in the Water: The Attica Prison Uprising of 1971 and Its Legacy.* New York: Pantheon, 2016.

———. The Racial History of Criminal Justice in America." *Du Bois Review* 16, no. 1 (Spring 2019): 221–241.

———. *Whose Detroit: Politics, Labor, and Race in a Modern American City.* Ithaca, NY: Cornell University Press, 2001.

Tinsley, Omise'eke Natasha. "Black Atlantic, Queer Atlantic: Queer Imaginings of the Middle Passage." *GLQ* 14, no. 2–3 (2008): 191–215.

Tuck, Stephen G. N. *Beyond Atlanta: The Struggle for Racial Equality in Georgia, 1940–1980.* Athens: University of Georgia Press, 2003.

Tyson, Timothy. *Radio Free Dixie: Robert F. Williams and the Roots of Black Power.* Chapel Hill: University of North Carolina Press, 2001.

Vogel, Shane. "Closing Time: Langston Hughes and the Queer Poetics of Harlem Nightlife." *Criticism* 48, no. 3 (Summer 2006): 397–425.

———. *The Scene of Harlem Cabaret: Race, Sexuality, Performance.* Durham, NC: Duke University Press, 2009.

Wade, Wyn Craig. *The Fiery Cross: The Ku Klux Klan in America.* New York: Oxford University Press, 1998.

Wailoo, Keith. *Dying in the City of the Blues: Sickle Cell Anemia and the Politics of Race and Health.* Chapel Hill: University of North Carolina Press, 2001.

Watkins-Hayes, Celeste. *Remaking a Life: How Women Living with HIV/AIDS Confront Inequality.* Oakland: University of California Press, 2019.

Webb, Clive, ed. *Massive Resistance: Southern Opposition to the Second Reconstruction.* Oxford: Oxford University Press, 2005.

———. *Rabble Rousers: The American Far Right in the Civil Rights Era.* Athens: University of Georgia Press, 2010.

White, Deborah Gray. *Ar'n't I a Woman? Female Slaves in the Plantation South.* New York: Norton, 1985.

Whiteside, Alan. *HIV/AIDS: A Very Short Introduction*. Oxford: Oxford University Press, 2008.

Whitford, David M. *The Curse of Ham in the Early Modern Era: The Bible and the Justifications for Slavery*. Farnham, UK: Ashgate, 2009.

Wiggins, Danielle. "'Order as well as Decency': The Develop of Order Maintenance Policing in Black Atlanta." *Journal of Urban History* 46, no. 4 (July 2020): 711–727.

Williams, Heather Ann. *Help Me to Find My People: The African American Search for Family Lost in Slavery*. Chapel Hill: University of North Carolina Press, 2012.

Williams, Rhonda Y. *The Politics of Public Housing: Black Women's Struggles against Urban Inequality*. New York: Oxford University Press, 2004.

Wolcott, Victoria. *Remaking Respectability: African American Women in Interwar Detroit*. Chapel Hill: University of North Carolina Press, 2001.

Woodard, Komozi. *A Nation within a Nation: Amiri Baraka (LeRoi Jones) and Black Power Politics*. Chapel Hill: University of North Carolina Press, 1999.

Woods, Jeff. *Black Struggle, Red Scare: Segregation and Anti-communism in the South, 1948–1968*. Baton Rouge: Louisiana State University Press, 2004.

Woods, Louis Lee. "Almost 'No Negro Veteran . . . Could Get a Loan': African Americans, the GI Bill, and the NAACP Campaign against Residential Segregation, 1917–1960." *Journal of African American History* 98, no. 3 (2013): 392–417.

Woolner, Cookie, *The Famous Lady Lovers: Black Women and Queer Desire Before Stonewall*. Chapel Hill: University of North Carolina Press, 2023.

Woubshet, Dagmawi. *Calendar of Loss: Race, Sexuality, and Mourning in the Early Era of AIDS*. Baltimore: Johns Hopkins University Press, 2015.

Wright Rigueur, Leah. *The Loneliness of the Black Republican: Pragmatic Politics and the Pursuit of Power*. Princeton, NJ: Princeton University Press, 2015.

Wynn, Neil A. *The African American Experience during World War II*. Lanham, MD: Rowman & Littlefield, 2010.

Index

Lomax, Michael, 127, 163–167
Look magazine, 85
Los Angeles, CA, 38, 91, 101, 122, 126, 141, 158, 177, 190
Los Angeles Sentinel, 38
Los Angeles Times, 76
Louisiana, 25, 92, 121
Loving v. Virginia, 117–118
Lowery, Evelyn Gibson, 172, 177, 180, 190–191, 243n15–16
Lowery, Joseph, 170–171, 180, 186, 190–191, 243n15–16
Lupton, Bob, 154
Lyons, Carl F., 111

Mallory, J. J., 72
Mangan, William H., 92
Marable, Manning, 174
March on Washington for Jobs and Freedom, 1–3, 83, 105
March on Washington for Lesbian, Gay, and Bi-Equal Rights and Liberation, 1, 4, 13, 206n2
marriage: interracial, 6, 33–34, 58, 77, 97, 110, 117–118; same-sex, 3–4, 97, 117–118, 195
Marsh, Cheryl Thompson, 177
Marshall, Billy, 37–38
Marshall, Bob: *The Sorrow of Selma,* 89
Marshall, Thurgood, 25
Martin, Bill, 156–157
masculinity, 113–116
massage parlors, 136, 142, 145, 147, 149, 151
Massell, Sam, 129, 132–133, 144
Masters, Robert E. L., 82
Mattachine Society, 100–101, 110
Maury, Ann, 141
Mayberry, Sara C., 79
McAuliffe, Hinson, 147
McCarthy, Joseph, 52, 81, 99
McConnell, James, 117
McCoy, Renee, 189
McCoy, Rodney, Jr., 175
McFadden, Mariah, 188

McGinnity, Terry, 121
McGuire, Danielle, 78
McMillen, Neil, 119
Meadows, K. N., 136
Meeker, Martin, 83
Memphis, TN, 47, 172
Metropolitan Atlanta Council of Gay and Lesbian Organizations, 165–166
Metropolitan Community Church, 129, 140, 155, 159, 163–164
Metropolitan Gazette, 157
Miami, FL, 152, 155
Miami-Dade County, FL, 122, 152, 230n21
Michigan, 19, 94, 176. *See also* Detroit, MI
Mikell, Robert: *Selma* pamphlet, 88–89, 227n94
military (US): blue discharges from, 22–24, 26–35, 38–39, 214n76; general discharges from, 24, 211n20; queer people in, 3–4, 8, 10, 15, 93, 97, 184, 189–190, 207n18, 211n19; racial inequality in, 19–23, 25, 36–37, 211n14. *See also* US Army; US Navy; veterans
Millican, Everett, 143, 147
Minority Business Enterprise Program, 165–166
miscegenation: and Christianity, 88, 107; laws against, 33–34, 39, 117, 214n78; rhetoric against, 9, 41, 45, 67, 118, 120. *See also* interracial relationships
Mississippi, 23, 42, 66, 72, 83, 107, 119. *See also* Jackson, MS
Missouri. *See* Kansas City, MO; Saint Louis, MO
Mitchell, Michele, 198
Mobile, AL, 79, 171, 243n15
Mobley, Carolyn, 164
Montgomery, AL, 60, 65, 68–71, 73, 75–76, 80, 85, 88. *See also* Selma-Montgomery march
Montgomery Advertiser, 72–74
Moore, Audley, 37
Moore, Harmon, 134, 136, 154
Moral Majority, 134, 159

Rivera, Sylvia, 129
Robeson, Paul, 37
Robinson, R. James, 92
Robison, Gil, 176
Robnett, Belinda, 171
Rockefeller, Nelson, 84
Rockwell, George Lincoln, 99–102, 104–106, 229n11. *See also* American Nazi Party
Roosevelt, Franklin Delano, 24, 34
Rosen v. United States, 82
Roth v. United States, 82, 226n80
Rowan, C. R., 78
Royal, A. R., 59
Royles, Dan, 170
Russell, E., 142
Russia, 195–196
Rustin, Bayard, 1–3, 39, 79, 83–85, 92–93, 95, 105, 170
Ryan, Seth D., 105

Saint Louis, MO, 26, 29, 41–45, 47, 50, 53, 120, 214n76
Saint Louis Argus, 56–59
Saint Louis Globe-Democrat, 50, 59, 219n42
Saint Louis Globe-Dispatch, 58
Saint Louis National Archives, 33
Saint Louis Post-Dispatch, 41–42, 59
Salisbury, Harrison, 71
Salo, Robert, 140
same-sex intimacies: and civil rights activists, 57, 66, 85, 88–89, 92, 197; and HIV/AIDS, 169, 180, 182, 188; in the military, 15, 20–24, 28–29; policing of, 7, 10, 128; visibility of, 82; and white supremacists, 96–99, 110
San Francisco, CA, 19, 31, 72, 95, 101, 109, 120, 129, 184
Save Our Children campaign, 122, 152, 159, 230n21
Scheuren, Frank, 159
Schlafly, Phyllis, 42
schools: communism in, 95; critical race theory in, 197; desegregation of, 2, 45,

60, 66, 70, 135, 143, 231n43, 233n79, 243n15; and HIV/AIDS, 182; and homosexuality, 66, 100, 129; sex education in, 119, 232n99
Schwerner, Michael, 107
SCLC/WOMEN: early HIV/AIDS work, 16, 168–176, 180, 182; NAMIETP (National AIDS Awareness Program), 176–179, 181, 183–184, 188, 191–192; RACE program, 169–170, 173, 183–192. *See also* HIV/AIDS
Seele, Pernessa, 178
segregation: in Atlanta, 128, 130–131, 135, 143; and Christianity, 73–74, 107–110, 230–231n43, 231n51; and color-blindness, 8; and HIV/AIDS, 185; Jim Crow, 36, 52, 78, 110; and masculinity, 113–116; in the military, 20–21, 28, 36; organizations opposed to, 19, 44, 48–51, 212n37; organizations supporting, 40–42, 45, 47, 77, 90–91, 95–96, 106, 118–119, 223n13, 230n32; in the press, 59–60, 70; in queer spaces, 128, 161. *See also* desegregation; *individual segregationists and organizations*
Self, William, 134, 136, 141
Selma, AL, 65, 68–70, 73, 85, 88, 102
Selma-Montgomery march, 65, 68–70, 75–76, 79–80, 85–89, 91–92, 94, 243n15. *See also* voting rights demonstrations (Alabama, 1965)
Servicemen's Readjustment Act. *See* GI Bill of Rights
Sex Information and Education Council of the United States, 119
Sexton, Melvin, 111
sexual psychopathy, 8, 10, 22, 27–28, 30, 53–55, 92, 128, 207n18
sexual violence: allegations against Black men, 33, 77, 114, 120–121, 243n16; Black male veterans prosecuted for, 39; against Black women by white men, 77–78; and children, 54–56, 159, 221n74; and slavery, 6–7

sex work: and civil rights demonstrations, 67, 84, 90, 113; decriminalization of, 155; and the federal government, 111; male, 55; policing of, 9, 144–145, 147–152; and religion, 139
Shah, Nayan, 5–6
Shannon, Margie, 177, 244n42
Sharp, John D., 134, 137–138, 154, 237n42, 239n94
Shelley v. Kraemer, 42
Shelton, Robert, 88, 106–107, 110, 112–113
Shroyer, Owen, 197
Shuttlesworth, Fred, 170
sickle cell anemia, 116, 233n79
Sides, Josh, 126, 142
Simmons, John Paul, 116–117
Sister Love, 178
Sisters of Charity of the Blessed Virgin Mary, 80
Skidmore, Emily, 116
slavery, 6–7, 14, 77–78, 106, 108, 149, 178–179, 206n10
Small, Sanda, 161
Smelser, E. L., 94
Smith, Gerald L. K., 41–42, 99
Smith, M. H., 74
Smith, Nadine, 1
Smitherman, Joseph T., 69
Snorton, C. Riley, 192
Snow, Jim N., 155
Socialist Workers Party, 155
Society of Professional Journalists, 76
sodomy laws, 7–8, 10, 12, 50, 53, 108, 111, 128, 235n10
Southern Christian Leadership Conference (SCLC): and Alabama demonstrations, 68, 70, 76–77, 79, 84; and Atlanta Gay Pride, 138–140, 153–154, 166–167; and gay rights, 189–190; and HIV/AIDS, 169–171, 174–175, 179–180, 183, 192; *SCLC National Magazine,* 189; and Washington demonstrations, 112. *See also* SCLC/ WOMEN

Southern Conference Education Fund, 79
Sparkman, John, 90, 224n52
Spartanburg (SC) *Journal,* 76
Spearman, Henrietta, 182
Spears, Kevin C., 190
Springfield, IL, 24
Stanley, Charles, 134
state intimacies, 185
States' Rights Council of Georgia, 47
Stearn, Jess, 82
Stein, Marc, 8, 129
St. John, Charlie, 129
Stockdill, Brett, 187
Stone, Clarence, 130, 165
Stoner, J. B., 99
Stonewall uprising, 118, 127, 129, 165
Street, Barbara Gervais, 156
Street Transvestite Action Revolutionaries (STAR), 129
Strickland, Ed, 80–82
Stromer, John A., 42
Stryker, Susan, xii
Student Nonviolent Coordinating Committee (SNCC), 68, 70, 88, 132, 163
Sweat, Dan E., 148–150
Swift, G. W., Sr., 92

Talmadge, Herman, 132
Taylor-Hines, Brenda, 177
Teague, Duncan, 164, 190
Tennessee, 47, 99, 106, 172. *See also* Memphis, TN
Texas, 38, 100, 104, 167
Thomas, Stephan A., 183
Thompson, James G., 21
Thurmond, Strom, 3, 83
Till, Emmett, 60
Tinney, James, 189
transgender people, xii, 83, 116–117, 129–130, 199–200, 206n2, 235n2
Truman, Harry S., 36–37
Trump, Donald, 196
Tuscaloosa News, 76
Tweed, Robert L., 31

Printed in the USA
CPSIA information can be obtained
at www.ICGtesting.com
CBHW020056030824
12615CB00005B/220